The Healing
Community

Richard Almond

The Healing Community

Dynamics

of

the

Therapeutic

Milieu

Jason Aronson, New York

Library of Congress Cataloging in Publication Data

Almond, Richard.
　The healing community.

　Bibliography: p.
　1. Milieu therapy. I. Title. [DNLM: 1. Milieu
therapy—Case studies. 2. Psychotherapy—Case studies.
3. Therapeutic community—Case studies. WM420 A449h]
RC489.M5A45　　616.8'915　　73-17733
ISBN 0-87668-111-9

For my parents, Dorothea and Gabriel Almond

CONTENTS

Preface

HEALING COMMUNITY is both a specific approach to psychiatric treatment, usually known to us as therapeutic community or milieu therapy, and a general pattern found in a variety of social organizations. As a specific, therapeutic community was developed shortly after World War II by the English psychiatrist Maxwell Jones. As a general phenomenon, organizations that qualify as healing communities can be found historically in other cultures, and in our own society outside formal mental health settings. In the main, this book consists of case studies of varied healing communities. I have used direct observations, interviews, questionnaires, behavior ratings, personal experiences, and published reports to extract some of the core features of healing community as a universal pattern. My emphasis will be primarily social and social-psychological, for healing community is a *social* therapy system. Further, as we shall see, it deals with a wide variety of problems and people, only a portion of whom qualify in our view as "patients."

This volume is an exploration, not a "how to" book. The settings in which therapeutic organizations develop are too varied for simple recipes. As the explorations here will show, it is the processes, not the specifics, that are the essence of healing community. My hope is that the reader concerned with developing a therapeutic community, or with maximizing the therapeutic qualities of a group in which he is involved, will apply the ideas and conclusions described here in a way that fits his situation. In working with psychiatric staffs and members of other groups, I have time and again found that the knowledge needed to develop specific changes grows best from the group itself, once general ideas have been stated.

Today we are in the midst of an era of change and turmoil in mental health. The impact of several successive waves of innovation and challenge—from psychoanalysis to community mental health to radical psychiatry—is still being absorbed. The recent opposition by the political right to large-scale federal support could easily lead back to a dehumanization of those who manifest deviant behavior. On the brighter side, there are hints that the postwar liberalization of attitudes toward mental health is being maintained and may even be spreading to attitudes toward prison inmates. These historical and political shifts give a certain moral urgency to the themes discussed here. As I shall elaborate in detail in the Introduction, past periods of enlightenment in dealing with psychological problems have been followed by long "dark ages" of fear and ignorance. We have an obligation, to ourselves and to those we help, to learn and to preserve what we learn.

The studies and observations included here span a period of several years of my own professional and intellectual development. I have tried to retain the freshness of observations where the material is firsthand. The overall sequence of presentation also reflects the sequence of my interests. Healing communities everywhere tend to be somewhat controversial or marginal. I have sought, not so much out of fairness as from the overall purpose of the volume, to minimize the polemical issues. A further justification for avoiding the most controversial aspects of healing communities is that the polemic tends to be a function of the newness of the particular group. My own viewpoint for observing healing communities has varied considerably and is reflected in the descriptions here. I have been a nursing

aide, activities therapist, medical student, psychiatric intern
and resident, day hospital director, ward administrator, and
consultant on a variety of psychiatric wards, as well as a
participant in, and leader of, a variety of encounter and
psychodrama groups. In general I have tried to take a step
back into objectivity in what I report here, so that the vantage
point will reflect the experience of the "patient" or "staff
member," as well as the leadership, of healing communities.

* * *

This work has benefited from the support, collaboration,
and inspiration of many colleagues. I owe most of the ideas
presented here to insights suggested to me directly or indirectly by my teachers, co-workers, patients, and students.
The form these ideas take in this volume is, of course, one for
which only I can take responsibility.

Frederick Redlich, as Chairman of the Department of
Psychiatry during my seven years at Yale, created an atmosphere of intense interest in social system phenomena and
individual-group interaction. He encouraged and supported
my developing interests in studying therapeutic community.
Hans Esser, a research fellow at Yale in 1962–1963, provided
my first experience in psychiatric research; his enthusiasm
and intellectual curiosity helped sustain my own directions of
study. Boris Astrachan, one of my first teachers in psychiatry,
has shared and encouraged my interest in therapeutic community as a social ogratization; he has also made helpful
comments on the manuscript of this volume.

Kenneth Keniston has been important to me in so many
ways it is difficult to acknowledge his help sufficiently. He has
been a patient teacher, a tolerant collaborator, and a sensitive
guide. This volume owes much of its conception to his constant encouragement and stimulating ideas. The empirical
research described in Part I was done in collaboration with
him. Sandra Boltax also participated in that research; without

her energy and initiative, much of the data collection and analysis would not have been possible.

Erich Lindemann has read the manuscript of this volume in several versions; more important, his enthusiasm and interest in the concept of healing community have sustained me through several years of writing and rewriting. He has often seen possibilities and connections that I had not noticed and has thus made criticism a widening, creative experience for me.

Thomas Detre, Daniel Levinson, and Gerald Klerman have been important teachers who aided my developing interest in social organizations and helped focus my interest in therapeutic community. Ingvar Løfgren, Melvin Kohn, and the late William Caudill each provided advice and encouragement for my pursuit of a social science view of healing organizations. Robert Lifton, by his personal example and by involving me in meetings of the Group for the Study of Psychohistorical Process, exposed me to a breadth of thinking that is unusual in an era of specialization. Through this group I was exposed to Erik Erikson, Robert Coles, Philip Rieff, Kai Erikson, and others; the scope of this volume reflects their influence on my evolving vision of psychological inquiry.

David Reiss, at the National Institute of Mental Health, encouraged this project and provided me time for initiating it. His descriptions of Navaho curing ceremonies provided the spark for the inquiries reported in Part II. David Hamburg at Stanford provided me freedom and support for continuing the work over several years.

My wife, Barbara, has tolerated the moodiness of an author and has been consistently encouraging about the work, and interested in the ideas involved. I cannot list all the many colleagues, friends, and students who have given ideas and encouragement or who have exemplified the patterns described here. Many have suggested other groups that would qualify for inclusion here as examples of healing community; although I have not been able to include most of these groups, I appreciate the fact that my concepts have been meaningful to others.

My gratitude also extends to several persons who have contributed crucial typing, editorial, and research aid: Mardith Louisell, Susan Nassau, Chris Grey, Suzanne Boughey, Judith Manzagol, and Jill Joseph.

Acknowledgements

THE AUTHOR is grateful to the following for permission to use material from their works:

Aldine-Atherton, Inc.: from *The Ritual Process*, by Victor W. Turner.

Charles C. Thomas, Publisher: from "The Use of a Psychiatric Unit in a General Hospital," by G. Saslow, in Albert F. Wessen (ed.), *The Psychiatric Hospital as a Social System.*

Connecticut Medicine: from "An Experimental Approach to the Treatment of the Acutely Ill Psychiatric Patient in the General Hospital," by Thomas Detre, M.D.

Cornell University Press: from *The Primitive World and Its Transformations*, by Robert Redfield.

Grune & Stratton, Inc.: from *Ego Psychology, Group Dynamics, and the Therapeutic Community*, by Marshall Edelson (by permission).

Holt, Rinehart and Winston, Inc.: from *I Never Promised You a Rose Garden*, by Hannah Green.

Macmillan Company: from *International Encyclopedia of the Social Sciences*, by David Sills; and from *Synanon: The Tunnel Back*, by Louis Yablonsky.

Simon D. Messing: from *The Highland Plateau Amhara of Ethiopia.*

Munson-Human Relations Area Files Press: from *People of the Middle Place: A Study of the Zuni Indians*, by Dorothea C. and John Adair Leighton.

Psychiatry: from "Patient Role and Social Uncertainty—A Dilemma of the Mentally Ill," by Kai T. Erikson.

Springer Publishing Co.: from *Moral Treatment in Community Mental Health*, by J. Sanbourne Bockoven. Copyright © 1972 Springer Publishing Company, Inc., 200 Park Avenue South, New York.

University of Toronto Press: from "A Socioadaptive Approach to Treatment of Acutely Disturbed Inpatients," by Thomas Detre, D. Kessler, and Jean Sayres, in *Proceedings of the Third World Congress of Psychiatry.*

Introduction: Concepts and History

CONCEPTS

IN THIS BOOK I shall describe and analyze a type of social organization that I call the *healing community*. In hospital psychiatric wards, we know it by the name *therapeutic community*. I have chosen a more general term because one important goal of this book is to demonstrate that this pattern of organization is a general phenomenon found in different cultures and in different niches of our society. Healing communities are small collectivities (usually between 15 and 100 members) characterized by intense commitment to the group and by a common interest in healing of some range of psychological, behavioral, or spiritual maladies. The healing community is distinctive in several ways. Patterns of internal organization, roles, handling of authority, relations between members, and the subjective experience of participation are all "special" in certain respects.

It is the search for a fuller understanding of the specialness of healing community, especially the qualities that recur in all such groups, that motivates the studies reported here. In this pursuit I shall use a variety of data and explore healing communities in a variety of settings. The data will range from participant observations, interviews, and anthropological descriptions to questionnaire attitude studies and behavior ratings. The explorations of different groups include the following:

Part I is a detailed study of one American contemporary therapeutic community in a general hospital psychiatric ward. Examined in greater detail than any other community in the book, this setting provides the first and richest source of ideas for a general model of the qualities and processes of healing community. Part II includes briefer descriptions of groups in three unrelated non-Western cultures: the Amharic population of Northwest Ethiopia; the Zuni pueblo of the American Southwest; and the Japanese community of Hawaii. These studies validate the idea that healing community is a universal phenomenon and give us a concept of the range of relationships between such groups and the societies within which they function. Part III returns to the United States to look at healing communities that have emerged recently outside the formal mental health establishment: encounter groups, Synanon, and the Psychodrama Workshop of Palo Alto. This last set of examples, in addition to demonstrating how healing communities spring spontaneously from unmet societal needs, brings up wider issues of alienation and frustration with dehumanizing institutions in our society and suggests the possible redemptive, restorative role healing communities may play in a culture that manifests widespread yearning for closer human contact and group involvement. The second part of this Introduction recounts two historical antecedents of therapeutic community in American-European experience.

Deviance and Institutions for the Mad

The afflictions we call "mental illness" are found universally in human societies and throughout man's history. Sociologically, the behaviors that we call madness or mental illness are part of a wider category: deviance. Deviance is a behavioral phenomenon. When an individual's behavior goes beyond a range defined as normal or acceptable in a given society, it is defined as deviant and usually evokes some sort of reaction—mild at first, stronger as time passes or as the behavior augments. The individual manifesting deviant behavior passes through a series of social "screens" in this process, as first family and kin, then neighbors and friends, seek to influence him. Eventually, if these first reactions are ineffective, two things happen: (1) He is brought to some more specialized societal institution for handling—a doctor or hospital, a court or prison; (2) He is labeled a deviant —he becomes a "patient," "criminal," "revolutionary," or "heretic."

As a result of these steps, the individual becomes characterized by his problem behavior. He is no longer an ordinary citizen with an eccentric quality; he is now a madman. As such, he may be dealt with differently; his deviance becomes the overriding consideration and he may be arbitrarily deprived of certain rights and freedoms. Handling him becomes the special province of experts in his sort of deviance. In our Western societies these changes are frequently manifest in placement in a special institution: in the case of the madman, a clinic or mental hospital of some sort. This action usually gives the appearance of a definitive resolution to the deviance problem: The individual is out of the way, and he is in a place where he may be helped to stop behaving deviantly. Three factors limit the latter outcome, however. First, as sociologists have pointed out repeatedly, the deviance-handlers have a vested interest in maintaining the problem they work with, and the easiest way to accomplish this is to keep the deviant behaving deviantly. Second, the deviant himself may find it difficult to change his behavior or to resume his prior life. Third, the family and home community may close their doors to the deviant's return. Much of the post-World War II reform effort in mental health has been devoted to changing this pattern, which too often ended in chronic hospitalization. Unfortunately, the changes made have primarily been administrative and geographic; it has too often been easier to do something new with madness than to do something really different.[1]

What is it about the madman that makes him a deviant? The behavior of those designated "mad" evokes anxiety in others. While violent behavior is the most prominent cause of uneasiness, it is the general tendency of the "mentally disordered" individual to be an unpredictable transgressor of his society's important norms that creates a deeper fear. "Nothing is sacred" to the madman; he may violate rules of dress, of social intercourse and ceremony, of language. He reminds us of the potential within each of us for impulsive, destructive, self-debasing actions; for passivity and dependence; or for paranoid mistrust of others (Bursten, 1965; Scheff, 1966).

The institutions of Western societies for handling madness have tended to respond to the anxiety of these primal themes by exerting massive, coercive control over the deviant's behavior and by removing him from contact with other citizens. The recurring struggle to change this pattern over the past two centuries is described later in this chapter. The general approach during the present modern era of reform has been to try to prevent or reverse the labeling process. This takes the form of crisis intervention, possibly with brief hospitalization, then return home. Frequently, less intense outpatient treatment is suggested. All too often this approach of de-labeling means doing nothing about pervasive difficulties in the person's psychological or social life. Pragmatically, these problems are discussed in terms of the "delivery of services." Scarce professional resources are allocated, like commodities, to a seemingly limitless market.

The healing community goes a step beyond the controlling or de-labeling approaches to deviance. Instead, the attitude is one of *redefining the meaning of the behavior* and *involving the person with a group of fellow sufferers* who aid each other in handling both the deviant behavior and the underlying threatening impulses. Integral to healing community is the involvement of the deviant as a member. Thus the processes of involving newcomers in the group, and the group's mechanisms for maintaining itself, are central features of healing community as a general phenomenon. These are the core interests in this volume: the individual and group processes that enable healing communities to redefine the nature of deviance and to bring it under control through voluntary conformity to the expectations of a peer group. In the healing community these two levels of process are interwoven. For the purpose of our understanding of healing, it is useful to separate what happens to the individual, over a period of time, from what happens to the group. Important for the effectiveness of such groups is a feeling of specialness in both specific interactions and the healing community as a whole. To capture this quality I shall use two borrowed terms: *charisma* and *communitas*. I have added the adjective *healing* to charisma, to indicate that the specialness of individuals implied by the term is largely directed at and around therapeutic activities. *Healing charisma*, thus, will be roughly equivalent to *therapeutic* in the healing community situation when we are speaking of individual members. *Communitas* will also be a synonym for *therapeutic* when speaking of the community as a whole (i.e., as in *therapeutic community*). Unlike *therapeutic*, the two terms carry with them certain meanings; using them is equivalent to proposing hypotheses about the nature of the treatment process in the healing community.

The individual healing process occurs against the background of this special sort of group life. While its specifics are a function of each group, three universal features recur. Each healing community has the task of getting the new member's *attention*. Once it is obtained, he is engaged in a process of *behavior change* through a variety of group influences. Making possible the redefinition of his deviant behavior, and altering or channeling it into an acceptable form, is the general *role* available to members of the community.

Healing Charisma

Therapeutic has at least as many different meanings as there are schools of therapy. Although used with conviction, it is infrequently defined. When the meaning of the term is specified, it is usually in the language of one particular school of therapy. The term thus lacks the generality needed in an investigation of universal therapeutic patterns. Jerome Frank speaks of persuasion and influencing processes as recurrent qualities of many varieties of psychotherapy (1973). He also points out that an important factor in healing is the patient's faith (see Part II). These ideas can be most accurately summarized by describing therapeutic activity as a charismatic process.

The sociologist Max Weber applied the concept of charisma to the special leadership qualities found in new religious and political movements. These qualities include a capacity to inspire awe in others and gain their following through this characteristic, rather than through force or rational argument (1946). Specifying exactly what charisma *is*, is difficult or impossible. The range of behaviors and qualities in charismatic individuals includes magical ability (Weber, 1946), persuasiveness (Tucker, 1968), distance-taking (Etzioni, 1961), and partial satisfaction of dependent or guilt-derived wishes (E. Erikson, 1959). What is common to charisma is its specialness and atypical quality, and the fact that it is an interpersonal phenomenon. Since every culture and every situation has different expectations, that which is charismatic can be expected to vary considerably in different settings and for each specific interaction. Despite this elusiveness, charisma is not only a real and general phenomenon but a psychological and social fundamental in human societies. Weber emphasized the drama of intense charismatic leadership, but other sociologists have indicated that charisma may be found in less dramatic manifestations:

Charisma, then, is the quality which is imputed to persons,

actions, roles, institutions, symbols and material objects because of their presumed connection with "ultimate," "fundamental," "vital," order-determining powers. This presumed connection with the ultimately "serious" elements in the universe and in human life is seen as a quality or state of being, manifested in the bearing or demeanor and in the actions of individual persons; it is also seen as inherent in certain roles and collectivities. It can be perceived as existing in intense and concentrated form in particular institutions, roles and individuals (or strata of individuals). It can also be perceived as existing in an attenuated and dispersed form (Shils, 1968, p. 386).

Healing charisma occurs in relation to physical or mental disorder. In general medicine, healing charisma can be recognized in the aura of mystery, omniscience, and omnipotence surrounding the physician and his patients' expectations of him (Parsons, 1956; Myerhoff and Larson, 1965). It is evident in the "placebo effect": positive objective or subjective responses to drugs or procedures that are biologically inert (e.g., sugar pills). Presumably, the effect stems from the patient's belief in the physician, a belief that often ignores the "real" limits of his powers.

Healing charisma in a hospital or other healing organization can be distributed in a variety of patterns (Etzioni, 1961). In the custodial hospital where control over deviant behavior, rather than therapy, is the goal, charisma may be entirely absent. It may appear on occasion in the form of a young, dedicated staff member or even in an unusual patient (see, for example, Clifford Beers' *A Mind That Found Itself*, 1935). But the pressures on such custodial institutions are such that charismatic, therapeutic programs or individuals are dissonant. They are usually extruded or encapsulated within a short time. In hospitals specializing in healing, charisma is located in the therapists and their sessions with patients. This is much the same pattern as in a general hospital, where, despite an elaborate technical and staffing structure, healing itself is attributed to the physicians. And, as in the general hospital, the patient is seen as the object of the charismatic process rather than as an active participant in it. The patient is not expected to do more than be present and, if he wishes, to speak. There is no specific expectation that the patient's experience in therapy will carry over to his behavior in the hospital ward. In fact, there is often an expectation in such psychotherapy hospitals that the uncovering work of therapy will be accompanied by more, rather than less, symptomatic upset.

In therapeutic community, charisma is not limited to individual psychotherapy and psychotherapists. This is often symbolized by explicit statements that "therapy is a 24-hour process." Healing charisma potentially characterizes any staff member and patient. A director of a therapeutic community may manifest an intense charismatic quality. Interestingly, this need not diminish the charisma of subordinate staff. On the contrary, the leader may accept or encourage the development of charisma in others. Nor does this decrease the leader's healing charisma; healing charisma is not limited, and greater charisma at one level does not mean less at another. As we shall see, the healing process becomes interwoven with the transmission of healing charisma through the community. The limits on healing charisma derive from those forces that have through history pushed for a punitive, restrictive, custodial approach to persons with unusual behavior. In reality, every healing community must contend with the issues of control and authority. More specifically, the spread of authority downward through the charismatic organization can be effective and charismatic only as it is balanced by the maintenance of member behavior within certain limits. This is done through powerful group processes that influence members' behavior through conformity pressure rather than through direct control.

Communitas

To refer to a group pattern in which all relations and individuals, ideally, are charismatic, I use the term *communitas*. This concept was recently introduced by the anthropologist Victor Turner to facilitate the understanding of the social process of ritual events. In analyzing observations of healing ceremonies of the African Ndembu tribe, Turner found that the central phase of the ritual frequently involved a temporary undoing of all distinctions: gender, family, rank, age, and so on. This pattern recurred in other ritual situations, suggesting to Turner that there is an implicit social organization counterbalancing the ordinary social order. This he terms "communitas" to suggest a group in which the usual differentiation of individuals by role, sex, and class gives way to a basic-relatedness:

> All human societies implicitly or explicitly refer to two contrasting social models. One, as we have seen, is of society as a structure of jural, political, and economic positions, offices, statuses, and roles in which the individual is only ambiguously grasped behind the social persona. The other is of society as a communitas of concrete idiosyncratic individuals, who, though differing in physical and mental endowment, are nevertheless regarded as equal in terms of shared humanity. The first model is of a differentiated, culturally structured, segmented, and often hierarchical system of institutionalized positions. The second presents society as an undifferentiated, homogeneous whole, in which individuals confront one another integrally, and not as "segmentalized" into statuses and roles (Turner, 1969, p. 177).[2]

An important feature of healing communities is their approximation of communitas. None achieves it completely, but communitas defines an ideal that acts on the organization powerfully. When we examine the real social structure of healing communities, we will find differences in status among members. But these differences are those of a communitas: externals that do not color the essential equality of relatedness. In the same way, the ideal of the healing community is for each individual and every interpersonal relationship to be charismatic. In fact, the existence of a communitas in the healing community and the presence of healing charisma are two sides of the same coin. Communitas inspires charismatic feeling by emphasizing basic equality and integral relatedness among members; charisma strengthens the communitas by providing a form for relatedness that is special and not dependent on rigidly defined social structures.

The differences that are recognized among individuals in a healing community have most to do with the group's healing procedures. *Newcomers*—sufferers—are not yet familiar with these and may not yet espouse them. *Members* fully accept and practice the group's beliefs. The charismatic *leader* or *leaders* maintain the crucial beliefs and practices, and promulgate new ones. These three levels are not necessarily recognized formally; there may in fact be another formal social structure. Thus, when the healing community is set in a hospital framework, we will find people designated by the usual medical hospital role categories: patient, aide, nurse, physician, director. Functionally, however, the therapeutic healing process operates in terms of the three informal categories. Coming from the opposite extreme, an encounter group like Synanon or Psychodrama may maintain a presumption of equality of members, but it actually functions in terms of these same three levels of experience.

A Model of the Healing Community

Both communitas and healing charisma are abstractions that must be translated into day-to-day behavioral events to have meaning. Communitas must be maintained and conveyed to new members as a set of behavior *norms*.[3] These norms concern those matters that symbolize the sense of unity and sharing within this group, and the general involvement in the group and in its practices and beliefs. Thus, there are norms in a group for how to act in various situations, for how to talk about problems, for the healing activities of the group. In the hospital therapeutic community these norms concern disclosure of the problems that led to admission, accepting the reactions of others, and supporting the strengths of other patients. In the Ethiopian Zar cult the norms involve espousing the leader's diagnosis that one has a particular Zar spirit riding invisibly on one's shoulder and assimilating the power of that spirit through the ritual *gurri* dance.

Healing charisma becomes a part of daily life in a healing community through its impact on the meaning of membership or *role*.[4] To be a member of a healing community is something special, elevated. *How* one is to act as a member is laid out by the norms. But that these actions are special and can induce healing changes in oneself and others is implied in the charismatic aspect of roles. These roles are enacted primarily in interactional situations. Healing charisma is the quality of experience in such interactions that makes them feel special, that enables participants to do things they did not think they could do; for example, the therapeutic community member confronts another member in a therapy group, the psychodrama actor becomes the protagonist's father, the mentally retarded Clown Fraternity member partakes in the sacred rituals of Zuni.

Schematically, we can represent relations among these aspects of group processes in healing community as follows:

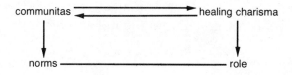

These concepts and relations will take on more specific meaning as we turn to the actual functioning of healing communities and will be reviewed in Part IV.

The social structure of the healing community is a framework for its healing process. Since the sufferer who comes to the healing community is distracted, the first step is gaining his attention. This is generally done by *immersing* the group's norms. Discussions, hypnotic dancing, chanting, drugs, or fasting may all be aspects of this attention-recruiting process. The response of the newcomer may be primarily imitative, but he begins to act in the desired ways. Initial involvement is most intense, often in protracted ceremonies or round-the-clock activity. In some healing groups, an awareness of making an open-ended, life-long commitment to the group achieves the same effect. The charismatic aura of the leader is a further contribution to recruiting the newcomer's attention.

Once attention is focused on members and leaders, they begin to respond selectively to the newcomer's behavior. A process of natural *behavior modification* occurs. The interaction again is guided by the group's norms for member behavior. Behaviors that are desired are subtly or openly encouraged, while those that are not are ignored or criticized. As time passes, a transition to member is made by emulating experienced members. Since roles are not separated by closed role boundaries, the new member may model his behavior directly on the *parallel roles* of the experienced ones. Psychologically, this identification is aided by communitas: Identification is easier with someone who is felt to be an equal. Finally, the newcomer becomes a member. He accepts the healing processes of the group, and he becomes a model for others. Both these aspects of membership reinforce changes he has made. In some healing communities, membership is open-ended and is integrated into the member's life patterns.

HISTORY

Reports of kindly, let alone therapeutic, treatment of the mad are limited in the history of Western civilization. Incarceration of some sort seems to have been the most common pattern, whether it was at sea aboard *narrenschiffen* (ships for the mad), within the towers of the town walls, or in special institutions (Foucault). At other times the mad were simply driven into the countryside by force. Not until the past 200 years do we find the emergence of occasional reforms in care of the severely disturbed. The first of these was the Moral Treatment movement of the late eighteenth and early nineteenth centuries, which has received increasing attention as a forerunner of the contemporary mental health movement. The second is a little-known development in early twentieth century Germany, *milieutherapie* (also known as *aktivere behandlung* or "more active therapy"). The third is the post-World War II development of therapeutic community in the hospital setting.

A common conception of the history of hospital treatment over the past 200 years depicts a steady progression of increasingly humane and therapeutic treatment, beginning with Pinel's unchaining the inmates of the Salpetrière and Bicêtre in 1793. A more careful examination of that history reveals that psychiatric institutions have run a far more uneven course. Both moral treatment and *milieutherapie* were passing episodes in a consistently neglectful and often brutal history of handling of the mad.

Moral Treatment

Perhaps because France was the center of revolution and social change at the end of the eighteenth century, Pinel became symbolic, at least in retrospect, of what was actually an international phenomenon. He was one of a number of innovators and humanitarian hospital directors who instituted dramatic changes in the care of the mentally disturbed in the late eighteenth and early nineteenth centuries. This movement, known as Moral Treatment, had wide influence on the care of the mad throughout Europe and America. It led to the establishment of institutions strictly for the treatment of the mentally ill. The best-known proponents of the approach are the Tuke family in England, who for several generations managed the York Retreat, and Benjamin Rush in America, who established the first psychiatric hospital in Philadelphia. All these institutions and their directors shared a new view of mental disorder and its treatment, strongly influenced by the Enlightenment principles of reason and brotherhood, and an Enlightenment conception of man as malleable in a benign environment.

Although moral treatment was never simply or clearly defined, it carried with it a number of definite meanings:

> . . . the early psychiatrist used "moral" as the equivalent of "emotional" or "psychological" . . . moral treatment was never clearly defined, possibly because its meaning was self-evident during the era in which it was used. It meant compassionate and understanding treatment of innocent sufferers.

> Moral treatment . . . was the first practical effort made to provide systematic and responsible care for an appreciable number of mentally ill, and it was eminently successful in achieving recoveries (Bockoven, 1972, pp. 12–13).

During the early practice of moral treatment, Pinel and other psychiatrists employed such uncomfortable techniques as cold-water dousings and painful straightjackets to manipulate patients into more rational behavior. As time passed, especially in English and American hospitals, moral treatment evolved into a more benign social therapy consisting of kindly care, fresh air, social intercourse among patients and staff, and sharing with patients of some responsible tasks.

Evidence that moral treatment was being used even before Pinel's time is seen in the following quotation from "the proprietor of an obscure madhouse" in 1789 England:

> Here all unnecessary confinement is avoided . . . every appearance of restraint avoided . . . coercion is never used but when absolutely requisite but is abandoned as soon as possible. Every indulgence as far as consistent with physical and mental operation is allowed; and it will not be wondered at that treated as a rational creature with attention and humanity, amused with art, the patient should gain his rational faculties, recur to his former habits and gradually become himself again (Faulkner, quoted by Walk, 1954).

Reports of 95 or 100 percent recoveries were not uncommon from hospitals using moral treatment. Even if we question these figures as inflated, or the improvements as temporary, it seems that moral treatment was a frequently effective technique.

In 1817 the first American hospital expressly for providing moral treatment was established by the Quakers at Philadelphia, the Friends' Asylum. Over the next 30 years, 18 hospitals were built for this form of treatment: McLean Hospital near Boston, the Hartford Retreat, Butler Hospital in Providence, and a number of joint state-private institutions including hospitals at Worcester, Massachusetts; Stanton, Virginia; and Utica, New York. The content and procedures of moral therapy are suggested by such descriptions as that of Pliny Earle, director of the Bloomingdale Hospital in New York:

> . . . the primary object is to treat the patients so far as their condition will possibly admit, *as if they were still in the enjoyment of the healthy exercise of their mental faculties.* An important desideratum for the attainment of this object is to make their condition as boarders, as comfortable as possible; that they may be less sensible of the deprivations to which they are

subjected by a removal from home. Nor is it less essential to extend them the privilege, or the right, to as much liberty, as much freedom from personal restraint that is compatible with their safety, the safety of others, and the judicious administration of other branches of curative treatment.

The most essential element of success in the establishment and maintenance of such a hospital is a corps of intelligent attendants, of kind dispositions, and good judgment . . . nearly all the young men who have been so employed during the last few years were from the country, and so well educated that they had been accustomed to teaching school in the winter (Earle, quoted in Bockoven, 1972, pp. 69–70; emphasis added).

In summary:

From the writings of Earle, Brigham, Woodward, Butler, Ray, it becomes clear that moral treatment was in no sense a *single technique*. Yet it had a definable goal—that of arousing the dormant faculties of the mind. Every available means was employed to achieve this end. The very matrix of moral treatment was the communal life of patients and hospital personnel. Every aspect of daily living was utilized by the physician for its therapeutic effect in awaking feelings of companionship in the patients. The chief modalities used in awaking such feelings were those endeavors which required the patient to invest interest in something outside himself in *cooperation with others*, namely manual work, intellectual work, recreation, and religious worship.

Psychotherapy, as such, was not mentioned, but it took the form of patients sharing past experiences with each other and discussing these experiences both in groups and privately with their physician. Ray and Butler, in particular, emphasized the need for the physician to know the experiences of each of his patients.

The moral therapist acted toward his patients as though they were mentally well. He believed that kindness and forebearance were essential in dealing with them. He also believed in *firmness and persistence in impressing upon patients the idea that a change to a more acceptable behavior was expected* (Bockoven, 1972, pp. 75–76; emphasis added).

What became of moral treatment in America? In part it was a victim of its own success. Between 1840 and 1860 militant reform advocate Dorothea Dix personally lobbied state legislatures across the country to build rural institutions for the mad, where they could receive moral treatment. Impressed by the fact that many of the poor or chronic cases were housed in jails, poorhouses, or family homes, she argued that the new state-financed hospitals should be large:

> She was rapidly successful in achieving the results she demanded, namely the construction of new, and expansion of already existing, mental hospitals. . . .

> Her immense emphasis on eliminating gross abuse of the insane had the most unfortunate effect of driving into the background any serious consideration of the requirements to be met in securing positive treatment. The inundation of mental hospitals with longstanding chronic cases ruined moral treatment. Neither the chronic cases transferred to the hospitals from jails, houses, cellars, and attics nor the new cases of recently acquired insanity could benefit from the art and therapeutic know-how which had been learned by moral therapists since the time of Pinel and Tuke (Bockoven, 1972, pp. 38–39).

The large, several-thousand-patient, state-supported hospitals that were the legacy of Dorothea Dix's work never became centers of moral treatment. A number of factors appear to account for this. By the middle part of the century, many of the leaders in moral treatment were aging or had died. The superintendents who took over the large state hospitals tended to be administratively orientated, concerned with controlling patients and running efficient institutions. At the same time that the institutional patterns of care were shifting, there was a major change in the patient population. With the increasing immigration of the middle and late nineteenth century, more and more of the clients of mental hospitals, especially of the large, free, state institutions, were "foreign insane paupers." These individuals were poor candidates for moral treatment; they spoke little or no English, and their cultural backgrounds were different from those of the hospital staff. The hospital budgets were completely dependent on state legislators who, after the initial enthusiasm, lost interest in underwriting expensive institutions. Hospital populations increased without proportionate budget allocations, so that the quality and quantity of staffing declined.

A third important factor in the change of treatment pattern was the shift in model of psychiatric illness that took place during the same years. This was embodied in the concepts of degeneration or dementia developed in France and Germany, respectively, about this time. Replacing the Enlightenment-inspired view of illness as a temporary, moral (psychological) aberration was one that saw illness as progressive, irreversible brain deterioration. As time passed, it became clear that some patients did not respond to moral treatment and that some indeed had neurological defects. The flowering German neuropathologic approach, emphasizing nerve tissue damage and diagnosis, also contributed to a shift in emphasis away from the individual and his history to his disease and presumed cellular pathology. The neuropsychiatrist, whose orientation was diagnostic and prognostic but not heavily therapeutic, became the specialist responsible for the mentally disturbed.

Toward the end of the century, even the minimum goal of Dorothea Dix's campaigning—decent care—had begun to slip seriously. Henry Burdett, an English physician, described care in American mental hospitals in his four-volume *Hospitals and Asylums of the World* published in 1891:

> Were it not for the lavish expenditure in sanitary matters, and the introduction of all the latest scientific appliances for minimizing labor and risk, it would appear lunatics in America were still regarded as a class to be confined first, and perhaps cured afterwards, rather than unfortunate beings for whose curative treatment these enormous buildings have been designed (Burdett, 1891, vol. 1, p. 110).

Burdett's thorough survey of American institutions depicts overcrowding, deteriorated physical facilities, extensive use of physical restraint and manipulation, and only occasionally a hospital with a therapeutic orientation.

The patterns described by Burdett, of course, continued well into the twentieth century. It is sobering to realize that a hospital reform movement with international scope could give way over a few decades to custodial, dehumanizing patterns of care that are still reflected in many of our state hospitals. Even in the smaller institutions where moral therapy had thrived, there was a similar reversal, more a result of the altered orientation of supervising physicians than of the political and economic forces that acted on large state hospitals.

Milieutherapie

We take up next a second period of innovation in the use of the institution as a vehicle for therapy. This movement is less well known to us because its spread was aborted, or at least deferred, by the rise of European fascism in the 1930s.

During the first two decades of this century Hermann Simon, a German psychiatrist, developed a system of hospital treatment that he called *activere behandlung* (literally, "more active therapy"). As superintendent of a state-supported hospital at Gutersloh, Simon saw patients' behaviors as responsive to the expectations of those around them. Each patient was carefully assessed not only for his psychopathology at the moment, but for recent and past work performance. He was then placed in a work situation suitable to his present status and social background. When he had shown competence at this activity, he was encouraged to undertake more demanding tasks.

Simon's descriptions of the application of *aktivere behandlung* show an awareness of the importance of the nursing staff in effecting this rehabilitative work program. He was also aware of the importance of maintaining among both patients and staff an atmosphere that supports recovery and good function:

> Nursing staff and caretakers are never supervisors of work, but are co-workers.

> Assigned work must take into account the ability of the individual patient. This is originally often reduced, and overexpectations may be harmful.

> If the caretaker sits next to him and shows him simple steps for a short period, the basis is laid for the next day.

> I can report from our experience that no symptom need be a stop to activity.

> Finally, all psychotherapy is nothing but training the patient with the goal of re-creating the will and the strength towards an ordered and useful self-realization (Simon, 1927, 1929).[5]

Simon's work became widely known in Germany during the 1920s and was described in three long papers in the *Allgemeine Zeitschrift für Psychiatrie,* the major German psychiatric journal 1927, 1929a, 1929b). His approach, which spread to other German hospitals, became referred to as *milieutherapie*, conveying awareness and use of the whole hospital environment. After Hitler's rise to power in 1933, the therapeutic movement in German institutions waned rapidly.

As had the earlier approach of moral treatment, the principles of *milieutherapie* appeared concurrently in different countries and settings. Working with institutionalized delinquents at Hollabrunn, Austria, Adolf Aichhorn, an educator and psychoanalyst influenced by Freud, used the social structure as a part of treatment strategy. Aichhorn made sensitive use of peer relations among adolescents and of the intensity of their transference feelings toward counselors (1965).

The same therapeutic optimism and interest in using the entire hospital environment was reflected in the development of "total push" treatment in the United States during the 1930s (Myerson, 1939). The entire ward staff was considered important in bringing pressure for change on patients in the total push approach. Similarly, the Menninger brothers introduced the German "milieu therapy" in their hospital work at Topeka, Kansas. Milieu therapy required a more specific prescription for each patient. Patients were treated with individual psychotherapy, and the therapist, on the basis of his treatment data, prescribed to the ward staff the manner of social interaction he felt would provide the patient with the most useful therapeutic experience (Menninger, 1936). Milieu therapy and therapeutic community, whose origins we take up next, are often confused. In many ways they overlap, although the historical continuity between the two appears minimal. Both acknowledge the importance and therapeutic utility of all aspects of patients' hospital experience. Perhaps the critical difference lies in the fact that milieu therapy retains the medical framework, with a physician (psychiatrist) using his diagnostic and therapeutic insights to instruct the ward staff in the best approach to each patient. Therapeutic community moves away from this medical model to emphasize group treatment and decision-making that often includes patients as well as staff.

Origins of Therapeutic Community

Like most phenomena examined closely, the beginnings of therapeutic community and its spread to the United States are more complex than would appear at first glance. Just as Pinel became the symbol for what we have recently discovered was a widespread Moral Treatment movement, Maxwell Jones' industrial rehabilitation unit at Belmont Hospital, England, has become the official birthplace of therapeutic community. Indeed, Jones' pioneering program embodied many of the crucial features that distinguish therapeutic community, and his book *The Therapeutic Community* (1953) discusses many important features of the technique. But why did Jones' example spread so rapidly in England and the United States? A number of confluent factors were responsible. First was a general post-World War II resurgence of therapeutic optimism growing from the triumph of democracy over fascism but, more specifically, from the spread of psychoanalytic concepts and therapy in psychiatric circles. Second, many psychiatrists had been exposed to great numbers of young men who were too mentally disturbed to be inducted into the armed forces or who became disturbed during their military experience. Thus the epidemiologic scope of mental problems was brought to attention in a way that academic training and office practice of neuropsychiatry or psychoanalysis never could. Third, professional and public concern sprang up about the conditions in large state hospitals where the great majority of care for the severely disturbed was provided in locked wards little better than mass jail cells. Fourth, the milieu therapy and total push approaches had already suggested the possibility and efficacy of using the hospital environment therapeutically. A final, little-known fact, which may have had wider impact than we recognize, is that during

World War II many state hospital wards, depleted of nursing personnel by the military, were run by patients.

The first major innovation in hospital psychiatry in this period was not, however, therapeutic community but what I shall refer to as the "psychotherapy hospital." Here, as in milieu therapy, the major change was the introduction of psychoanalytically oriented psychotherapy with inpatients.

Widespread interest in psychoanalytic therapy had engendered new therapeutic optimism about severe mental illness. Harry Stack Sullivan's work with schizophrenics in the hospital setting had included emphasis on the part played by the environment in treatment (1933), but his followers placed greater emphasis on the challenging work of psychotherapy and the psychodynamics of the severely disturbed patient (Fromm-Reichman, 1950; Knight and Friedman, 1970). Application of psychoanalysis to the hospital first generated the psychotherapy hospital, the best-known examples being Chestnut Lodge in Maryland and Austen Riggs in Massachusetts, along with the Menninger Foundation in Kansas. Many academic hospitals followed in this direction and placed strong emphasis for young psychiatrists-in-training on intensive psychotherapy with severely disturbed inpatients. While the theoretical, educational, and therapeutic significance of the psychotherapy hospital was considerable, certain limits and problems had become clear by the 1950s. Such care was expensive, since it required an entire therapy staff, usually in addition to the existing staff. The addition of psychoanalytic therapy to the hospital created new problems in patient care, epitomized by the conflict between a permissive therapy orientation and a medical, controlling hospital orientation. These problems raised the question of whether the psychotherapy hospital pattern could or should be widely extended to other institutions. Put another way, the therapy approach had the attractive feature of appearing to be simply an addition to the program of a hospital. To facilitate experimentation with concepts like Jones' therapeutic community, which entailed a complete reexamination of hospital functioning and staff roles, required the evolution of new psychiatric settings in a period of rapid expansion of psychiatric services of all sorts.

Jones' description of the program at Belmont and subsequent descriptions of innovative therapeutic community programs in the United States, bring out certain recurring features that go beyond simple program development. It is these features that I want to stress here, since they will be the focus of inquiry in Part I, and in my view are the essence of therapeutic community—far more than are particular meetings, ward schedules, or therapy approaches. Of the latter it can be said in general that therapeutic communities inevitably have a variety of group meetings and activities. These may include group therapy sessions, large meetings of the entire community, patient government meetings, activities programs, job training, psychodrama, family group meetings, planning meetings, recreational and social groups, and so forth. The particulars of these meetings and activities are a function of both the sorts of patients involved and the interests of staff. But inevitably there are a number of such meetings, and staff considers them of prime importance in the patients' hospital day. Individual therapy, on the other hand, is either minimized, held to a supportive role, or used in the service of the patients' wider ward experience.[6] The point is that the staff demonstrates through the program, and its attitudes toward various therapies and meetings, that groups and the community as a whole are very important. Usually there is at least one "community meeting" or "patient-staff" that includes everyone involved. Whatever happens in this meeting—and again this varies—the meeting symbolizes the unity and coherence of the entire aggregation of patients and staff. (Wilmer, 1958; Artiss, 1962; Daniels and Rubin, 1968). At such meetings a second purpose, which may or may not be explicit, is to convey and reinforce the "culture" of the community (Saslow, 1965). Frequent aspects of this culture include: a stress on pragmatism; facing real-life problems in the community and in patients' lives; a here-and-now emphasis on present manifestations rather than on origins of problems; informal sociability and friendliness, rather than arbitrary edicts from "on high" or sympathy and commiseration; immediate responses to patient behavior and ward problems. As Jones observed, "the more the patient culture approximates to the Unit culture as represented by the staff, the greater will be our effectiveness in treating new patients" (Jones, 1953, p. 51).

In general, practitioners of therapeutic community have recognized the importance of the newcomer's entry, often devising special ways for easing the transition to the hospital setting. As John and Elaine Cumming, who developed therapeutic community units in a Canadian province hospital, say of the situation of the new patient:

> . . . his immediate problem is that, like a migrant, he is a stranger in a strange place. He greatly needs to see an acceptable image of himself reflected in the responses of those with whom he deals and to understand his relationship to this milieu (Cumming and Cumming, 1962, p. 138).

Another universal feature running through the descriptions of therapeutic communities is the importance of role definitions for both patient and staff. Properly, I should say "role redefinition," for inevitably the behavior expected of doctors, nurses, aides, patients, and others in the therapeutic community is different from that generally expected in hospitals. The Cummings emphasize, for example, that in traditional large hospitals, nursing aides make most decisions about patients but must attribute these to higher staff (see also, Strauss et al., 1964). In the therapeutic community, the responsibility of this staff role is accepted and reinforced. The nurse, too, is seen as moving from being a passive implementer of medical orders, and an observer of behavior, to an active, therapeutic role. Similarly, the patient is seen as an actor, initiator, collaborator, and manager of his own affairs (Cumming and Cumming, 1962).

In the same way the description of the roles of senior personnel—chief psychiatrist, nursing director, chief social worker—in therapeutic communities is different from that in other psychiatric services. The symbols of rank—the white coats, private offices, "professional" reserve—are often absent, replaced by an informal, egalitarian style of interaction with patients and other staff members. These senior personnel do a great deal of teaching or training; their roles become less those of medical professionals and therapists, and more those of educators in the ways of therapeutic community and models for others. A further aspect of the roles of senior personnel is more often reported about them than by them: In many instances, they have a charismatic, inspirational quality.

Therapeutic communities proliferated during the 1960s. Most developed in new settings: overhauled state hospital admission wards, new general hospital psychiatric units, community mental health centers. Recently trained psychiatrists, charged with setting up and administrating these units, were aware of the many studies of asylums and psychotherapy hospitals revealing the extraordinary complexity of structure and functioning and the frequency of antitherapeutic patterns in these institutions (Stanton and Schwartz, 1954; Caudill, 1958; Goffman, 1961). The growing pool of experience in the United States and in England led to more frequent and more sophisticated interpretations of therapeutic community. At the Yale-New Haven Hospital in 1959, Thomas Detre was appointed director of a new inpatient treatment unit that was also to be part of the training program of the Department of Psychiatry of the Yale University School of Medicine. Part I comprises a close examination of the therapeutic community Detre developed, providing our most accessible and carefully observed example of a healing community.

NOTES

1. I do not mean to gloss over the massive impact of psychoactive drugs. The drugs, however, primarily control symptoms; that is, they are a more subtle, individualized way of diminishing deviant behavior. As such they make many persons amenable to other sorts of treatment and change, and they have also no doubt contributed to a growing acceptance of the mentally ill in society.

2. The sociologist will recognize a familiar dichotomy here, identified by Toennies as *gesellschaft* and *gemeinschaft*. For further discussion of this general theme, see Chapter 23.

3. *Norm* refers to a concept of desirable behavior or attitude shared among members of a group or organization. In the study of psychiatric settings, we and others have often used the term *value* for the same idea. However, it is more consistent with the usage of anthropology and sociology to reserve *value* for broader concepts of the desirable that are often reflected in sets of specific norms. Thus, individualism is a major American value; leaving home to go to college is a norm for members of the American upper-middle class that is one reflection of this value. Although some norms are shared by a whole society they are generally maintained within specific social institutions such as the family or the school. Other norms apply only within the bounds of a particular group. For example, the highly confrontive, attacking style of Synanon meetings would be considered rude and bizarre in most American social situations. Following the same logic, I shall refer to what has often been called the "hospital culture" as a "norm system." This will refer to the beliefs shared by members of the therapeutic community that have to do with mental illness and, especially, healing.

4. *Role* is a term that bridges social groups and individuals. It refers to the existence of expectations, usually shared between an individual and a group, for directing individual behavior. A role—in our case almost always the role of sufferer (e.g., patient) or healer (e.g., staff)—is a set of behavior patterns that are expected and therefore predictable. A role concept is shared by the enactor and by those in the situation where the role performance is expectable. For our purposes, roles are extremely important. If a hospital maintains, as part of its norm system, a concept of the patient role as unpredictable, dangerous, irrational, childlike, and untrustworthy, the staff is unlikely to notice or encourage more positive behaviors. Similarly, if patients expect staff to be distant, punitive, arbitrary, and hostile, they may not notice or respond to friendliness or encouragement. For further discussion of role theory, see Sarbin and Allen, 1968.

5. Translated from the German by Dorothea Almond.

6. Marshall Edelson has written extensively about therapeutic community—or sociotherapy—as a companion to psychotherapy (1964,

1970). He sees the hospital staff divided into two groups, one addressing the intrapsychic level of the patient's experience, the other addressing the patient's social relationships. Both Edelson's and the author's experiences indicate that this combined form of therapeutic community has difficulty at the interface of the two therapies and functions best when there is a central leader who can negotiate conflicts between them.

PART I

A Therapeutic Community

The nine chapters that follow comprise a series of descriptions, research findings, and conceptualizations that explore one therapeutic community in considerable detail. The data available for Part I are more complete and varied than for any of the other examples in this volume: I had the good fortune to be "on the scene" when the Yale-New Haven Hospital Psychiatric Service opened in 1960 and to be on the ward staff in roles (activities therapist, medical student) that permitted me to observe, without many of the pressures that bear on staff from day to day, during 1961 and 1962. From 1962 to 1963 and again between 1964 and 1967, I was actively involved as a researcher studying a number of facets of the ward, its patients, staff, and program. In this role I could observe the ward informally, as well as through structured research tools and procedures. In addition, my research collaborators—Hans Esser, Sandra Boltax, and Kenneth Keniston —each knew the ward well and each offered observations from different vantage points. Finally, follow-up observations and interviews of patients who had been hospitalized were conducted between 1967 and 1970, giving some idea about the long-range effects of patient experiences during hospitalization.

2

The organization and material of the following chapters has been determined by the natural sequence of insights into the ward as they emerged and by the general goal of discovering and demonstrating the core processes of therapeutic community. The focus moves frequently among at least three levels of discussion: (1) specific descriptive examples of behavior and ward life; (2) research data and findings; (3) concepts and models. We begin with an overview of the history of Tompkins I, focusing on initial plans, purposes, and experiences as the therapeutic community program developed (Chapter I). Next we consider the "culture" or norm system of the ward. In doing this we discuss three dimensions or themes that every large social organization must contend with: authority, nurture, and communitas. Prior observations and studies of mental hospitals show that emphasis is generally skewed toward one of these dimensions more than toward the others. Thus the asylum stresses authority through its rigid and limited conception of patient and staff roles and their relations; the sanatarium, Veterans Administration hospitals, and to some extent the psychotherapy hospital emphasize nurture through material or intangible dependency benefits. Chapter 2 explores how the Tompkins I therapeutic community emphasizes the dimension of communitas, in an institutional framework of communitas. We are particularly concerned with how this dimension of communitas is translated specifically into the norms that govern individual and group behavior in the day-to-day life of the ward. One important form this takes is in role expectations for various participants in the ward (Chapter 3). Again, our concern is not simply with the definitions of roles but with a theme running through the definitions of all roles in this setting: their specialness, unusualness, or, as we are calling it, "charismatic" quality, given conventional training or expectations. Specifically we shall examine how the roles of director, psychiatric resident, nurse, and patient are each given healing charisma.

Thus Chapters 2 and 3 bring out how the general qualities that I impute to healing communities are manifest in this specific setting, its norm system, and its role definitions. Chapter 4 brings these qualities to life as parts of a dynamic ward process. To do this we look at the experience of the patient as he progresses into, through, and out of the therapeutic community. The data we use include descriptions by patients of their own experiences, observations of patients by staff, and findings from studying the attitudes and behaviors of an aggregate sample of 60 patients. Similarly, the time perspective shifts from a moment-to-moment analysis of the first minutes of a patient's arrival at the ward, to an overview of major phases of hospitalization. In Chapter 4 we begin to see the outlines of more general individual and group processes in a healing community. Examination of entry to the ward brings out the importance of making initial contact with the patient, getting his attention in a way that will make him maximally responsive to his environment. The experiences of patients in the midst of their hospitalization demonstrates how norms and roles serve to create a system of behavior modification by using powerful social reinforcements. Backing up this system is a second motivating principle: the parallel charismatic quality of all roles. Put simply, if a doctor or nurse can be something unusual here, why not a patient?

The following three chapters (5-7) comprise three case studies of specific individuals. These "hospital career studies" bring the formulations developed in Chapters 2-4 to bear on real individuals as they encounter the therapeutic community. The primary purpose here is to find out what really happens when individuals come into this therapeutic community. These hospital career studies both bring out the ways in which the general processes that were elaborated apply in specific cases and begin to suggest patterns of individual response to therapeutic community. To explore this latter idea, that there may be recurring patterns of patient-hospital interaction, I have included in each chapter findings for a group of patients whose hospitalizations had features in common with the individual described in that chapter. In this way our discussion moves from "how" the therapeutic community works to "how it works for whom."

In Chapters 5-7 and Chapter 8 follow-up findings are reported for the three carefully described individual experiences and for a larger cohort of patients. These data begin to suggest where the overall experience of therapeutic community fits into individual lives. They also provide some general answers to inevitable questions about outcome: how well the system works. A final review (Chapter 9) allows us to summarize some of the central findings that can be drawn from looking closely at one therapeutic community before we turn to the series of briefer examinations of similar systems in very different places and styles that comprise Parts II and III.

CHAPTER 1

The Development of a Therapeutic Community: "Tompkins I"

Most descriptions of therapeutic communities are presented as accomplished facts. In the case of the ward we shall be examining, enough information is available to depict in some detail the beginnings of the program and the influences that led to certain changes and innovations during its first few years.

The idea of a short-term psychiatric inpatient treatment service in the Yale-New Haven Community Hospital was conceived by the hospital administration and Dr. Frederick Redlich, chairman of the Department of Psychiatry, Yale Medical School, during the late 1950s. The unit opened in January 1960, under the medical direction of Thomas Detre and a small staff, including Christine Ferriter, nursing supervisor, and Nea Norton, chief of social work. Detre's views on the nature of the mental disorders that would be treated by the unit and his ideas on treatment of acute mental disorder are conveyed by remarks he made in explaining the program to his fellow faculty members:

> The goals and objectives of treatment must be based on the clear recognition of what the society around us can tolerate, and members of the staff must make every effort to make not only

their aims but also their techniques of treatment comprehensible to all who participate in the therapeutic process. . . . The recognition that the model for most mental illnesses is not pneumococcal pneumonia but rather something like rheumatoid arthritis, where remissions and relapses are the rule rather than the exception, is a sobering experience. . . . We have learned that disorganizing anxiety is not an essential requirement to attain motivation for treatment, and, in fact, it is in the climate of reduced suffering where many of our most ambitious goals can be best realized (1959).

Detre's earlier training in the Yale Department of Psychiatry included an extensive period of work in the Yale Psychiatric Institute during the late 1950s. There, severely disturbed patients, many of them young schizophrenics, were being treated with intensive psychotherapy and minimal use of antipsychotic medication or group techniques. Patients remained in the hospital for lengthy periods of one to several years; psychotic and self-destructive behaviors were common occurrences, viewed by the psychiatric staff as inevitable in the working through of the considerable intrapsychic problems of their patients. William Caudill's book, *The Psychiatric Hospital as a Small Society* (1958), based on an extensive study of the Yale Psychiatric Institute, suggested that much of this patient behavior was related to organizational patterns and staff expectations (see also Rubenstein and Lasswell, 1967; and Berkowitz, 1969). Detre felt strongly that an atmosphere that tolerates or encourages symptomatic behavior would not be effective for brief hospitalization. He also believed that the psychiatrist-patient relationship should not be patterned after the psychoanalytic model but should focus on such immediate matters as the patients' symptoms, his relations to family and work, and his daily ward life (Detre et al., 1961). He felt that acute illness and consequent hospitalization are only the first phase of treatment, one in which relief symptoms and restoration of functioning are primary. Implicit in Detre's orientation was a therapeutic focus on ego psychological concepts like mastery and coping. He viewed all available treatment modalities—psychological, social, and somatic—as legitimate means to the end of restored functioning, discharge, and out-patient therapy (Astrachan and Detre, 1968).

The patients who were accepted for treatment ranged in age from 10 to 80. Their disorders were severe, that is, acute psychoses, severe depressions, and neurological conditions with behavioral effects. Both sexes were accepted, with female patients more common by about 2:1. Few chronic patients were admitted, unless they had had an exacerbation of their condition. Patients were referred to the unit primarily by private psychiatrists, by clinics, and by the medical and surgical wards of the hospital. Because the cost of treatment on Tompkins I is high, the patients admitted were usually middle to upper class, with Blue Cross and welfare making possible some lower-class patients' hospitalizations.

Unlike their counterparts in most hospital situations, the Tompkins I nursing and social work staffs—responsible for day-to-day patient care and family contacts, respectively—were supervised or trained by Detre. This meant that the unit was highly self-contained and that one therapeutic approach could be suggested for all staff members. Detre not only supervised the work of the psychiatric residents who had primary responsibility for patients, but met with nurses and aides twice a week for training. His rationale of treatment was carefully explained, including full information on the effects and side effects of medications.[1]

Patient-staff meetings at first were held twice weekly. The concept of "staff" itself was broadly interpreted to include all nonpatients working on the ward, so that not only nurses and aides, but even kitchen workers who had frequent informal interactions with patients, attended patient-staff meetings. Discussion focused on formal administrative issues affecting patients and/or staff and at other times on issues the patients brought up. Initially the format of such meetings was unstructured; with time, the staff, finding that unstructured discussion encouraged disruptive or symptomatic behavior in some patients, increased their guidance of the meetings. Later a mimeographed outline of topics was introduced, and the meetings became part of a community decision-making process. Emergency patient-staff meetings were called at times of any major individual or unit-wide crisis. These included such issues as locking the unit door because of a patient's behavior, elopements, or suicidal feelings.

Group therapy was conducted twice a week from the outset. Shortly after opening, "we decided to divide the group and to have each resident conduct group therapy with his own patients. We hoped that this would promote group cohesiveness that might otherwise be difficult to achieve with a rapidly changing population. We also felt that patients' rivalry for their own doctor's attention, perhaps otherwise overlooked on a fast-moving service, could be brought into the open and dealt with in this way" (Detre et al., 1961).

Continuing contacts between patients, staff, and families have been viewed as critical for rapid resumption of functioning and return home. The unit's program in this respect quickly moved away from the traditional model of social worker-family contacts isolated from the psychiatrist and the patient. Accordingly, two therapies were developed toward these goals: (1) "four-way meetings" including the patient, members of his family, the psychiatrist, and a social worker; (2) multifamily group meetings attended by one resident, his patients, their families, a social worker, and nurses. The four-way meetings allow intensive focus on the problems of an individual patient and his family, and are especially useful in dealing with emotionally charged family issues. Planning for discharge is also a frequent purpose. The frequency of such four-way meetings depends on staff appraisal of a particular family's needs. Family members are required to attend multifamily group meetings held regularly twice each week at convenient evening and weekend times. These meetings give family members a taste of the patient's experience on the unit, a reassuring contact with relatives of other patients, and opportunity to share problems with other patients' relatives in a supportive, accepting context.

Somatic treatments, especially antipsychotic tranquilizers and antidepressants, were actively used from the outset. Detre felt that extensive use of medications—and even electroconvulsive treatment—is necessary not only for specific therapeutic reasons but for maintaining adequate control over patients' behavior in the setting of a (generally) open-door ward on the main floor of a busy general hospital. An additional reason for active use of medications is to make patients accessible to the social contact required for involvement in ward life. Thus, when possible, tranquilizers that avoid strong sedative effects are chosen. Side-effects of drugs, or the "zombie" effect of overhigh dosage levels, are checked for frequently and treated promptly. Detre put much responsibility for choice and dosage of medication in the hands of the nursing staff, who are in the best postition to be aware of the patient's behavior and the effects of medication. Four seclusion rooms were converted, one by one, to offices as the staff found it possible to manage acute upsets with social contact and medications.

Use of individual therapy is evaluated for each particular case and such therapy is offered when staff feel it will contribute to that patient's progress. Outside therapists do not continue treatment while the patient is on the ward, with the exception of the period before discharge. Some patients are seen for a full hour two or three times weekly, while others are not seen at all beyond brief chats for administrative purposes. Individual therapy is viewed as potentially offering a way for patients to withdraw from the active and demanding social atmosphere of the unit. When the staff senses this, individual treatment, if offered at all, focuses on the patient's avoidance of the community. At other times individual therapy meetings are seen as critical in building a patient's trust and confidence to the point where he will engage with others.

The integration of these varied components of the early ward program were summarized in descriptions by Detre and his colleagues:

> Most acutely ill patients deteriorate in their social functioning prior to hospitalization. Transactions with important others in his life are disrupted, performance at work or school is impaired. By the time the patient is admitted not only is he poorly organized and isolated but so are those in his environment who attempted to cope with him. Indeed, in the great majority of cases the patient's difficulties are not limited to any single important relationship but have in fact extended into all the areas of his life so that he suffers from massive social dysfunctioning and can no longer cope with the problems of living in the outside world.
>
> In some ways, therefore, the hospital phase of treatment can be described as an attempt to deal with those issues which make separation from the community necessary. The expression "hospital phase of treatment" is purposely used because it is obvious that restoration of the patient's social competence is not the only treatment goal. It merely serves to emphasize that a more thorough exploration of his characterological problems should be postponed until after discharge, when dangers of passivity, institutional dependency and desertion by family and freinds are no longer threatening.
>
> Thus, the initial approach of the hospital to the patient must be structured. The patient will have to experience a less stressful interchange with others. In the midst of his chaos, he must observe some order about him. A careful diagnostic evaluation will be important. The patient's biologic rhythms will be observed, organic factors investigated, and dynamic issues approached. Somatic treatment modalities will assist the patient to arrive at some more comfortable level of integration

and to participate more actively in the treatment program (Detre, 1959).

The programme that has evolved over the past year might best be characterized as a socio-adaptive approach to hospital treatment. This term implies that the mentally ill person is seen as one who has failed to adapt in some way to prevalent standards of normality as defined by his particular social-familial setting. While it is true that what brings the patient to the hospital is usually a major change in his "psychopathology," which has disrupted a pre-existing equilibrium between patient and family, this change is either preceded or accompanied by major shifts in the patient's immediate social contacts. Symptoms, then, are regarded as important insofar as they impair the patient's ability to interact comfortably and effectively in his milieu (Detre, Kessler, and Sayres, 1965).

These descriptions depict the ward and its program as it began. Before we turn to an account of the early years of the ward and the additions and changes made as the therapeutic community evolved, a mention of the atmosphere of the unit is important. From the start, the unit was characterized by high staff *esprit de corps* and considerable loyalty to Detre and one another. Initially, when the program was innovative and controversial, there was a sense of being part of a revolutionary, but eminently sensible, enterprise. Detre was initially available on the unit many hours a day and frequently during weekend and evening hours. He did much of the formal teaching and emergency supervision. Within a year, the unit's approach—both for specific situations and as a general "ward culture"—was well enough understood for Detre to transfer much day-to-day decision-making to other psychiatrists and to the chiefs of nursing and social work. Psychiatric residents, assigned to the unit for a year, were put in a pivotal role that included medical responsibility for five to 10 patients, leadership of these patients in group therapy and multifamily groups, and individual and family therapy for specific patients. The residents' multiple interactions with patients and families made them, in a sense, the focus of a subunit of the ward and allowed them to develop their own style of leadership.[2] In general, staff members were encouraged, on the one hand, to be themselves as naturally as possible and, on the other, to present a consistent set of expectations to patients. The result was that rather than appearing in the conventional "professional role," staff tended to appear to patients, visitors, and other newcomers as a varied group of individual personalities espousing a common attitude in relation to the central activities of ward life. This pattern of "universal specialness" is discussed in detail in Chapter 3, "Roles and Healing Charisma."

Next, what of the ward program of Tompkins I? The system of meetings and patient statuses developed and changed rapidly during the early years. A "buddy system" was adopted on the suggestion of a patient. A patient with buddy privileges could go off the ward accompanied by other patients at a time when he was not eligible for solo passes into the community. Initial experimentation with family group meetings included the following: meetings without the patient member, meetings continuing following discharge, and meetings of specialized types of family constellations. Eventually, the system of twice-weekly, multifamily group meetings was settled on, with four-way meetings in addition for those families needing special attention. During the first year the length of hospitalization increased from the intended three to an average six or seven weeks. This somewhat longer time appeared to be necessary if the staff were to achieve the multiple goals of controlling acute upset, evaluating patient and family, adapting patient to the unit and engaging him in its processes, preparing him and his family for the readjustment of discharge, and testing out the patient's readiness through passes of increasing duration.

On the evening of a staff party celebrating the second

anniversary of the unit, a graduate student, who had been readmitted only days after his recent discharge from a three-month stay, ran off the unit and successfully committed suicide by throwing himself in front of a train. The patient had returned to the unit depressed, but no one on the staff had a sense of urgency about the degree of depression. This tragic event, the first suicide of a patient or ex-patient of the unit, was initially experienced as a shattering blow to the sense of omnipotence of staff members. The suicide was also an implicit challenge to the reputation and confidence of the staff, especially of Detre. It could well have been the stimulus for a major shift in unit policy toward more control, screening out of risky admissions, or reducing patients' responsibility in the ward. Instead there was an interesting and quite different reaction.

The suicide patient happened to have been hospitalized during the time when patient social contacts were being closely observed as part of a research study. A careful record of seating positions of all patients at lunch and dinner was made daily for a six-month period in the communal dining room. Week-by-week analysis indicated a variety of interaction patterns. However, almost all patients showed some preferences for one or two mealtime "friends." A careful review of this patient's social patterns was made, in a search for retrospective hints that might have predicted his behavior. The patient's hospital course had been characterized by three distinct social phases. In the first, he was an active member of the social group of young male patients on the unit, although others often found him irritating. After making a verbal homosexual advance, he became something of an outcast from the young male group and socialized almost solely with new, markedly disturbed patients. During this time his overt behavior became less bizarre and obnoxious. Thus, patients and staff experienced him as less difficult than in the earlier phase of his stay. During the last month of hospitalization, this patient's social pattern became "randomized." His social contact pattern was no different from what it would have been had he made his social contacts purely by chance. No other patients had such a pattern, even during the final week in the hospital. In retrospect it was concluded that randomization reflects a severe disruption and alienation from the social life of the unit (Almond and Esser, 1965).

Detre and his staff drew an interesting conclusion from these findings. Rather than turn to increased staff vigilance and patient restrictions, they concluded that the mistake had been in not recognizing an important source of information about the patient: other patients. It was concluded that other patients on the unit must have had some awareness of this man's unusual socializing pattern, had they only been asked. What emerged out of this experience and the staff's appraisal of it were innovations in which patients' responsibility for one another in decision-making processes was *increased*. Detre believed that what was needed was not simply the *opportunity* to communicate concerns about others—these already existed in patient-staff meetings—but the *responsibility* for doing so as a regular part of ward life.

To implement this view a "Patient Advisory Board" was established in 1963. The seven-member board is elected by the patients as a whole, with members serving terms of one week or more. All decisions on any change in patients' statuses are to be passed on by the board. Thus, requests to be moved from the "specialed" status, requests to be placed on the buddy system, and requests for passes to go off the ward individually are all brought before the board. Patients desiring status changes are required to submit these in writing to the Patient Advisory Board. The board's decision is based on a careful discussion with the patient and the entire patient group. The only staff member at board meetings is the activities therapist (who spends the great bulk of her time as a board consultant, since advisory meetings take up much of patients' free time). Factors considered by the board in its decisions about a change in privilege status include other patients' comfort about this change, how well the patient meets the ward behavior norms, whether he has made the prescribed arrangements for outside treatment and work, and so forth. The board votes on the change; the vote is then reported at a larger general meeting of patients and staff, where the issues may be rediscussed. If no questions are raised about the change, a patient's privilege request, once approved by the board, is automatically effected. While staff maintains a veto privilege, the decisions of the Patient Advisory Board are accepted or only slightly modified unless there is serious staff concern. Staff influence on the board is effected by observing its overall decision-making competence. Should the board make what the staff views as consistently poor decisions, all passes are briefly withdrawn and the community is asked to reconstitute the board.

Another related change in the unit program at this time (1963) was the development of a system of patient monitors. This role can be described most succinctly as a sort of "psychiatric trustee." The monitor is a patient who, for a given time period, performs certain nursing duties. These include "specialing" of severely disturbed, usually newer, patients. Most patients who required continuous observation, it was felt, could be observed by other patients rather than by staff. Staff was relieved of much of the burden of specialing disturbed patients, and the input of information about such patients was maintained by including the patient "specialer" as a participant in nursing reports. Monitors are also assigned to check on patients who need to be intermittently observed; to make a general report at change of shift to the oncoming nursing and monitor staff; and to report to the community on specific problems that develop during weekends and evenings, when fewer staff are available.

Another example of expanded patient responsibility was

the introduction in 1964 of leaderless group therapy. The same group that attended therapy together with a resident psychiatrist met twice weekly without the therapist, but with the expectation that they would have a therapy session. Patients initially resisted this new activity; one patient went so far as to urinate on the floor during one of the first meetings. The staff, however, continued to convey consistently their expectation that patients could manage these sessions. Soon leaderless meetings were part of ward routine, conducted in as businesslike a way as staff-led therapies. A comparative study of leaderless meetings, led meetings, and family meetings gave support to the impression that the leaderless meetings were similar in quality to other meetings, except that patients were in some ways more active than in led meetings (Astrachan et al., 1967a).

Between 1962 and 1964—the period during which many of these innovations were implemented—the average length of stay increased from seven to ten weeks. Much of the increase can be attributed directly to the additional time required for patients to experience the monitor and Patient Advisory Board roles. Although many patients were treated and discharged without experiencing one or both of these assignments, the latter were increasingly seen as useful hurdles for testing a patient's readiness for progressing toward discharge. Additional hurdles were added around the interface of patients' ward involvement and imminent discharge: It became a prerequisite for discharge, and even for predischarge full-day passes, for patients to (1) resume work, school, or household activity; and (2) begin or resume visits with an outside therapist.

These specific hurdles and new activities and responsibilities for patients reflect a more general, underlying process that was evolving during the first three or four years. By 1964 a transition had taken place and fewer changes in the program were made thereafter. This transition involves a vision of the patient as a person who *becomes part of* the ward community, rather than someone who is *acted upon* by the staff of the ward. To pursue the implications of the conception of patienthood and therapeutic community, we will turn in the next three chapters to the guiding principles of ward life: its norms; how they are used to define roles; and the way these roles are learned and affect individual behavior. At the same time we shall be continuously developing a picture of the cohesive social system of therapeutic community as it interacts with individual attitudes and behaviors.

NOTES

1. For a description of the administrative development of Tompkins I, see Schulberg (1968).

2. A description of the varied styles developed by one set of residents is available in "The Psychiatrist's Effect on the Behavior and Interaction of Therapy Groups" (Astrachan et al., 1967b); an analysis of the training possibilities of such a resident role in a day hospital setting is found in Almond and Astrachan (1969).

CHAPTER 2

Norms and Communitas

In any organization there exist norms for the behavior of members. Large organizations tend to formulate these norms in extensive and usually rigid bureaucratic rules and role descriptions. In smaller organizations like psychiatric wards or small hospitals, the same may be true, but it is also possible to rely more on unwritten, word-of-mouth transmitting of norms. The latter is the case in the therapeutic community. We shall see, in this and the following two chapters, that the sharing of a system of norms informally and the process of bringing patients into the norm system of the community are interwoven with therapy and the functioning of the community. For the norms of the community instruct its members in how to behave—and it is, after all, the behavior of the patient that has brought him, directly or indirectly, to the hospital. Thus, in trying to understand a psychiatric unit such as Tompkins I, which addresses itself to altering behavior rather than changing internal dynamics, we have a special interest in the norm system. [1]

To establish a framework for discussing psychiatric hospital norms, and specifically those of therapeutic community, we shall consider briefly the patterns of norms found in social organizations. Studies of organizations suggest three recur-

rent dimensions of institutional life, which we shall refer to
here as *control, nurture,* and *communitas.*[2] Every social group
deals in some way with these dimensions in its norm system.
In hospital terms the issues are posed as follows: How is the
behavior of members of the organization (especially patients)
controlled? What sort of care—material and psychological—
is provided? What degree of cohesion—sense of
"we-ness"—exists among the membership or its subgroups?
To a considerable extent the hospital, or any organization for
that matter, can be characterized by the emphasis it puts on
one dimension over the others.

CONTROL

Institutions for the mad have tended to emphasize the
dimension of control. The behavior of those who come to
mental hospitals evokes anxiety in others because it implies
the loss of some degree of internal control. Thus, the first
worry of society, one inevitably transmitted in the mandate
given the institution's staff, is the imposition of external limits
to counter the inferred loss of inner limits. Consistent with
this, every modern study of a mental hospital has identified
the pattern of authority as an important feature of the institution, and the attitudes of members concerning control as an
important aspect of the system of norms.[3] In many questionnaire studies dealing with such things as hospital atmosphere, values or goals, a dimension emerges that correlates
strongly with a personality measure, authoritarianism, that
emphasizes external, paternalistic control (the "F Scale"). No
matter whether one is measuring patient, staff, or citizen
attitudes, or finding the scores high or low, the control dimension appears to be universally relevant. Traditional
asylum staff attitudes about control convey a mistrustful, distant view of patients, a belief that mental illness is incurable

and makes patients different from "normals," and that staff must be vigilant to prevent violence (Gilbert, 1954). Traditional patient attitudes on control are somewhat different, but related. Patients see their disorder as a temporary problem, something they are not responsible for, and best covered over with a conventional facade (Levinson and Gallagher, 1964). They rely on staff to control and heal them, accepting the authority of staff over them and hoping it will be used benignly and for their benefit.

Erving Goffman has described as total institutions, or asylums, those organizations operated with control as the major dimension of life. In such hospitals most human activities are conducted in the guise of authority relations. The hospital norm system acts "as though" control were the only important activity taking place. In such institutions the line between staff and patients is clear, and completely different sets of norms operate for each. Needs for nurturance or friendship between patients and staff are disguised or suppressed. Such patient needs, if met at all, are met within the patient group or through informal relationships between patients and staff.[4]

NURTURE

Nurture is a second major dimension of organization life: What does one "get" for being a member? In most work organizations, members are paid or rewarded materially, and this is the central factor in the relation of member to organization.

The first concern of mental hospital reformers has generally been nurture. Does the hospital at least provide a decent life for its patients? Are the staff concerned, kind, gentle, giving? The "sanitarium," where healing occurs through good care and removal from the stresses of everyday life, embodies the idea of nurture as a dominant theme of hospital life. As we saw, nurture was an important element in moral treatment, but one that became tragically confused with the treatment itself in the attempt to expand its application. For many chronic patients, Veterans Administration hospitals and the better state hospitals have become residences within which adequate amounts of nurture—both literal and symbolic—are available (Daniels and Kuldau, 1967). Patient behavior in these institutions is more a function of whether or not nurture is adequate and secure than anything else. Patients will specifically (although not necessarily consciously) present themselves as sicker if they are told discharge is being considered. On the other hand they will appear less sick if they believe the question of open versus closed ward is being decided (Braginsky et al., 1969).[5]

In the psychotherapy hospital, patients and staff may operate under different assumptions about the meaning of therapy in norm terms. The staff views psychotherapy as offering the patient a special two-person relationship within which the patient may work on his problems. There are special norms in the therapy hour: The patient may say anything he thinks or feels and the therapist maintains a nonjudgmental attitude. The patient's hospital life, as well as the therapist, becomes part of the transference material. The relationship also may be seen as a corrective experience counterbalancing earlier, conflictual family ties. Thus the therapist may experience his treatment relationship as a dyadic communitas system. Patients, however, often see therapy as a part of the hospital's nurturance. They receive the direct satisfaction of an accepting relationship, one in which the therapist is totally concerned with them; and, as in the more comfortable asylums, they may see therapy as the "price" they pay for remaining in the pleasant hospital situation. Clearly, nurture is a double-edged sword. Especially when a goal of the hospital is rapid restoration to the community, emphasis on the nurturant side of hospital life or of therapy may be a problem.

COMMUNITAS

Communitas is a third dimension of organization life. In other sorts of groups such as religious congregations, many political campaigns, or social movements, it may be dominant. Communitas is a sense of being part of a group of essentially equal members who are important to one another. In asylums we find little development of communitas. Where it exists, it is within staff or patient groups or subgroups, and it is not necessarily related to the goal of patient improvement. Similarly, in psychotherapy hospitals little sense of wider communitas develops. Instead, there are three or more overlapping subcommunities: staff, patients, and therapy dyads. It is obviously therapeutic community that strives to put a primary emphasis on the communitas norm dimension. Communitas values a sense of belonging, of membership in the community, as playing a central part in one's life. One not only belongs but feels a sense of responsibility for others and for the intactness of the group as a whole. Another aspect of the communitas norm system is espousal of the particular ideology, beliefs, or practices of the group. These, of course, may range from sectarian dogmatic convictions, to political positions and tactics, to special ceremonies and patterns of interaction considered beneficial in healing. The remainder of this chapter will be devoted to exploring the norms of therapeutic community, especially those of Tompkins I.

To elucidate the communitas norms in the Tompkins I therapeutic community we drew on a variety of sorts of data. We interviewed staff members from different roles and ranks. We interviewed patients at several times during their hospital stays about their hospital experiences and reactions. We looked at the training material given to new staff members, the introductory material given to all new patients, and published descriptions of the ward. From these observations we derived 60 items that stated, in positive or negative terms, attitudes and behaviors that seemed to reflect the ward's norms. Another group of items was drawn from other studies to tap the dimensions of control and nurture.

A series of 65 patients filled out questionnaires with these items at four times during hospitalization: (1) within 48 hours of admission; (2) at one week; (3) after a month; (4) at discharge (which averaged 10 weeks after admission). A representative group of staff members was also tested. The repeated patient testing was a way of examining the acceptance of ward norms over the course of hospitalization (see Chapter 4). Here, we are interested in identifying the norms of the ward and the interrelations among the norms.

We found that the items we had devised were indeed meaningful to patients and staff. Strong agreement was shown, especially by staff, with items that expressed trust and involvement in the community; the importance of social interactions on the ward; the value of sharing problems, feelings, and activities with others, both patients and staff; and a belief in patient responsibility. Items expressing mistrust, social withdrawal, and dependence on staff for help were strongly rejected.

To assess whether the norms these items reflect comprise a coherent communitas dimension, a statistical technique, factor analysis, was used to identify groups of items that were highly intercorrelated in the responses of the patients.[6] Most of the new items we had introduced to tap the Tompkins I norm system grouped together around a single dimension whose themes are those of communitas. In addition, groups of items reflecting the dimensions of control and nurture appeared as they had in the studies where these dimensions had first been identified.

The themes of communitas on Tompkins I are suggested by listing those positively phrased items that most intensely reflect the overall factor dimension:

"Each patient's major problems should be known to the staff and other patients."

"The more a patient can open up about his problems the better."

"I shouldn't mind when my personal problems are brought up in the group."

"I like to go to lots of hospital activities such as OT and dances and patient government."

"For a patient who has to be hospitalized, groups are the most important treatment."

"Other patients can help me get well just as much as the staff can."

"Everyone here—patients and staff alike—is trying to help me get better."

"A patient should prefer talking with any other patient over reading a book."

"The staff here is trying to make a permanent improvement in my life."

"A patient should not worry about whether the things he tells his doctor will remain confidential."

"If I do not get better, it will be my own fault."

"It is most important to take an active part in helping other patients get better."

Almost all of these positive items convey directly or implicitly the importance of patients; feeling themselves to be members of the ward community. In this community patients should be very *open* about themselves and their problems. Such openness is accompanied by *trust* in other patients and in the staff: that they are important, that they can help, that one can help them. A basis of this trust is a sense of *responsibility* on the part of patients as well as staff. Interestingly, responsibility for oneself is as much a part of the dimension as is responsibility for others, or acceptance of their aid. *Involvement* is an expression of this sense of responsibility and trust in others; participation in social activity is valued over individual activities. Family involvement in the ward program is important as well.

Many negatively phrased items also reflect the communitas dimension (i.e., its opposite pole). Most express beliefs antithetical to those just listed ("Patients shouldn't have to tell each other about how they came to be on the ward."). In addition, the negative items suggest that a certain degree of conformity is part of the norm system ("There should not be so much pressure here for patients to conform to the system of the ward.").

When we put this analysis of Tompkins I norms in the context of descriptions and studies of other therapeutic communities, it becomes clear that we can distinguish two aspects of the therapeutic community norm system. The first aspect reflects communitas: valuation of active membership in a group of individuals who are equals as human beings, who are close, who care about each other, who trust each other. The second apsect of norms concerns more specifically how people are to pursue the goals of therapy and change. One part of communitas is the sharing of these particular beliefs. Thus communitas is found in a variety of communal organizations such as kibbutzim (Spiro, 1956), utopian communities (Kanter, 1972), and religious and political groups (Turner, 1969). These obviously differ on what is important in daily life, but they share the quality of communitas, including strong commitment among members to the particular goals and activities of the group. Similarly, we expect to find communitas norms in all therapeutic communities, but different styles of "being therapeutic" in them.

For Tompkins I, norms for the specific therapeutic intent of the setting include the valuing of facing problems, discussing them realistically, and finding reasonable solutions or compromises. In the original Belmont therapeutic community, Rapoport identified four major "value themes": communalism, democratization, permissiveness, and reality confrontation.[7] The first two are expressions of communitas. Permissiveness has its origin as a therapeutic style in psychoanalytic ideas and is shared as a norm with many psychotherapy hospitals, but not—as we have seen—with Tompkins I. Reality confrontation, on the other hand, is very much a feature of the Tompkins I norm system, and of most therapeutic communities. It corresponds to the "facing problems" theme we found in our interviews and questionnaire results. Another area of variation among communities concerns the importance and degree of family involvement. An experimental therapeutic community at the National Institute of Mental Health in Bethesda, Maryland, treating persons with recurring hospitalizations for schizophrenia, put great weight on family involvement, essentially requiring that the family become part of the community. Tompkins I insists on family involvement at a less intense level. Other therapeutic communities lay even less stress on family participation.

The differences between Belmont and Tompkins I in the area of permissiveness, and to some extent in that of democratization, bring up an important issue. Both the earliest and some of the most recent interpretations of therapeutic community are puristic about the range of permissible behaviors and about decision-making. A frequent conclusion in the application of psychoanalytic theory has been that repression or suppression of impulses is "bad" and leads to mental disorder. Similarly, a conclusion in the application of democratic concepts in the hospital has been that, ideally, patients ought to have full and equal voice in all matters. Both of these beliefs, of course, stand in stark contrast to the oppressive, controlling patterns of the asylum. Yet in practice they seem to lead to problems. At Belmont, Rapoport observed oscillations between times of permissiveness and times when patient misbehavior forced staff to clamp down severely. In American state hospital settings, therapeutic community units high on permissiveness and unsupervised patient

decision-making have failed either in terms of patient outcome (Spadoni and Smith, 1969) or in terms of survival of the
program (Ludwig and Farrelly, 1966). My own experience in
the introduction of a decision-making Patient Pass Committee in a Veterans Administration psychiatric ward is indicative of the problem here. When staff, in a "democratic" move
gave this committee decision-making power, patients on the
committee initially voted unanimously for every pass request.
Inevitably, some of the patients had trouble during their pass
time away from the hospital, discrediting the committee.
When staff became actively involved by reviewing the
committee's decisions in open patient-staff meetings, the
committee became more selective in granting passes. Peer
loyalty—the "code of chronicity" as Ludwig and Farrelly call
it—is powerful and can be overcome only with staff help.
Patients' symptoms, by the time of hospitalization,
have become part of their lives, a way of dealing with their
social environment.[8] Often the symptoms permit the patient
a position of dependency or irresponsibility he would otherwise be denied. Left alone or encouraged by a strong norm of
permissiveness, the patient group will protect the symptoms
of its members.

In situations like Tompkins I where there is a time limit
on the length of hospitalization, permissiveness and the consequent support of patients' symptomatic behavior would be
counter to the ward's primary goals. Furthermore, as Detre
noted even before the unit opened, a ward within a general
hospital must be sensitive to pressures from its immediate
environment. Reflecting this, staff and patients on Tompkins
I scored low on items that expressed a cathartic letting-go
attitude. At the same time, the ward's emphasis on facing
problems implies acceptance of a certain amount of genuine
feeling and expressed emotion.

Thus on Tompkins I a balance is struck between permissiveness and repressive controls. This is a norm on which
therapeutic communities vary from one another. The varia-

tion reflects both the ideological variations of the leaders and staff of different settings and their reality contexts. In Tompkins I and many other therapeutic communities, norms reflect a belief that it may be both clinically unproductive and locally unacceptable to maintain a high level of symptomatic behavior. A recent resurgence of the permissiveness norm has occurred around the ideas of Ronald Laing (1967). Because of his belief that many psychotic experiences are part of personal growth, Laing and his followers oppose the suppression of external symptomatic manifestations of inner struggle and conflict. They emphasize, however, that care is needed to protect the patient and to help him make his experience meaningful.

The balance maintained on Tompkins I was reflected in the relationship between questionnaire items and factor dimensions reflecting control, and those indicative of communitas norms. Those items that suggest staff exert authoritarian, arbitrary control—even for benign purposes—are negatively correlated with (opposite to) the communitas norms. Items reflecting *self*-control are neutral in relation to communitas, probably because some of the items express self-control as a suppressive denial of problems. Those items that express self-control as a positive step that follows dealing with problems (e.g., "I feel I understand most of my problems now even though I was confused on admission.") are closer to the communitas dimension. In other words, dangerous or self-destructive behavior in a therapeutic community is handled *neither* by imposing staff controls *nor* by rejecting controls completely. Instead, behavior is affected by emphasis on involvement in the community, an involvement that in itself aids and expects a growing capacity for self-control as a by-product of involvement. Where an individual has continuing difficulty, the mechanisms for achieving compliance are those generally used to induce conformity in close-knit communities: encouragement and praise for small positive steps, on the one hand, and shaming and threat of exclusion, on the other. Patients' behavior that is too disruptive to individual progress or to community life is discussed in patient-staff meetings, and ultimately the patient may be discharged or transferred elsewhere if no change occurs (see, for example, Chapter 7).

Turning to the issue of nurture and communitas, our results indicate that patients on Tompkins I experience staff as warm, concerned, giving individuals. This perception is separate from the communitas norm. In fact, staff prefer to de-emphasize this perception, scoring far lower than patients on sets of items that reflect nurture. This corresponds with the businesslike attitude of the ward staff: Patients are here to work on problems; being an involved, responsible but temporary member of the community is valuable to this end; feeling too much warmth from staff may make leaving more difficult. On the other hand, items expressing the idea that the ward or the staff are exploitative or depriving to patients, that is, the inverse of nurture, obviously are counter to a feeling of community, and indeed such items correlate negatively with the communitas dimension. As with the control dimension, nurture is de-emphasized at Tompkins I by the espousal of communitas as the primary concern of the norm system.

NOTES

1. What is referred to here as "norm system" has usually been called "culture" or "hospital culture." The latter usage reflects the early tendency to view the therapeutic community as a "small society" unto itself. It is more accurate to recognize that the community is always part of something larger—a hospital, mental health center, or local society. Similarly, what we refer to as norms are often called "values," but again this confuses a term applied to belief systems of entire societies with more specific sets of attitudes and beliefs about life in a specific institution.

2. The present discussion of dimensions and analysis of norm systems is a modification of that of Etzioni (1961).

3. Descriptive studies include those of Dunham and Weinberg (1960), Goffman (1961), Caudill (1958); questionnaire studies include Gilbert (1954), Sommer and Hall (1958), Caine and Smail (1966, 1967, 1968a, 1968b), Ellsworth et al. (1968), Levinson and Gallagher (1964), Canter (1963), Carstairs and Heron (1957).

4. This pattern of finding informal, semihidden ways of meeting needs for nurture and sociability in an asylum is portrayed extensively in Goffman's *Asylums*, in the section "The Moral Career of the Mental Patient" (1961). In psychotherapy hospitals, patients' nurture and communitas are also hidden from staff view (see, for example, Caudill, 1958; Green, 1964).

5. In a number of experiences with wards in such institutions, I have found that nurture is also a central staff issue. The high proportion of chronic patients they deal with provides little satisfaction of staff members' needs for "results," since the patients have a vested interest in remaining "sick." At the same time such patients, for whom the hospital has become a home or home base, present a continuous stream of requests for services, care, and attention. Forcing such patients into a therapeutic system rarely works. Instead, I have found that staff members will be more satisfied and effective when they can share with one another their sense of being constantly drained by patients. They can help support one another in dealing with hospital and outside problems and develop their own sense of communitas as a staff.

6. Factor analysis is a method for grouping items, not a test of significance. Items that "factor" together in a given sample can be used to define common dimensions of response, that is abstractions that condense themes running through the sample's reactions to the list of items as a whole. By examining those items that "load" most strongly for each factor, we can infer the qualities of each of these common themes.

7. *Democratization* refers to the ideal that each patient or staff member of the community share equally in the exercise or power in community decision-making. Actually, Rapoport demonstrates that, in reality, the community oscillates between conditions under which this goal is met and conditions under which the staff is forced to reassert control. *Permissiveness* refers to a belief that members of the community should tolerate in one another a wide range of behaviors that would not be acceptable by outside norms. Again, the real situation for this value varies between times when wide swings in behavior can be tolerated, and other times when the staff is forced to limit behavior extremes in order to maintain order. *Communalism* refers to the unit's belief that its functioning should be characterized by tight-knit, communicative and intimate relationships. Sharing of amenities, informality (e.g., universal use of first names), and "freeing" communication are prescribed. Included in communalism is the importance

of "self-expression of pent-up emotions for its cathartic value." Finally, *reality confrontation* refers to the unit's belief that "patients should be continuously presented with interpretations of their behavior as it is seen by most others" (Rapoport, 1960).

8. Silverman et al. have demonstrated changes in perceptual style correlated with long-term institutionalization suggesting that chronicity has a neurophysiological component (1966).

CHAPTER 3

Roles and Healing Charisma

Norms are abstractions that must be translated into behavior to have meaning as part of a therapeutic system. This is true whether we think of the psychoanalytic concepts of transference and working through, or the valuation of openness and mutual responsibility in a therapeutic community. Real individuals functioning and interacting in a social system experience sets of norms as defining *roles*, that is, expectations for their behavior. In the last chapter we found that the norms of Tompkins I were determined by strong emphasis on the dimension of communitas, the specialness and oneness of the ward community. Similarly, we find that role expectations for individuals working in, or being treated at, Tompkins I have a universally special quality that will be referred to as *healing charisma*. In this chapter we shall look at several of the most important positions on Tompkins I—director, psychiatric resident, nurse, patient—and see how the role concept for each reflects this charismatic quality.

The term "healing charisma" is used in this chapter, and subsequently, to point up qualities of roles that go beyond the ordinary definitions of psychiatric staff or patients. As Weber (1946) and others have pointed out, the traditional, existing roles may have a charismatic component, referred to as "of-

fice charisma." In psychiatric settings, office charisma is almost invariably associated only with the psychiatrist or
therapist, by virtue of special professional background. Healing charisma is a function of the setting and its emphasis on
communitas, that is, on a feeling of specialness, real or potential, in *all* participants.

THE DIRECTOR'S ROLE

From the outset Detre was a dramatic figure on the ward.
He was central in the unit for the first few months, as patterns
of care were evolved. The professional staff was initially
small, and residents were assigned to the unit only on a
part-time basis. Detre made individual contact with each patient and then was active in suggesting the strategy of treatment. In his interaction with patients, Detre might be warm
and supportive one moment and devastatingly sarcastic
another. Staff saw him as exciting, knowledgeable, and un-
cannily accurate in his clinical decisions. At the same time,
Detre was directly educating the medical and nursing staff in
his views on drugs, side-effects, observing and responding to
patient behavior. Suggestions from staff members or patients
were integrated into the program. Thus Detre's charismatic
role had several elements: (1) the natural respect and excitement surrounding the director of a new, innovative ward; (2)
his personal charm, drama, wit, and rich Hungarian accent;
(3) his clinical savvy, which appeared to go beyond the usual
psychiatric expertise; (4) his willingness to encourage and
train others to expand their roles.

That the director's charismatic role is not unique to Detre
is suggested by reports of other therapeutic communities.
Sheppard Kellam developed a therapeutic community at the
National Institute for Mental Health about the same time.
Both Kellam and his successor, Jack Durell, are described by
those who worked with them as dramatic, magnetic, often

emotional, and as evoking great loyalty from patients and nursing staff.

These charismatic aspects of the leader are not simply individual characteristics, but become a part of the leader role. After several years of directing the program, Detre took a year's sabbatical leave. The acting director quickly became viewed with the same charismatic aura. His behavior became charismatic, although modified by personality differences between the two men. Personally, he experienced great stress as he sought to meet the charismatic role expectations of the staff (Astrachan, personal communication). A similar phenomenon was reported by another physician who moved into the ward administrator role of the NIMH therapeutic community after Durell left the unit. The new administrator found that staff continuously related to him in ways that clearly expected him to evidence charismatic behavior. He felt pressure to make arbitrary, blanket evaluative statements; to evidence publicly his emotionality, especially in relation to patients; to engage in heated, intense personal interactions with staff and patients; and to defend the unit from the world outside it (Epstein, personal communication).

In general, the charismatic leader of the therapeutic community behaves in ways that go far beyond the ordinary role expectations of a unit chief. He may strike a dramatic figure in public situations. He will take stands with certainty and definiteness where others are more hesitant. His language may be colorful and emotional, while he remains cool in the midst of crisis. He retains, even when he is intermittently present, unquestioning trust in his staff and patients, and in the performance they will bring to their tasks. In his behavior with patients he is likely to be direct, unusual, and often "unprofessional." He may raise issues with them that others fear to discuss. He defines the ward's norms, including nontraditional definitions of staff roles.

More than any other, the director's charismatic leadership role is central in the therapeutic community. In any

organization the person or persons in higher-ranked positions tend to be central to all aspects of institutional life. This is
specially true in a ward organization emphasizing communitas norms, since traditional expectations for authoritarian control norms, or nurturant norms, must be constantly countered. Thus the leader role and the ward norms
are in a constant interplay: The communitas norms define the
specialness of his role, while he symbolizes through his
charismatic behavior the importance and validity of the
norms. Put another way, the personal bonds that tend to be
an essential element of communitas are paralleled by the
mutual support between leader and others in the community
as they assume charismatic roles. Marshall Edelson makes
this same point:

> The Chief of Service, or whoever has an analogous role in the
> therapeutic community or whatever staff person shares this
> role with him, must represent these values in group
> discussion—just as the psychotherapist does, in individual
> psychotherapy. He must contribute continuously his aware-
> ness of any process that threatens these values and in doing so
> make clear to the group that the values upon which treatment
> itself depends are being ignored, undermined, or opposed by
> behavior, attitudes, assumptions, or interactions in the com-
> munity.
>
> In addition, because he comes to represent in part the treatment
> values of the community, his participation becomes crucial at
> certain times to begin or support aspects of the program. . . .
>
> That it is helpful to him to have other members of the staff
> understand and represent treatment values to the community
> is obvious, and much of his function has to do with bringing
> this about (Edelson, 1964, p. 127).

Edelson cites the importance of the chief of service personally investing innovative aspects of therapeutic commun-

ity programs in order to make them a success. He also notes
that there is a tendency to blur reality and symbolism around
the words of the chief:

> In many discussions in which patients flinched from exposure
> or sought to protect each other from awareness or pain, the idea
> was expressed by the Chief of Service that it was better to be a
> weed that could survive in all kinds of soil and conditions than a
> fragile flower. That this was not experienced as depreciating by
> the patients was evidenced by the fact that "weed gardens"
> sprang up in room after room on the hall and that patients
> attended these green patches assiduously and with pride (Edel-
> son, 1964, p. 127).

Other descriptive and anecdotal data from therapeutic
community units indicate that this interchangeability of
norms and charismatic leadership is universal. This also helps
us understand how it is that some therapeutic community
units can function without a single charismatic leader—they
have adopted a normative system sufficiently intensive so
that symbolizing them in an individual is not critical. It also
explains how other units can function with a charismatic
leader, but a poorly defined set of norms—the unit is sufficiently small, and the involvement of the leader with his staff
sufficiently frequent and intense, that the guidelines for behavior can be maintained within the leader and not formu-
lated into social norms.

In relation to his staff and patients, the charismatic leader
models behaviors that deviate from usual expectations.
Furthermore, he makes clear his high degree of trust and high
performance expectations from staff. He relates to them in
ways that open possibilities of their viewing themselves as
more effective and more charismatic than they might expect.
The sense of charisma—the capacity for saying to oneself, "I
am more than I thought"—is transmitted downward to the
middle-ranking, and ultimately to the lowest-ranking, members of the community: the new patients. These altered expec-

tations of staff members, just as those of patients, are maintained and supported by the role definition for each staff group on the unit.

RESIDENT PSYCHIATRIST'S ROLE

Returning to Tompkins I as it evolved such a pattern of charismatic "flow" outward from the director, the observations of Ezra Vogel, a sociologist who knew the ward during its first years, are useful. Vogel saw Detre as a charismatic leader and saw the central task of the unit, after a year, as the "routinization of charisma" (Vogel, unpublished paper, 1961). That is, the ward needed to develop rules and standardized ways of operating, so that Detre's presence would not be so critical and his decision-making role could be shared with others. With assignment of several full-time residents and a chief resident to the unit (later, an assistant director with faculty status), Detre began to share the leadership functions with other psychiatrists. As I have already described, these residents were given a central role in relation to a subpopulation of the ward, usually some five to ten patients. The transfer of this considerable responsibility to residents required that they be trained, or retrained, to the norms of the unit and to the assumption of a charismatically defined role.

Support for the assertion that charisma is delegated to the resident psychiatrist in the form of charismatically enhanced role definitions is found in a study of group therapy behavior on Tompkins I (Astrachan et al., 1968). In comparing groups led by different psychiatrists, it was found that those variables differing significantly from one resident's group to another indicated the "style" of the group and its leader. This style determined how each group during its meetings went about working on the issues raised by the general norms of the unit. In our terminology the small group meetings can be seen as a site for the development of the resident's healing

charisma. As group leader, invested with charismatic importance by the director and the ward norms, the resident is
experienced by patients as closely symbolic of those norms.
The quality of each group's behavior reflects a combination of
the unit's norms and the particular personality style of the
given resident.

In the three groups studied, it was found that one resident generated an "instrumental" style of group problem-
solving, another an "adjustive" style, and the third and "expressive" style. Each of these styles was applied to the universally important activities of problem-solving, group involvement, and openness about problems and feelings. That
the resident's particular charismatic style extends beyond his
physical presence in meetings is indicated by the finding that
in unled meetings, the stylistic differences among groups
were maintained. For Tompkins I, the small-group program
can be understood as one channel through which the unit's
norms were relayed to patients. The process comes about
through charismatic investment of the group therapist, who
is the psychiatrist responsible for each group member and
who serves as model and as one important norm-giver in the
group sessions. The group accepts these norms and interacts
around them in a way that is determined by the norms and by
the personality of the norm-giver.

NURSING STAFF ROLES

The nursing staff is treated in a special way, quite different from what might be expected by the traditional psychiatric
nurse, by nurses on adjacent medical units, or by nurses
working in psychotherapy hospitals. The nurse takes an active part in daily ward rounds; her comments and opinions
are not only taken seriously but are frequently more respected
than the opinions of higher status professionals who have less

data on patients' behaviors. For example, nurses frequently make the decisive suggestions about medication choices and dosages, and about such major issues as discharge.

This enhancement of the nurse's role is again a manifestation of the special, nontraditional, charismatic meaning of being a nurse on Tompkins I. Because nursing training is so powerfully oriented toward a subordinate, non-initiating role, the ward makes a special retraining effort.

Within the nursing staff there is clear expectation that nurses will behave and think in a way different from the ordinary for members of their profession:

> Nurses on Tompkins I have the exciting and challenging opportunity to be a member of a psychiatric team whose leader encourages each member of the team to use his or her professional or non-professional skills in an atmosphere of mutual respect. Opportunity is given to each member to express his opinions and group staff decisions are the general rule.

> Nurses assigned to Tompkins I are permanently assigned to this service. They are not expected to be asked to cover any other area in the hospital. By the same token, when illness prevents a staff member scheduled to report on duty from arriving, it is understood that a member of our staff volunteers to work an additional shift. . . .

> On Tompkins I the supervisor or head nurse find themselves in the position of *making many medical decisions* or *guiding other staff members in making judgments that in many hospitals only the medical staff would make.* The medical director, as leader of the health team, encourages this activity and lends support and guidance in all cases as their decisions are discussed in conferences. The nurse is not threatened, her reasons are explored and only if the group disagrees with her plan or decision, are her recommendations or actions altered or vetoed. As a result nurses feel free and secure in recommending or planning nursing aspects of the

treatment program for each patient. In emergency situations she functions much more effectively, intelligently and with greater skill (*An Introductory Manual for Nursing Students and New Staff Members*, Ferriter; emphasis is added).

Thus, new staff members learn quickly that there are expectations for capacities and behaviors that are an expansion of professional role. It is also made clear that the unit chief will strongly support nurses as they attempt to meet these expanded expectations. In the same outline of introductory material, we find a description of the expected transaction that should occur between nurse and patient.

> Nurses are taught to deal realistically with ward situations. A nurse's attention is focused on helping the patient find appropriate ways to express his feelings and difficulties as well as to help him discover healthier ways to interact with others. The nurse encourages patients to function up to their capacity, thus avoid regression. Limits and controls of patient behavior are set by the nurse when this is therapeutically valuable. The nurse "mothers" patients when appropriate, being a source of help, security and protection when indicated. She conveys by her attitude and behavior that the staff are in control when ward emergencies arise (Ferriter).

Note that the description here emphasizes the active role of nursing in therapeutic encounters with patients. Although nurturance is mentioned, it is secondary to a primary emphasis upon assisting patients in altering their behaviors and meeting higher standards in relation to handling problematic social situations. While these descriptions tend to sound rather pleasant and typical of therapeutic hospitals, it should be clear that the implied role expectations for nurses are strikingly different from those for which nurses are trained. Nursing school training orients to a role in which the doctor's orders are accepted unquestioningly and carried out with maximum efficiency. Nurses are not expected to initiate therapeutic activities themselves, although they are expected to be highly nurturant to patients. Even the reality of the medical ward often does not correspond to this last description: Often the nurse "knows" better than the intern what treatment a patient needs. But in this therapeutic community the nursing role is openly and clearly defined as different.

Thus, by virtue of becoming a "therapist" in accordance with the norms of the ward, the nurse adds a charismatic component to her role. And the nurse—just as the director and the resident—is encouraged to be herself, to use her own personality traits in the charismatic manifestations of her role. On Tompkins I, nurses tend often to be brusque, bantering, and confronting, perhaps to emphasize that they are not to be expected to act like more traditional nurses.

The nurse who has successfully reoriented to the role expectations in the therapeutic community is likely to be a good model for patients who are faced with a similar task. Having herself tested and been trained in behaviors that are likely to be able effectively to convey similar sets of expectations to patients.

THE PATIENT'S ROLE

Kai Erikson draws attention to a conflict intrinsic to the usual patient role: Because of his disorder, he wishes (or someone wishes him) to be accorded some sort of "sick" role. Once the patient is hospitalized, a number of other motives come to bear. He may find it possible to behave "normally" for considerable periods, and he finds he is expected to be an active participant in the psychotherapy process. But behaving "normally" will lead quickly to anxiety that he will be viewed as entirely well, that the legitimacy of his illness will be lost.[1]

But the mental patient is in double jeopardy. He acquires recognition as a "sick" person only at a considerable emotional price, if at all; later, he is able to withdraw from this recognition only with extreme difficulty, for he then faces the widespread conviction that legitimate mental illness cannot be completely cured anyway. Moreover, the mental patient's treatment is often designed to effect comprehensive ego changes rather than simply to restore him to his former state of health, so that on several counts his experience with sickness may become crucial to his developing sense of direction and identity. The danger is that patienthood may become a model for his image of the future rather than a provisional shelter in which he resets himself for a life already in progress (K. Erikson, 1957, p. 270).

As a result, steps forward are frequently followed quickly by behavior that clearly revalidates the sick role:

Like Penelope, who wove a cloak by day only to unravel it at night, the mental patient often portrays the insecurity of his position by staging, after every advance of this kind, a dramatic retreat into impulsivity and destruction (K. Erikson, 1957, p. 266).

This dilemma contributes to the phenomena that potentially plague psychotherapy hospitals: patients' need to legitimize their sick role contributes to a pool of ready resources for collective or individual disruption of the hospital organization.

This dilemma is dealt with on Tompkins I by seeking to legitimize for each patient a different patient role. Malfunction—depression, psychosis, anxiety, etc.—is accepted as explaining why the patient required hospitalization. But in every way possible—through the use of drugs, social sanctions, and positive rewards—the "healthy" side of the patient is legitimized as the acceptable patient role on Tompkins I.

Patients entering a mental hospital are confronted with an entirely new social setting. Those we interviewed had expectations of either a medical hospital ward or a "snake pit" asylum setting. As a newcomer, the patient must resolve a whole variety of issues about how he is to live in the hospital (Pine and Levinson, 1961). While we may tend to think of patients who are acutely ill as "sick" and thus unable to make such choices, in reality we rarely find a patient who is so psychotic or depressed that he is truly incapable of interacting with the environment. Even before the present era in which patients can be rapidly restored to contact with drugs, a whole variety of responses to admission could be outlined (Denbo and Hanfman, 1935).

To delineate the special, charismatic qualities of the patient role on Tompkins I, we can examine the items that were closely associated with the communitas norm dimension. The following paragraphs do this by listing questions that a new patient must deal with in the hospital, along with the answers supplied by the communitas items:

(How should I deal with my symptoms and my illness?)

First, you should try to get your behavior under control. You should not allow yourself to spend a great deal of time in isolated fantasy or hallucination. You should take some responsibility for speaking out in meetings about yourself and your problems. You should open up verbally about your problems with yourself and your family.

(What are appropriate activities here?)

Attending the varied unit meetings and therapies. In free time, socializing with others rather than isolating oneself. At any point taking an active stance in relation to the hospital or outside environment and in particular your problem areas in it.

(How should I regard the hospital as a whole?)

The hospital is a place where you can briefly avoid some of the responsibilities and pressures that may have made it difficult to deal with problems. This is not a place to rest, relax, or be taken care of. This is a community of staff and people with various psychiatric problems who are seeking to help themselves and each other with these problems.

(How should I view patients and staff, and what are the differences between them?)

Patients are here for treatment; staff to facilitate it. You should regard staff as human beings who have a special interest in aiding patients to return to their prior life situation. Patients are individuals who have difficulaties like yours, but also can help you and others, with the same help staff is paid to provide.

(How should I relate to the people here?)

You should join, be a member, transact socially with patients and staff. You should care about others here. You should trust in the efficacy of the unit for helping you with your problems. You should value the community itself.

(What should I do about problems—mine and others'?)

With everyone, be open about yourself and your problems. Trust staff and patients as people with whom you can talk about your problems, and from whom you may receive valuable insights. Initiate questions to other patients about their problems and offer suggestions to them. Be loyal to patients' improvement rather than help them protect themselves from anxiety. With staff you should be open also about difficult issues—your own and other patients'. You should not look to staff for magical relief from problems but rather for guidance on how to approach problems. With family, try to bring them into the community and relate to them with greater openness and a problem-solving attitude. They should take part in treatment with you.

These patient role expectations are conveyed in a wide variety of situations, as the next chapter, dealing with learning the patient role, will show. The charismatic component of the patient role, much like that of nursing staff, is reflected in the concept of the patient as therapist for himself and others. The role behavior listed above is primarily concerned with membership and with how to "do therapy" in the style of the ward. Perhaps most important of all is the expectation that patients will be therapists for one another, formally, in such situations as leaderless groups, Patient Advisory Board meetings, and informal interactions.

Finally, we can observe that there is a circularity to this transmission of healing charisma throughout the unit system. The behavioral acceptance by new patients of the unit's expectations is visible testimony to its effectiveness. It rewards all those who have already committed themselves to the unit's value system and, of course, supports, gratifies, and enhances the charismatic healing aura of the individual leader. Thus the efficacy of the system supports the charismatic going-beyond-the-ordinary-self of all unit participants, which, in turn, provides support for maintaining the process.

NOTES

1. In this reaction patients apparently are reacting the way laymen do to the idea of mental illness, seeing it as an either/or phenomenon. Surveys of public attitudes reveal that most people are not sure about the symptoms of mental illness, but that if a person is "mentally ill" it is incurable. This view conflicts with that of mental health professionals, who regard such disorders within the medical model of illness and the sick role as a transient state.

CHAPTER 4

Learning the Patient Role

The abstractions of therapeutic community norms and roles discussed in Chapters 2 and 3 come to life when we begin to examine the actual experience of being a Tompkins I patient. In this chapter we will look at this experience in a number of ways: through interview descriptions and direct observations of brief encounters at the time of admission, by understanding the privilege system a patient must deal with, by looking at changes in attitudes on norms and changes in behavior for a sample of patients, and, finally, by using questionnaire data to discover the sequence of these changes over time.

PATIENT SELF-REPORTS

A perceptive patient speaking about her entry to Tompkins I:

When I first came in I didn't understand the community at all. The hospital wasn't at all what I thought it would be like.

. . . I thought there would be people obviously crazy: the typical idea of a mental hospital. I was very surprised to see some natural-acting people. . . . To me the first day—it was so overwhelming I thought it was hopeless and I didn't think one could actually do it. I very quickly learned it was a community—that people were very understanding, staff as well as patients, with the older patients having more insight and experience—and they were quite easy to talk with. I read the constitution and discovered that it was really community living and while this was being taken away from your natural environment with the pressures of everyday living removed, you could learn to function with this ward. This was explained to me by very sympathetic people and I began my process of getting into the community.

. . . I was so surprised to realize, for instance, that in spite of how I felt, I could still attend these meetings, but I was much too wrapped up with my own feelings, my own problems, so it was just attending the meetings and talking with people. I was quite taken aback when people would come up and say to me, "Why were you brought here?" because I wasn't even sure that first day. . . . As I said, that first day was the most overwhelming.

About the next few days she says:

I think the first shock subsides—and I realized that I was hospitalized. I began attending all the various meetings and functions of the community on the ward and began to feel interested. At the time, I was on the five-minute check system. I was admitted on staff or patient special. I began talking with very many people, patients and staff alike. I began seeing the problems that I had, having been removed from the pressures of everyday life. I was becoming more objective. I had never been quite so clear. I could see what I was doing outside of the hospital, what got me into this illness, so I became much more objective and I could really talk about it.

. . . It has always been easy for me to talk so that it wasn't too much of a problem, and I also began talking with young people as well as people my own age, and I found it very easy. I had accepted fully that I was in the hospital because of my behavior: things that I had said and have done. I thought it would be a long time, a long process to learn the various symptoms. Then I began to find out that it wouldn't take so long. I began to feel better very fast. It was through talking actually; the intensity of this ward is impressive. The meetings with doctors and patients, patient-staff meetings and leaderless groups, and ones with the doctors, and at least two private conversations with doctors, and talking with patients in the evening or at lunchtime or at dinner, etc., keeps things so intense that you do adjust quickly and begin to see your own problems more objectively because you're constantly thrown into situations where you must talk about them.

Another patient describes his admission:

Before I came in I was having anxiety attacks and sleeping poorly—it was strange how quickly that changed when I was admitted. I don't know why, maybe because I had made a decision. When I was admitted, I felt that doctors would help me; after three days I realized it's up to me.

(Where did that idea come from?)

I think it was group therapy—people talking about their problems, the doctors saying, "What do you think?" I felt good about this. The more I talked, the more I thought. . . .

I was depressed, disgusted with myself, ashamed, I didn't talk with anyone.

. . . I had all sorts of ideas about the staff in a psychiatric hospital, that they don't care, that they're underpaid. Here they're marvelous, they really have the patient's interest at heart. I was frightened about that when I came in.

(Can you recall what kinds of experiences you had with other patients during the first days you were here?)

I was looking—like Smith, he shot himself in the mouth. I tried to think if I could do something like that—what feeling would a person have to do that? I talked with him when he came in—I became sick. They asked me to be his sponsor, I said no. I was running away. Then an hour later I went to his sponsor and said I'd like to. I ate with him, talked with him, played as his bridge partner. That night I got nauseous, dizzy. I did the same with Jones—projecting myself onto their position.

(What do you think it is that helps patients get better?)

Concentrated group therapy. Always talking about your problems, every day, and other people's. Seeing your doctor every day, talking and thinking about why they're here. The more you think about your problems and why you have them and how to change, the more you do that, the more chance you have to change. Some patients never get the picture for a long time. . . .

(Where does the impetus come from to listen?)

You project yourself into other patients' positions. . . . They tell you to talk with patients, ask them about their problems. After the first day I did, I became curious. I questioned people. I would open conversations with, "Why are you here?" Other people did it. "Misery loves company." . . . They tell you to be with patients, socialize. When I came in I just wanted to be by myself, but patients began questioning me.

The constitution of the unit is handed to the newcomer by another patient, a "sponsor," who shows the newcomer around the ward. On the second page there is the following statement:

This pamphlet, written by the patients, is an attempt to make you and your family feel comfortable by acquainting you with the atmosphere and procedure of the ward.

Tompkins I is devoted to intensive treatment of persons who are emotionally disturbed. Although numerous means are used in the treatment of such persons within a general hospital setting, the emphasis is on group therapy, the use of medications and community living. T-I is just that, a community, comprised of all patients and staff. A community whose goal is that each can learn how to be responsible for himself and is able to help himself through helping others.

You will find that families and friends are encouraged to participate in therapy in special meetings. At the beginning your family or friends will be uneasy. Yet after one or two family meetings, they will realize the important role they play in therapy.

Upon first entering the ward many patients feel lost, lonely and sometimes even frightened. But in a short time you'll find the other patients become your friends and that the staff respects your feelings.

There follows a detailed description of the interviews, physical examination, check of belongings, role of the "patient sponsor," description of patient governing structure, and detailed information on "who is who" among the staff, including the title and profession of each. The following page lists and describes 11 different sorts of meetings held on the unit, including individual therapy, small group meetings, advisory board meetings, patient-staff meetings, and family meetings of different sorts. The brochure also outlines the specific privilege statuses patients may have. All in all, the new patient is introduced rapidly to the program and personnel of the ward, with a minimum of mystery.

The assimilation of a patient into the Tompkins I community is a two-sided phenomenon. The ward has a general role concept for patients that it transmits to newcomers; the newcomer has his special characteristics that interact with these role expectations. To illustrate how this ward-patient interaction takes place, we can look at the first few moments of one particular patient's hospitalization. The exploration of "what this patient is like" by the unit, and a similar exploration by the patient of "what this hospital is like" and "what a patient may be here" begin with the first encounter between the patient and the unit. The following example is taken from the study of a patient whose hospitalization will be described in greater detail in Chapter 5.

INTERACTIONS IN DETAIL

Mary Wheeler is a registered nurse whose admission followed a serious suicide attempt. She had been in outpatient therapy for some months, but her desperateness had not been taken seriously by her husband or her psychiatrist. Following her overdose, she developed pneumonia and required five days of medical hospitalization before coming to Tompkins I. She was interviewed on the medical ward by the Tompkins I psychiatric resident who was to be her physician there. The atmosphere and program of the psychiatric ward were explained to Mary to prepare her for the transfer, which can be described as follows:

> Mrs. Wheeler arrives by wheelchair at the study unit, on transfer from a medical ward where she has been recovering from the medical complications of her suicide attempt with barbiturate overdose. She meets her Tompkins I physician in the corridor of the unit, and is told that a ward meeting is about to begin. She is helped to her feet from the chair and somewhat unsteadily accompanies the physician toward the meeting room. After a few steps she inquires, "What would you do if I

fell down?" The psychiatrist replies quite spontaneously, "You wouldn't do that to me." Mrs. Wheeler then continues without difficulty to the meeting.

What follows next is an analysis of this transaction in "slow motion" in order to understand the first events of hospitalization. We must acknowledge, of course, that even this description represents a very summarized version of what actually transpired, which included many nonverbal cues and qualities of inflection and tone that are not captured here. [1] On the left below is the description we have just given and on the right comments conveying our inferences about the significance of the behavior described.

Initial Encounter Description	*Comments on Behavioral Transactions*
Mrs. Wheeler arrives by wheelchair at the study unit, on transfer from a medical ward where she has been recovering from the medical complications of her suicide attempt with barbiturate overdose.	The study unit staff are confronted with visible evidence of Mrs. Wheeler's medical patienthood, sure to remind them of the life-threatening nature of Mrs. Wheeler's problem. Mrs. Wheeler has been told about Tompkins I by the psychiatrist who will be working with her.
She meets her Tompkins I physician in the corridor of the unit,	The place of greeting deviates from the medical ward situation, where the patient is more likely to be in bed when the physician arrives.
and is told that a ward meeting is about to begin.	The physician immediately orients the patient to an aspect of the unit other than the doctor: a patient-staff group meeting. Implicit, of course, is the communication, "You will be expected to attend, and may not remain a passive medical patient." The doctor's information also serves to invest the group meeting with considerable implied importance, since the doctor brings it up immediately and gives it priority over any other procedure of admission to the unit that the patient might expect.

She is helped to her feet from her chair and somewhat unsteadily

Mrs. Wheeler had indeed been in bed for five days, and could be expected to be shaky on her feet. She may be exaggerating her unsteadiness, however, in order to communicate that she is or has been quite ill, and may continue to be rather unsteady as a person. On the other hand, she may be truly weak and a bit dizzy, and her performance may represent an effort to convey about herself, "I wish to be a good patient, and follow your expectations."

accompanies the physician toward the meeting room.

The physician can be said to have accompanied the patient, as well. By doing so, the doctor underlines the importance of the meeting. In addition she assumes a behavior in relation to the patient that may be somewhat unexpected; she personally accompanies her, rather than delegating this task to nursing staff. This not only indicates that the doctor is not a distant medical authority, but by implication indicates that patients and psychiatrists in this setting are part of the same world.

After a few steps

Mrs. Wheeler reveals in action that she *can* walk. And that she will do so on the staff's request.

she inquires, "What would you do if I fell down?"

Having established her initial compliance and having indicated that she can stand and move, the patient now explores how stoutly the staff will continue to expect her to function normally and move from the role of medical patient to something new and more active. Note that she did not say, "I may fall down," or, "I feel dizzy." She is more specific in asking, "What would you do . . . ?" There is a challenge implied by the form of the question. While the challenge on the one hand is a test of the staff's messages to this point, it is also a new step: The patient is letting the doctor know that she is a person capable of challenging authority, even while she appears to be complying with it.

The psychiatrist replies quite spontaneously, "You wouldn't do that to me."

The doctor has picked up the challenging tone of the patient's question sufficiently clearly and comfortably that the response is given unselfconsciously. The possibility of real weakness is ignored, and the reply is completely directed at the challenge. The phrasing used by the doctor is striking. It appears to respond to the patient's challenge directly as a threat. In addition it reasserts the nonmedical role relation, by implying that the patient could, through her action and illness, embarrass or hurt the doctor (". . . to me."). At the same the bantering tone of the comment implies that doctor and patient already have another level of relationship established and that there is a shared ability to look at what goes on between them with some perspective.

Mrs. Wheeler then continues without difficulty to the meeting.

This reveals that the patient is not going to make a showdown at this point. It reflects the effectiveness of the staff's pushing her to act like an ambulatory member of the community. Through her compliance, the patient had disqualified herself from future behavior that would put her in a passive role, unless she is willing to renege on what she has conveyed about herself this far.

This example brings out some important aspects of the behavioral transactions that occur in the therapeutic community. Within some 30 seconds, patient and unit (primarily represented by the doctor, but in the supporting presence and awareness of patients and staff) have transacted a great deal of business around the issues of initial impressions of one another. Just as important, a precedent has been set for the style of future interactions (see Chapter 5). The unit conveys rapidly to the patient that the medical patient role is not available, but that there are strong expectations for active participation at meetings. The interchange hints at a patient-doctor relationship different from that of medical patient and physician.[2]

The self-reports from patients suggest another recurring experience that contributes to the initial impact of the unit's expectations—an experience in which the newcomer is approached by more experienced patients who say something like "Why are you here?" This is a question that most new patients expect only from a staff member, particularly a physician. Facing it in public, from a patient, immediately conveys two things. First, the question asks for a response, that is, indicates that the new patient should be able to formulate an appropriate answer and that he should convey it to the other patient. Second, by asking such a question, the more experienced patient models a patient role in which *patients* ask the sorts of questions usually expected from *staff*, and ask the questions in a stafflike manner.

During the first day—even the first hours—in the hospital, the newcomer sees that patients are "natural-acting people," while staff members wear no special uniforms and are frequently and informally interacting with patients. Almost immediately, the newcomer takes part in a group or ward meeting in which patients are active leaders and participants. The norms of the meetings will be quickly apparent: rationality, forceful but friendly confrontation of patients' problems, openness about such problems, efforts at problem-solving and planning. Other than meeting times, unless the newcomer is put on "staff special" status, he will be observed initially by another patient, a "monitor," thus formalizing the stafflike appearance of an experienced patient.[3] Even if the new patient has a staff special, he will have a patient sponsor who conveys information about procedures, makes introductions, shows him around.

All this has an impact on the newcomer: "I began to feel better very fast. It was through talking actually; the intensity of the ward is impressive . . . you do adjust quickly and begin to see your own problems more objectively because you're constantly thrown into situations where you must talk about them." Many patients have this experience within hours or days of admission. Others, whose attention is more withdrawn from their environment or whose defensiveness is greater, may take longer. Although individuals' timetables vary, something we will see dramatically in individual case studies, the ward has a core of responses to all patients. On a moment-to-moment level this response pattern is enacted by staff or other patients constantly, with the norm-role system of Tompkins I as a guide. That is, both patients and staff feel responsible, as members of the community, for the changing of behavior that does not conform with the ward's expectations for "nonsick" behavior. This, by necessity, means that staff and healthier patients must approach newcomers and be able to relate to them in a way that conveys an anticipation that their behavior will change in the direction of less deviant patterns. The difficulty of this is suggested by the second patient quoted at the beginning of this chapter. He spoke of approaching a newcomer, a patient who had shot himself in the mouth in a suicide attempt. This approach was difficult: The patient balked at first, then forced himself to confront the newcomer. Afterward he felt nauseated and shaken. He had put himself in the other patient's place, allowed himself to wonder how it would feel to do something like this.

Staff members also find such contact threatening and upsetting, although they are trained to encounter individuals manifesting bizarre behavior. Definitions of staff roles tend to provide structured ways of relating to such behavior—ways that create sufficient psychological distance for comfort. This is maximally true in the asylum, where great distance and significant power imbalance protect staff from the personal impact of disturbing behavior. It is also the case in most other hospitals. In the psychotherapy hospital, although cure is the ultimate goal of the treatment program, staff members are encouraged to look on symptoms—the most personally threatening and upsetting aspect of patients' behaviors—as surface manifestations. As such, there is no clear mandate for responding to them. They are to be ignored, in some situations interpreted, and when necessary controlled. Tompkins I cannot accept such a laissez-faire attitude: Continuing symptomatology is a problem. For this reason patient behavior over longer time periods—days or weeks—is the basis for advancement or stasis in privileges, and movement toward discharge. But most important of all are the strong role expectations for everyone of contacting and confronting the behavior of others.

THE PRIVILEGE SEQUENCE

The privilege system of Tompkins I reinforces explicitly the ward's clear set of patient role expectations. There is a highly specific sequence of privilege statuses that are outlined to a new patient early in his hospitalization. The ground rules of this privilege system also contribute to clarifying role expectations. Essentially, these rules are that a patient will progress rapidly to statuses of increasing freedom and responsibility as long as his behavior is progressing in conformity with the ward's norms as they apply to the patient's particular situation. Motivation for progress thus stems from social approbation as well as internal desire for improvement. Diagram 4.1 outlines this sequence by suggesting specific patient behaviors that are often used as the basis for unit decisions on advancing in privilege status. A given level of conformity to unit norms is not necessarily associated with a given privilege status. Rather, a change in behavior is taken as evidence for progress and grounds for advancement to whatever is the next status level. To a considerable extent, the guidelines indicated in the diagram inform people about the salient issues for a patient at a given time. Knowing these issues, the norms then provide some idea of how to interact with a patient and help him work on the issues. If, for example, a new patient is able to talk to others but withdraws easily, this is the point that others can focus on. Family relations, inner experiences, job problems—all these can be deferred if the patient's present problem is defined as withdrawal, in a setting that offers help through social interaction. Knowing

DIAGRAM 4.1 PATIENT MOVEMENT THROUGH THE WARD

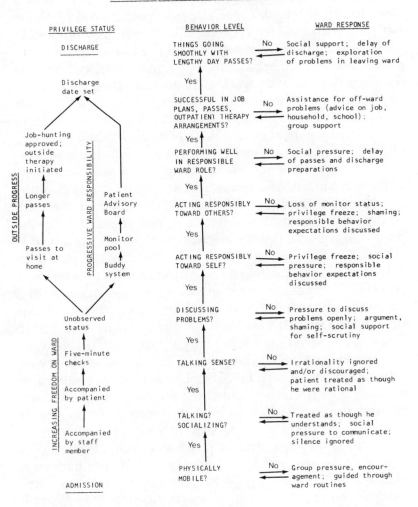

PRIVILEGE STATUS	BEHAVIOR LEVEL	WARD RESPONSE

DISCHARGE

THINGS GOING SMOOTHLY WITH LENGTHY DAY PASSES? No → ← Social support; delay of discharge; exploration of problems in leaving ward

Discharge date set

Yes

SUCCESSFUL IN JOB PLANS, PASSES, OUTPATIENT THERAPY ARRANGEMENTS? No → ← Assistance for off-ward problems (advice on job, household, school); group support

Job-hunting approved; outside therapy initiated

Yes

PERFORMING WELL IN RESPONSIBLE WARD ROLE? No → ← Social pressure; delay of passes and discharge preparations

Longer passes

Patient Advisory Board

Yes

ACTING RESPONSIBLY TOWARD OTHERS? No → ← Loss of monitor status; privilege freeze; shaming; responsible behavior expectations discussed

Monitor pool

Yes

Passes to visit at home

Buddy system

ACTING RESPONSIBLY TOWARD SELF? No → ← Privilege freeze; social pressure; responsible behavior expectations discussed

Yes

Unobserved status

DISCUSSING PROBLEMS? No → ← Pressure to discuss problems openly; argument, shaming; social support for self-scrutiny

Five-minute checks

Yes

TALKING SENSE? No → ← Irrationality ignored and/or discouraged; patient treated as though he were rational

Accompanied by patient

Yes

TALKING? SOCIALIZING? No → ← Treated as though he understands; social pressure to communicate; silence ignored

Accompanied by staff member

Yes

PHYSICALLY MOBILE? No → ← Group pressure, encouragement; guided through ward routines

ADMISSION

OUTSIDE PROGRESS

PROGRESSIVE WARD RESPONSIBILITY

INCREASING FREEDOM ON WARD

where the patient stands in the sequence of statuses helps others to focus on this issue and thus to aid the patient in dealing with his withdrawal—or, more likely, the feelings of mistrust, self-doubt, anxiety, or hopelessness that lie behind the withdrawal.

The level at which a patient enters the system can vary considerably, from staff special to no observation at all. Some patients, such as Mary Wheeler (Chapter 5), may be capable of responsibility for themselves, and even for others, shortly after admission; other patients may remain immobile or mute for some days or even weeks. An acutely schizophrenic patient might pass through all levels of the diagram in a relatively steady way, with a week or 10 days at each level. More likely, such a patient would have plateaus, backsliding, and rapid forward movement at different times during hospitalization. A seriously depressed patient often remains immobile or incommunicative for some time, and then moves rapidly as the depression begins to lift. An adolescent patient, who will be described at length in Chapter 6, moved steadily up the privilege sequence until arrangements began for his return to school. Confronted with imminent discharge, he had difficulty; the "as if" quality of some of his earlier progress was revealed. He remained for many weeks at this stage as he and the staff dealt with crucial issues in his relations with his parents and in their marriage. Another patient, described in Chapter 7, moved only reluctantly through the privilege sequence, and balked at the point of taking responsibility for others. Assuming such responsibility became a condition for discharge, with which he ultimately complied. He never went through the final two levels, but was discharged after making one symbolic gesture to take care of another patient.

Each of these patterns of progress through the privilege system of Tompkins I is indicative of a different pattern of ward-patient interaction. Whatever the pattern, two regularities emerge: (1) The ward *comes to* the patient, it responds to him and to his reactions; (2) the ward's response individuates around each patient, both initially and with the passage of time. The combined effect of the ward's norms; the active, charismatically invested staff; and the program of scheduled meetings with patient decision-making process at their focus—all create a responsive environment. To get a response, the patient need not go far in experimenting with his behavior. If the acutely psychotic patient emerges from his room and has a quiet conversation with another patient, he is likely to be praised and rewarded for it soon. If he becomes anxious and withdrawn, he is quickly reassured and offered company. If a patient near discharge has a difficult time on his first weekend at home, he and his family will have opportunity—and some pressure—to discuss this on Sunday evening at a family group meeting with a member of the nursing staff. The difficulties that developed can then be pursued during the week in the patient's various therapy situations, including family meetings.

To individualize this active response to patients, the ward collects two sorts of data about each patient. At admission a great deal of information is gotten about recent events in the patient's life and his earlier history. During the first days of hospitalization, the ward staff observes closely how the patient is responding to this particular environment. It is the latter data that most influence the initial responses and pressures from the ward. They determine where in the privilege sequence the patient is begun and how quickly he moves through the initial phases. As time passes and the patient becomes involved in the ward system, the ward begins to be influenced increasingly by prehospital events. On Tompkins I the important historical events are usually considered those that took place shortly before admission. Disruptions in family relations during the period of decompensation, such as marital strife and alienation, or parent-adolescent conflict, or problems in a work situation are frequently the focus. These problem areas may be examined directly, and some in-hospital pattern may develop as a sort of "transference" onto the hospital situation of such outside conflict. For example, problems with authority and responsibility can easily be evoked by the ward's system of sharing decision-making with patients. The process of focusing on problem areas and seeking change is complex and subtle. It involves estimates of a patient's capacity, of the ward's therapeutic leverage, and of the best timing for working toward change.

BEHAVIOR CHANGES

What evidence is there for the effectiveness of these efforts toward general improvement or resolution of specific problems? To answer the first part of this question we can look at ratings of behavior over the course of hospitalization. The indices of behavior listed in Table 4.1 are derived from a number of staff members' weekly or daily ratings—doctors, nurses, activities therapist. *Condition* indicates the level of symptomatology and global judgments of how a patient is doing; *community membership* includes ratings of sociability and involvement; *responsibility* combines taking care of one-self and helping others. On all three measures, significant change occurs within the first month of treatment. Of the total change for each index, a greater proportion of eventual total change occurs for community membership and responsibility during the first month than for condition. This suggests that change may occur first, or more rapidly, for behaviors that reflect the ward norms than for behaviors having to do with

		Change	
Table 4.1			
Changes Over Hospital Course			
for Three Behavior Indices			
(n = 42)			
		First to	First to
Index	*First Week*	*Fourth Week*	*Final Week***
Condition	15.6	+ 2.9*	+ 5.3*
Community membership	16.3	+ 2.7*	+ 4.1*
Responsibility	7.8	+ 5.0*	+ 6.8*

*All changes are significantly different from admission at $p<0.01$ (paired t-tests).
**Average length of stay, 10 weeks.

Table 4.2

Scores and Changes on Three Norm Dimensions During Hospitalization
Mean Score Change from
Admission Score[a]

Dimension	Mean Admission Score[b]	At One Week	At One Month	At Discharge
Communitas	4.72	+ 0.16[c]	+ 0.39[d]	+ 0.60[d]
Nurture	5.19	− 0.10	− 0.28[e]	+ 0.13
Control	3.44	− 0.05	− 0.34[d]	− 0.33[f]

[a] t-tests for paired observations (two-tailed test of significance).

[b] computed by scoring 1 for "strong disagreement" through 7 for "strong agreement"; 4.00 = neutral.

[c] $p < 0.10$
[e] $p < 0.05$
[f] $p < 0.01$
[d] $p < 0.001$

one's overall condition. In all, the data indicate that behavior change does occur in Tompkins I patients.

The next logical question must be: What is the meaning of these changes? Is this the improvement seen in acute patients in most hospital settings, or does it have any relation to the special norm system of Tompkins I and its efforts at norm change? The fact that normative behavior changes, and does so more rapidly than general condition, would suggest this. To understand this further, we can look at changes in patient norms during hospitalization. Table 4.2 presents scores on the *communitas* dimension, along with *nurture* and *control* measures; changes in these scores are charted in Figure 4.1. In this case we have scores at the time of admission, at the end of the first week, at one month, and at discharge. Patients' attitudes on the communitas dimension change quickly, dramatically, and in the direction of a staff "ideal patient" score of 5.9. Changes in the control score are also distinct and probably reflect the degree to which the communitas dimension is opposed to the control dimension, as measured by these items. On the other hand, nurture changes only during the midst of hospitalization, reflecting the fact that patients' sense of staff as giving and kind decreases as they are most involved in intense, realistic dealing with problems.

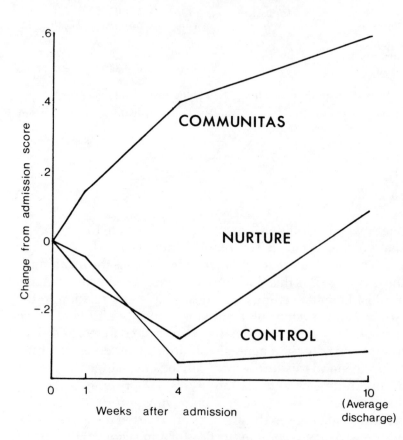

Thus we have documented role acceptance at the level of norms as well as behavior. Over an aggregate of patients, acceptance of the Tompkins I patient role as a concept begins quickly and grows steadily. In view of the parallel finding that actual behavior changes also, we can now ask: Which changes first, attitude or behavior? The natural assumption is that patients would first be induced to change their beliefs, and then their behavior would change. This, after all, is the common assumption about attitude change, propaganda, advertising. Our data indicates the opposite: Behavior change appears to precede attitude change.[4] Changes in both general condition and in behaviors reflecting ward norms appear to precede change in attitude toward the norms, when we consider the whole span of hospitalization.[5]

If we go back to the level of analysis used in examining the first moments of Mary Wheeler's admission, the relation of behavior and attitude becomes somewhat clearer. The quality of the ward is such that a given bit of patient behavior—a withdrawal to his room, a highly depressed statement, angry abuse of another person—will be responded to almost immediately. The response not only "comes to" the patient, but it seeks to move him away from the behavior directly. There is no intermediate step of convincing the patient that he should "stop doing that because it's not good for you and others." Rather, the initial change process is behavioral: a behavioral response to patient behavior. Most of these behavioral responses are verbal, but the effect is direct and not mediated by a translation to the attitudinal level.

ATTITUDE CHANGES DURING HOSPITALIZATION

Despite what has just been said, attitudes play an important part in the change process. They both prepare and confirm the behavior changes that occur. Also they guide patients as well as staff in behaving in ways that will be effectively change-inducing. The ward norm system, then, is an orienting framework for everyday behavioral transactions. Attitudes and behavior are two different aspects of a change process, not competing hypothetical causes of change. To understand the sequence of the change process in more detail, we can examine norm changes at different times during hospitalization.

Gross changes in the communitas norm items and behavior indices show only the broadest sweep of orientation change during hospitalization. We can begin to sketch in some of the detail of this change process through changes in specific questionnaire items. Findings for phases of role induction are depicted in Diagram 4.2. At the left are a series of role issues. Changes in responses to these issues, occurring at different times during the course of hospitalization, extend across the page. The statements listed are inferred from items

DIAGRAM 4.2 PATIENT CHANGES DEDUCED FROM MAJOR SHIFTS IN ITEM SCORES DURING DIFFERENT PHASES OF HOSPITAL STAY

	First Week	Weeks 1 - 4	Week 4 - Discharge
TIME-PERIOD:			
Relation to:			
The ward as a whole	I have less doubt about its helpfulness.	It is important to be a member of the community.	I have faith in this ward. This system is helpful, but it's hard to leave.
The staff	Nurses are not just nurturant.	I accept the nurses' observing, evaluating role. They need not be supportive and motherly to be helpful.	The doctor is kind and gentle, but not necessarily an adviser or guide.
Other patients	I accept the ward's emphasis on socializing, not staying alone. I am developing concern for other patients.	I have a strong feeling of responsibility for others; to question them about problems, to help them.	I would tell the staff about another patient's problem. I prefer to avoid sick patients. I don't feel so responsible for other patients anymore.
		Patients are not so touchy.	I can get involved with the
	My problems should be known to others here - patients and staff.		
Problems	Suppress symptoms; control them.		I feel healthier.
	Something is seriously wrong with me. I will have to work on problems to change myself.		I understand my problem better. The pressure to face them was needed
	I got myself here. My family can help in this.	My family should participate; they have problems too.	
		I feel less restless and nervous.	

on which the questionnaire-tested group shows significant changes during the time intervals shown. Most of the statements in the diagram use the language of the items themselves.

The role expectations outlined in the diagram, especially those that show change during the first week, appear to focus on the tendency of entering patients to form an alienated relation to the hospital. Patients are expected to socialize and reveal their problems to others. Thus their sense of stigma is countered by having them relate to others in a way that reduces their sense of peculiarity. At the very same time, patients are told that there is something seriously wrong in their way of adapting, that they will have to work on this, and that they played a part in those patterns that led to hospital admission. During this first week on the unit, patients are best able to reject negative aspects of the above role expectations. That is, they do not yet actively support these expectations as much as they reject alternatives to them, alternatives that generally represent alienated responses. Another example of patients' acknowledgment of those role expectations de-emphasizing passivity and dependence is the changed view of nurses—a *lessened* view of them as primarily kind, gentle, nurturing figures.

During the next three weeks of hospitalization, emphasis shifts from patients' problems to their involvement in the therapeutic community. Membership in the community is an important aspect of role expectations that patients acknowledge. Patients accept considerable responsibility for other patients in a variety of ways—questioning them about their problems, helping them, refusing to see them as touchy, getting involved with them. Patients feel less upset and acknowledge that there are problems in the family that make important the involvement of families in treatment. Within the community, staff—especially nurses—are accepted as important evaluators of patient progress; the expectation that nurses' primary function is a nurturant one continues to diminish.

Between one month and discharge, patients further confirm their acceptance of a role as a member of a therapeutic community, but begin to acknowledge the readjustments necessary for adapting to the realities of discharge. They continue to express confidence in therapeutic community as a treatment, but express also the difficulty of giving up the sense of membership. Although they see involvement with, and responsibility for, other patients as important, they view this as being in the past. Subjectively, they feel healthier and believe that they have some grasp of their difficulties, recognizing that it took social pressure for them to face these difficulties. The doctor is seen as a warm but real person; his role as an authority figure or magical healer is de-emphasized. During this later phase, the majority of item changes are in a positive direction; that is, patients have reached a point where they can actively assert their acceptance of therapeutic community role expectations for themselves and others rather than simply reject the negative alternatives.

An appropriate question at this point is: Why attitude-norm change? Why is behavior change not enough? After all, the goal of a two-month hospitalization is not to produce a patient well trained in therapeutic community, but to enable the patient to return home. The answer lies in the role of the patient group itself in therapeutic community. No matter how large a ward's staff nor how busy its program, a great deal of patients' time is spent with other patients. The flaw discovered in so many studies of therapeutically oriented hospitals has been that the patient group remains separate, especially as a normative group, from staff. Its norms act as a shield from the effects of staff norms on patient behavior. The extreme example of this is Hannah Green's fictionalized portrayal of "Ward D" and its norm system at Chestnut Lodge Hospital:

Deborah lay in bed, and her thoughts returned to the puzzle.

Dust motes blown and floating all the patients were, but even so there were some things that were not done. Deborah knew very well that she could never ask Miss Coral why she had thrown the bed or how it was that Mrs. Forbes' arm had been intruded upon by that bed. Beating, stealing, swearing, blaspheming, and sexual eccentricity were not sins on D ward. Spitting on the floor, urinating, defecating, or masturbating incontinently in public aroused only passing annoyance rather than horror, but to ask how or why was not forgivable and to oppose another patient's act was a sign of crudity at best and at worst a kind of assault—an attempted mayhem at the barriers which were the all-costly protectors of life. Lee Miller had cursed Deborah for the burnings which had resulted in the whole ward's restriction, but she had never asked why they had been done or expressed a wish that they be stopped. There was ridicule and anger, but never intrusion. Miss Coral could never be confronted with throwing the bed, and her friends, such as they could be, would henceforth delicately expunge the name of Mrs. Forbes from their conversation in the presence of the one who had caused her to be hurt (Green, 1964, p. 184).

This was a ward of chronic patients in a long-stay institution. We would not expect more acute patients to develop such an antitherapeutic culture, if only because their time in the hospital is too brief. But the potency of the patient peer group is demonstrated.

In a therapeutic community like Tompkins I, an attempt is made to use this normative influence of the peer group for therapy and change. To do this the patient group must be brought into the same norm system as staff.[6] We see this happening in the analysis of norm changes over time in hospital; the changes begin passively—the patient begins by accepting that he need not act "sick" and ineffective. By the middle period he is active, involved in mutual aid with other patients, working alongside staff toward the same goals. This bringing-together of the staff group and the patient group achieves two major ends: Staff can transmit a charismatically invested role concept to patients; the charismatic potential of the patient group is enlisted in the service of therapy. This explains the importance of the norm system despite the fact that enculturation of patients to the norms alone is not directly therapeutic.[7] The norm system also provides the focus for patient-staff cohesion; the very sharing of it binds the group together, presenting newcomers with a "solid front." Finding few weak points in the hospital social system, the patient is most likely to begin to attend to the patterns of that system rather than to the prior maladaptive patterns of relating to the environment that led him to the hospital.

This brings the analysis of the Tompkins I social system full circle. Diagram 4.3—which represents a process, not an actual time sequence—summarizes the conclusions of Chapters 2-4. When the patient enters, "sick," he is immediately acted on by a variety of social and biological influences (A). These lead him to become a community member (C), accepting the beliefs and enacting the norms of the ward staff; and to "get better" in terms of symptoms and/or ability to cope (B). The former (C) directly facilitates return home (D); the latter (B) facilitates the community as a whole (E), and the treatment of other patients (F). Finally, success in working with patients enhances the staff, the community as a whole, and the director (E) and (G), aiding their ability to work with patients (H). This rather complex picture can be summarized by saying that there are two interwoven processes here: the treatment experience of the individual patient, and the maintenance of an effective community. A truly complete picture of the operation of the entire ward would include more staff processes: the inculcation of roles and norms in staff, their maintenance in staff meetings, the psychological benefits staff gain from being members themselves. This analysis has been in terms of an "average," or "modal" patient. Aggregate data from 65 patients, with widely varying problems and hospital experiences, have been the basis for this mode. In the next three

DIAGRAM 4.3

THE PROCESS OF THERAPEUTIC COMMUNITY

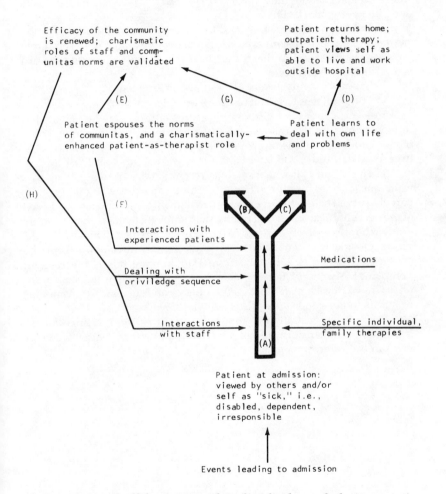

Efficacy of the community
is renewed; charismatic
roles of staff and comm-
unitas norms are validated

Patient returns home;
outpatient therapy;
patient views self as
able to live and work
outside hospital

(E)   (G)   (D)

Patient espouses the norms
of communitas, and a charismatically-
enhanced patient-as-therapist role

Patient learns to
deal with own life
and problems

(H)

(F)

(B) (C)

Interactions with
experienced patients

Medications

Dealing with
oriviledge sequence

Interactions
with staff

Specific individual,
family therapies

(A)

Patient at admission:
viewed by others and/or
self as "sick," i.e.,
disabled, dependent,
irresponsible

Events leading to admission

chapters we shall look at real individuals and their experiences as Tompkins I patients. The system we have described
will be seen in operation, adapting to the real responses of
several types of patients.

NOTES

1. For microanalysis of the first moments of an outpatient evaluation interview that includes these qualities of speech and paraverbal expression, see Pittenger et al. (1960).

2. In Mary Wheeler's case, and to varying extents in other cases, the norms of the ward are conveyed to patients before admission itself. From patients' reports it is clear that the actual experience of arriving at the ward is a far more powerful one.

3. "Special" status means 24-hour accompaniment.

4. This finding is based on results of a technique involving comparison of "cross-correlations" of different measures (attitudes and behaviors) at different times. In this case we found that correlations between early behavior and later attitudes were significantly greater than correlations between early attitudes and later behavior (see Almond et al. 1969).

5. This result is like that of some recent studies of role-playing as a technique for bringing about change. Cigarette smokers who role-play the part of a patient being shown x-rays of a malignant tumor and being advised of the necessity of an operation reduce their smoking far more than a control group who are passively exposed to the same information (Janis and King).

6. Obviously staff must be highly consistent themselves in acceptance of the ward's norms. Our data from staff indicate this is the case for Tompkins I. My observations of other settings indicate that staff consensus on norms is critical both for therapeutic efficacy and successful transmission of norms to newcomers (see also Caudill, 1958).

7. As a demonstration of this, we found that norm change for the communitas dimension did *not* correlate significantly with behavioral measures of improvement.

CHAPTER 5

Individual Hospital Careers: Mary Wheeler

In the last three chapters we have examined the hospital experience of a "modal" or "typical" patient. Doing so has made it possible to understand the workings of social therapy in a therapeutic community. The modal patient's experience reflects an important reality, namely, that a large part of hospital process in the Tompkins I therapeutic community concerns shared program experiences, shared interaction processes, and a shared norm system. Patients are, however, heterogeneous individuals who differ not only in their pasts and their problems, but in their reactions to hospitalization. This chapter and the two that follow will each present an individual hospital experience. Through these three cases we can examine how the general patterns apply and are modulated in specific situations. The three cases are not only of interest in themselves, but also typify three major types of patient-hospital interaction.

The hospital career studies that are the basis of these three chapters differ from a usual case history in several important ways. A fundamental difference between the two types of case study is in the "stories" they seek to tell. The case history relates the patient's life, extending the tale into the hospital only in conclusion; the hospital career study tells in detail the story of the patient and the hospital system as they interact over a relatively brief time. In fact, both the case history and the hospital career study are distillations from larger amounts of data. Implicit in each are a series of assumptions about dynamics: in one case, the dynamics of the individual's psychology; in the other, the dynamics of interaction between individual and social system. In the hospital career studies that follow, the data presented have been selected because they depict aspects of a core patient-hospital interaction process we deduce in each case. [1]

Hospital career studies were based on the following data: routine hospital record (which includes detailed data obtained at admission, daily and weekly behavior ratings by a variety of staff members, progress reports by the ward physician, nurses' notes on every eight-hour period, and a record of all drugs prescribed during hospitalization): the ward physician's diary describing both formal treatment contacts and informal contacts; changes in privilege status and associated group discussion; social relations with other patients and role in the patient advisory system; patients' subjective experience of the socialization process. Much of this data was collected through research interviews. These interviews focused on the subjective experience of patienthood. Expectations of what hospitalization would be like were sought out, along with information on what the patient had actually been told about the ward before arriving. The patient's earliest interactions with staff and other patients were explored, with special emphasis on the patient's reactions to these contacts. We asked how the patient perceived the privilege system of the unit and the various therapeutic and governmental meetings. We also inquired into the patient's perception of his illness and its relation to hospitalization. In the later phases of hospitalization, we asked how the patient related his improvement, if any, to the social processes of the unit. Finally, before discharge, we were interested in how the hospital experience related to resuming contact with home environments.

Hospital career studies have a number of major limitations. Ours were restricted to the patients of one physician who, as a research collaborator, could record detailed observations of her patients and her own actions and responses.[2] We selected three very different patients for the close scrutiny of the career study, but were quite aware that this number could never encompass the varieties of patients who come to the ward. These three patients exemplify three different patterns of hospital-patient interaction that we discovered in our larger patient sample. We found that the pattern of patients' scores on the communitas scale was a good basis for distinguishing major patterns of response to Tompkins I. The profile of scores at admission, at one week, at one month, and at discharge indicated the patient's reaction to the norm system of the ward and separated the sample studied into more homogeneous groups.[3] We found that 48 of 58 patients fell into one of three major patterns. The first group we termed "preconverts." These were individuals (exemplified by Mary Wheeler, whose hospital career is examined in the present chapter) who scored high on the communitas scale the first week on, as though they accepted the ward's norms almost immediately on arriving. The second group did not accept the ward's norms until after at least a week of hospitalization had passed, and often as much as a month. This group (exemplified by Bill Putnam in Chapter 6) we termed "unit converts." A third group consisted of patients who did not accept, or accepted and then rejected, the ward's norms: "rejectors" and "renegers," respectively (illustrated by Charles Lawrence in Chapter 7). Figure 5.1 depicts the profiles of these groups.

In presenting these cases and patterns of patient-hospital response, the hospital career study will be given first, followed by data on the characteristics of patients who, based on

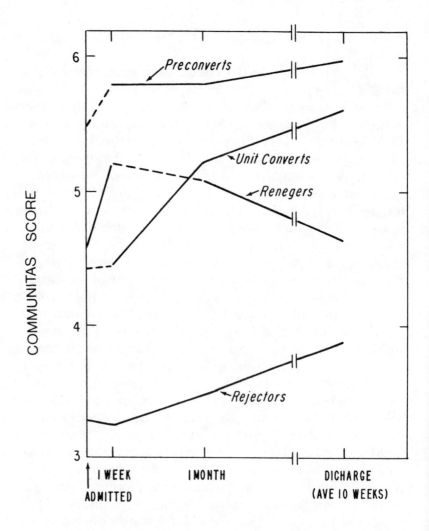

their profiles, had a corresponding experience. In addition, two sorts of follow-up data will be discussed in Chapters 5–8. The first sort was derived from the large sample of 60 patients who were interviewed about a year after discharge; the second, from the three hospital career patients who were interviewed five years after hospitalization.

HOSPITAL CAREER STUDY 1: MARY WHEELER

Mrs. Wheeler was a 34-year-old married mother of three when she was admitted to Tompkins I. She had functioned competently during the last 10 years as a nurse, as a housewife, and as an active participant in community organizations. About a year before her hospitalization, Mary began to feel depressed. She became increasingly alienated from her husband. Mary's parents, who lived several hundred miles away, were emotionally inaccessible to her, but she had several close female friends with whom she could discuss some of her marital problems. Seven months before hospitalization, Mary entered psychotherapy with a private psychiatrist, whom she saw once a week. In psychotherapy Mary examined her relationship with her parents—for example, her mother's defensive emotional withdrawal—and how it affected her marital relations. During this time, she made two relatively harmless suicide gestures. The first created some alarm, but the second was ignored by both her husband and her psychiatrist, who saw the gestures as rather childish, hysterical outbursts that reflected the issues she was working through in therapy. Six days before admission, Mary swallowed a dose of barbiturates sufficient to kill her, had she not been discovered unconscious. She was hospitalized on a medical ward, where she required treatment for both the barbiturate coma and a secondary pneumonia. When after five days she was physically recovered, a transfer to the psychiatric service was arranged.

Mary Wheeler's first moments on admission to the unit have been described in Chapter 4. To the staff, Mary presented herself as competent, in good contact with reality, sharp-witted, and challenging. Of her own style, Mrs. Wheeler said, "I feel that it's very much of a defense. You know, it kind of shakes the other person if you say something very nasty to them right off. . . . I guess that I'm sort of afraid that people will take advantage of me and beat me down, so therefore I do it before they can. . . . I can be nasty—I think it comes very naturally to me." Mary was actually quite frightened in the new situation of the psychiatric unit. She recognized rather early that patients were expected to discuss problems, not only with the staff but with other patients. During one of the history-taking sessions with her doctor, she revealed what for her was a major secret—that she masturbated. To her ward physician this appeared to be an invitation to discuss internal problems, as she had done in outpatient individual therapy. The ward staff had decided quickly that a major factor in Mary's depression was her marital relationship, though the probable psychodynamic origins of Mary's depressive response were recognized as including her relations with her parents. The staff felt that the individual therapy approach to such causes had been unsuccessful and that a more realistic goal during a brief hospital stay would be to focus on the marriage. The doctor listened to the masturbation "confession" rather indifferently and made little response. To avoid reproducing the unsuccessful outpatient experience, she did not see Mrs. Wheeler individually after these first meetings except for brief interchanges in the hallway. Instead, in group meetings she encouraged Mary to discuss her marital relationship, and made arrangements for conjoint therapy meetings.

    In effect, the ward responded to Mary in this way: "You have been effective in your life by having high expectations for yourself and trying to meet them. We will ally ourselves with this pattern of strength by encouraging you to be active and effective in the protected setting of the hospital and by not offering you an individual therapy relationship that might evoke your more primitive, dependent impulses." By not making individual therapy regularly available, the ward was making Mary the judge of her need for individual contact with her ward psychiatrist.

    At admission Mrs. Wheeler had been assigned to a room with other recently admitted patients. She found herself both fascinated and frightened by these other patients, many of whom were more overtly disturbed. She was intrigued by a patient who, after a blatantly psychotic phase, showed no interest in her earlier, "sicker" behavior once it was over. Speaking for herself, Mary said that she would have been eager to know how she had acted. Of a patient who screamed during the night, she said, "It just seemed to go right through me every time . . . . I—maybe I put myself in her situation. I wouldn't want to be in bed losing that much control over myself." She recognized that the staff responded differently to different patients and that they responded to her by accepting her competence and "needling" her. As she was to say later, "I just found that most of them were very sarcastic." It is interesting that in talking about her parents, Mary said:

> They sort of have the feeling that "Mary can take care of herself. We don't have to feel sorry about her." Therefore I never did really bother them with everything, and I think now they realize that I can't take everything. . . . My father's attitude always is "be strong, be strong and everything will be all right," but it didn't work.

Because she was composed and in apparent self-control, Mary passed through privilege status levels rather rapidly. She saw her psychiatrist at two group meetings each week as well as at community meetings, but became increasingly uneasy at not having individual sessions. On her 11th day of hospitalization, she asked to see the psychiatrist and was given an appointment the next day. At that time she cried —unusual for her—and asked whether she would be seen individually. The doctor told her that she would not, that the conjoint marital sessions would be the most important part of her ward therapy. Mary apparently accepted this and continued to become involved in a highly competent way in the unit's governing system. At times she expressed anger toward her doctor through sarcastic comments. The psychiatrist responded to such communications minimally, assuming that they reflected Mary's resentment at taking increasing responsibility for herself and others without major support from her doctor. During her third week on the unit, she was elected president of the Patient Advisory Board, reflecting how impressed the community was with her competence. However, Mary allowed the responsibilities of this position to interfere with her visits with her husband on the unit. Mr. Wheeler brought this up in family therapy, and Mary's doctor pointed out that this was an avoidance of what she considered the central issues to be dealt with during hospital treatment.

Apparently Mary was "being strong" in the first weeks of her stay on Tompkins I. She said, for example, about being president of the advisory board, "It's a very simple thing for me to do because I'm sort of in control of the situation." Mary thus appeared to be making an initial adaptation to the unit that replicated a way she had been encouraged to behave by her father, a way she had sought to use rather unsuccessfully in her family life—being strong, ignoring her passive and dependent impulses, being psychologically tough on herself and others.

The Tompkins I staff was taking a position much like that of Mary's parents. They were allowing, even encouraging, her to "be strong," to maintain a seeming control over the situation. At the same time they were emphasizing to Mary the one relationship where she could realistically expect closeness and support—that with her husband. By not offering the temporary support of individual therapy sessions, her ward doctor thought to push Mary toward working on improving the marriage relationship.

The strain of having this mode of adaptation accepted by the psychiatric unit emerged in Mary's irritability. During research interviews in the second and third week of hospitalization, she was sarcastic, critical, and somewhat paranoid. She assumed, despite the denials of the interviewer, that the tape recording of the interview would be played for the entire staff. Her defiance of the unit's approach was apparent in her avoidance of her husband during the visiting hours. In effect, she was showing that she could beat the unit at its own game. If she did not receive the individual care and support she desired, she would use the ward involvement expectations to avoid the area her doctor considered most vital—her marriage. She spent most of her free time with a patient who avoided involvement with the unit by insisting on his greater involvement in his outside psychoanalytic therapy. This patient had been admitted to the unit after a severe anxiety attack, apparently prompted by the vacation of his psychoanalyst.

This resistance to the ward program continued, as we shall see, and gives some evidence about the compliant quality of Mary's ward adaptation. The fragility of this adaptation in the face of postdischarge life events was revealed only on follow-up (see below).

Mary Wheeler's adaptive abilities and her ways of thinking about herself were superficially highly syntonic with unit expectations. She could take some pleasure in being a "good" patient, in the same way she had been a "good" daughter, then a good nurse, wife, and mother. Mary could appear strong, independent, and undemanding of nurturance from others. But signs that Mary's pattern of adjustment to the unit would not last indefinitely began to emerge increasingly during the third and fourth weeks of her hospitalization. In addition to avoiding Mr. Wheeler, with whom her doctor felt that the most important work of therapy should be going on, Mary became increasingly irritable in a variety of situations. For example, the advisory board of which she was chairman was censured by Dr. Astrachan, the assistant director, by the suspension of all passes for one weekend. This was a response to the staff's judgment that patient responsibility and self-control were slipping, a judgment suggested by a series of poor decisions on passes and by the elopement of one patient. By this time Mary was identifying strongly with the staff and their techniques for bringing about changes in patients. Thus the censure came as a distinct blow. Her response was an angry one, expressed in her usual style of sarcasm. She referred to Dr. Astrachan as "Dr. Alcatraz." She expressed her pain at the implicit criticism of her leadership by describing her chairmanship as, "I'll be the teacher this week." She complained at having to be interviewed by medical students while paying $50 a day for her treatment.

During the fourth week of hospitalization, Mary became more visibly angry. She verbally attacked a male patient, in a very hostile way, during a group meeting. She complained about microphones used to tape record group meetings and about the presence of observers in the meetings. On the 25th day of hospitalization, Mary's anger reached a crisis point. She was chosen to be interviewed by a medical student in a seminar of students and faculty members from the ward. Because she had visitors at the time of the interview, Mary refused to participate. Her doctor, who was participating in the teaching session, insisted that she come and finally sent a male aide to bring her to the meeting. She very reluctantly agreed. In the meeting she attacked the student interviewer with her sarcasm and eventually made it impossible for him to conduct the interview. The ward chief, Dr. Detre, commented to her that she was behaving quite "nastily."

According to Mary, immediately after this comment she experienced a major change in how she looked at herself. She suddenly could acknowledge her stubbornness and nastiness. That evening, in a conjoint session with her husband, she listened far more intently than previously to his comments and after the meeting conveyed to him her feeling of needing more emotional support. He spoke to the ward therapist about the possibility of Mary being seen individually. The doctor saw Mary the next day, during which time there was a great deal of discussion of her "nasty" pattern of behavior. The day after this, her husband was able to express

for the first time his guilt about his past behavior toward
Mary. She was able to respond to him with a plea that he
listen to her more. Many observers, both patients and staff,
noted a change in Mary's whole manner: Where before she
had been harsh and tough and brittle, she was now easier and
quieter. In a research interview on day 29, she appeared
markedly changed. Her suspiciousness and sarcasm were
gone, her voice was soft and gentle.

> *Interviewer:* How are things going?
> *Mary:* Much better.
> *Interviewer:* Better? Better than . . . .
> *Mary:* Than they were.
> *Interviewer:* What's better?
> *Mary:* Well, I'm beginning to really understand myself better
> and the problems I have. One of them is being nasty. I never
> realized how nasty I was. I know you did.
> *Interviewer:* Pardon?
> *Mary:* I know *you* did.
> *Interviewer:* Is it something that you've sort of been thinking
> about since last week?
> *Mary:* Yes, when it was brought to my attention.
> *Interviewer:* How did that happen?
> *Mary:* I was being very nasty. One of the things was when Dr.
> Boltax asked me to go in the room with the medical students
> to interview me or ask me some questions. I really didn't
> want to go. I didn't like the idea. . . . At this point I don't
> really know why, but I got very angry, and I was told that if I
> didn't come by myself, that the orderly would take me in.
> Then I was so angry at that—about the situation—that when
> you come here—this is a teaching and research ward and you
> have to make yourself available to anybody or anyone for
> teaching or research or whatever—and I became somewhat
> angry about it, but I started to be angry before the students
> asked me questions. I was being very stubborn and now that I
> realize how I get stubborn—I think maybe it will be some-

what easier for me to cope with it. I was always too concerned
with my own rights and now anybody . . . . I realized how
stubborn I act and there's really no reason for it. And I felt
somewhat badly for the students . . . . I'm sure I wasn't
being asked to do something that terrible that it warranted
the way that I acted.

Interviewer: Do you think this kind of experience on the ward
here has any connection with your outside life?

Mary: Well, I think it is the way I talk to my husband, definitely.
I would be apt to say "no, I won't, no I will not, and don't try
to make me"—and I realize this—without really giving him a
chance to say too much.

The remainder of Mary's hospitalization can be seen as a
working out and repetition of this crisis. For example, on the
next weekend she sought out her doctor to inquire whether
she ought to have sex with her husband during her first
overnight pass. Apparently, in accepting a more dependent
relation to her doctor and her husband, Mary put herself in a
childlike status. Her doctor rejected the parental role by saying that Mary should do whatever it would be natural to do
with her husband when she was at home. It may well have
been that intercourse represented not only being an adult but
also coming closer to losing control. Since Mary had so recently given up her primary mode of keeping control—her
sarcasm and nastiness—she may well have had fears of what
would happen if she took part in an activity which also involved loosening control with her husband. Her doctor was,
of course, maintaining the unit's attitude toward her, which
had been established at the outset, by saying in effect, "You
can handle it yourself." Thus, although Mrs. Wheeler's "nastiness" had been challenged and broken down, it was not
replaced with a passive role but rather with a reorientation
toward her competence. Even after her "crisis," Mary felt that
it was up to her to do most of the changing in the marriage.
She recognized that she wanted different things from her

husband, but that to get them she herself would have to behave differently. Her husband was apparently able to voice some of his anger about this time. And it was he who, in a joint session, brought up their sexual relationship for discussion.

There was a smaller crisis around discharge planning, concerning the question of what kind of follow-up therapy would be appropriate. Mary requested individual therapy, but by this time her husband agreed with the ward staff on the need for couple therapy. The crisis was resolved in favor of couple treatment, and Mary was discharged after seven weeks of hospital stay.

The Wheelers were advised to continue attending the unit's family meetings twice weekly for two weeks after discharge. They missed the first such meeting following a marital argument. The doctor called Mary after this and asked why she had not come to the meeting. Mary told her doctor, "I was too upset to come. It doesn't matter anyway." The doctor responded, "It matters to me." The Wheelers attended the remaining family group sessions, and the transition to outpatient treatment was otherwise uneventful. In their last family group session, Mary created a final crisis by asking whether she could go to see her former individual therapist, rather than the therapist she and her husband had been referred to at discharge. In a final research interview, she gave some indication of the motivation for this request. She was feeling the lack of opportunity to talk to an individual doctor and in retrospect wished she had heard, in individual therapy sessions, more of the things she had learned about herself on Tompkins I. While this on the face of it makes some sense, the rather lengthy course of individual therapy prior to admission indicates that her request had other meanings. It was in a sense an acknowledgment of her limitations; a statement that although she could rationally acknowledge the value of her hospitalization, leaving and facing a new, relatively unknown psychiatrist made her feel frightened and wishful of returning to someone more familiar, perhaps someone who would be available to her alone. In fact she was left to handle this dilemma by herself and did enter joint therapy with the recommended therapist.

FOLLOW-UP

Mary Wheeler's last five years have been difficult. Following discharge she was seen in conjoint marital therapy but received individual therapy also. She continued to have severe depressive periods, and at one point she was rehospitalized elsewhere for depression. Approximately six months after her Tompkins I discharge, the Wheelers moved to a different city. There, because of further severe depression, Mary was hospitalized a third time. She received individual psychotherapy as an inpatient for six months. For another four months she was at the same hospital in day care; shortly before termination of day care, she made another serious suicide attempt. She was returned to inpatient care and finally treated with a course of electroshock therapy. Apparently during this hospitalization (before the shock treatments), she was overtly psychotic as well as depressed. She improved from this phase of illness gradually but remained in day treatment for a year and a half. Since that time she has continued in once-weekly psychotherapy. She has continued to recieve both tranquilizers and antidepressant medication. Her children, now in early adolescence, have only recently been returned to Mary's household from the care of relatives.

During the five-year follow-up interview, Mary acknowledged that she could not disentangle her Tompkins I stay from her considerable later hospital and therapy experiences. She felt that her illness had been underrated while she was at Tompkins I and that it had not helped her: "Nobody realized how horrible I was feeling; I never could go back."

Mary also said that she felt she had not been as sick while she was at Tompkins I as she had later become. She seemed genuinely pleased to speak with her ward physician during the follow-up interview and remembered several staff members and other patients warmly.

There are several ways to understand what happened to Mary Wheeler. We can speculate that her initial hospitalization occurred during an early phase of a severe psychotic depression. Or it could be speculated that the Wheelers' departure from the New Haven area added a further stress that precipitated further upset. It is also possible that marital conflicts and Mary's long-standing internal problems had simply not been adequately worked out in therapy.

In denying Mary individual support and concentrating on therapy work around her marital relationship, the staff put the degree of her underlying depression to the test. In the face of this test, Mary responded positively—while she was a member of the community. Her anger came to a head, was confronted, and she could then admit her neediness more readily. But the ward was also relying on Mary's guilt-driven pattern of competence to enable her to return home to her family life. Outpatient therapy, couple *or* individual, proved inadequate to handle the emerging depression. The ward took a gamble that succeeded briefly and then failed.

The staff assumed that she had sufficient capabilities and strengths to resume outpatient treatment and homelife rather quickly. Her defensive facade, of course, facilitated this assumption. Further time and return to home revealed the limitations of the "conversion experience" that Mary underwent while on Tompkins I. Religious conversions, too, are notoriously unstable unless they occasion a permanent commitment to a group or institution. It should be added that growing understanding of depression indicates a considerable role for biological factors in the course of such disorders. Mary's Tompkins I hospitalization may have occurred early in the course of a continuing process.

Tompkins I took its most natural path in dealing with Mary Wheeler. Her capacity to cope was bolstered, and provisions for aftercare were made. In doing this the ward reinforced her defenses and disregarded the possibility that Mary's competence had a counterfeit quality, that from a dynamic point of view her coping was based on guilt rather than a sense of herself and her life as genuine. In restrospect it could be argued that Mary needed then the more extensive hospitalization she ultimately required. It could also be argued that Mary's lengthy period of depression was a needed period of intrapsychic reorganization, such as Laing postulates for young schizophrenics. But even now our prognostic skills would not enable us to predict that Mary's problems would worsen or that the total experience could be beneficial.

Mary Wheeler's hospitalization—but not her life since —exemplifies in many ways the experience of the group of patients we call "preconverts."[4] Preconverts are characterized by high communitas scores at admission or by the end of the first week of hospitalization. A second defining characteristic of the preconvert profile is that the high score continues through discharge. Such early and continuing acceptance of a therapeutic community orientation we interpret as reflecting either considerable flexibility or a prior acceptance of the philosophical and normative orientation implied by communitas norms. Preconverts are adults in the age group 25–35, upper-middle class, and most often with values similar to those promulgated on the unit: hard work, social participation, responsibility for one's fellowman, and acceptance of responsibility for personal upset. For example, at admission this group has a significantly lower score than do other groups for the hospital-related authoritarianism measure. Diagnostically, a significantly smaller proportion of this group fell into the psychotic category; the majority (10 out of 16) were depressed.

During the first week on the unit, preconverted patients

adapt quickly. They are judged by staff to be in relatively good condition and are already joining the unit community in a responsible way. For such patients the fit between their capabilities and the ward's expectations of good patient behavior is a close one. Whatever degree of disorganization the patient experienced in the crisis preceding admission, it is likely to diminish considerably in the highly structured, friendly atmosphere of the unit. Many norms and role expectations of ward life are familiar to these patients from school, camp, church, and family experiences. Mary Wheeler, for example, referred to the Patient Advisory Board as "playing school" and conveyed her understanding of the responsible patient role when she said, "This week I am playing teacher." In fact, Mary was so attuned to the expectations of therapeutic community that her involvement in patient government became a way to avoid marital problems the staff considered important. Preconverts are of great value to the unit. They are immediate acceptors of the unit's ways and quickly come to be the good models of the patient role who are so effective with newer patients.

The middle phase of hospitalization for preconverts is characterized by continued good condition and a high level of community membership. By the fourth week of hospitalization, members of this group achieve ratings for responsibility as high as those achieved by members of any other patient group at the end of hospitalization. Mary Wheeler's election to the presidency of the advisory board illustrates this. Just as was the case for Mary, relatively few in this group receive a great deal of individual therapy time: Fewer than half are seen by their physicians individually more than one hour weekly.

With respect to the process of hospitilization, the preconverted group follows one of two paths. If the crisis that led to admission appears to the staff to have resolved, and potential for future difficulty is relatively low, staff may not press for greater change than the patient make suitable aftercare therapy arrangements. On the other hand, if—as in Mary

Wheeler's case—the staff feels that the patient's good adaptation to the ward conceals a more serious set of problems, and especially if the crisis that led to admission involved a serious suicide attempt, then the unit may participate in bringing about a more critical confrontation. The patient is not passive in the choice between these two options. The good fit between preconverted patients and the unit may offer sufficient relief and protection to suppress any patient motivation for using the unit to explore problems and to make further change. However, patients in this group are likely, as was Mary Wheeler, to sense the possibility of change and participate unconsciously in bringing it about. In such cases the result can be an intense "struggle," in which individual and social system are intensely involved, and in which the potential for change in the patient is greater.

The low confrontation version of the preconvert ward experience is exemplified by a patient with whom Mary Wheeler spent considerable amounts of time in the early part of her hospitalization. This man, who had experienced a period of agitation and upset precipitated by his psychoanalyst's vacation, adapted rapidly to the unit, while limiting more active discussion of his problems. No great effort was made by unit staff or other patients to break down his reluctance to participate, and he was not kept on the unit for a long period in order to achieve this. Instead, he was discharged after his analyst returned from vacation.

Mary Wheeler, on the other hand, had a more dramatic experience of hospitalization. To the research interviewer and many of the ward staff, the change she experienced during her fourth week, following her increasing anger and confrontation with her "nastiness" in the hospital, was analogous to a religious conversion. After observing Mary's experience, we found ourselves using the term "conversion" to characterize the central events in hospital process. This comparison is not simply coincidence: There are a great many features common to dramatic therapeutic changes and religious conversion.

Descriptions of the religious conversion process in certain individuals could equally describe Mary Wheeler's hospitalization (James, 1958). Most individuals who experience religious conversion in a sudden crisis have previously been religious but in a peripheral way. The sudden change is only a surface manifestation of a more gradual, unconscious change-process level.

> Emotional occasions, especially violent ones, are extremely potent in precipitating mental rearrangements. The sudden and explosive ways in which love, jealousy, guilt, fear, remorse, or anger can seize upon one are known to everybody. Hope, happiness, security, resolve, emotions characteristic of conversion, can be equally explosive. And emotions that come in this explosive way seldom leave things as they found them. (James, 1958, pp. 163–164).

For preconverts such as Mary Wheeler, the confrontation process, like the religious conversion, engages a prior defensive-adaptive stance of the patient as the focus about which a struggle takes place. In the struggle, the therapeutic community members play an important role, while in the religious conversion the subject is grappling with internalized values and experiences. However, it may be that, psychologically, the religious community of the late nineteenth-century converts parallels the therapeutic community of the late twentieth century. In Mary Wheeler's case there certainly was a concerted and intuitively coordinated response by the ward physician, the nurses, and, to some extent, the other patients. All of these pushed Mary's prior adaptive style to the limit. Like the religious convert, she experienced a buildup of tension, irritation, and dissatisfaction—even the strong opposition to the values of the community that James found in studies of religious converts just prior to their conversion. Like a convert, Mary had come to the end of her rope when she made a fool of a medical student before the eyes of her physician and the chief of the unit, a particularly provocative behavior for a woman trained as a registered nurse. In the research interview three days prior to this incident, she was, like many religious converts, in a state of excitement and heightened sensation. She was angry and irritable but at the same time excited and elated about her conflict with authority figures on the unit. In the next research interview, she appeared quite changed. Her manner resembled the self-surrender of converts. For example, she attributed great understanding to the research interviewer and assumed that he had anticipated what she now understood. This positive feeling contrasts strikingly with her earlier suspicious and challenging attitude.

As with a religious convert, Mrs. Wheeler did not become a different individual but rather changed her orientations towards herself and others while remaining the same person she had been before. And, like a convert, there was no guarantee that the change would endure. Her old personality patterns reasserted themselves quickly after discharge. Judging from the low frequency of such continuing difficulties in the one-year follow-up of preconvert patients, this group as a whole has a far more favorable outcome than Mary. There are two ways to look at Mary's "conversion." One is to say that, for all its drama, it was an experience with little impact on her. The other is to say that the impact was great, but that it was not sustained. Unlike the religious convert, who proceeds to adopt an organized system of belief, social organization, and ritual, Mary returned to her "old" situation with few changes made. Her dilemma is very much that of the encounter group member who makes a "breakthrough" to feelings, openness, and closeness but then has a traumatic "reentry" on returning home (see Part III).

Mary Wheeler's relatively brief hospital stay (seven weeks) was characteristic of the preconverted group, whose average stay of 10 weeks was significantly shorter than that of any other group. The length of their hospital stay undoubtedly is a function of the rapidity and degree to which members of this group improve. During their discharge week, the staff rates this group as showing the best condition of any group at any time during hospitalization. Not only do preconverts leave the hospital in strong agreement with the Tompkins I orientation—this follows automatically from the definition of the group—but they also leave with the most positive feeling about the nurturance of the unit. They continue throughout hospitalization strongly to reject the authoritarian view of the hospital. In retrospective staff judgments, this group receives high improvement and prognosis ratings.

When retested at follow-up 15 months after hospitalization, preconverts continue to have higher communitas scale scores, suggesting, as we have noted before, that the attitudes of this group are inherently in congruence with those of the unit. Measures of condition at follow-up again confirm the healthiness of this group of patients. Here, Mary Wheeler is clearly *not* typical of this group. Although differences in follow-up condition among groups are not striking, the preconverts are consistently performing better. For example, they are rehospitalized very infrequently (*one* of 16) and have the highest porportion of time functioning adequately at work. They participate in the greatest number of social group activities outside the family and are rated as having the best social functioning by the follow-up team. This group tended most often to be referred to a therapist in sympathy with the Tompkins I views. In parallel with this, they tended on follow-up to see Tompkins I as having been helpful and having changed their views.

In summary, preconverts are patients who, although they arrive at the hospital with an acute disturbance, are less crippled by their emotional problems than most patients. Their backgrounds tend to let them fit comfortably into the culture of Tompkins I. These two factors appear to account for their briefer hospitalizations and for their apparent good performance in the hospital. Depending on a variety of factors, preconverted patients may go through their hospitalizations relatively uneventfully or may become involved in an intense interaction. In the latter case, dramatic changes may occur in a short space of time. Preconverts interviewed on follow-up most often saw the unit as having influenced, helped, and changed them. It is impossible to say whether the frequent good outcomes for this group on follow-up can be attributed to hospital treatment rather than to intrinsic strengths. However, it can certainly be said that hospitalization did not foster malfunction in this group. We have noted comparative outcomes between preconverts and other groups, but it should also be pointed out that the absolute level of functioning in this group was extremely high as measured by a variety of outcome variables.

NOTES

1. Examples of such patient career studies have been few. Closest to this approach is Caudill's study of the hospitalization of a single patient, "Mr. Esposito," in a psychotherapy hospital (1958). Stanton and Schwartz have several analyses of portions of individual patient's hospital experience (1954). Sifneos has described the psychological experience of an ulcerative colitis patient in his book, *Ascent from Chaos* (1964). Hannah Green has described her hospitalization at Chestnut Lodge in fictionalized form; the account is valuable for its sensitivity and its presentation of social system aspects of hospital experience during a three-year period (1964). Barbara Field Benziger has presented a similar "patient's-eye view" of several hospitalizations in a nonfiction autobiographical account (1970).

2. Sandra Boltax, M.D., contributed much of the data and many of the ideas presented in the hospital career studies reported in Chapters 5-7.

3. This separation was achieved by applying the mathematic grouping technique, cluster analysis, to "raw" scores and change scores on the communitas scale. Cluster analysis separates subgroups that have internal homogeneity on the variables used; i.e., in this case the profiles of scores that most closely reflect the norm system (for details, see Almond et al. 1969b). Cluster analysis is a classifying technique, not a test of significance;

its results will have meaning only if we find they yield meaningful group-
ings when we look at other characteristics of members.

4. Mary Wheeler is taken as an example of this type, but her hospitalization ended before we had developed the questionnaire used to classify
patients. Some of the discrepancies in her outcome may stem from the fact
that she was not actually a preconvert but, in a sense, a "pseudo-
preconvert."

CHAPTER 6

Individual Hospital Careers: Bill Putnam

Bill, a 15-year-old only child, was admitted to the hospital after he handed his mother a letter to mail to a close friend of his and instructed her to "be sure to mail this and don't read it." His mother read the letter and found its language rather bizarre. Mrs. Putnam consulted Dr. Detre for advice. He recommended that Bill come to Tompkins I. Bill was admitted the next day after his mother told him of her conversation with the ward chief.

Bill was an isolated child. He stood out in school because he always wore a tie and coat. His academic record was poor—he had repeated the third grade and was repeating his first high school year when admitted. He had seen the school social worker weekly for a year when he was 11 years old. Over the four years before admission, Bill had become increasingly withdrawn. There was considerable family difficulty in the background: Mr. Putnam had a chronic, though mild, alcohol problem that had become worse when it was discovered that he had a severe valvular disease of his heart. When Bill was 12, Mr. Putnam underwent open heart surgery. He was postoperatively close to death, and then for a time psychotic. Repeated admissions were required to deal with the complications of surgery. Only a year before Bill's

99

admission, Mr. Putnam had been seen in the hospital emergency room with suicidal impulses and was admitted briefly to the nearby state hospital. Bill's mother had physical defects secondary to childhood polio. Bill felt burdened by his parents' difficult problems, and he worried about their marital tensions. He had isolated himself increasingly from peers and from school. Bill was close to his mother, who confided to him doubts about her marriage, but was also acutely anxious about his father's health: initially his drinking and then his heart problems.

Bill described his feelings and experience of admission to the hospital in this way:

> *Bill:* Well, my mother was the one who decided on Tompkins I. It wasn't me. I didn't choose to come here. When I was told about it, I figured I'd be in a private room and see my private psychiatrist once in a while. That's what I thought it would be like. I didn't know the residents were in charge. I thought there were regular psychiatrists . . . .
>
> *Interviewer:* When you first came in, what were your reactions?
>
> *Bill:* Well, I was quite bewildered. That was all. I mean I didn't know how it was run, you know, the first day I was here. I think there were too many meetings and most of them are ludicrous.

Bill was a neatly dressed, somewhat obese adolescent who looked hostile, fearful, and depressed. He was somewhat aloof and his speech was slightly pompous and formal. During the first week, Bill socialized little with other patients; he talked most easily with a nurse who had teen-age children herself. In an individual session with his doctor, he spoke primarily of Tompkins I and his fears that although people were nice, he could not trust the ward. He condemned the ward but immediately had to reassure himself that he had not offended his doctor by this. He was initially placed on "patient special" status but was changed the next day to five-minute checks. He petitioned to be taken off five-minute checks at the end of the first week in the hospital in a written request that he "be removed from these five-minute checks inflicted upon my person." Bill's ward physician took the initial view that his problems reflected an adolescent turmoil rather than an imminent schizophrenic episode. She hoped that in the protected and supportive environment of a therapeutic community, he would make use of possibilities to develop greater social skills.

During Bill's second week in the hospital, however, he showed very little diminution of defensiveness. This was most clearly symbolized by his continuing to wear a sports coat and tie at all times. He also continued anxiously to seek out his physician to check when his next appointment would be, and was unable to participate actively in group therapy or informal situations. Toward the end of the second week, after staff discussion of Bill's progress, his doctor decided, "He's sicker than I thought," and began Bill on a low dose of anti-psychotic medication (perphenazine, 16 mg daily).

She had already been seeing Bill in twice-weekly individual therapy meetings because of his shyness and a feeling he would need a close adult relationship to work on his relationships with his family. Immediately following initiation of medication, Bill appeared to relax somewhat. He relaxed enough to have a heated argument with an adolescent girl who was a new patient of his ward doctor. During the next week he was able to express feelings of loss when an older female patient in the group discussed her imminent discharge. He told his doctor that he was enjoying the family group meetings. The nursing staff noticed that Bill was friendlier but that he now was overcomplimentary, anxious about alienating anyone. It would seem his doctor's acknowledgment that Bill had a real illness, symbolized by the initiation of medication, allowed Bill for the first time to accept being a patient on Tompkins I.

At the end of his third week in the hospital, his medication was increased to 24 mg daily, a dose generally used and considered more effective by the ward staff. The following day, Bill wore a sweater rather than a coat and tie for the first time. In a psychotherapy session he told his doctor, "I'm going to like it here—but I wouldn't hesitate to leave." When he was asked, "What do you like?" he replied, "It's a friendly atmosphere which is different for me. School is usually un-friendly. I don't usually trust people, but I am beginning to trust them here. I hope they trust me—I always have an adverse comment to say." He was also able, for the first time, to acknowledge how close to madness he had come: "It is a good thing my mother read that letter. I was so confused. Something serious would have happened. My mind couldn't think. Fantasy was on my mind. I felt sick every time I wrote a letter like that. Something had to happen. I was on the edge of something." (*What were you afraid would happen?*) "I don't know. I might have gone crazy. So many pressures—so mixed up—couldn't think."

During this fourth week Bill was put on the "buddy system," enabling him to leave the ward with another pa-tient. He began to enjoy gym activities with other patients and to flirt more openly with the adolescent girl in his group. As though these relaxations took a toll on Bill, he became anxious in the middle of the week and asked to see his doctor. She saw him individually to discuss his anxiety and increased his medication to 32 mg a day, a dose used for moderately psychotic patients. Late in the week, when his doctor was out sick, Bill expressed a wish to be discharged and voiced great hopelessness about his treatment. At the same time he also asked for more medication. During this week a ward social worker had begun to meet with Mr. and Mrs. Putnam and was encouraging their desire to discuss some of their marital difficulties in family group meetings. Bill was strongly op-posed to this and expressed this with his doctor and directly to his parents. Following the increase in medication to 32 mg, however, Bill talked about his parents for the first time. Specifically, he could acknowledge his anxiety about his father's health and how this fear led him to want to see his parents daily.

During his fifth week in the hospital, Bill was elected to the Patient Advisory Board. He continued to socialize with his ward "girl friend" and began to talk with a medical-student patient whom he admired. Bill's parents brought up their family problems in a group meeting, and Bill accepted this. For the first time in individual therapy, he looked ahead toward leaving the ward and talked about plans for returning to school.

During weeks six and seven of Bill's hospital stay, there was an apparent slowing of his new pattern of progress. He became somewhat depressed when a rival for his female friend appeared. In individual therapy, however, he continued to discuss important issues such as his father's impending operation for a chronic infection. Part of the reason for the slowed progress emerged in a family meeting when the Putnams spoke for the first time of Mr. Putnam's alcohol difficulties and Mrs. Putnam's tendency to confide her worries to Bill. In a research interview about this time, Bill presented a cynical, defensive view of himself and the unit. He questioned the purpose of the unit's governing activities and his own role in them. Most notably, he denied that the ward had had any impact on how he related to, or thought about, his parents. He also denied that there was any importance in his relationship with other patients. Despite his depression and his hostility to everything about him, Bill was still able to acknowledge that the unit might help some patients and that he really did hope it might help him.

When during his seventh week the Patient Advisory Board turned Bill down for a pass to go home, he spoke with his father and returned with the threat, "If I'm not discharged in a month, my dad will sign me out." He then said that he felt he could talk to other patients "now that I know I will be going home." It became clearer after Mr. Putnam's agreement with

Bill to sign him out in a month, against medical advice, that Bill's depression and slowed progress were related to his growing anxiety about separating himself from his parents. Bill revealed in individual therapy that although he could now accept himself as a patient, he was increasingly preoccupied with, and anxious about, his father's health, had to reassure himself about it, and needed—in a phobic fashion—to remain close to his parents. That is, his father's history of life-threatening illness and Bill's intimacy with his mother created a situation in which Bill became guilty and anxious as soon as he began to distance himself from his parents. In a research interview at this time, he emphasized how much he wanted to go home and that nothing else of importance was happening to him on the unit. In this interview Bill could acknowledge that he was talking more freely with others and could realize some of his problems. He was able to describe his behavior on the advisory board and recognize that he had become more constructive in how he viewed other patients. He could acknowledge the change that had been coming about over the past few weeks, although its origins were not clear. He related it to the fact that he had decided to cooperate and talk with other people. He also acknowledged that his family was changing, in particular that his father had stopped drinking during his weekend visits at home, and that he could now talk to his parents about his problems, notably some of his feelings about them and their behavior.

Once again a critical aspect of this second breakthrough in Bill's progress appeared to have been a change in his drug regimen. The day after Bill reported that his father would sign him out in a month, he was begun on a low dose of antidepressant (imipramine, 75 mg daily). In this case the symbolic meaningfulness of the medication was even more clear than before. Although this drug has little effect for 10 to 14 days, Bill's behavior began to change within a day or two. In his small therapy group he admitted, "I feel sad because I have found my life has been an act. I have been putting up a front. I don't know what I am really like. I try to look and act older, but I don't feel that way. I find I am more scared about my dad's coming operation than any of the others, but I feel I don't have to retreat into a fantasy world. I feel I can cope with it." His increasing ability to verbalize the purpose of the unit's system of treatment was apparent in his comments about Tompkins I in research interviews. On a weekend pass he was able to look at his parents more realistically, instead of denying their difficult behavior and idealizing them. In another research interview a few days later, he was able to express many positive feelings about his doctor; about the medical students working on the ward, whom he had formerly resented and criticized; and about the way the ward handled people. He now felt that it would really be possible for him to consider dealing with his problems and to take on increasing responsibility in life. In informal situations on the unit, Bill was experimenting socially with a variety of patients, including a fatherly middle-aged man, a woman in her thirties, and a female patient a few years older than himself.

An interesting incident occurred at this time that suggests Bill was reenacting feelings about his parents with staff: Bill's doctor presented his case at the departmental "grand rounds." As part of the presentation, Bill was interviewed by the ward chief before the 70 persons present. Following the interview, he was asked if he would answer questions from the audience. He refused to do this. On returning to the unit, Bill became extremely anxious. He was relieved only when his doctor spoke to him and commented that in the discussion at the conference there had been an optimistic view about his future. Although Bill could not explain why he had refused to accept questions at the presentation, he feared that by refusing he had damaged his doctor's career. This accounted for his anxiety afterward and his relief when he learned that his refusal had neither destroyed his doctor nor sealed his own doom. Bill's reaction was analogous to his feelings in relation to his worries about his father's illness. In discussing these fears, Bill described how he had once found his father apparently dead after a fainting spell. Just as he had viewed himself as potentially damaging or murderous in relation to his father, he had imagined that he might be able to do professional damage to his doctor.

During Bill's 10th week on the unit, another small crisis occurred around the question of whether he would indeed be discharged after the month's interval he had discussed with his father. Bill and his parents let this "showdown" pass, in part by provoking limits from the ward: Bill presented a Thanksgiving weekend pass request with inadequate planning, so that he was instead given several day-passes. While Bill was at home, Mr. Putnam drank heavily. Following this the issue of discharge in the near future was dropped by tacit mutual agreement. In the next family meeting, Bill was able to criticize his father for the drinking. After the meeting, when his father left for home, Bill became massively anxious about his father's health and asked permission to telephone home. He was allowed to do so under the condition that he not apologize for having confronted his father. Shortly after this, Bill for the first time asked another patient how she felt. He also established a relationship with an outside therapist, part of preparation for discharge. He was able to weather a difficult first meeting during which he said little to the new psychiatrist. In the second meeting, he spoke about this difficulty talking and then found that he could indeed talk.

By this time Bill revealed in research interviews considerably more perspective about his participation in the unit. For example, he noted that when he participated in group meetings he found them much more interesting. He was able to bring up other patients' problems in group meetings when he felt it would be useful. Bill noticed that other patients were becoming more open in telling him things about himself. He could report to the research interviewer that there had been a change not only in himself but in his parents and in the capacity of people in his family to talk openly with one another. His increasingly positive view of the unit is illustrated in the following excerpt:

> *Interviewer:* What are your thoughts these days on the ward, what kind of place the ward is?
> *Bill:* I like the ward. What about it?
> *Interviewer:* About the way the government works and the advisory board?
> *Bill:* I approve of it, I think it's good.
> *Interviewer:* You're on the board now? How's it been this week?
> *Bill:* It's been good. I like being on the board. I like making decisions about other people, as well as myself. I feel responsible enough to take this. I enjoy it.

Bill could now report that he voted against some patients' requests for privileges and was even willing to go against the majority if he felt strongly enough.

Because of the gradual pace of Bill's improvement and the fact that Mr. Putnam was entering the hospital shortly for minor surgery, a very gradual discharge from the unit was planned. Bill was begun on a second tranquilizer at this time, because the staff felt that in response to his father's operation he was somewhat more paranoid (chlorpromazine, 150 mg daily). A few days later Bill signed up to return to his old high school; during his 13th week on the unit, he successfully returned to school, *not* wearing his coat and tie. The return went successfully, despite Bill's apprehensions about his father's imminent surgery for drainage of an infection. Bill weathered his father's hospitalization without difficulty. However, Mrs. Putnam became quite anxious and depressed, and was begun on a low dose of tranquilizer by Bill's ward physician. Bill continued on a partially hospitalized status for an additional three weeks prior to his discharge to outpatient treatment. During this time, he did a certain amount of testing of his imminent discharge by skipping school one day. The Putnams, similarly, showed their ancitipation of separating from the unit by missing a family group meeting. In his final group meetings, Bill briefly returned to his earlier defensive, withdrawn pattern of behavior. With encouragement, however, he was able to admit that he would miss the group and that he very much hoped he could have some sort of group experience after he left the unit.

Bill Putnam has had a relatively stable course since his Tompkins I discharge. He was able to return to high school, where he had experienced such difficulties prior to his hospitalization. He attended a private school where he did well enough to be promoted each year and to make plans for college. Following discharge, Bill received outpatient treatment that included occasional family meetings. After one year his therapy was terminated and the medications he had been taking were discontinued. Five years after his admission, his basic style of life has changed very little. He still dresses carefully, lives quietly at home with his parents, and has few close friends. He does not date girls to this time. An event that may indicate some limitations on Bill's psychological flexibility occurred recently. During his senior year of high school, Bill had been accepted at a college several hundred miles away. Only a few weeks later, he had a car accident while driving alone on a wet road. The degree to which the accident was indeed "accidental" is not clear. In the accident his leg was broken, requiring several hospitalizations and a protracted convalescence. This led to a change in college plans; Bill now plans to attend a local college. Despite the limitations that the Tompkins I staff observed, Bill reads a good deal and is writing a novel. He still occasionally talks on the phone to some patients whom he knew on the ward.

Bill remembers Tompkins I in a way that is quite close to how he experienced the ward during the first phase of hospitalization. He described it as "detrimental to my overall mental state." He still likes and respects the ward chief and his ward doctor, but resents the other physicians who were not directly involved in his care. Bill criticizes "everyone knowing too much of everyone else's business."

Superficially, it would seem that the role of the Tompkins I experience in Bill's life remains rather obscure. But it is possible that this is an individual who under other circumstances of hospitalization might have become overtly psychotic and become fixed in a chronic paranoid state or paranoid personality pattern. This certainly did not happen during the Tompkins I experience; Bill had some of the most intense and meaningful relations of his adolescence while on the ward. In fact, it would seem that in Bill's case, although both he and the staff tend to question the efficacy of hospitalization, its limits were more imposed by the necessity of discharge and the constraints of his family situation. In Bill's case, Tompkins I again addressed itself to the social situation of the patient in a very realistic way. Bill was the fulcrum of his parents' difficult relationship and shared the pressure of his father's long-standing medical problems. Instead of encouraging greater distance between Bill and his parents, the hospital worked considerably at opening up more emotional contact between members of the family. This enabled Bill to reassure himself about some of his magical fears that he was responsible for his father's illness and could directly affect it through his anger. Going away to college was apparently too threatening to the delicate family equilibrium, but there are signs that Bill is maturing and developing gradually, along with his continued closeness with his parents.

The ward provided Bill with a number of qualities his parents could not: authority figures against whom he could safely pit himself; nurturant figures who did not depend on him; a peer group that could tolerate his ambivalence. He could even test his parents' loyalty to him by enlisting his father's backing in his desire to leave at one point. Bill could also have first flirtations in the protective setting of the ward. Overall, it would seem that hospitalization provided Bill with several experiences important in adolescent development, while possibly averting a progressively more isolated social style and more psychotic thinking pattern.

Bill Putnam exemplifies a second group of patients in the

questionnaire sample whom we call "unit converts." Such
patients enter the hospital with lower communitas scores
than do preconverts. During the first week, their scores do
not change notably. Sometime following the first week, unit
converts have an upswing in score. For the majority (12 out of
17), this rise in score occurs between one week and one month
of hospitalization. For the remainder, the rise occurs between
one month and discharge. By the time of discharge the mean
score of unit converts is only slightly below that of preconverts. This group of patients is distinctively young (average
age = 20) and single (13 out of 17). Their social class level is
roughly the same as that of the preconverts: upper-middle.
Over half of these patients were diagnosed psychotic on admission. When they arrive at the hospital, they admit to more
turmoil than patients in any other group; they experience the
unit as less nurturant than do other groups of patients. Despite having the greatest amount of subjective turmoil, unit
converts are rated during their first week on the unit as in only
slightly worse condition than preconverts. Thus, unit converts are adolescents who arrive in a considerable state of
subjective upset, and although their social backgrounds are
similar to those of preconverts, they do not find the unit's
norms so naturally syntonic with their own. Their age alone
may account for this difference: Bill Putnam had had very few
of the adolescent and adult socialization experiences that
probably made participating in the social life of the unit easy
for Mary Wheeler.

The effect of this difference in initial orientation is illustrated by the slow progress of Bill's first few weeks. Where
Mrs. Wheeler was active and overaccepting of the ward's
value system, Bill resisted any accommodation to the ward
until it responded to him. Only when his doctor acknowledged and legitimized his "sickness" by prescribing tranquilizers, did Bill show any change in his behavior. Another
difference between these two patterns is that ultimately a
confrontation was more or less inevitable for Bill, while for

preconverts confrontation is optional. The social system of the unit presents to the adolescent patient an adult-derived set of behavior norms. For the isolated, disturbed, immature adolescent, the norms may represent a considerable threat or challenge.

In Bill Putnam's case, the confrontation between patient and ward initially was played out around the issue of how his patient role would be defined and the related issue of medication. When Bill's doctor observed his lack of progress, she decided that he was "sicker than I thought." As an empathic physician, she had preferred to give Bill the benefit of the doubt, diagnostically, and to envision his problem as a temporary crisis that might respond to the unit's social opportunities alone. His lack of progress led to a redefinition of Bill as someone with a prepsychotic, schizophrenic potential. Bill experienced this shift not in terms of the ward's abstract notions about his illness but in terms of his patient experience: Now he received tranquilizers, as did most other patients. As became apparent later in hospitalization, Bill viewed himself in an important, powerful role in relation to his parents, especially in connection with his father's heart disease. It may have been unacceptable for Bill to accept patienthood for psychological problems alone. Unconsciously, he felt responsible for his parent's relationship, his mother's anxiety, and his father's survival. How could he justify taking part in an outside social situation like the ward simply in the service of his own needs? When he received a legitimization of his illness in a concrete, familiar, medical form—the kind of medical care his father had received—he could loosen his rigid defensiveness and begin to take part as a patient on the unit.

Bill's case begins to suggest an explanation for the difference in hospital course of unit converts. The adolescent patient has a heavy anchor slowing the pace of his change: He is still intimately and actively involved with his parents, even when he is not living at home with them. Family studies have repeatedly revealed that there is a considerable interplay between the pathology of the child and that of others in the family as well as the whole system of family dynamics (Lidz et al., 1965; Wynne et al., 1958). These family disturbances frequently lead to difficult and distorted relations between members of the family and the extrafamilial environment (Reiss, 1971).

The sluggishness of Bill Putnam's response to the socializing forces of the therapeutic community and the characteristics of hospitalization for unit converts can thus be seen as a result of two factors. (1) For the adolescent, socialization to the norms of the unit is a *first experience*, not (as with Mary Wheeler) a repetition of familiar patterns. Bill was breaking completely new ground when he began engaging more closely with people on the unit. As he explored the possibility of discussing his problems—first with a physician, then with older "parental" patients, and finally in his small therapy group and family group therapy—he was enacting *for the first time* a concept of himself as a social being. (2) Processes of change for a young patient usually include the family of origin, in order for the patient to change individually. For Bill Putnam the development of new individual potentialities prerequired the participation of the family in a gradual series of readjustments in which Bill played a complex and central role. A steady process of change began only after a number of changes had occurred for his family as a whole: Bill himself was in a patient role he found acceptable, despite protestations; his parents began to reveal marital difficulties to others; the family received support around the needs of each member. As a result the interplay between patient and ward was spread over a longer period of time and varied aspects of hospitalization.

The delayed and gradual quality of change going on within Bill Putnam was further revealed in research interviews. Although Bill became actively involved in the social activities of the unit some four to six weeks after admission, his response to questions about the usefulness of the ward program lagged behind even this pace. It was only during this third month on the unit that he began to acknowledge the possibility that the pressures on him earlier in his stay might have been helpful in reaching a point when he could "pick apart problems and dissect them," as he put it later in his stay. When he had reached this point, he could also acknowledge the importance of changes in his parents to his own hospitalization. This delayed ability to accept unit norms is part of the definition of the unit converts. Other features of the gradual and delayed change that this profile suggests, and that were found in Bill Putnam's case, are also found consistently in the unit converts. They are inevitably seen for individual therapy sessions by their doctors, usually (15 out of 17) over one hour a week. They receive more individual therapy time than do other groups of patients. They invariably have stays on the unit longer than two months, often longer than three (average = 14 weeks).

These statistics suggest that the processes of Bill Putnam's case apply in general for this group: The initial resistance to the unit's norms is responded to by offering more individual therapy time. The same patient mistrust that leads to individualized therapy contact may also contribute to the longer hospitalizations in this group. The greater length of stay also supports our observation with Bill that change for such patients may require the participation of their families. Since the family's experience with the unit, even when twice-weekly family group meetings are supplemented with individual family meetings, is a diluted one, it may take more weeks in the hospital for the necessary changes to occur throughout the family system. In fact, although we do not have exact data, it is our observation that the parents of these young patients, like their offspring, receive a considerable amount of extra attention from the unit's staff. These contributions from the staff's side provide the leverage for change in the patient-family unit that is manifested in the patient's altered orientation to the norms of the unit in the middle or later part of his hospital stay. The dramatic change we observed in Mary Wheeler is unlikely when the system being treated is a multi-person, two-generation one. Out of this more gradual process may come significant change, just as may happen with the preconverted type of patient. The confrontation process may lead to an altered defensive-adaptive stance for the patient. For example, Bill Putnam's wish for some sort of group experience after hospitalization strongly suggested that he had made a major change in his outlook—a change he hoped to continue in his posthospital life. This request reflected far more than an altered sociability pattern; it embodied a shift in family dynamics that involved all the Putnams.

Staff ratings for retrospective improvement and prognosis are the highest for unit converts. When followed up at 15 months after discharge, patients in this group were doing relatively well, but they do not live up to the staff's high hopes for them. On a variety of measures of follow-up condition, these patients are doing moderately well, but not as well as the preconverted group. They are likely to be continuing in treatment and to have missed some time from work or school. Patients in this group have had fewer months of rehospitalization time compared to all other groups except preconverts, who had almost no readmissions. The group splits in its view of the impact of the Tompkins I experience; half feel the ward had a profound effect on them while the other half denies much impact at all. Unit converts' mean score on the communitas dimension at the time of follow-up has dropped off markedly—more than that of any other group—to a point close to their admission score. Thus, although the change in scores for this group appears to help define their hospital experience, this attitude change itself does not seem responsible for any enduring improvement. That the patients in this group are generally improved is suggested by their fairly successful readjustments to outside life, despite the fact that they are a group that entered the hospital with relatively severe diagnoses. Bill Putnam himself did relatively well following hospitalization; he and his family continued in outpatient therapy, and he was not rehospitalized. There were no more instances of acute crisis and disorganization. Bill returned occasionally to say hello to staff members and retained contact with patient friends. This suggests that although unit converts may show an extinction of their acceptance of unit norms, the relationships developed on the unit retain significance.

CHAPTER 7

Individual Hospital Careers: Charles Lawrence

Charles Lawrence was a 50-year-old laboratory technician whose work performance had deteriorated because of heavy recent use of barbiturates and alcohol. These problems had worsened in the weeks prior to admission, and his supervisors had become concerned. Although he had previously used barbiturates regularly for insomnia or to overcome anxiety, Charles had functioned adequately within the limitation of his job and few social contacts. He had lived for most of his life with his mother, now 68 years old, a woman who drank heavily. His only other regular social relationship was with a male friend whose role in Mr. Lawrence's life never became completely clear. No recent upset in these relationships was described by Mr. Lawrence; he attributed his difficulties at the time of hospitalization to a recent virus and a resulting increase in his use of phenobarbital.

Charles' admission occurred under unusual circumstances: He was brought to the hospital by another employee at the request of his supervisor. He strongly resisted the suggestion of psychiatric admission, agreeing to it only after a two-hour series of negotiations in the emergency room. During these negotiations his physician-to-be from the unit, along with his superior at work, presented him with the alternatives of a voluntary admission to Tompkins I or a commitment to the state hospital. It was unusual for a Tompkins I physician to be part of such a negotiation and for admission to be manipulated in this way, but Charles was something of a special case because of his highly sensitive job. As was the case for Mary Wheeler, these first events surrounding admission foreshadowed what would happen later in Charles' hospitalization: denial of problems, refusal to accept the recommendations of his ward physician, and action only when presented with a choice between two inescapable alternatives.

As Charles Lawrence saw it, he came to the hospital for admission to a general medical ward for a physical work-up. In fact, he acknowledged that he knew he would be going to the psychiatric ward only after signing the voluntary admission agreement. Although it is quite likely that Mr. Lawrence was still considerably under the influence of an unknown combination of barbiturates and alcohol, his initial orientation to the unit was not markedly different from the pattern he showed once he had been withdrawn from medication. He described his expectations and experiences on admission as follows:

> *Charles:* Well, it all went so rapidly—I was so confused over the turn events had taken—I was only interested in what I immediately had to do when I got here—as far as finding a room and a bed and a locker. A sponsor came to me with the constitution, and the regime about temperatures and blood pressures and so on. I was all taken up with that in the beginning.
> *Interviewer:* Well, how about when somebody said "psychiatric ward" or "hospital" to you? Did certain ideas come to you of what it was going to be like, or what you would expect? Did you think about it?
> *Charles:* No, I was so busy with the immediate things that they gave me to do; I didn't go very much beyond that.

Interviewer: What about the first few days? What would you say you experienced, learned, all of that?

Charles: Well, I learned the general routine for the day, with regard to blood pressure, medication, time meals were served, and half-hour rest period after lunch, after dinner. I learned about making my own bed, trying to figure out in the morning when I could get into the lavatory and shave and shower before too many other people got in there. I learned where the linen was stored, began going over some features of the constitution and how to figure the day from the schedule typed and put on the bulletin board. Also signing in and out sheets there, and the patients have passes, you know, activities in the evening, which evenings, all general things like that.

Interviewer: What would you say was most important in those first few days?

Charles: Mr. Smyth was in that third room with me and he has been very helpful.

Interviewer: How was that?

Charles: Well, he explained to me more about the constitution, about the five-minute check that I was on then, and moving to a no-status position, what the requirements are to join the monitor pool and after that what one does about specialing the patients.

Interviewer: Anybody else? Was he your sponsor too?

Charles: No. Mrs. Benson was my sponsor.

Interviewer: Was she helpful?

Charles: Yes, maybe even too much so because I hadn't been in the door more than five minutes when she approached me with a copy of the constitution. I thought, "Well, you don't expect me to take that all in right away, do you?" and she said, "No, it'll be a couple of days yet before you begin to get used to it." She went over the main features of it, and I think when one comes in here to begin with, he's so preoccupied with his own immediate troubles—it takes a day or two before he becomes more aware of what's all around him.

Compared to most other patients Mr. Lawrence was concerned with himself and his daily routine, not the social life of the unit, which he tended to ignore. When questioned specifically about his first contacts with other patients and staff, Mr. Lawrence was notable in that, according to him, he listened more to their problems than he spoke about his. This reflected his continuing guardedness and his concern about "knowing what was the right thing to do and when was the right time to do it."

During the first three days of his hospitalization, Charles was regarded by staff as quite seclusive. He maintained an attitude of aloof defensiveness toward others and differentness from them. At the time of admission, his doctor noted that he had a bad smell and appeared not to have changed his clothes for quite some time. He was obviously disregarding and resisting the norms of socializing, committing oneself to helping others and facing problems. For relief he looked to his medication (he was being withdrawn gradually from barbiturates) and to his visitors, his mother and friend. On the fourth day of hospitalization, another struggle took place, similar to the one that had taken place around admission to the unit. Charles refused to take his medication—the barbiturates prescribed in the withdrawal program. The ward physician again found that the only argument that would lead Charles to acquiesce was to suggest transfer to another hospital. Later she realized that she had not considered the alternative threat of intramuscular injection of medication. (She admitted later that she would have been as happy to have Charles transferred.) However, Charles acquiesced again.

After this "showdown," the doctor began creating pressures for him to orient towards the unit; she limited the number of phone calls that Mr. Lawrence could make to, or receive from, his mother and his friend. After a week of hospitalization, Mr. Lawrence was still "bored" and totally uninvolved with the ward. His mother was complaining to the senior personnel about the restrictions on her visits and her doubts about the unit. The nursing staff and other patients observed that Charles sat looking at a book for most of the free time, never turning the page but fending off other patients this way. On his ninth hospital day, he submitted a request for coming off five-minute checks. This was his first active acknowledgment of the unit. However, when he presented his arguments for the status change, the Patient Advisory Board rejected the request on the ground that he was isolated from others and gave "insomnia" as a reason for hospitalization. Three days later he acknowledged to a nurse that he was "getting help" from his therapist and from another patient. At this time the phone restrictions were being gradually lifted and he was making many phone calls out.

At the beginning of this second week, the phenobarbital was discontinued, and Charles began on a low dose of tranquilizer (perphenazine, 16 mg daily). Thus, by the end of his second week of hospital stay, Mr. Lawrence was beginning to acknowledge that he was a patient, perhaps because he was beginning to be treated in the sort of medical manner he could accept. His mother had meanwhile requested that a private psychiatrist outside the unit assess the need for hospitalization. This evaluation occurred at the end of the second week, and the need for hospitalization was supported. The ward physician at this time noted that Charles was "still not a member of the community." She increased his medication markedly, to 40 mg daily. There was a strong attempt made to induce Charles' mother, who had previously resisted, to come to family group therapy meetings. At the end of the third week of hospitalization, however, Charles submitted a request for discharge against medical advice. By the rules of the hospital, the staff was required to release him within no more than 10 days or to seek a court commitment. The next day Charles' physician told him that in order to be discharged, he need only perform one action of the sort desired in the unit, for example, one day's rotation as a member of the monitor pool. She also began him on Antabuse, an aversive treatment of alcoholism. The ward psychiatrist decided definitely not to seek a court commitment, but did not mention this to Charles. Instead she emphasized her request that he make one symbolic gesture of acceptance of the ward. This most likely reflected the frustration of the ward psychiatrist, caught between her superiors, who had made Charles something of a special case, and Charles' resistive attitude.

Two days before the discharge request would take effect, Charles joined the monitor pool, meeting the condition for discharge. The day before his deadline, his doctor suggested a discharge date three days later. Charles accepted this. He was discharged after one month in the hospital on the date suggested by the staff. When interviewed just prior to discharge, Charles continued to maintain his low appraisal of the therapeutic community. He said, for example, when asked about the relation of group meetings to his treatment, "I keep asking myself, 'What is group therapy going to do to cure my insomnia?' " Charles found leaderless group meetings most difficult. He felt that his doctor was the factor primarily responsible for any improvement, saying, "I feel better than I did when I was first admitted. That is, I feel better physically."

Charles returned for a follow-up group therapy meeting four days after his discharge. At that time he showed a behavior pattern remarkably different from the one he had demonstrated as an unwilling inpatient. He behaved exactly in the way that the unit's norms would have patients do in small groups. He was active, interested in other patients' problems, supportive of the unit's values, and more relaxed than usual. Nevertheless, he missed all future group meetings and was reported to have later discontinued Antabuse and the aftercare psychotherapy that had been initiated during the final week of hospitalization.

Charles Lawrence's life since discharge is as great a surprise as Mary Wheeler's—in an opposite way. As might have been predicted, Charles' difficulties continued after his rather unsatisfactory hospital experience. He had more trouble handling his job and continued to use barbiturates and alcohol as self-medication. After several months he was again hospitalized for one month on Tompkins I, with very little further change. Outpatient therapy following the second admission was of little help, and finally he was hospitalized at a nearby state hospital for a four-month period. Here again his experience was negative; Charles states that this was the "nadir of my life." He left the state hospital against medical advice, because "there was nothing the hospital could do for me." He took no medications following his discharge, returned to live with his mother, and did not resume working. After a few months he took a night course at a local college and received a "B" grade. Following this, he began a full load of courses toward a master's degree and continued to receive "B" grades. After successfully earning a master's degree, he was able to locate a good job in his new field, a job that required relatively little responsibility and allowed him considerable quietness and lack of interference. He functioned well on the job and after a year received a promotion. Although his personal life remains as it was before hospitalization, Charles has been able to continue effectively at work and is now trying to improve his ability at public speaking and relating to people.

After five years Charles' memories of Tompkins I are interesting for their ambivalence. On the one hand, in comparing this attitude to the atmosphere of the ward, he continues to state that "a more complete dichotomy can't be imagined." He still feels that it is deleterious for patients to be herded together and remembers his own "claustrophobia" during hospitalization. On the other hand, Charles recalls how interesting it was to observe the group interactions and to learn about mental illness. He states that Tompkins I "is the best thing that ever happened to me; I should have done it years ago; it shook me up and got me out of it. I was a victim of inertia." He is referring apparently to the fact that he was quite unhappy with his prior job but could not bring himself to leave its security. Thus he acknowledges that his sickness helped change his life in a way that was ultimately beneficial. He even remembers one patient-friend he had during hospitalization whom he recalls as having been quite helpful.

In Charles Lawrence's case the dynamics of his illness and surprising recovery remain rather opaque. There is nothing to suggest that Tompkins I, with which Charles interacted so minimally and ineffectively, brought about major changes. In fact, it seemed to be necessary for him to pass through a period of real self-destructiveness and inaction before he could begin a new direction in his life. But his assertion of being "shaken up" suggests that regardless of the impasse that held for most of Charles' stay on Tompkins I, the confrontation of his prior pattern of life had an effect.

Charles Lawrence represents one of two groups whom we shall discuss together because they are quite similar. These groups we refer to as "renegers" and "rejectors." Renegers are defined by early acceptance of unit norms similar to that of preconverts (before or during the first week), and a subsequent dropoff during the latter part of hospitalization. Rejectors are defined by a consistently low score on the communitas scale. Renegers and rejectors differ from each other in certain respects, but in many ways they are similar. Separately or together they contrast distinctly with preconverts and unit converts. They will be discussed separately only around variables where there are marked reneger/rejector differences. Thus, although their specific patterns and the absolute levels of norm scores are quite different for the two groups, the fact that they *never accept* the norms of the unit fully, or accept them and then *give them up*, seems to indicate some commonality of hospital experience. Findings for these two groups must also be taken with somewhat more caution than those for the previously discussed groups, since the numbers in the separate groups are smaller (renegers—9; rejectors—6).

Within the therapeutic community of Tompkins I, these groups can be considered "deviants" in that they do not conform to the desired expectations of the unit's culture. Thus a number of interesting and important questions come up around these groups: (1) What are the limits of what the unit can handle? and (2) How does the unit adjust to patients who do not conform to its ideal model?

In demographic characteristics these groups are distinctly different from the preconverts and unit converts. Renegers' average age is 30, similar to that of the preconverts. Rejectors' average age is 39; they are distinctly older than the rest of the patient population. About half of these patients are married, a low proportion considering that this is an older group. Social class status of this group is the lowest of all groups, although the differences among groups are not statistically significant. Social class in itself need not contribute to a different sort of hospital adjustment, but it may be that the correlates of class—for example, a greater tendency toward authoritarian personality styles in middle- and lower-class individuals—will influence the nature of the hospital experience. It is also striking that five of the seven patients who in the sample identified their religion as "none" were in the reneger/rejector group.

Diagnostically, almost half of this group received psychotic diagnoses at admission. These are, however, predominantly depressive illnesses, especially in the older rejector group. Both groups are in considerably poorer psychiatric condition during their first week of hospitalization than are preconverts or unit converts. The rejectors enter the hospital denying much upset and having a greater preference for an authoritarian hospital structure. These observations, especially for the rejectors, fit Charles Lawrence at the time of his admission. In his life he apparently had few experiences with organizations patterned along the lines of Tompkins I; he dealt with staff as though they were manifestations of one global authority figure. His social class background corresponds to the mean of the rejector group, Class III (Hollingshead-Redlich` classification). At admission he denied being upset, and although he expected to get things from the unit and its staff, he anticipated such nurturance being provided through a benign but autocratic framework.

Patients in these two groups had the lowest behavior ratings of any groups during the first week. On indices for community membership and responsibility, they score considerably and significantly lower than the other two groups at this time. By one month of hospitalization, these differences have been reduced somewhat—although they remain, especially for the rejector group. Community membership ratings of rejectors, although higher than at admission, remain lowest of all groups and never reach the level of preconverts or rise above the admission of unit converts. In responsibility, an important aspect of the patient role as the unit defines it, both of these groups remain lower than other patients through the first month. By discharge, however, the renegers have come up to the responsibility levels of other groups in the eyes of staff, while the rejectors continue to be rated lower. That these patients are benefiting, as did Charles Lawrence, from being in the hospital is reflected in staff ratings of condition. Both groups here rise sharply from their initial rating level, which would rate them as considerably sicker than preconverts or unit converts. Although even in the final week of stay these patients are in the poorest condition, the differences among groups are not significant.

We have here a strong suggestion that patients in these two groups make their way through the hospital experience quite differently from others. Their stay in the hospital was relatively long, almost as long as the unit converts'. Unlike that group, however, they receive considerably less individual therapy time. That is especially true for the reneging patients, only a third of whom received much individual therapy. Looking back on hospitalization and ahead to the future, staff rated these patients as having shown less improvement and having poor prognoses.

Patients in the reneger/rejector group are older than the average for the unit, and they come from middle-class rather than upper-class or upper-middle-class backgrounds. They are both less flexible in adapting to the ward and, ideologically or attitudinally, less ready to do so. Their recalcitrance to adopting the ward's norms is perceived by staff. It leads to lower ratings for improvement and prognosis. Many of these patients do not do as well as those from other groups, but on the whole they, too, are in relatively good condition a year after their hospitalization.

Hospital process for these two groups is likely to be less intense than for preconverts or unit converts. Charles Lawrence's marked alienation from the norms of Tompkins I is illustrative of how a patient may have a standoff with the ward and appear relatively unaffected by its processes. Yet Charles did absorb the ward's norms; once he was an outpatient, he revealed that he had learned much more than he was willing to show while in the hospital. He did not accept and agree with the ward norms. This parallels a tendency to deny problems in general. Behaviorally, patients in these groups improve considerably. Staff do not rate their improvement and prognoses as high as the other groups, and indeed these patients do not do as well after discharge. Thus, because of their psychiatric condition, or because of their backgrounds, renegers/rejectors do not become actively involved in the attitude-change aspects of Tompkins I.

In actual follow-up performance, these patients are not doing as poorly as might have been anticipated. They do, indeed, have the greatest amount of rehospitalization after discharge, especially the rejector group. They also have the least amount of time working. The one suicide in our sample was a rejector.

SUMMARY

These three hospital career studies cannot be viewed as a cross-section, especially since the patients were all in the care of the same ward psychiatrist. For example, Mary Wheeler's conflict over dependency and anger and Charles Lawrence's struggle over ward norms may have been affected by counter-transference feelings in the doctor. In the first case, she was dealing with a woman who was threatening to collapse rather than cope, and the response of denying individual therapy may have in part reflected discomfort with the issues Mary was dealing with. In Charles Lawrence's case, his resistance to treatment could have evoked the doctor's latent doubts about the conformity demands of the ward. Her sympathy and patience with Bill Putnam may have reflected her greater interest in child psychiatry and empathy for the situation of a suspicious adolescent. Nevertheless, in each case we can see the working of the general therapeutic community pattern: the ward norms as a strong press on doctor and patient alike, the role expectations of the ward and their different impact on each patient. We can also see through these specific careers that the ward does modulate its expectations and the applications of its norms for each individual. That this is true in general is shown by the study of three types of patient-hospital pattern. Not only do different patients react differently to the ward, but the ward responds varyingly, albeit according to certain patterns. Our sample and methods of analysis were limited, so that we could delineate only three or four such patterns.

When we look back with the perspective of five years on the career study patients, it becomes clear that a hospitalization is only one brief episode in a life history. Tompkins I, operating under constraints of Blue Cross coverage and high costs of private hospitalization, offers care for a relatively brief period. Problems that have taken years to develop are obviously not going to be "cured" in a brief hospitalization. The ward takes a pragmatic attitude of dealing with the problems at hand and seeking to restore the patient to an outside setting. Occasionally, referral to more lengthy inpatient treatment is made if it is clear that the rehabilitative goal is not going to be met quickly. In the next chapter we will look at the status of Tompkins I patients a year-and-a-half after discharge. This will give some indication of how the ward experience interacts with patients' life histories for a larger group and during a time period in which the hospital experience can still be expected to play some significant part.

CHAPTER 8

Follow-up

The long-range follow-ups on three patients discussed in the last three chapters raise questions about the place of the Tompkins I experience in patients' life histories. A follow-up study of the larger series of 65 patients should reveal more clearly the general impact of the hospital experience.

Of the 65 patients in the group whose hospitalizations we studied, one committed suicide and one died following heart surgery in the 18 months since admission. A vigorous effort was made to contact every living patient: 58 of 63 were ultimately interviewed (92%). The follow-up findings can be taken as reflecting relatively accurately the outcome of all patients admitted over a six-month period.[1]

In general, the follow-up results depict a group of persons struggling with serious psychiatric problems, but functioning quite well. No patient was hospitalized at the time of the follow-up interview. Of the 18 patients rehospitalized in the 15 months since discharge, the distribution of rehospitalization time was as follows:

% time rehospitalized in follow-up period

none	*0–25%*	*25–50%*	*over 50%*
40	6	5	7

Yet in some ways, rehospitalization is a poor index of success. The patients transferred to other hospitals had, for the most part, made a positive decision with the ward that further inpatient therapy would ultimately be advantageous. These patients were referred to longer-treatment hospitals. Readmission, too, can be as much a success as a failure, if it reflects a capacity of the patient and his family to recognize a recurring need for help.

Referral to outpatient therapy is a prerequisite for discharge. One measure of success is whether these referrals "took."

% time in therapy during follow-up period

over 75%	50-75%	less than 50%	none
40	5	9	4

Similarly the finding that 31 of the 58 were continuing in outpatient treatment at the time of the follow-up can be interpreted as reflecting success in convincing patients of the need for extended care, rather than reflecting failure in achieving definitive "cure." Appropriately, those patients with more severe disorders were more often those who continued in outpatient therapy, and who continued to take medication. Eighteen patients were taking medication at the time of follow-up; 21 had discontinued in the course of outpatient treatment; only two had stopped medication against their therapist's advice.

Hospitalization, outpatient treatment, and medication tell us more about the ward's success in educating and arranging effective aftercare than about psychological condition itself. This can be estimated in a variety of ways. First, what of patients' subjective evaluation of how things are going? In response to a global inquiry about their state of mental health, the sample reported the following:

Responses to follow-up interview question: "Overall, how would you rate your mental health now?"

excellent	good	fair	poor	declined to answer
21	20	11	2	4

Since this global estimate could be distorted by a variety of factors, we inquired about self-evaluation in the two important life areas: work, and interpersonal relations. Of 51 who were working, 44 rated their performance good or excellent; 7 rated their work fair or poor, as did the 7 who were not working at the time of the follow-up. That 51 of 58 (88%) were functioning in role-appropriate work activities would indicate a considerable success in patients' return to the community. In terms of work performance over the entire follow-up period, the results were:

% time working since discharge[2]

100%	75–99%	50–74%	25–49%	0–24%
13	18	17	7	4

Of the 51 patients working at the time of follow-up, 49 reported no need for special supervision or modification of work conditions. Job changes, another possible index of effective work role-performance, were relatively few, with 46 patients having no change of job; two having one change; and only three patients with three or more job changes.

In the area of interpersonal relations, the self-report was again largely positive, though not to the extent of the work area:

Satisfaction with close relationships

excellent	good	satisfactory	low	unsatisfactory
12	16	8	16	6

Describing a typical week, only 8 reported that they would have no social contact outside the home, and 9 others reported just one contact. Involvement in formal nonwork groups in the community (clubs, charities, etc.) was as follows:

Organized group involvement

two or more	one	none
18	8	32

Social function is a more debatable index of condition than
work function. The latter says something about capacity to
survive in a society that expects adequate role performance.
Sociability, while a positive in the American value scheme,
may say little about condition. Perhaps most informative is
that only 10 patients expressed dissatisfaction with their interpersonal lives.

How did patients evaluate their experience at Tompkins I
a year later? The interviewer asked each ex-patient to say how
helpful or harmful the experience had been:

Effect of Tompkins I experience

very helpful	helpful	neutral	unhelpful	very harmful
14	14	20	5	5

A second question put to the interviewee was how much the
hospital experience had altered his outlook on life:

Changed life outlook from Tompkins I experience

great or very great	considerable	very slightly	no change
11	15	17	15

Thus, almost half the sample looked back after 18 months on a
hospital experience that averaged 10 weeks as having considerable impact, and that impact positive. On the other hand, if
we combine those who felt Tompkins I was unhelpful or very
harmful, the one suicide, and the four patients who refused
follow-up interview (from which we can assume negative
feelings), we have 15 who viewed hospitalization's impact
negatively.

In brief, the picture derived from the follow-up study is

that of a relatively successful, functioning group of ex-patients.[3] The great majority are working at full-time jobs or in school, handling the full demands of the work. Most report considerable satisfaction with work and social lives, and believe their psychological condition is good. Ex-patients have received a good deal of continued treatment since discharge; almost a third have been readmitted to a psychiatric ward, usually briefly. The great majority have continued therapy and many continue medication. Ex-patients remember the hospital as helpful and influential more often than not, but a few felt unhelped, unaffected, or hurt by the experience.

We also retested our sample on the hospital norm questionnaire. The results were striking: The average score for the communitas scale had returned to exactly the admission level. This was true even when we examined preconverts, unit converts, and renegers/rejectors separately; each group at follow-up had returned to its admission average. Nor did acceptance of the communitas norms during hospitalization or on follow-up correlate with objective condition at follow-up. This finding confirms the earlier conclusion that norm change is a by-product of hospital experience and not critical to improvement itself. Once he has left the ward, the ex-patient is no longer in a situation where the communitas norms will be useful. They may, in fact, be a problem if he tries to be open and confrontive in a family, work, or social situation that does not understand such a style.

The questionnaire scale measuring hospital authoritarianism correlated negatively with functioning both during hospitalization and at follow-up. To the degree that this scale reflects a denying, passive, distant relation to figures in authority—in this case hospital staff or outpatient therapist—it may explain poorer condition on follow-up.

Follow-up functioning is highly correlated with variables that reflect the severity and duration of illness at the time of hospitalization. Such indicators as psychotic or schizophrenic

diagnosis and previous treatment or hospitalization are correlated significantly with poorer follow-up status. This is not
unexpected, unless one envisions the hospital experience as a
universal panacea. Similarly, *condition* in the hospital, as reflected in staff behavior ratings, is highly predictive of
follow-up status. Behaviors reflecting integration into the
ward—*community membership* and *responsibility* ratings—are
correlated strongly with follow-up, suggesting that adaptability in the ward is indicative of adaptability elsewhere. Patients
whose behavior comes more into line with ward expectations
later in their stay do not do as well on follow-up as those who
conform early. Yet, given the more serious disorders of these
patients, it is likely that their follow-up condition *for them* is as
meaningful as the good condition of less impaired patients.

Follow-up findings comparing the three types of hospital
experience described in Chapters 5–7 add little to what has
been said already. To the extent that there are follow-up
differences between groups, they can be explained by the
distribution of more serious psychopathology and prior
treatment in the groups. Other findings that could be of
prognostic significance are staff appraisals of improvement
and prognosis made just after discharge. Next after actual
condition ratings during hospitalization, the staff's improvement and prognostic estimates had the highest correlations
(.39, .44, respectively; both significant with $p < 0.01$) with
follow-up condition.

The conclusion to be drawn here is a familiar one in
outcome studies: Past behavior is the best predictor of future
behavior. Our follow-up results suggest that if Tompkins I
has an impact, it is a general one: Previously healthier persons
are doing very well; previously more troubled patients are
having some difficulty but are much better, on the average,
than before admission. They are continuing therapy. That the
ward is no panacea is indicated by the one suicide, but that it
may well avert chronic institutionalization is indicated by the

fact that none of the sample were hospitalized after 15 months. Finally, our outcome results—including the five-year follow-ups on three patients—indicate that the proper unit of outcome analysis may be *not* the treatment, but the patient. Only by accepting the uniqueness of every life history and accumulating longitudinal data on a large number of individuals might the part played by any given therapy setting become more clear (Keniston et al., 1971).

NOTES

1. The issues and problems in outcome research are subtle and complex (Keniston et al., 1971). Most critical, of course, is the fact that we have no control group with which to compare our Tompkins I sample. Other issues concern the timing of the follow-up interviews: If they are too close to the time of discharge, they may not reflect on the real challenge of returning to the community; if they are too long after discharge, the impact of brief hospitalization may be obscured by intervening events. For an overview of evaluation studies, see Dent (1966), Kelman and Parloff (1957).

2. "Work" includes school and household activities.

3. In a five-year follow-up of 39 first-admission schizophrenics who received Tompkins I treatment and were discharged, Soskis et al. found 2 suicides, 5 refusal of interview, 3 in hospitals, 29 living at home (1969). In general, the findings were consistent with ours: Work function was somewhat poorer and rehospitalization more common, reflecting the more seriously disturbed patient group. Compared to prehospital condition, this sample, like ours, was doing considerably better.

CHAPTER 9

Tompkins I as a Healing Community

What have we learned about the healing community from our examination of Tompkins I? To answer this we shall return to two models of healing community processes: one for the function of the community as a whole, the other for the experience of the individual as he passes through the community. We shall also look at a number of specific issues and questions that arise from the Tompkins I studies.

SOCIAL PROCESSES

Recall that the uniqueness of the healing community could be described in terms of two abstract concepts: communitas and healing charisma. These in turn are translated into daily life through specific patterns of norms and roles:

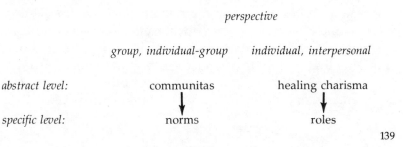

We can now look at the elements of this model as illustrated by observations and findings from the Tompkins I therapeutic community.

In the ideal of communitas, members are related to each other, and each to the group, as unique but essentially equal individuals. Loyalty and sense of membership are high. The only major status differences that exist are those of experience in the group's major activities—in our case, healing activities. In the healing community, presumably anyone may heal, but some are more experienced at it than others. In Tompkins I we found clear evidence for the presence of communitas as we delineated the ward's norm system: Highly valued are involvement in ward life, faith in the ward program, responsiveness to others, participation, and responsibility. Active efforts are made to enculturate all newcomers, including patients, to these norms. For, as a psychotherapeutic system that will influence patients' behavior, the communitas norms will be effective in proportion to the extent that they are shared by all the ward population—patients as well as staff.

The norms of the community are strands of one fabric. Still, these strands can be divided into two major groups. In the first group are norms that directly maintain communitas; in the other are the norms of the actual therapeutic approach. As might have been expected by the definition of communitas, these two parts are inextricable in the actual experience of a ward participant; to be a member of the community is to espouse its therapeutic beliefs. In the first group are such beliefs as responsibility, involvement, faith in the ward. Responsibility implies involvement in the lives of others; involvement takes the form of responsible reaction when another member is upset, self-destructive, or hurt. Faith in the ward stimulates receptivity to help from others while implying that each individual's contribution to the group will be valuable. Together these norms exert a pull on the sufferer: to attend to others in the group, to attend to himself as a member of the group, to be loyal to the community as a whole.

In the second group of norms are those that serve as instructions for the major concern of the ward: therapy, or in a wider sense, healing. These norms, in the case of Tompkins I, emphasize direct, open communication between individuals and the restoration of troubled persons to family and work, to life outside the hospital. Direct, open communication at times becomes forceful confrontation of difficult feelings and behaviors. This norm of openness and confrontation facilitates the belief that each patient's problems are, in a sense, everyone's problems. These norms instruct members in how to act in a variety of formal therapy meetings and informal situations, and in how to think about their difficulties on their own. Implicit in these norms are a set of assumptions about psychological processes. These assumptions include beliefs about (1) the interrelation of inner life and outer behavior, (2) the value of serious, rational analysis of problems, (3) dealing with the emotional issues raised by problems, and (4) solving problems as the result of a process combining rational analysis and emotional working-through. These specific norms for enacting healing on Tompkins I are closely linked to the more general norms that concern the maintenance of a communitas of close, caring, equal individuals. That is, one aspect of the more general communitas norm is the *sharing* of these specific therapy norms. The sharing of specific therapy techniques is an aspect of each member's commitment to the community. Thus the model can be expanded:

communitas	healing charisma
↓	↓
communitas norms	roles
therapeutic norms	

In delineating the norms of Tompkins I, we saw also the relation between communitas-derived norms and norms often more prevalent in dealing with mental disorder—norms that emphasize control and nurture. We saw that in the therapeutic community which effectively emphasizes communitas norms, control and nurture issues are subordinated and dealt with through these communitas norms. Thus, control is achieved, whenever possible, through social pressure and support. Nurture is given through therapeutic interaction and involvement rather than unquestioning, loving care. For the purpose of exploring the model of healing community in relation to Tompkins I, we have not stressed the control and nurture activities of the ward. The case studies make clear that these exist and are needed to make the communitas-oriented processes effective. This is illustrated by the extensive use of medication, which, as we say, plays an important role in both control and nurture. Drugs directly reduce the level of disruptive, threatening behavior; that is, they serve a control function. They are also a form of nurture, something staff "gives" to patients. These are seen by staff as ways to make more effective the communitas-oriented wark program.

The concept of role has been helpful in understanding how both types of norms are translated into actual behaviors. For any member of the Tompkins I staff organization— patient, aide, nurse, ward psychiatrist, director—the general communitas-supporting norms and the specific therapy-guiding norms instruct individuals in dealing with their daily questions about how to play their role in the ward situation. We have dwelt very little on those aspects of role that are traditional and structured: the medical duties of the ward psychiatrist or the nurse, the relinquishment of certain rights and freedoms of the patient, the administrative responsibilities of the director. Instead we have examined how the norms of the ward modify traditional role expectations into new patterns. What results is a redefinition of role at each level and for each staff position. Whether the member be the director or the newest patient, the role expectations that influence his behavior are enlarged by the influence of communitas. Each role is influenced by the value placed on great involvement in the ward community, by the expectation of each person's responsibility for others, by the special expectations of the therapeutic potential of all members. This is communitas at work: The special expectations of this psychiatric unit apply equally to each individual as he plays his part on the ward.

The discrepancy between "ordinary" (i.e., traditional) role definitions and those of Tompkins I, we have called *healing charisma*. For it is around this discrepancy—between what might ordinarily be expected and what individuals actually do in this setting—that individual charismatic aura and charismatic processes proceed. There is a two-way process here. Roles defined in extraordinary ways make possible the unusual interactions that the norms encourage. For example, if a nurse is specifically encouraged to interact with staff and patients in a way that is generally reserved for physicians, and if these behaviors are indeed accepted by the rest of the staff, they will have a striking effect upon patients. Several patients we interviewed commented upon this; our questionnaire results indicated that patients decrease their expectation of conventional nursing behaviors as they spend more time on the ward. The extraordinary quality of such behavior and of interactions with nurses in turn magnify their impact on patients, that is, increase the potential therapeutic effect. The other side of this two-way process is that an enhanced impact on patients leads to behavior change and to espousal of the ward norms. The extraordinary quality in the nurse's performance is her healing charisma, and her therapeutic impact on patients is a charismatic interaction. The same can be said for interactions between the director and his subordinates, nursing supervisor and staff nurses, and so forth. In terms of the model, we can now add:

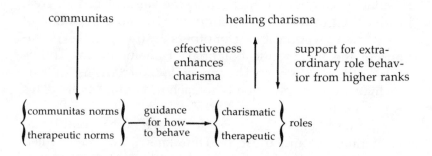

    As the diagram indicates, efficacy in such expanded or
altered roles in the therapeutic community confirms the enhanced subjective charismatic sense of each member. The
same process works between patient and patient. A newcomer to a psychiatric unit does not expect to be a therapist.
To the extent that he is doing this after a few weeks, he is
experiencing himself charismatically and projecting a charismatic appearance to later newcomers. When he is successful,
his ability to play a therapeutic part with others will contribute
to his own enhanced sense of himself and will be of obvious
therapeutic value to him. "Playing therapist" on the ward
does not directly cure or resolve the problems that lead to
admission; it does give the patient a sense of confidence he
was almost inevitably lacking when he arrived and thus enhances his capacity to deal with those problems that brought
him to the hospital.
    Healing charisma can be conceived of as a motive force or
energy that moves in its own way through the social system of
the ward. It is distinct from, and at times opposite to, formal
patterns of authority or professionalism. The ward director is
vested with formal authority over all others in the staff. Yet he
gains his special abilities and enhances the special qualities of

the unit by virtue of his charismatic aura. This stems in part from his greater experience as a psychiatrist, from a professional source of charisma. But in addition, as he enacts his role, he behaves unusually and in terms of a special relationship with the unit. The dominance of charismatic authority patterns over traditional ones is parallel to the presence of communitas. This dimension is antithetical to a hospital authoritarianism dimension that embodies power and cure in proportion to status in the medical hierarchy,and asks unquestioning obedience to authority on the part of the patient. Not only does the charismatic process in the community run counter to authoritarian hospital attitudes, but it is— somewhat surprisingly—distinct from emphasis on the hospital and its staff as a source of nurturance. Close examination again makes this understandable: For a patient to be taken care of implies that the staff are caretakers. Such a division of labor creates a role dilemma for the patient—the prospect that improvement will lead to the loss of nurture. The healing charismatic process implies a *parallel* between members at any level. Every person is in turn both enhanced by, and a model of, something special. He transmits expectations of enhanced self-concept to others, especially newcomers. Thus, charisma is a flow of enhanced regard for self and others that the spirit of communitas makes possible through norms and role definitions.

Two forms of healing charismatic flow can be distinguished.[1] One operates horizontally, laterally between individuals of similar rank or experience. As such, it is a direct element of communitas. It makes every member of the ward community and any member of a subgroup, such as a regular therapy group, feel that he is strengthened and enhanced by his involvement in the community. The other form of charisma operates vertically. The charismatic leader is the focus of this vertical charisma flow. Contrary to our usual idea, he is simply the most intense nidus of vertical charisma. The leader's charisma is nonexistent without a responsive following.[2] He must be most sensitive to the flow of vertical charisma. On the one hand, he must constantly sense whether he is effectively transmitting charismatic qualities to his followers—the members of the group; on the other hand, his own charismatic image must be sustained constantly—by his inner sense of himself, by the devotion of the members, and by the efficacy of the group in dealing with newcomers. These two forms of charisma are interdependent. This is manifest in the matter of roles. Enhanced roles are shared among a group. All nurses can and must support each other in transcending traditional role patterns. This process is aided by the horizontal charisma of the nurses as a group and as members of the ward staff group. At the same time, the enhanced role definition of the nurse is constantly supported by her formal superiors, the psychiatric staff and the nursing supervisory staff. Finally, it is supported by the fact that nurses may transmit altered role expectations to patients, sharing with the patients many of their nursing responsibilities. Diagram 9.1 includes these observations, allowing us to take the model one step further by linking communitas and healing charisma.

DIAGRAM 9.1

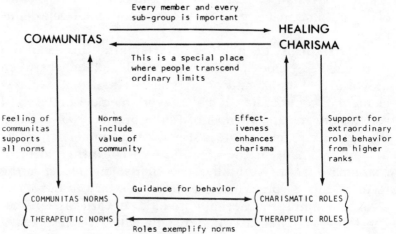

INDIVIDUAL PROCESSES

In the analysis of social processes, the individual patient and his hospital experience are only elements in a complex system. Much of our study of Tompkins I has focused on the general experience of patients with that system, that is, average findings for a large series of patients, and the specific experience, in considerable detail, of three patients. We turn now to a review of the processes that occur around individual patients as they go through the experiences of hospitalization in the Tompkins I therapeutic community.

Engagement of newcomers to Tompkins I proves to be a different process from that which might have been expected. From our emphasis on norms, one might have assumed that newcomers would first be taught the norms of the setting and would then gradually alter their behavior in accordance with those norms. Instead, behavior patterns are the initial focus of most interactions. In other words, the primary attention of the staff is on patient behavior and on influencing behavior patterns through action responses. At the same time, a strong effort is made to convey clearly to patients the ward's activities and to give them a clear picture of their new environment.

From the moment of a patient's arrival, he is dealt with in terms of a patient role concept unlike that of most mental hospitals. He usually expects to be a "patient" in the traditional, medical sense, that is, passive, needy, out of control. Instead, almost every interaction he has, moment to moment or week to week, conveys to him that he is expected to be competent and to be a therapist to himself and others. He finds his attention pushed away from his inner turmoil or family conflicts and into the active life of the unit. Much of his day is spent in a variety of meetings, often with few or no staff present. He finds himself frequently doing things and acting in ways that he could never have expected before admission. Examined vis-à-vis any particular individual, this process is more complex. But the ward is indeed successful in steadily engaging the average patient as an increasingly active participant. This gives him new strength for dealing with the inner side of his crisis. The ward's attention to his family further strengthens him in dealing with outside situations that contributed to the hospitalization. Much of his time is spent on administrative issues concerning himself, other patients, and the ward as a whole. Requests for changes in status at any point in hospitalization are the subject of considerable discussion and debate in Patient Advisory Board meetings and patient-staff meetings. As one patient put it, "The intensity of this ward is impressive!"

Thus, the first effort of the ward is to get the *attention* of the newcomer, to involve him in the ward's processes, regardless of his diagnosis, symptomatology, or inner state. This is done by saturating his field of external stimuli (and to some extent by influencing his inner state to make him amenable to these stimuli). At the same time that he is being exposed to this saturation with ward-defined stimuli, his behavior is being reacted to intently and actively. The moment-to-moment interactions of staff and experienced patients are guided by the norm-role system; his overall progress, by the privilege system. Together these comprise a pervasive *behavior modification* program, one with social approbation, friendship, and increasing individual freedoms as its rewards. George Saslow has observed, in a similar sort of therapeutic community, that change is achieved through an operant conditioning approach, with the ward reinforcing desired behaviors and extinguishing undesired ones (1965).

A third process that generally comes to bear on the patient midway in his stay involves his taking on more therapeutic roles in relation to others. This occurs both in structured ways—as monitor, sponsor of new patients, member of the advisory board—and informally, as he translates the ward's norms into a concept of a patient-as-therapist in groups and casual situations. Here he becomes an active participant in the charismatic flow. He identifies himself with the patients and staff who have interacted with him in a therapeutic way and tries this role himself with others. As a general process we can refer to this as *role paralleling*. That is, the patient is implicitly trained to see his role as he sees the roles of others, to adopt a set of approaches that are in common use around him. Our studies indicate that this has a double function: first, to enable him to be an effective member of the ward community; second, to aid him in dealing with the problems that concern him specifically. These include his own particular psychological problems and his return to some sort of outside life.

There are distinctly differing patterns of actual patient experience with the ward. For every patient the ward can be a rich transference screen for enacting the inner issues and conflicts of the moment. But unlike the psychotherapist, the ward does not strive to be neutral and uninvolved in the patient's life. The ward presents definite behavior expectations and norms to the newcomer. Some patients indeed seem to share the norms when they arrive, or at least they are able to learn them quite rapidly. This does not in itself guarantee a successful hospital experience. Such patients do extremely well after discharge, but this seems at least in part related to their relatively good condition in the past. Other patients experience a change towards greater acceptance of the community concept during their hospitalization. A third and fourth group do not increasingly accept the norms of the unit. More vital than norm acceptance, however, are change in behavior during hospitalization and the degree of intensity reached in the interaction between patient and ward. Yet even these do not guarantee what will happen when the sufferer returns to a home or work environment that differs in many ways from Tompkins I. Most patients leaving the ward report a jarring change when they again encounter the normative assumptions of other situations. Their newly learned patterns of openness and confrontation may be dissonant.

They miss the sense of involvement in a caring, cohesive community. What happens next is very much a function of the individual life history: Is the patient past the worst phase of a life crisis? Are there ways for him to continue dealing with the problems that were clarified and worked on in the hospital? Did the support and involvement of hospital life simply cover over the extent of vulnerability and fragility? Follow-up study provides no ready answers. Some patients do better than others; some diagnostic categories fare differently from others; but much of these differences can be attributed to qualities of the patient that existed before admission.

COMMENTS ON THERAPEUTIC COMMUNITY

In our interest in the internal processes of healing community, we have de-emphasized the important fact that Tompkins I operates in a specific milieu that determines many of its limits and influences its internal function. To do this area justice would require an extensive presentation of new material tangential to our focus on the community. Nevertheless, certain broad points can be made. When initially opened, Tompkins I was an innovative approach to psychiatric problems that was welcomed for its originality, but opposed because of some of its untraditional features. Detre himself stressed the importance of respecting the limits of tolerance of the ward's surrounding context. The brief, intense hospital experience as a model of treatment was, in the early 1960s, an intriguing alternative to prolonged hospitalization. Experience here and elsewhere has indicated that many patients require repeated or continuing contact with psychiatric facilities, although rarely do they require chronic, full-time hospitalization. The Yale-New Haven Hospital has emphasized development of follow-up outpatient services over the past few years. The effectiveness of short-term hospitalization has encouraged development of other services such as day and night treatment, halfway houses, and brief hospitalization (one or two weeks). The ward's heavy use of medication is in part a function of its location in a general hospital and in part a result of the time limits imposed by Blue Cross hospitalization coverage that finances many patients' stays.

The results suggest that there are some patients for whom a single Tompkins I admission is helpful and sufficient, given the availability of some outpatient treatment. But for those who need the availability of more frequent, flexible, and continuing help, discharge from the hospital may also mean the loss of much that is valuable. A closer and longer-term scrutiny of the three patients whose hospital careers are presented in Chapters 5–7 suggests that the problem is complex: Acute psychiatric crises *may* occasionally be transient. Often they are only part of a longer process. A particular hospital experience that occurs early in a troubled phase of a life may or may not avert further problems. Part of the pressure for complete discharge from the community comes from a continuing negative attitude toward mental illness in our society—mental illness is bad, and better "gotten over" than acknowledged. Detre himself makes this point in stressing that serious psychiatric problems are more like rheumatoid arthritis than pneumococcal pneumonia. Hospitalization is, then, only a phase of care; continuity of involvement and availability are clearly needed (Astrachan and Detre, 1968). This principle has been recognized in the theoretical model of the community mental health center, with its provision of emergency, 24-hour, day/night, and outpatient care. Too often, however, patients are processed or shuffled back and forth between these units, and the strong sense of membership in a community is lost. As we consider healing groups in Part II, it will be of interest to see how these two issues—duration and flexibility of involvement—will emerge.

We also see the workings of the wider milieu in the treatment norms of the community. The limited tolerance for "abnormal" behavior in the outside world leads to pressures for decreasing such behavior during hospitalization. Similarly, the realities of most patients' outside situations and the American valuation of work performance make return to job an important goal during the inpatient experience. Part of this is inescapable: Patients and ward are part of the same wider culture. It may be the patient as much as the ward, his job, or his family that creates pressure to return to work.

Another issue raised by our analysis is the coercive quality of the social pressures that the Tompkins I therapeutic community can exert. Are we simply exchanging the authoritarian system of the asylum for the dictates of a monolithic system of brainwashing? The career studies suggest that there is strong pressure for patients' adopting attitudes shared by the ward staff. In Charles Lawrence's case, for example, the ward psychiatrist manipulated his symbolic acceptance of the patient role.

Analogies between the process of Tompkins I and "brainwashing" are apt, but can be carried too far. The similarities are primarily those of process—not so much those of purpose.[3] Brainwashing makes use of physical coercion, forced confession, isolation from outside contact, and social pressure (Lifton, 1961). Its goal is ideological change. The goal of Tompkins I is behavioral change toward the end of returning the patient to the wider community in a happier, more capable state of mind. That the healing process of the ward is a potent influencing technique cannot be ignored. In our case studies we observed several instances of deliberate manipulation. There is also no doubt that the community norm system exerts a strong conforming pressure upon patient members. Our cultural attitudes, strongly influenced by the theme of individualism in the wider culture, lead us to respond with some distaste to social pressure. As Saslow indicated, every treatment seeks in some way to influence the patient. Even in the most "nondirective" therapy, closer scrutiny reveals a subtle process of reinforcement and influence (Frank, 1973). The danger, then, lies not in the use of social pressure itself, but rather in the ends toward which it is used and the extent to which the individual is controlled or abused in the process. Here the therapeutic community staff member must struggle with the same issues as his or her counterpart in any other hospital situation. As Saslow says in discussing the same dilemma:

> In general, the procedures used by thought reform (brainwashing) emphasize coercion and exhortation whereas the procedures on our ward emphasize therapy and self-realization, but all of these procedures are used in thought reform and all are used on our ward. . . . If our staff wishes to act out its stated democratic assumptions, it will need to be continuously vigilant to encourage therapy and self-realization and to minimize coercion and exhortation. . . . The ethical dilemmas of control will remain and psychotherapists will have to deal with these problems in the same way persons working in other agencies of social control in our society have for a long time had to do. Those who deny that psychotherapy involves control are perhaps more comfortable, but would appear to a detached observer to be self-deluded and not any the less controlled (Saslow, 1965, pp. 142–143).

One aspect of brainwashing that is found also in Tompkins I is the encompassing quality of ward life. Privacy, both physical and psychological, is minimal. Withdrawal is an invitation to inquiry, and every action is potential "grist for the mill" of therapy meetings. As we saw in Chapter 3, the ward "comes to" the patient, responding in some way to him whether he is acting upon the environment or holding still. In brainwashing, this responsiveness of the environment is manipulated constantly to maximize the greatest influence in the one goal of confession and ideological change. In Tompkins I the goal is not brainwashing—acceptance of one totalistic conception of all experience—but changed behavior and departure from the ward. The procedures used toward these goals frequently stereotype the patient or subject him to a set of responses that do not acknowledge his real subjective or objective situation. We saw this in the career studies. Yet two things may be said for the active, encompassing quality of the ward: (1) It is less monolithic than the dehumanizing asylum with its authoritarian stereotyping of patients. It is also, in general, more flexible than institutions that use one sort of therapy alone. (2) The intense attention given to every sufferer in this system is a form of caring that replaces more regressive nurturance or dehumanizing control and is more respectful of the patient's potential for recovery.

NOTES

1. This analysis of charisma in an organization setting follows Etzioni (1961).

2. Western psychological thinking, with its emphasis upon the individual separate from his environment, has tended to emphasize charisma as an individual attribute. Yet almost every classical example of a charismatic leader brings out the fact that charisma is a process involving a leader and a following. T.E. Lawrence ("Lawrence of Arabia"), who at his height led thousands of Arabs against the Turks during World War I, became an obscure soldier in the British army in later years.

3. The mass executions of World War II are as much due to the efficiency of the bureaucracy that supervised the process as to the savagery of the individuals in charge. Yet bureaucracy is not, therefore, by definition as evil as that of the concentration camp system.

PART II

Non-Western Healing Communities

In Parts II and III we move from depth of analysis toward breadth and variety. Part II includes descriptions of healing communities in three extremely different cultural settings: the Amhara region of northwest Ethiopia, the Zuni pueblo of the American southwest, and the Japanese community of Hawaii. Despite the very different sort of data we shall be using and the foreignness of culture and concepts, the purpose remains consistent. We mean to discover other manifestations of the healing community, and to check whether the model of its process holds for these very different situations. In fact, this search for other examples of healing community began with the observation that such treatment could be found intermittently in the history of Western psychiatry; moral treatment and *milieutherapie* are examples of healing community as well as historical precursors of therapeutic community as such.

Transcultural psychiatric material has special advantages—and certain problems. The advantages stem from the perspective of distance and differentness. We have our own cultural blinders that lead us to take for granted that what is called "therapy" is indeed therapeutic. Much of the purpose of Part I was devoted to searching out the actual process of healing, a therapy within the complexity of a

156

psychiatric ward run as a "therapeutic community." In Part II we shall be interested in discovering whether similar processes can be identified in much less familiar situations. In Part I we had the advantage of intimacy: We could talk with patients and staff, distribute questionnaires, observe meetings. In Part II we have the advantage of perspective. The belief in Ethiopia that bizarre behavior represents possession by a Zar spirit riding on the sufferer's shoulder is sufficiently outlandish to us that we can recognize the underlying social process at work in the group ceremony that coaxes the spirit to come under the sufferer's control. We do not share the belief of a member of the Tensho sect that their leader, Ogamisama, is a deity, but we shall be able to recognize the charismatic processes that these beliefs reflect.

The problem of this sort of data is in limits on available information. We rely on the reports of anthropological observers, who in turn rely on informants and a few direct observations. Each of these intervening screens between the actual events and the report contributes distortions. We have counterbalanced this by using several different examples. In general, examples have been selected for which the descriptions of the group's activities, concepts, and processes are most complete.

The earliest meeting ground between mental health and anthropology was psychoanalysis. Freud and his early colleagues were interested in materials from other cultures as support for the universality of their ideas and as sources of new insights. In turn, psychoanalysis provided the anthropologist with a rich model of man's psyche and a model of therapy (Sapir, 1949).[1]

Foremost in using transcultural practices like "faith healing" as data relevant to a search for the universals in therapy has been Jerome Frank. His observations have gone far to clarify the role of healer and to draw meaningful parallels among a wide variety of healing activities in our society and other cultures (1959, 1973). Healing of mental (and sometimes physical) maladies, Frank argues, is dependent less on the rational application of specific therapeutic technique than on the presence of four general factors:

1. Cultural definition of the sufferer's ailment as a legitimate, treatable disorder.
2. Social agreement on the appropriateness and efficacy of the therapist and his techniques.
3. The therapist's faith in his technique and his ability to help the patient.
4. The patient's trust in, and need for, treatment.

These four factors contribute to a "persuasive" effect upon the patient, who develops "faith" in the healer.[2] Frank suggests that the effect is the same whether this faith is is used to achieve individual change in psychotherapy, faith healing, brainwashing, or the cures of primitive ceremonies.

Frank is not concerned with any one set of techniques of processes as a paradigm for what good therapy should be or should include. Instead, he is arguing that there are certain conditions of involvement for all the participants in a therapeutic process, conditions that must be met in order for therapy to be effective. His interest, like ours, is to discover the elements of a therapeutic process and then to see how this process functions in relation to its purpose and the culture in which it is operating. Frank emphasizes individual therapy as the important Western therapy process and examines non-Western healing with that technique in mind. One purpose of Part II will be to carry Frank's comparative analysis further by examining most closely those cross-cultural healing practices which employ groups or more complicated social systems. Just as Frank was concerned with understanding the core process of individual psychotherapy, we shall be seeking such processes in these reports of group healing.

What are the comparative themes we are interested in identifying before we turn to the transcultural data? First, of course, we are interested in finding parallels to the processes described in Chapter 9. For example, we shall learn much of how communitas norms interact with specific therapeutic norms by observing them in several different cultures. Charismatic interactions recur, as does communitas, but the social organization of the different healing communities varies. We find that in these groups the healer himself is frequently a sufferer, an "ex-patient." We also find that these groups in general take a different attitude toward time, specifically toward the issues of recurrence and chronicity that emerged as problematic for the therapeutic community.

Finally, what new understanding of the healing group will be gained from these further examples? If it is a *type* of social organization, the healing group should appear differently in different environments, and we should learn new things about it in each one. For example, Tompkins I is conceived as a medical-psychological organization. Many non-Western groups are wholly or partly religious in purpose. What does this tell us about the healing group and about madness? Does it have implications for healing communities in our society?

NOTES

1. In fact, psychoanalytic therapy techniques became the yardstick with which anthropologists observed and evaluated primitive healing. As a result the healer or shaman was the central focus of observation, and the standard of therapy was psychoanalysis. The professionalism and emotional stability of the analyst was compared with the frequent report of madness or its symptoms in the shaman (Kroeber, 1952; Kiev, 1962). The techniques of treatment were held up to a psychoanalytic ideal of insight and working through. Therapies using catharsis, environmental manipulation, and confession were implicitly inferior. Now that we embrace a wider variety of techniques as therapeutic tools, many "primitive" therapies look quite legitimate. The evidence for a relativistic view of non-Western therapies is by now persuasive (Kiev, 1968; Silverman, 1967).

2. Where Frank has used the terms persuasion and faith, I have used the concept of healing charisma. The difference stems largely from Frank's paradigm of individual psychotherapy as against our focus here on individual-group processes of healing.

CHAPTER 10

The Zar Cult of Ethiopia

There are two reasons for examining the healing activities of the Amhara population of Ethiopia.[1] First, this region supports one of the best-described parallels to therapeutic community—the Zar cult. Second, illness is handled by four different systems of medicine, each with its own practitioners, techniques, theory, social patterns, and range of the spectrum of illnesses. The Amhara culture provides both a cross-cultural perspective and a degree of social and medical complexity comparable to that of Western societies. Thus, in this first cross-cultural case it is possible to consider issues dealing with both the internal processes of a non-Western "therapeutic community" and the relationship of the group healing system to its surrounding culture.

BACKGROUND

"Amhara" describes both a people and an area of northwest Ethiopia. This poorly accessible plateau region is populated by a number of ethnic and racial subgroups; the Amharic-speaking are the most populous and are culturally dominant. The region numbers some four or five million of the roughly 16 million population of Ethiopia. The dominant religion is Coptic, an early form of Christianity. Although the majority of residents of the region are Amharic-speaking, of Coptic faith, and ethnically Amharic (Caucasian), several other languages, religions, and ethnic groups are represented in the area. There is frequent contact with members of the Muslim and "pagan" population of the country. Sudanese (Blacks) populate other areas heavily but are also found in the Amhara. The area has a complex history in which diverse racial, religious, and ethnic forces have struggled for domination back and forth over the land and have intermingled to create a complex caste and class system. At the same time, the rugged, mountainous geography of the northwest and the warlike nature of most of its cultural groups have blunted the impact of large-scale colonial assaults from the Mediterranean area. The fierce fighting in Ethiopia during the Italian invasion of 1935–1936 is only the most recent episode in a long history of resistance to sudden conquest. Muslim domination of Northeast Africa during the great expansion of Mohammedanism around the Mediterranean met its stiffest resistance in this region. Later colonial expansion by Western European powers similarly failed to make deep inroads. European economic and religious colonialism and proselytizing during the past several centuries achieved only a partial penetration here. Thus the Amhara represents a sort of "cultural museum" in which can be found living side by side early Christian, Hebraic, Muslim, and native African cultural elements.

French-educated Haile Selassie, who became regent in 1916 and later emperor, pursued a policy of national consolidation of the diverse regions and groups of Ethiopia, begun in the late nineteenth century. He introduced many Westernizing cultural patterns in government, military, and education, thus adding a new acculturative complexity. Again, because of the mountainous geography of the country and the cultural resistance to forces of change, Selassie's efforts have been more successful in the area of Addis Ababa and in other urban regions.

CONCEPTS OF DISEASE AND TREATMENT

The Amharic categorization of disease is as complex as the culture of the region. Some physical problems may come to Western-type medical personnel, including midwives and physicians in the few cities. The bulk of healing is still done by four specialized types of native healers, who may be consulted for different but overlapping groups of illnesses. Most of the clearly physical problems are treated by the "woggesha," a healer akin to our general practitioner. He does minor surgery and dentistry, and treats a variety of complaints with herbs. The woggesha learns his herbal skills from his father, to whom he is an apprentice. He raises, transplants, or collects his remedies, and memorizes a complex formulary. His treatments are administered directly, in a primarily one-to-one fashion. Like the general practitioner in rural America, a good woggesha knows his patients well, relates diplomatically to their families, and maintains good relations with other healers to whom he may refer patients.

The "dabtara" is a scribe in the Coptic church. His healing activity is secondary to his religious function but may be his major source of income and prestige. The dabtara's healing role stems from literacy and religious knowledge, which enable him to write texts for amulets used against a variety of demons. Again, the healing transaction is dyadic, with the sufferer's family, at most, interested bystanders. Demon-caused ailments that may respond to amulet treatment include fevers, hemoptysis (spitting blood, secondary to tuberculosis), dysentery, eye infections, "evil eye" causing learning problems, unexplained decline in health, barrenness, puerperal fever, stillbirth. A dabtara's diagnostic domain somewhat overlaps that of the woggesha. Although the herbal skills of the latter should give him a therapeutic advantage over the former, the legitimization of religious affiliation and power keeps the dabtara in business.

Other healers are involved with evil-eye sickness, or "buda." The diseases attributed to this cause cover both the psychological and physical spectrum, in particular, forms of withdrawal and apathy unresponsive to the Zar treatment, which we shall examine in detail. The buda spirits are more malign than the Zar. They are transferred to their victim by persons possessing the evil eye. The buda suck the blood out of their victims, thus accounting for such symptoms as nosebleed. The buda is exorcised in a ceremony conducted either by a dabtara scribe or a 'tanqway" sorcerer. Through negotiation, the buda is induced to leave the body of the victim permanently in exchange for an appropriate sacrifice or payment. The buda is then transferred to some vegetation, where it can seize another victim. The ceremony in which a buda is exorcised focuses on the victim alone and does not involve other buda sufferers. The techniques used in the exorcism depend on the therapist. If he is a dabtara scribe, then amulets and prayers as well as religious threats may be made. The tanqway sorcerer, on the other hand, uses magical techniques. He is the most primitive—and has the lowest social status—of the healers we have encountered among the Amhara.

Tanqway sorcerers also treat a disorder known as "ganyen" or "evil spirit disease." This, too, is due to spirits who, like the buda, are wholly evil. Such spirits are more specifically malicious and cause their victims to attack others destructively. The ganyen spirit is exorcised by being treated with contempt and by being given such insulting gifts as a meal of ashes.

THE ZAR CULT

The major treatment for what Western medicine identifies as psychiatric disorder is the Zar cult. The illnesses treated in the cult are attributed to "Zar spirits," or "Zars." These are analogous to, but of a different species from, the demons treated with amulets. Zar treatment is most specific for "hysterical" symptoms (meaning immature, childlike behavior—not hysterical conversion symptoms); withdrawal (presumably depression and catatonia), miscarriage or barrenness; change of personality (grandiosity, paranoia); bizarre behavior like self-injury, "pica" (eating dirt), running out in the night "to roam with the hyenas"; running amok (directing aggression towards others). Highly aggressive behavior may also be diagnosed as "buda" or "ganyen," possession states that are out of the Zar domain and are treated instead by the dabtara or by the tanqway sorcerer.

The great bulk of this section will be concerned with a description of the Zar cult. Although I shall emphasize Messing's description of the cult as it is found in the northwest Amhara region of Ethiopia, especially in the town of Gondar, Zar ceremonies can be found in many areas of Africa and the Middle East, including the Sudan, Egypt, Iran, Saudi Arabia, and the Yemen (Torrey, 1967). The cult is also thought to be related to healing groups found as far west as Nigeria. Since the word "zar" has linguistic origin in Ethiopia, it is assumed that it spread from that region. The cult has been known for over a century in Ethiopia, but probably has existed for much longer. Torrey has classified three varieties of the Zar cult found within Ethiopia as "conversion Zar," "seer Zar," and "group therapy Zar" (1967). These variations in the cult may explain its wide distribution and may reflect adjustment to the variations of cultural and social patterns within Ethiopia and in surrounding regions. The emphasis here will be upon the third form of the Zar cult, the "group therapy Zar." Although this form is relatively specific to the Gondar region of northwest Ethiopia, a very similar Zar ceremony has been described by Kennedy at Nubia, in the Sudan (1967).

Certain features of the Zar ceremony—such as the use of dancing and trance states, and at least a limited view of the

Zar spirits as having a complex existence and demonology-
—are common to all three varieties of the cult. In fact, the Zar
ceremonies described by Messing and Kennedy involve, as
we shall see, not simply a ceremony but a cosmology of spirits
and spirit worlds that maintain a subtle and complementary
relationship with everyday life. Furthermore, the Zar cult as a
social institution is interwoven with many facets of Amhara
culture and social institutions. Before we describe any of these
wider aspects of the cult, let us look at the experience of the
cult as a treatment institution.

The initial onset and handling of a hysterically excited
woman is described in the following manner:

> Symptoms of hysteria usually begin at night, and take the
> pattern of seeking escape. The patient tries to run out of the hut
> at night, with great clamor and drama, to "roam with the
> hyenas." (Hyenas are associated with the most malign spirits
> in the Zar cosmology and with the "buda" possession—more
> sinister than most of the Zar afflictions.) Restraint results in
> rage, even self-injury. Kinfolk usualy tie the patient with ropes
> until contact with the Zar doctor can be made. The latter usu-
> ally has cultivated a stare that can calm cases of hysteria so that
> diagnosis can proceed. (This intense stare is associated with
> the "evil-eye," that is with special, magical and powerful
> forces, here being used to subdue the Zar that has possessed
> the sufferer.) Without saying a word, the doctor grasps the
> upper arm of the patient (for male Zars attack the shoulders
> first and then squat on the patient's back until they descend
> into the victim, during the period of full possession). When the
> patient has been sufficiently calmed, the doctor loosens his
> grip and lightly caresses the upper arm and shoulder. This
> indicates that he is unafraid to establish contact with the spirit,
> and that the situation is well in hand. Most victims of hysteria
> are women (Messing, 1959, p. 322).

Disorders we would term depression or catatonia are also
dealt with rapidly:

Extreme apathy indicates possession by an evil Zar. The patient, often a woman, withdraws into a corner of the hut, sits there huddled, refuses food. Kinfolk immediately come to her aid, for if she were to remain long in this state her Zar could "ride his horse to death." Therefore, until a Zar doctor can be sent for, kinfolk and neighbors come quickly, sing to the patient, dance for her, try to move her into joining them, promise her whatever she desires, and never leave her alone (Messing, 1959, pp. 322–323).

These are only two examples of the onset of Zar possession. In other instances there may be grandiose or aggressive behavior, usually regarded as possession by a male Zar of a female patient. Menstrual disorders, barrenness, and still-births may also be taken as prodromal signs of Zar possession, again by a male Zar.[2]

THE ZAR CEREMONY

The Zar ceremony is arranged as soon as possible, often the next evening.[3]

When darkness has fallen the patient is brought to the hut of the Zar doctor. Here the Zar disciples, mostly women, are assembled, seated quietly, perhaps talking in subdued tones or spinning cut thread. The scene inside is warm with illumination, burning incense, and the assembled membership of the devotees, all chronic cases themselves. A relative hands an entry gift, referred to as "incense money," to a disciple, who passes it quietly to the doctor behind a screened platform. The doctor ignores the new arrival . . . there is a low rhythmic drum beat, occasionally broken by chants accompanied by rhythmic handclapping. Member after member rises individually, "when the spirit moves her," and begins to perform her "gurri" with slight variations according to her particular Zar. The "gurri" is a movement that begins with shoulders (typical of Amhara dancing), while the performer is yet seated, and continues while she rises. Head and shoulders move forward and backwards, sometimes in horizontal direction, sometimes rotating clockwise, sometimes counter-clockwise. During the orgiastic climax the possessed proceeds to twirl like a top, faster and faster, until she drops in a heap. Habitués can go on for twenty minutes, and be ready for another movement an hour later.

While watching this over and over again, the patient may herself in time be moved to do likewise, though at first clumsily. This is a good sign, for it means that her Zar has consented to dismount from his "riding" position, and is beginning to "descend" into the possessed person himself. The "gurri" is regarded as the "victory dance of the Zar," much like a hunter who has wounded and felled his deer. There is a strong element of struggle in the "gurri" dance, like the frantic death throes of an animal about to surrender its individual existence. It is also the climax of the magical coitus (much like the bride who is "conquered" on her wedding night).

. . . only then does the doctor emerge, her eyes bright and curious, her gestures commanding. She greets her flock and orders drinks for everyone. The male reader-composer of liturgy of the Zar cult intones old and new hymns of praise to the Zar. He is accompanied by the rhythmic handclapping of the worshippers. This ritual recharges the interrogation whenever the latter becomes difficult.

The patient is now in a trance-like state, considered in communication and partly identified with the Zar, but yet open to urgings by the doctor. More incense is burned, closeby, to make the new and as-yet unidentified Zar feel cosy and put him in a benevolent, cooperative mood. Great care must be taken prior to the diagnosis. For this reason no poetry is sung to him and no gift-giving as yet, for the wrong kind might insult him—he insists on his own, individual cult. When the patient dances subsequent "gurri" the Zar doctor becomes increasingly certain whether the Zar is male or female, evil or mischevious, "neglected" or offended (Messing, 1957, pp. 609–610).

The ceremony now moves to a more specific diagnostic phase, in which the name and characteristics of the Zar are discovered.

The specific personality and identity of the Zar is revealed later during the course of the diagnosis, when the Zar, using the body of the patient, dances the "fukkara" dance. This is considered the equivalent of the "boasting" dance of the Amhara warrior on the eve of battle, which goes by the same name. Thus the Zar reveals his "faras sem" (war name; lit., horse name, i.e., knighthood name), much like an Amhara feudal knight. Since formal "boasting" is highly individualistic, this means that the Zar has come out of hiding, like a warrior who emerges from ambush. The dance itself is just as individualistic and irregular, therefore called "dankira," and may include the brandishing of sticks (as if they were spears) or jumping up and down.

Once the patient has proceeded to such expressive behavior, the Zar doctor claims that he "knows" the identity of the Zar. The doctor now asks the Zar a series of leading questions, and the patient usually does not fail to respond with the "truthful" answers. Finally the name of the Zar is openly proclaimed. Certain Zars are stubborn, hide their identity in various subterfuges, so that the battle of wits between the Zar doctor and the Zar is a lengthy and difficult one. But the former nearly always wins out and announces his diagnosis (Messing, 1957, p. 611).

In this interchange with the patient speaking for the Zar, the doctor, by alternately threatening and praising the spirit, makes him confess shortcomings (of the sufferer, not the Zar) "such as neglect of family, of kinfolk, of the church, and of course of the Zar himself, who may have been insulted in some unintentional way . . . sometimes several nights are needed to achieve this final expression."

The Zar doctor does not proclaim the final diagnosis until he has also studied the social and economic status of the patient. For an important part of the doctor's function is to match the social class of Zar with the socio-economic class of patient. The Zar of poor and low-class members usually belongs to the class of "pages serving great Zars" (Wuresa). Such poor patients may work off their dues by "serving in the trade." Sometimes when a doctor regrets his earlier overestimate of a patient's financial position, he may "transfer" his expensive Zar to another devotee better able to bear the offerings demanded (Messing, 1959, p. 326).

Thereupon the Zar doctor proceeds to decide what course of treatment to follow. The Zar is asked, through the mouth of the patient, what offense has been committed against him; what he would like to receive as "maqwadasha" (love-gift) in order to "pardon" the iniquity or as damages for the "insult" or "neglect." Finally the Zar is asked what he will demand in regular offerings in order to remain on good terms with the possessed, to plague her less and only at regular intervals, and, perhaps, to become her protective spirit. On the basis of the replies, the patient is assessed membership fees in the Zar congregation headed by that particular Zar doctor. The patient thus becomes a devotee of the Zar ("Yazar Welaj") (Messing, 1957, pp. 611–612).

The symptoms of the patient are thus channeled in such a manner that will fulfill both his psychological and social needs. He is not made into a deviant from society. He learns to accept his ailment and come to terms with it. His new social role within the Zar society is similar to his position in the social hierarchy of the outside community. He now has the backing of the Zar subculture and social organization. The acceptance by the patient of his new role is ritualized. The Zar doctor helps him to transform the Zar spirit into an attitude of benevolence, of protection (wequabi). The aim is to reduce the sufferings in frequency and severity, in exchange for periodic offerings of animals, ornaments, incense money, etc. Most Zars are never exorcised. This is attempted only in a few stubborn cases, where possession is attributed to certain evil female Zars, whose "contracts" are regarded as unreliable anyway. In this case the doctor transfers the spirit to a spot near the path in the bush, where he can pounce upon an unsuspecting stranger. In his place, the patient is assigned another Zar as protective spirit, from among the Zars currently available in the house of Zar society, and without a "horse" to serve them (Messing, 1959, p. 326).

THE MEANINGS OF MEMBERSHIP

Since Zar possession is a chronic state, entrance into the Zar cult introduces permanent changes into the life of the sufferer. In order to appreciate fully the legitimacy and function of these changes, I shall describe briefly some aspects of Zar cosmology and mythology.

According to Amhara myth, the Zar spirits originated in the Garden of Eden at the same time man was created. Eve is believed to have had 30 children. One day God (in some versions, the Virgin Mary) came to visit. Eve, in apprehension, hid the 15 most beautiful and intelligent of her children. As punishment, God condemned the hidden children to be eternally invisible, nighttime creatures. These ancestral Zar spirits went on to procreate and populate the world with their descendants. They have a society that mirrors that of the Ethiopians. They are more powerful and more beautiful than man and know remedies for ailments, but envy their uglier and weaker human brothers and sisters who are daytime "children of the light."

The Zar myth suggests one psychological function of membership. One of the ingredients of most Zar afflictions is low self-esteem, often a function of low status associated with being of a subordinate race, class, and/or sex. The Zar spirits combine both the sufferer's low self-view and his wish for a grander experience of himself. The spirits are "invisible," just as is the cult member, who may be ignored by, and thus feel invisible to, her husband or more prestigious classes. The Zars are envious and "ride" their victims just as high-status feudal lords ride on horseback.

In the Zar ceremony of a new initiate, the spirit is induced to possess the sufferer fully; but by virtue of being induced into a negotiation process, the spirit becomes amenable to the control of the Zar doctor and ultimately the sufferer and the cult. Such negotiating is a familiar experience in Amharic life and brings the Zar into a psychological world that is familiar to the sufferer. The result of this negotiation is ordinarily that the sufferer, through the mediation of the Zar doctor, achieves some control over the spirit, and in fact may turn it to a protective or helpful purpose. The victim (1) achieves a symbolic victory over the forces he feels are controlling him; (2) incorporates a sense of higher status by achieving full Zar possession; (3) gains real advantage through the terms demanded by the Zar for settlement. As settlement for assuming a protective relationship, the Zar spirit may insist on some material benefit from the family such as clothes or jewelry, or the sacrifice (and therefore festive consumption) of an animal. The beneficiaries are both the new member and the cult as a whole.

The actual advantages consequent upon Zar possession and subsequent participation in the cult can go far beyond these. For a great many women, diagnosed as possessed by sexually desirous male Zars, there is a whole sexual and marital symbolism carried through the ceremony. Thus the orgiastic gurri dance has many physical parallels to sexual intercourse and orgasm, and can be seen as an overt, socially acceptable sort of grand hysterical fit.

> One of the basic relationships with the Zar spirit of the opposite sex, the "magical coitus," is solemnized by the Zar doctor in a "marriage communion." The possessed is then referred to as "musharra" (newlywed), and is attended by two "mize" (best men, like in a human wedding) from among the circle of the society of the possessed, who ever thereafter are in attendance every time another possession occurs, so that the patient "does not get hurt" in the violent twirling (much as the "mize" protect a wife against her husband). The Zar spirit appreciates these acknowledgements and is thus open to negotiations, especially during the "honeymoon" (Messing, 1957, pp. 608–609.).

Thus, as Messing observes, the Zar cult is far more than a treatment:

> The Zar doctors do not limit themselves to treating . . . mental ailments. They organize the afflicted before, during, and after "cure," into Zar societies, which bear the earmarks of a religious cult, and to which the individual belongs henceforth until his or her death. Here he finds the warm companionship of the fellow-afflicted; opportunity for expressive behavior; the religious feeling of having been of service; the personal attention of a personal possessive and protective spirit; and the visible leadership of the Zar doctor who heads the organization unit (Messing, 1957, p. 597).

These advantages of Zar possession and cult membership carry over into life outside the society. For example, a woman with marital incompatibility may use the possession by a male Zar as the occasion for legitimizing divorce proceedings.

Amharic women are married off early in life, and after marriage join the village and family of the husband. In cases of poor marital relationship, divorce is possible but frequently difficult to initiate; once complete, it leaves the woman in a vulnerable position. Zar possession can thus both legitimize the divorce psychologically and provide a social supportive group for the divorcee. Since Zar possession is accepted as legitimate throughout Amhara culture, advantages and facilitations provided by the cult are not contested.

Other women may not be interested in divorce but may find the subordinated, inhibited role of the Ethiopian housewife discouraging and burdensome. Membership in the Zar society legitimizes their absence from home (often for entire nights) and the exciting experience of the Zar ceremony. Husbands may resent this but cannot complain too much lest the Zar spirit make another attack. Furthermore, many husbands "admit that their wives are thereafter easier to live with, indeed more beautiful when the 'wequabi' (inspiration) is on their face."

Analogous advantages exist for individuals with other sorts of afflictions. For example, some possibly schizophrenic individuals find legitimate roles within the cult, roles in which they can express bizarre behavior in a socially sanctioned fashion:

> A Zar doctor, especially a male one, is regarded as particularly arrogant in personality. When walking on a trail, he walks in great strides. His hair stands up stiff like that of a warrior, or, if his "Zar" is a Muslim, is covered with a flaming-colored turban. Unlike other Amhara men, he wears an ear-ring, of bright metal, in one ear. He seems absent-minded, distracted, inward-looking, greets no one. However, when greeted, he may reply with a tirade in "Zar" language. Sometimes he claims to have just returned from a magical voyage, e.g., to have just visited the home country of a visiting foreigner, so that he knows all about it (Messing, 1957, pp. 603–604).[4]

Since all Zar doctors are themselves afflicted with Zar spirits, such patterns may well be the chaneling within the cult of initially more diffuse, disorganized and deviant behavior.

> A male Zar doctor had, in the past, a place of honor at the table of feudal chiefs who often consulted them—perhaps more because of the doctors' knowledge of humans and public opinion than because of their spirit world. Even today, the social status and income of a Zar doctor in rural areas and provincial towns is high, and he can afford such expensive European attire and apparel as a folding umbrella, laced shoes, a ring of silver or gold, etc. He may break rules of politeness, even utter mild insults and commit familiarities without repression and penalty, for no layman can know whether or not it is the spirit who speaks through the doctor in any given situation (Messing, 1957, pp. 604–605).

There are other, yet more general benefits of Zar membership, again illustrating the intriguing psychological and social complementarity between the cult and the culture. An important social institution in the Amhara region is the "mahabbar" communal worship society. These are fraternal groups, with primarily male membership. Their ostensible function is religious, but their activities are primarily social. Membership in such societies, especially older, well-established ones, is extremely useful and important. These groups gather for rather festive social occasions in which the bonds of fraternal association are celebrated. But beyond this:

> According to traditional law, the mahabbar inherits any property left by a deceased member who leaves no blood kin (consanguinal), in preference to any relatives he might have by marriage (affinal). The mahabbar acts as a mutual aid society for its members, as banker, making loans to members in financial need by raising internal subscriptions, and will even pay for the "tazcar" memorial feast forty days after a member's

death if his family cannot afford to do it properly. Family and personal problems of all kinds are discussed among "brothers" and "sisters," thus crossing the usual kinship lines of confidence and trust. Marriage arrangements between extended families having eligible youngsters are often first informally broached by women "sisters," who then agree to ask their husbands to act as intermediaries (Messing, 1957, p. 396).

The groups of chronically possessed individuals who meet regularly in Zar ceremonies become a special society, called "aqwadash." These groups serve many of the same functions as the mahabbar societies, and a system of artificial kinship develops here as well. Within it, job-finding, matchmaking, and mutual emotional support occur in a stable social framework. Further mirroring the dominant social institutions, the leader of the Zar cult, usually a woman, invests the cult with solidarity and spiritual significance by virtue of her complete mastery of one or usually several Zar spirits.

The Zar complex to the Amhara mind, represents the shadow side of the visible human world, making it complete. Hence just as the Coptic Christian (and also the Muslim) church emphasizes the male-dominated, patriarchal side of society, so does the Zar complex represent the obverse, the female-dominated, matriarchal side of society (Messing, 1957, p. 645).

This is further reinforced by the subordinate sociopsychological position of the Amhara woman. She may not enter the church. Her daily labors are largely limited to routine, manual, monotonous tasks. Only noble women are exempted from the social position of the "commoner" female, and therefore are not found in the Zar cult—which therefore has a lower-class connotation in the basic two-class Amhara society.

Thus the female Zar initiate becomes part of a supportive social group, in which a woman usually serves as model for the possibility of feminine power and leadership, even in a sufferer. The individual Zar allows the acknowledgment of many culturally suppressed impulses. Through the legitimization of Zar possession, these impulses can then be expressed outside the cult, leading to improvements and changes in the member's life in general.

Further, the member may achieve specific economic improvement through jobs within the cult, or arranged through the cult.

> As a result of her exposure to businesswomen, the men folk in her family will not shunt her aside when talking business, or legal or kin matters. Some women devotees whose bent is more feminine, become midwives, "experts" in domestic obstetrics and primitive gynecology. There are many ways in which the women's social status improves. No longer is she a mere hauler of water and hewer of wood. This change usually relieves her mental ailment—and this cure is ascribed to the Zar doctor and the Zar complex (Messing, 1957, p. 646).

Those initiates who show special skills in the possession ceremonies may develop into assistants, apprentices, and finally may become Zar doctors themselves.

SUMMARY

The "group therapy" version of the Zar cult, found in Gondar and the northwest Amhara region of Ethiopia, is an extraordinarily complex and sensitive social institution whose purpose includes treatment of what we would consider to be the psychiatric spectrum of disease. Around this official and primary function, the cult serves a variety of other needs, thus adding an indirect healing component to its more direct effect. The cult is made up of sufferers and ex-sufferers of a variety of psychic, neurological, and gynecological disorders who serve as patients, audience, staff, and leaders in the treatment system.

We can identify the following important features of the Zar cult: (1) It has an acknowledged place in the traditional medical care system of the region. Certain behaviors and ailments are regularly attributed to Zar spirits. Interestingly, the cult is also open to individuals who wish to join for their own reasons. (2) Within the cult, procedures exist for emergency care, for the "diagnosis" and intensive treatment of newly afflicted sufferers. In the initial treating ceremony, a subtle procedure of inducing spirit possession is used to involve the sufferer with the group and the leader. Through imitating the ritual gurri dance, and then through the negotiation with the Zar spirit, the sufferer's attention is focused outside himself. The "diagnosis" and naming of the Zar make it familiar and less threatening. The negotiation that brings it under control is a familiar interpersonal experience in the general culture, since bargaining and negotiation are present in almost any Amharic relationship, as is the theme of control. (3) In ceremonies the leader, the members, and the new sufferer all become possessed by their Zar spirits. Those with greater experience use the possession in the service of themselves or others. Since the edicts of the Zar spirits during possession are accepted by those outside the cult, continuing involvement in the group is reinforced for old-timers. "Social mobility" exists from newcomer to leader—the only criteria for advancement are the quality of one's possession states and ability to manipulate one's Zar. If we replace "Zar spirit" with "charisma," we have exactly the pattern of the healing group. By becoming possessed, the cult member becomes "more" than before. He becomes internally strengthened—now the Zar's strength is his; he becomes externally strengthened—he may act and look differently and request more from the home situation. (4) The advantages, cures, and reassurance of group life contribute to solidarity among members. Involvement in the cult is not limited to the period of acute suffering but continues indefinitely. This is symbolized in the continuing possession by the Zar spirit. Enduring involvement provides the Zar cult member with support during such social stress as divorce, offers economic opportunity, and in general parallels in function an important social organization, the mahabbar fraternity. Put in our terms, the Zar cult has many elements of communitas: membership in a close, supportive group in which members all share an important characteristic.

NOTES

1. The descriptions and analyses of Amharic culture and healing presented here are drawn primarily from Simon Messing, *The Highland Plateau Amhara of Ethiopia*, Ph.D. dissertation, University of Pennsylvania, 1957. Unless otherwise indicated, quoted sections are from this source.

2. Some of these disorders may be what would be regarded in Western psychiatry as postpartum depression or psychosis.

3. The description quoted here is that of Messing (1957, 1959). The sequence of diagnosis and negotiation with the Zar can be varied by different forms of the Zar cult, and even from one cult leader to another. In the Nubian Zar ceremony, diagnosis occurs in a private interview with the sheikh (leader) of the cult prior to the ceremony itself (Kennedy, 1967).

4. Zar "language" is not word salad, but like the whole Zar cosmology, uses Amharic-style grammar, forms, and phonemes in its own vocabulary.

CHAPTER 11

The Tensho Sect of Hawaii

Tensho is a religious movement that developed around the inspirational leadership of a Japanese farmer's wife after World War II and spread to Hawaii in 1952.[1] In 1965, it had about 500 members participating in its weekly meetings, study groups, and in the public dancing ceremonies that have earned it the name "Dancing Religion." Tensho is of interest to us because of the high incidence of health problems among its recruits and the reported frequency of cure, improvement, or transcendence of illness. Almost every member has been depressed and discouraged in the months or years before joining Tensho. Although the sect's emphasis is put on salvation, that is, a religious goal, healing is cited by most members as evidence of benefit. It has many features in common with other healing communities and is of particular interest because one of the factors members must deal with is the acculturative tension between Japanese and American cultures.

BACKGROUND AND DEVELOPMENT OF THE SECT

With the end of World War II in Japan, there developed a considerable number of religious splinter groups, some of which have since grown into major social movements. They appear responsive to the major psychological readjustments of the postwar period, with its continuing Westernization. Most of these groups are religious in some degree. While some (like the major movement Soka-gakkai) have a strongly political flavor, others, including Tensho, are therapeutic in style.

Mrs. Sayo Kitamura, the founder and leader of Tensho, was an unusual person. Before the war she had been a village leader and something of a feminist. During 1942 the family lost all its wealth in a fire, and in the same year her only child, a son with whom she probably had her closest emotional bond, was drafted. These losses led Mrs. Kitamura to hours of daily prayer and then to the belief that a god had entered her and was guiding her through creating abdominal pain when displeased. Eventually the spirit instructed her to carry this guidance to others, and Mrs. Kitamura began walking about the streets of her town, preaching. Although most laughed at her or thought her mad, a few followers appeared. When the war ended, Mrs. Kitamura, now known as Ogamisama (Great Deity), revised the doctrines of her group to increase its religious emphasis and began to proselytize more openly. She met with rapid success.

Tensho came to Hawaii in 1950 when an islander visited the sect's headquarters and became convinced that Ogamisama represented the religious answer she and a loosely knit group of friends had been seeking. Members of this group had in common their involvement with a local Hawaiian clairvoyant. With the aid of a few loyal converts, some of whom made pilgrimages to Tensho headquarters in Japan, the movement grew gradually. Ogamisama made occasional visits to Hawaii, there publicizing, proselytizing, and making extensive contact with recent converts.

The appeal of Tensho in Hawaii has a good deal to do with the situation of the Japanese community there. Many Japanese had gone to Hawaii prior to World War II in hopes of economic success. Traditional Japanese culture was intially retained by these immigrants to a considerable degree, although Westernizing influences were present, as they were in Japan. World War II was a devastating and confusing experience. Many families were arbitrarily interned, yet many young men served in special Japanese brigades that fought in Europe. Japan's defeat was a blow to the self-esteem of many, while those who had espoused the American cause had to deal with discriminatory and distrustful attitudes during the war.

The war, however, only intensified the conflict between two distinctly different cultures. Traditional Japanese emphasis on filial piety, loyalty to the emperor, and perfect role performance contrasts with American ideals of independence, establishing one's own family, and individual accomplishment. By the postwar period the extended family and ethnic solidarity had both lost some ground. Cultural tensions were experienced differently by those who had immigrated from Japan, those who were born in Hawaii but reared in Japan, and those born and reared in Hawaii.

Two highly relevant areas of cultural tension were family relations and health, both areas that impinge intensely upon individual psychological life. The traditional Japanese family ties, in addition to stressing respect for parents, delineate specific roles depending on sex and sibship rank. Interpersonal relations involve triads rather than dyads as in the American family. The classical mother, son, daughter-in-law grouping contrasts directly with the dyadic American nuclear family, in which each generation becomes independent of the preceding. The effectiveness and subjective happiness of individuals in society is in many ways related to the acceptance of these family constellations and their respective roles.

For the Japanese, illness plays a specific function of allowing release from otherwise rigorous role demands. Thus, hypochondriacal or psychosomatic disorder is frequently a solution for life's stressful crises. Americans, on the other hand, view most illness as a sign of weakness; the American hero triumphs *despite* his disability or disease. These different perspectives again create stress for the Japanese-American in Hawaii, both in handling the pressures of life and in coping with real illness.

The role of these and other factors is seen in the characteristics of Tensho members. Compared with the Hawaiian Japanese population as a whole or with the members of a "control" Buddhist religious congregation, they tend to be (1) from lower socioeconomic backgrounds; (2) themselves lower in education and socioeconomic status; (3) financially poorly off due to failure at work or business; (4) in poor health, or having family members in poor health; (5) involved in tense family situations, such as marriage with a much more or much less acculturated spouse; (6) faced with family difficulty such as widowhood, divorce, or childlessness. Almost universal in members' self-descriptions prior to conversion are low self-esteem and alienation from important others. Future Tensho members are also characterized by a searching for solutions to their problems in religious movements and by discouragement with traditional religious groups and official health agencies.

BECOMING A MEMBER

Joining Tensho frequently begins with the individual searching for a religious solution to his subjective situation. He is exposed to the sect in some way and attends a meeting. Those directly exposed to Ogamisama on such an occasion report the most dramatic conversions:

> I went there, after cleansing my body. But my spirit was unclean, my spoiled conscience kept me from entering the house. Then I heard a voice from inside, saying, 'Come in. I won't scold you.' The moment I saw her face, I knew this was what I had been awaiting for a long, long time. Her face was radiating

with overwhelming compassion. I wished I could rush into her
arms (Lebra, 1967, p. 253).

In other cases the convert "goes through the motions" in the
desperate hope of being helped, but is intellectually skeptical.
He may nevertheless receive considerable material or
psychological assistance. For example, Ogamisama or
another member may intervene in a family feud on his side
and provide backing with which to sever relations or prevail
in the dispute. Tensho members may provide nurturant care,
such as massage for chronic ailments, or professional aid.
These forms of aid evoke a sense of obligation or *on*, a powerful motive in Japanese psychology. Relations with other persons, with one's family, and in commercial transactions are
always accompanied by specific balances of indebtedness.
Thus the initiation procedures of the Tensho sect make use of
an important psychological theme of Japanese culture. There
are no membership dues to the organization, thus further
intensifying the new member's sense of indebtedness.

In addition to the specific benefits, there are more subtle
ones, such as physical procedures during which the new
member's body is patted or pressed as part of the diagnosis of
the spirit afflicting him. Social gratifications are frequent,
since each member becomes an important element in the
Tensho movement as a whole. The initiate may be allowed to
discuss his problems, both his suffering and his social or
family difficulties, at length with a member.

Most early converts have the treasured memories of what
Ogamisama said to them in their first encounter with her. The
meaning of the verbalized content does not necessarily seem to
count. Many did not understand Ogamisama's particular
dialect and yet felt as if "struck by a thunderbolt." The affective
exposure to vocal stimulation from the whole congregation
chanting a meaningless phrase is another example (Lebra, 1969,
pp. 8–9).

During this intense period most members experience a moment of commitment to complete belief in Ogamisama:

> I had never gone back to Japan since I came to Hawaii at eighteen. I felt as if I were having a reunion with my mother at long last. No, my delight was much more than that.

> Every sentence, every phrase, every word from Ogamisama's mouth struck the bottom of my heart. Ogamisama recognized me because I was sitting in the front row. She said, smiling, "You understand what I said, don't you?"

> I wanted to be with Ogamisama every moment, I could not think of anything else. Whenever I was not with her, I missed her like my mother. In fact I missed Ogamisama more than my parents (Lebra, 1967, p. 253).

Following this initial phase of joining, during which there is much direct attention given to the sufferer by Ogamisama or experienced members of the sect, there is a gradual change in how the initiate is handled. Access to Ogamisama may decrease and another member may become a go-between for communication. While this decreases the direct impact of the deity-healer of the organization, the communications relayed to the new member by the third party take on intense meaningfulness and influence.

> In fact, this form of communication can be even more effective than a direct one in that the third person with better knowledge of the potential or new convert can adjust or modify the information to be transmitted (Lebra, 1969, p. 9).

At about this time the convert is introduced to Ogamisama in front of a large audience. Here Ogamisama may utilize the audience's response to motivate the new candidate further by playing on his particular psychological needs or vulnerabilities. Thus, candidates may be flattered at times or shamed in front of the group at other times.

All these early experiences frequently lead to some improvement in the member's health. The improvement may actually be a physical one, or it may be the result of a changed attitude toward his illness. Moreover, many converts experience an improvement in their social life and in the general richness of their day-to-day experience through the Tensho participation. These changes are associated with Tensho and most commonly with its leader, Ogamisama, who becomes *inochi-no-onjin*, the lifesaver. Although no formal obligations are contracted through membership in the sect, this particular form of *on* carries with it a subjective feeling of eternal obligation: Such *on* can never be fully repaid. To repay the *on*, a member must become further committed, healthier, and a helper of others. Public statements of benefit and indebtedness to Ogamisama and the sect tend to have the psychological meaning of repayment of part of this debt. The recurrence of symptomatology or illness, once a convert has become a regular member, is experienced with guilty embarrassment.

Ogamisama is also a model for converts. She suffers from illness herself, but through her heavenly transformation she has gained control over it. She reminds her followers that she has never missed a day of her calling despite illnesses.

As a human being subject to illness, Ogamisama plays two roles. She takes a typically "exemplary" leadership role . . . by stressing that she has attained absolute salvation and by telling her followers to emulate her. She says, "Come up where I am. How good I feel!" . . . One of the local pilgrims to the headquarters testified that while there she had been scolded by Ogamisama for "using" sickness, for not attending the daily disciplinary meeting. She was told that she was indulging herself. Seventy-nine years old, this informant could not get out of bed because of pain and sickness throughout her body. After learning of Ogamisama's scoldings, through a go-between, she made up her mind to attend the meeting and even participated in yardwork which all pilgrims were assigned (Lebra, 1969, pp. 10–11).

Ogamisama's legitimate religious status within the cult allows new members to give up their religious involvements outside and invest emotionally in their relationship with their leader-deity and her followers.

BELIEFS AND NORMS

The sect's theology is rudimentary. In part this can be attributed to the fact that Ogamisama is alive; most converts have opportunity to attend ceremonies she leads and even talk to her individually on some occasion. Since Ogamisama is multifaceted in her personality, relating critically to one and supportively to the next, there seems to be little need for a complex belief system now. Ogamisama is said to be the daughter of the absolute God of the Universe. Further, both a male and female deity entered Ogamisama's abdomen; she is equivalent to Buddha, or Christ. This millenial quality is counterposed to the spirits that afflict members and give rise to their illnesses or misfortunes. These spirits may emanate from deities, living persons, dead persons or animals. Possession by one such spirit may be

> benevolent, malevolent, or neutral, and thus sickness may be taken as a sign of the disciplinary intent of a fatherly supernatural, as an attack by a hostile spirit often holding a grudge or jealousy, or as a gesture of a dead person's spirit trying to call attention and solicit help from the living person (Lebra, 1969, p. 3).

Although the supernatural system of Tensho is still developing, the norms of group behavior and role expectations are more specific. The good Tensho member attends meetings, fulfills leadership roles on occasion, volunteers evidence of his past demoralization and present state of grace—thanks to Ogamisama. Further, the good member is prepared to overcome his illnesses in order to participate in ceremonies or do work for the sect. Beyond these requirements the expectations of an individual are adjusted to his particular situation. For example, some members are compelled to make a break with family, while others are told to conform to the expectations of the traditional roles.

The Tensho member is an equal: "We *doshi* (comrades) are all equal, regardless of class differences in the outside world" (Lebra, 1967, p. 350). As an equal he participates in the Tensho community. One member described it: "Every Friday evening I feel revitalized, I gain power from that nightly prayer by so many members all at once. If I prayed alone, the *horiki* (power) of the prayer would be much less" (Lebra, 1967, p. 350).

MEETINGS AND ACTIVITIES

Three sorts of meetings are held regularly:

1. A two-hour meeting, which all are required to attend, is held every Friday evening. The meeting is member-led on a rotating basis. The activities include chanting of prayers in a repetitive fashion that induces an altered, trancelike state in many; "spontaneous" statements by participants of the improvements that membership has brought about or of incidents illustrating Ogamisama's magical powers; and a tape-recorded sermon by Ogamisama from headquarters in Japan.

2. Study groups meet weekly also, but attendance is voluntary. Here the atmosphere is less formal, with free discussion among a smaller group. Members inquire of each other's recent experiences and relate these to Tensho beliefs. The interactions are frequently a give-and-take of the following sort:

A1 My son collapsed at school. His teacher was frightened that he might die, but I was not disturbed at all, because I was convinced it was an ordeal. They gave him a close examination at the hospital, with no results. It was indeed evil spirits that caused the trouble.

B1 What a good experience you have had, Mrs. K.! Learned doctors cannot diagnose spiritually caused diseases. They are ignorant. A Japanese doctor would have immediately judged your son "epileptic" wrongly (Lebra, 1967, p. 113).

New initiates are most often introduced to Tensho in these meetings, where there is opportunity for inquiry into problems and for a more personalized response to the newcomer. Leadership in study group meetings is not formalized—the host may take some of the initiative, or the group may look to a particularly well-educated or experienced member for guidance.

3. Once monthly all sect members on each island gather at a public park for go-iambi (consolation day), which is dedicated in gratitude to Ogamisama. This meeting consists of dancing with eyes closed to the singing of one member, and of group chanting of Tensho prayers. The activities continue through most of a Sunday. The ceremonies are interrupted only by a one-hour lunch period, during which members sit in small groups and consume a Spartan meal of rice balls and pickles.

Other activities of the Tensho group include extra study group meetings, informal get-togethers, and marriage and funeral services. When Ogamisama visits, there are many special individual meetings with her, as well as proselytizing public meetings.

In addition to the specific group religious activities, there is social life with other members. Many members report a dramatic, almost magical improvement in financial condition after joining. On the spiritual level Tensho membership creates a sense of "symbolic salvation," which reinvests life with meaning and supplies an evaluative framework for events. Negatives such as acculturative stress, the enduring burden of Japan's defeat, the threat of nuclear conflict are subsumed in apocalyptic visions of a third world war in which 90 percent of the world will be destroyed. At the same time, emphasis is put on salvation during life; a millenial era with Tensho leading the way. All of life's events can now be accounted for by the belief system of the group. For example:

> Recently I have had trouble all the time with my car. It goes out of order. I think this is because some spirit is trying to possess me, but, instead, possesses my car. In other words, my car is keeping me safe from the spirit (Lebra, 1967, p. 362).

This complete cognitive framework enables members to relate to the world in a new way, "in it, but not of it." Specifically, the intensity of member involvement makes possible solutions to some of the acculturative stresses facing members. In some cases this solution takes the form of return to traditional patterns:

> Under Ogamisama's ever watchful eyes, I began to reflect upon myself and recalled all the things I had done to hurt my husband and his parents with my selfish desire to live apart from my in-laws (Lebra, 1967, p. 425).

> Ogamisama states, "Take your choice, which life would you prefer?" There was but one path for me to follow. In August, we moved back with the folks. With my changed frame of mind and the determination to follow Ogamisama's teachings, I no longer hated the house nor minded my mother-in-law's talk of Mioshie. At times, perhaps, I may have tried too hard to please, but since then I have learned to accept my role as the daughter of the house (Lebra, 1967, pp. 426–427).

In other instances the dilemma is resolved the opposite way. With Tensho support, a member makes a complete break with traditional family expectations.

Opportunities for leadership exist within Tensho, especially in the Hawaiian setting. The possibility of identification with Ogamisama contributes to improved work role and even to rising status at work. Similarly, the positive experience of group membership improves individual self-esteem. For example, the positive attitude expected from members toward Tensho may indirectly alleviate their sense of ethnic stigma as Japanese in postwar Hawaii. All these changes together lead to an improved sense of health and potency.

The striking feature of Tensho as a healing community is the central figure and leader, Ogamisama. Her charismatic capacities are considered by members both the healing force and the binding link of the group. Yet she is only occasionally present in Hawaii. Her healing charisma has clearly spread to others and has become embodied in ritual activities, so that healing and worship continue with effectiveness in her absence. Communitas is clearly present, but the bonds of comembership are overshadowed by the charismatic bonds to Ogamisama. The shared dilemmas of acculturation, low social status, and physical maladies all play their part in creating a sense of community. As in the Zar cult, the expectation of permanentness of involvement, especially the intensity of such commitments for the Japanese, adds to the sense of communitas. A sense of obligation for cure or services received adds to this, along with the obligation to the group itself.

Like the Zar member, Tensho's leader shares the history of her own suffering and cure, through mastery of the spirits responsible. Many members progress from the role of initiate to what we would consider a "staff" sort of position in the Tensho organization. The expectations press members toward greater responsibility and toward maintaining the progress they have made. Older members model these expectations for newcomers, both informally and in Socratic training meetings.

As in the Zar cult, rhythmic chanting and dancing are part of the important ceremonies. Such activities seem expectable in the far off Ethiopian plateau country; in the city parks of Honolulu they are more startling. These seem to serve the purpose of inducing an excited, perhaps hypnotic state shared by the whole group. For newcomer or old member, these ritual activities must inevitably take attention away from the aches, pains, and problems of daily life. This shift in attention readies the newcomer for involvement in the behavior expectations and beliefs of the group.

Both Zar and Tensho healing communities are marginal to society. Tensho has flourished in the context of the acculturation process of the Hawaiian Japanese community. Its appeal is primarily healing and religious, but it provides economic aid and adaptive alternatives for some of the casualties of acculturation and social change. Here we see a parallel with the Zar cult, where members could often better their lot in life as a by-product of initiation. In the following chapter we learn of healing groups that are different in this respect. The Zuni Indians have a variety of medicine societies. These play an important part in the sacred life of the Zuni community as a whole, as well as providing specific therapeutic activities.

POSTSCRIPT

Tensho has grown far larger in the years since this study. The movement now claims 326,000 members and is led by Kiyokazu Kitamura, Ogamisama's granddaughter. She is known as Himegamisama (Honorable Princess God) and was selected as successor by her grandmother, who died in 1968. Himegamisama has studied at two American colleges and is now studying in London.

NOTES

1. The descriptions of Tensho (formally "Tensho-kotai-jingn-kyo") in this section are drawn from the doctoral dissertation of Takie Sugiyama Lebra, *An Interpretation of Religious Conversion: A Millennial Movement Among Japanese-Americans in Hawaii*, University of Pittsburgh, 1967.

CHAPTER 12

Zuni Healing Societies: The Clown Fraternity

by Carmen Acosta

A complex network of permanent treatment groups, which meet both the moral exigencies of the belief system and the requirements of social order, exists within a native American culture. The groups are made up of lifelong memberships devoted to the management of chronic behavior disorder. Pathways to treatment and the rationale for diagnosis and assignment of group are discussed below through historical and contemporary case examples.

The concept of community mental health is not peculiar to modern America. It has been an integral part of Zuni Indian social organization since ancient times. Under the traditional Zuni system, deviant behavior, which would in Western society have been isolated in mental institutions or prisons, has been systematically incorporated into the ongoing, daily social arrangements of Zuni society. Furthermore, incorporation of such behavior has been accomplished without show of force or hardship to individuals.

SETTING

The Zuni peublo is located in New Mexico near the

Arizona border. The old pueblo is built of stone and adobe. It consists of subterranean rooms, elevated roofways for drying and conversation, and interior plazas where the sacred dances take place. Modern ranchstyle homes have been constructed in suburban patterns on the periphery of the old pueblo.

In social organization the Zunis resemble the Hopi villages farther to the west, but in language they resemble no one, for no linguistic affiliations have ever been established. The Zunis continue to speak their own language, practice their own religion, and carry on the business of their own tribe. They are quick to point out that theirs is not a tribe but a nation in its own right, composed of approximately 4900 people living in four villages and a central city. They have, at times, been conquered or converted, but always they have maintained their old ways.[1] Zuni social structure is extraordinarily complex, in part because it retains all the elements of the period when the Zuni were a nation of seven tribes, and in part because the most important social level for Zuni is not the independent individual or the family but the social group. Among the small population of the Zuni pueblo there are an amazing variety and number of social organizations.

The complex social organization of Zuni includes the interactions of religious societies and priesthoods, the farming villages, kachina cults, political councils and factions, households, matrilineages, clans and linked clans, occupational organizations such as the sheep, cattle, and water associations, the irrigation ditch organizations, the lumbering and housebuilding interests, veterans' clubs, farmers' classes and lobby groups, PTAs, school and tribal bands and booster clubs, police, construction workers, the governmental offices, and white traders and missionaries.

Marriage arrangements, ceremonies, and problems receive little fanfare and gossip; courtship, marriage, adultery, and divorce are all casual and of little interest outside the matrilineal family. Religious ceremonies, on the other hand, are often public and inevitably arouse general interest. For example, the most important factor in economic success is summer rain. Its arrival is attributed to the diligence, correctness, and power of one or another priesthood. Thus the prayer retreats of different priesthoods take an interest for every Zuni.

Within this complex fabric it is to be expected that institutions for the control of problem behavior would also be complexly organized, and in fact this is the case.

RATIONALE FOR THE TREATMENT OF DEVIANCE

The moral basis of Zuni interpersonal relations may be found in the ancient religious beliefs. Like many non-Western societies, Zuni is still essentially a sacred society. A tribal religion, such as the traditional Zuni "way," corresponds closely with the social organization. This is why respondents can say, when asked what religion they belong to, that they don't belong to any religion, just their own. It also explains why it is easy for Zunis to be Christians for an hour on Sunday morning and still maintain their traditional religious beliefs, since the latter require a way of life while the former require only a particular ritual.

This aspect of Indian religion has been termed "totalizing," since its mode encompasses everything in the Zuni world. There are no large exclusions from the realm of the sacred, as there would be in a secular society. The usual Christian boundaries of good and evil do not adequately describe a world in which every detail, no matter how dirty or how fearful, is viewed with interest—even though the reason for its importance may remain unknown.

Since every little thing was put into this world for some purpose, everything must have a place somewhere in the scheme of things. When applied to human behavior, this premise results in the encouragement of a very wide range of

individual life-styles. It is part of the Zuni "way" to observe
the minute details of human behavior acutely and to be sensitive to, and expressive of, subjective experiences, for all these
details must be important in the Zuni world.

BEHAVIOR PROBLEMS

Nevertheless it is a fact of human social life that some of
the variations of behavior are very hard to live with, and some
are viewed as a clear threat to the continuance of the traditional Zuni way of life.

It is probably inevitable that when so many people live in
a densely populated habitat, the exigencies of daily social life
will cause mental and physical anguish. Individual Zuni
medicine men and women do a thriving business in the pueblo, setting the bruised feelings, choked emotions, and tight
stomachs to rights again with herbal preparations, massage,
prayers, and other techniques. These problems appear to be
transitory and are accepted as cases by private practitioners,
often priests of the medicine societies, who charge fees in
goods or services.

However, sometimes illness worsens, or the treatments
that are successful in acute cases do not rectify the difficulty,
even when repeated over a long period of time. In such
instances of more severe, chronic behavioral disorders, the
family will call in a medicine society to perform a series of
ceremonies on behalf of the sufferer. Arrangements must
then be made for him to be initiated into the same society in
order to preserve the healing secrets of the group and maintain the sufferer's improvement. In this way, many deviant
individuals are treated by integrating them into an appropriate medicine fraternity. There, problem behavior is subjected to patterning as the new member learns and rehearses
the required prayers, rituals, and public performances of this

fraternity. Once he is an initiate, a severely disordered person may be required to spend the major portion of his waking time, for the rest of his life, in programmed activities with his fraternity. This has the effect of relieving the community of the strain of accommodating to unpredictable behavior.

When such persons are taken into a fraternal organization, they remain at the lower levels of performance and competence while the more able members carry out more demanding tasks. Nevertheless it is possible for disordered persons, by virtue of their membership, to carry out sacred duties that preserve Zuni traditions and thus bring blessings on themselves as well as the community. If they wish and are able, they may become priests or medicine men themselves through further lengthy training. In this way deviant behavior is treated according to the Zuni moral requirements, and its place in the divine scheme of things is recognized.

The quote below from a man active in Zuni politics expresses this moral injunction to work with deviants and shape their behaviors to "right ways."

"This is our law. Troubles are measured under our law, not little piece by little piece, but over the long haul as a whole. People who give trouble are measured under our law not little act by little act, but as a whole, over the long haul. The purpose of our courts is to make good members of this community out of any members who get into trouble with our courts.

"It is not the practice of this community to put on any offender at any time the full penalty which the law of this community makes possible. But the power is there to do that when the good of the community makes it necessary. Nineteen times out of 20, the courts of this community are content to make an offender swear on his knees that he will give up bad things and be a right member.

"Our officers know how to go easy sometimes. Our officers also know how to wait. This often helps bring an offender to right ways."

Thus the overriding ethic of inclusion of problem behavior through patient efforts to shape behavior to traditional patterns is expressed by tribal councils. The possible exception to this ethic is witchcraft. Yet in the final analysis, even the witchcraft complex has its place in the "middle ant heap," as the Zunis call themselves.

THE MEDICINE FRATERNITIES

The medicine fraternities are secret organizations, as are all the sacred aspects of this virtually sacred society. There are three major types of religious organizations in Zuni: the *kiva societies* of masked gods; the *kachina priest cults*; and *medicine fraternities*. Descriptions of the fraternity system are available in the writings of the first students of Zuni society, Mathilda Coxe Stevenson (1904) and Frank Hamilton Cushing (1896), who were admitted as sympathetic observers to the less important aspects of the rituals. Their recorded observations have been approved by the Zunis to the extent that their books have been consulted on occasions when details of ritual were called into question.

Thus without violating religious requirements of secrecy, we may sketch the outlines of the fraternity system in order to expose its function as a complex of lifetime treatment groups for deviant behavior. There are 12 Zuni healing societies. Each derives its power from an animal god, usually a beast of prey. These gods are considered the source of disease and death. They also give man medicines and magical powers, which members of healing societies can use to control maladies. Each cult has a special area of disorder; some treat injuries, some infections. If an individual is considered seriously ill, he may be "given" to the society. Then, if he is cured, he will be initiated into the group that saved him. This will make the cure permenent and also secure the secrets he has observed during his own treatment.

INTERRELATIONS OF THE FRATERNITIES

Each of the 12 medicine fraternities carries on a cycle of fasts, retreats, prayers, rituals, and public dance dramas that dovetail into one another and into the other ritual activities of the tribe. A bit of village conversation illustrates the network of patterned interaction that regulates the interrelationships of the various religious bodies and the medicine fraternities:

"Rain priests have to be very peaceful. They can't argue with anyone or hit them or get mad. They can't even kill an insect. They never dance [in the sacred dance drama] or appear in public together.

"There goes A.K. He looks mad as usual, but he's a war priest and he can be as mean as he wants. He can argue and be mean, but the rain priest never speaks up at public meetings. So they [the rain priests] hire A.K. [the war priest] to speak for them. He does their public talking. That's one of his jobs."

The war priest group is privileged to be mean, even to get angry. One of the war priest's duties is to speak the opinion of the rain priests, who are forbidden to show emotions or take part in public affairs.

Each of the medicine fraternities is devoted to one or a group of related patron supernatural figures. These supernaturals are endowed with specialized knowledge that aids in curing, special duties that must be performed on his behalf, and special privileges. The members of the fraternity devoted to that particular supernatural become the privileged stewards of the supernatural's esoteric knowledge and acquire his sacred duties and privileges as well. In the above quote it can be seen that the war priest group is privileged to be mean, even to get angry, and that one of its duties is to speak the opinion of the rain priests, who are forbidden to show emotions or to take part in public affairs.

GODLY PERSONALITIES

The Zuni supernaturals, unlike remote Christian supernaturals, have interesting and distinct stylized personalities. There is, for example, the great and handsome lover, the fool, the rascal, the glutton, the good-natured one, the pretender, the blunderer, the stingy one, the angry man, and the one who is "kindly yet grave, with a look of endless contentment on his face and anger gone forever from his heart."

Each fraternity guards a group of masks and costumes representing its patron supernaturals. An impersonator, through years of apprenticeship, prepares himself to care for the mask and costume, and to wear them on ritual occasions. The supernaturals themselves are said to hover as a breath of life in their individual masks until the times comes around for them to be impersonated. For the period that the mask is being worn, the life breath of the supernatural dominates that of the impersonator, so that he actually is believed to transform himself into the supernatural, with that supernatural's personality.

Every facet of the godly role must be performed with precise accuracy, for to fail would cause the mask to stick to the impersonator's face, and in four days insanity and death would ensue. This is said to have actually occurred, so that no one takes up an impersonation lightly.

RECRUITMENT TO FRATERNITIES

Certain complex kinship ties figure prominently in recruitment to membership in one or more of the medicine fraternities. But after kinship considerations, it is the personality of the patron supernatural that dominates the decision of the family to "give" a relative to the fraternity.

When a behavior problem has been identified and the treatment of a medicine fraternity is thought necessary, the personality characteristics of the individual are matched as congenially as possible with those of a particular patron supernatural. The following description by a Zuni fraternity member of the procedures followed by the member who joins because of a behavior problem, may be taken as the general pattern of recruitment for all the medicine fraternities.

"Coyote is a medicine group. The time they initiate is the time a man is acting silly. Probably some years ago his relatives called them [the Coyote fraternity] for K.E. They take him to the fraternity house. They treat him secret. They have him vomit. Especially when a person goes crazy like a coyote [exhibits seizures similar to epilepsy] they think the yellow stuff inside his stomach makes him like that. He's vomiting and praying. He might have a headache [i.e., his seizures seem to start with a headache]. Finally it might go some way [a seizure might develop].

"They keep them in a secret place. Another fraternity man has to look after him for days. They wash his hair and he's prepared to be initiated.

"They set the date for initiation, maybe a year until you prepare for everything [he has passed into the lowest grade of the fraternity with the command to prepare himself to enter the next higher grade]. He goes home. He has to wait about two or

three years before the time comes. He spends his time getting
food and everything ready [learning the prayers and ritual in
the company with his group]. Then there's initiation. After
initiation they take him back [to his home] and his father's the
one who took care of him when he was sick [the man who
treated him becomes his ceremonial father with the right to
request services and care from his ceremonial son]. He [new
member] takes him [ceremonial father] home and they give him
corn, buckskin, and a blanket. After that he really belongs to
that group. Any time they get together, they call upon him. He
has to join them [he spends a major portion of his time in
programmed fraternity activities]."

Thus we see that decisions to "give" an individual to a
medicine fraternity are made by the matrilineal kin group,
and are dependent in the first place upon whether the relatives of the individual can afford treatment. The costs to the
family include not only the ceremonial gifts of corn, buckskin,
and blanket, but also feasts for the entire fraternity for long
periods of time during the various phases of induction.
The new initiate is inducted into a pseudokinship role in
which a leader of the curing rites becomes his ceremonial
father, and the other members of the fraternity become related as brothers or cousins. Like kinship, these relationships
adhere for life and encompass many aspects of the initiate's
activities outside the fraternity chambers. Frequently the
ceremonial father of the new initiate is already related to the
initiate. Thus the new relationship is doubly irrevocable and
draws the support of the entire kin group.
When a matrilineage decides to give a relative to a curing
fraternity and when the complexities of kinship have been
unraveled, then it is the type of problem behavior or style of
personality of the individual that determines the choice of
medicine fraternity. Further we have seen that the personalities of fraternity members are modeled after that of their
patron supernaturals. Through lengthy learning and daily

patterning, the new initiate can say, "At first they just called me Clown, but thereafter I became Clown."

CLOWNING FRATERNITIES

A cluster of medicine fraternities act as clowns, or delightmakers, for the Zuni community. It is their place to invoke laughter from the spectators of their public performances. Yet "the dancers aren't doing it just for fun," say the people. They are working for the community. The laughter of the assembled crowd so charms the gods that they send their blessings once more to the waiting village. The favors for which the Zunis pray are continual replenishment of vigorous life for the people, the crops, the domestic animals, the game animals, the wild desert plants, the salt, precipitated moisture of all descriptions. In short, these prayers concern all phenomena which make up the beloved world of Zuni. The delight-makers are distinctly curative in their avowed purpose, for vigorous, regenerating life is health indeed.

MYTHS AND RITUALS OF THE CLOWNS

Each fraternity is legitimized by its place in the ancient origin myths and stories of the peregrinatives of the tribe. The sacred dancès act out and celebrate these myths. According to myth, the patron supernatural of the Clowns originated in the following way:

There was once in the first fraternity two men and one woman. They were old and alone. The two children of the Sun said to them, "It is too bad you are all alone. Take the rubbings of your skin. Make of them a little figure. Cover it up and sing over it." They did this and a little boy came out. He was never still. He talked all the time. What he said was all the same to him, he did not care about the effect. The little boy was the first Clown. And today, although none takes offense, a Clown is regardless of all rules. He will say the very opposite he means . . . the name of a deceased person, speak in foreign languages (Stevenson, 1904).

The public performances of the impersonators of First Clown, or the *Newekwe* fraternity, are marked by what has been called "excessive buffoonery." They are essentially scatological rites. The performers are painted in white striped patterns; their hair is knotted to stick out above their ears like whiskbrooms. They emerge onto the dance plaza and begin to perform impromptu pantomimes, utilizing the most serious subjects as objects of their buffoonery.

For example, even though English is taboo within the hearing of a masked dancer, yet the clowns use exaggerated English to mimic the Indian agent talking to Washington on the telephone about his troubles with the Pueblos. Latin is used to recite a Catholic baptism, substituting a huge bowl of urine for holy water; pancakes of the dung of the sacred deer are eaten with gusto, doused with bottles of syrup from the trading post. Only those with great power would dare to tamper with such dangerous behavior.

Another major order of clowning groups is that of the Mudhead Clown, whose antics are modeled after persons with severe mental deficiency. According to myth, when the world was young and the people first emerged from the last underworld in search of a place to build their village, a maiden and her brothers were scouting ahead of the rest of the people. As she rested under a tree, her brothers were tempted by her beauty and, as the Pueblos say, they made a mistake. The result of this incestuous union was the first Mudhead, an absolute idiot. The contemporary dancers, in their grotesque masks made of mud, play like "men with baby minds"; people laugh at their childish antics and everyone's feelings are raised up.

BEHAVIOR PROBLEMS TREATED BY THE CLOWNS

Most members are said to join the Clowns through the necessity of serious illness, for popular opinion is somewhat disgusted by the scatological rites and may shrink from the thought of participating in them. Nevertheless, their numbers have been greatly augmented by the returning veterans of World War II who have sought treatment for behavior problems.

Swaggering about, speaking out on religious subjects, being unmindful of the feelings of others and hard to get along with, speaking foreign languages, using dirty words, talking too loudly, and drinking openly on the streets and in the bars of white towns—all this seems, to the Zuni, to belong under the aegis of the Clown associations.

The most serious problem that the Zunis associate with the Clowns is the Zuni style of alcoholism:

"Ever since the World War ended, things are different, because we were restricted from going into the bars when we were sent to the army. When we returned, we could go into the bars. It was a very queer thing to see each other coming out of bars, white men's bars. Navajo with long hair. Now it don't look strange because all Pueblos drink. At first the woman's shamed to come. Just a few younger boys. But finally some people even they have their own religious leaders, dance leaders they come into bars. Same with woman. They make a mistake they won't even remember. When I got a lot of worries, get to thinking, I get to drinking, but afterward when I sober up, I wonder how many people's feelings I have hurt."

There are two dangers connected with alcoholism, which mark it as a problem behavior in traditional Zuni thinking. One is that, while to drink enhances one's sense of autonomy ("no one can stop me"), there is the danger of going too far. Being drunk does not excuse one from the penalty for direct aggression, not even aggression which takes the form of hurting people's feelings:

"Here's the thing. Lotta times they used to call upon the

medicine man because this person has done something wrong while intoxicated and someone has placed a curse on him."

Thus transitory emotional upset may be caused by one's own drunken behavior. If this occurs, a medicine man can probably treat the condition effectively. The second danger is far more serious, however. One may get to liking alcohol so much that he becomes careless of tradition; this is a crime against the commonweal.

"Her husband died. He died of drinking. He was drunk while dancing. Silly thing [extremely careless behavior] to see a dancer do a thing like that. The night dancing in the winter time, when he got home about 1 A.M. her father told him to stay out, so he got mad and they started to fight in front of the house. We all watched. Her father probably hurt him [introduced a slow acting poison] in that fight. A week later he died. I guess he was asking for something like that. Then the people believed the gods gave him some kind of punishment."

Women associated with the clowns are reported to drink excessively and to be indiscreet:

"The Pueblos live a different life because of drinking. They dislike each other. They used to be peaceful. We have big problem because of drinking. They come together on Monday and Wednesday night to join Mexican and American dances; they start drinking, forget their husbands and children and run all around and dance. Most all Pueblos are married women come to town. Folks try their best to do something, but they have lost their power."

In order to save a person from social exclusion or even death, his relatives might act: "They gave him to the Clowns, thinking they could cure him of his drinking."
Associated with the Mudhead dance group are several severely retarded individuals. Their personal uncleanliness,

uncontrolled laughter, and delayed responses fit in well with the required public performances. They are considered to do a good job. In return for their efforts in the public ceremonies, the performers receive equal shares of the presents that the grateful villagers shower upon them. The presents consist of groceries and blankets, which help meet the cost of their room and board. In addition to their ceremonial duties, severely retarded individuals are called upon to participate with their group in hoeing parties, irrigating parties, and grinding bees; they chop wood, carry water, run errands, do bead work, and add whatever they can to the work of their households. No instance was encountered of a kin group voluntarily surrendering even the most severely retarded individual for care in a government institution. One retarded man was recently institutionalized, but the commitment was made at the request of a white trader's wife, and on the Indians' side there were many regrets.

In the following narrative a man who was a talented musician invoked an analogy with the second guise of the patron supernatural of the Clowns, that of Sun musician or the Man with the Flute. The incidental presence of an epileptic condition was considered fortuitous in view of the requirements of the clowning role:

"One time he was playing Clown. Had an epileptic fit. They take him inside the house. They initiate him because of different kind of illness [epilepsy]. He had fit every so often, around every month. Sometimes when they do funny things people laugh. They make people happy and enjoy them. The Clowns make people laugh in order to help feelings. When I have trouble with sadness, I see funny things; I laugh and happy things will change. Other people didn't know. Those who knew him and his fits, they were scared."

While the epileptic seizures were frightening, this man's family felt they were doing their best to help him by giving him to the Clowns.

SUMMARY

The clowning fraternities are a complex of groups whose activities are legitimized by ancient Zuni myth and ritual. The supernatural figures associated with the fraternities provide behavioral models for the characters of the sacred dance drama, as well as for the recruitment of likely members. The resulting groups are characterized by the personality of the patron supernaturals: Mudheads (idiots); Man with a Flute (musicians and epilepsy); Newekwe (veterans and alcoholism).

The behavioral clues that are considered diagnostic in determining treatment strategy are such matters as dirty talk, loud talk, drinking openly on the streets of Gallup, excessive buffoonery, and other actions considered to be problems in the native Zuni system. The diagnostic categories overlap but do not coincide with the categories of modern psychiatry and cannot be properly understood as a translation of modern Western medicine.

Furthermore, the purpose of the associations is not to stop the problem behavior, but rather to control it in such a way that it can be placed in its proper niche for the good of the people. Individuals who join the fraternities may continue to exhibit problem behavior, but under the aegis of the fraternity such behavior is controlled and turned to the good of the community in public performances and secret rituals. Thus individuals whom Western medicine might classify as severely retarded, alcoholic, or epileptic find a useful role within the complex social organization of traditional Zuni.

POSTSCRIPT (by Richard Almond)

Perhaps the most impressive aspect of Zuni medicine societies and their relation to individual behavior patterns is the positiveness of the processes that go on. Unlike our culture, which sees the patient entering the hospital as *mal*functioning and *mal*adjusted, problem behaviors in Zuni have a variety of potential benefits. For the sufferer there is, first, relief for his problem and reassurance from others about it. Second, the sufferer becomes a member of a new group; he is trained as a priest in the appropriate medicine society. While this may be an expense for him and his family, it is a valued step in the Zuni framework. In other words, the end result of "patienthood" for the Zuni is an expansion of the sense of self. For a person in a culture that emphasizes group involvement, this is an especially important addition to the self-concept and undoubtedly offsets negative feelings about the self that may contribute to problem behavior. Just as in the therapeutic community, such change occurs first behavior-ally, then attitudinally: "At first they just called me Clown, but then I really became Clown." That is, first one is given to a fraternity, initiated, involved in rites; then one begins to feel the impact on one's sense of self and to experience member-ship as an internal event.

As in the Zar cult or Tensho sect, membership can lead to "advancement" that goes beyond overcoming the initial problems. Not only does membership provide outlet for his behavior, but there are opportunities for advancement. Once a member, a Zuni joins each ceremony of the society and may become an ever more proficient member. If he wishes, he may, after much training, become a medicine priest who knows many prayers, remedies, and the sleight-of-hand tricks for removing illness from patients. Healing is one area where ambitiousness and individuality are tolerated by the Zuni. By virtue of his social utility, the medicine priest can express his ambition, but at the price of many years of training from the experts. Even then, the power of this healing is attributed to the group, not to his individual skill or expertise. Along with these advantages of membership in a medicine society goes an acceptance of the behavior involved. The sufferer need not change completely; he is simply aided in bringing his behavior into a socially approved channel.

Zuni society benefits also from the process of handling problem behavior. First, there is reassurance that the behavior will not get out of hand. Second, there is vicarious satisfaction: The aggression that is expressed by members of war and hunting fraternities gives vent to such feelings among others. Third, one is reassured tᵗ at one's own quirks or impulses will not lead to exclusion. Corresponding with these benefits for individual and society is the centrality and complexity of Zuni healing groups. Overall, the culture seems to expend much time, energy, and resources on dealing with problem behaviors. A Zuni would not see it this way, since to him the activities of multiple medicine societies are integral to the Zuni "way."

NOTES

1. Military and other contact by Americans with Zuni has been minimal. The Zuni have continued to use any means possible to maintain the continuity of their traditions. As the first ethnographer, Frank Hamilton Cushing, wrote about them in the year 1880: "The Zuni faith, as revealed in this sketch of more than 350 years of Spanish intercourse, is as a drop of oil in water, surrounded and touched at every point, yet in no place penetrated or changed inwardly by the blood of alien belief that descended upon it. . . . He adjusts other beliefs and opinions to his own, but never his own beliefs and opinions to others; and even his usages are almost never changed in spirit, however much so in externals" (Cushing, 1896, p. 339). Cushing's extensive data on Zuni were acquired by becoming a Zuni himself for two years, and publication of their ceremonies has left them increasingly secretive about their religious activity. This has limited our access to healing ceremonies, which in Zuni are religious occasions as well. It determines the omission here of any specific descriptions of chants or prayers, which, by being reproduced, would lose their strength in Zuni practice.

CHAPTER 13

Review

The contention that healing community is a general phenomenon is supported by the above descriptions of three such communities found in non-Western cultures.[1] We can review similarities and differences among these groups through reference to the therapeutic community processes delineated in Part I.

GROUP PROCESSES

The size of these groups varies between tens and hundreds of members. Functional units, most especially specific ceremonies, include a more limited range of 12 to 50 individuals. When the overall movement is larger, there is a tendency to have important ceremonial activities performed by subgroups, whose size is in this range. The Tompkins I therapeutic community numbered 20-30 patients with about 20 staff. Large ward meetings involved about 35 persons. The parallel to hospitals where moral treatment was practiced is also striking: The patient population of these institutions was usually far below 100. And, of course, moral treatment as a form of therapy did not survive transplantation to institutions housing hundreds or thousands of inmates.

A group of 12 to 50 individuals is small enough to make possible face-to-face contact between all members but large enough to give members a feeling of security in the group's viability. Such a group size also is large enough to be a "small society," a potentially or actually autonomous unit within whose boundaries one may feel protected from the many otherwise inescapable expectations of one's usual social situation. This may, in fact, represent the size range for achieving a sense of communitas.

Composition is interesting in these healing communities: Generally, the membership is a mix of more and less disturbed persons. This follows from the open-endedness of membership, which requires participation of recovered members as well as acutely disturbed ones. In addition, the severity of problems at entry seems quite varied. There appears to be a diversity of degrees and types of psychopathology. In the Zar cult we find not only initiates whose Zar spirits have given them symptoms we would associate with depression, catatonia, or hysteria, but also those who have had their Zars transmitted from mother to daughter with economic gain—a relatively transparent motivation. Other members have had physical symptoms. In Tensho there is a similar mix of spiritual, psychic, or physical suffering among members. The mix of varieties of disorder and degrees of severity provides a nice complementarity within the group. That is, there will be some members similarly afflicted, but many not; some recent initiates, some old-timers. The latter help maintain continuity through their familiarity with group norms and by modeling role expectations.

Entry into a group is a significant event, usually experienced with both ambivalence and a sense of necessity. Although there may be no immediate sense of inner change, the sufferer, his family, and members of the healing community view passage over the group threshold as special and significant. One form this transition takes is a special ceremony focused on the new member—as in the Zar cult or Zuni fraternity. The transition to membership is a significant event, especially when we consider that it is usually a crisis, an emergency, or failure of other treatments that has led to this step. Despite his desperation, the sufferer must often wait for initiation and is not greeted with open arms. The healing ceremony may have to wait until expensive or complex arrangements are made, or until it fits in with the routine of the group. At the same time, the permanence of commitment expected in most of these groups further heightens the significance of joining. In most of these groups, the newcomer has some idea of the beliefs of the community; in the case of the Zar and the Zuni, such beliefs are part of the wider culture. Experiencing the beliefs as actual norms within the group, however, is a different and powerful experience. Because the group and membership are so vivid, communitas and communitas norms are less openly emphasized than in the therapeutic community, where it must constantly be made clear that "this is *more* than a psychiatric ward." Yet communitas is present in each of these groups.

In Part I we distinguished norms that reflected the presence of communitas: involvement, group loyalty, faith in the group. These are all to be found in the examples of Part II. Group loyalty is often valued over strong kinship ties that are usually dominant. Other norms we've designated as particular to a given group; in the case of Tompkins I, these were the norms guiding the open, confronting style of therapeutic interaction. Such norms exist for each group discussed in Part II and are markedly different for each. One theme recurs despite the exotic quality of many of these specific norms, that is, a valuation of some sort of exposure or self-disclosure. At times—in Zuni or Zar, for example—this is done symbolically during the acknowledgment of spirit possession. In Tensho there is pressure for direct confession and self-criticism. Thus some sort of confession activity may be a universal, perhaps even another communitas norm.[2]

Adoption of the role of group member begins almost

immediately with initiation. During the initial ceremony, other members model proper behavior, and/or the leader may guide the newcomer specifically in some sort of individualized interaction. This process involves a coming to terms with the illness or with the spirit blamed for the malady. The afflicting Zar spirit is induced to enter the sufferer's body completely, rather than ride on his shoulder. These changes occur through an interaction process involving the initiate, the leader, and members of the group, and are facilitated by the intensity of the initiation ceremony. The goal of this process is twofold: the beginning of mastery over affliction, and commitment to the healing community. The role behavior of the new member is modeled on that of more experienced members, including the leader. This patterning of behavior is facilitated by the newcomer's knowledge that his condition is shared by other members in some way: All Zar members have Zar spirits; all Tensho members have some trouble or illness.

The role of member in a healing community is such that within the group there is no limit imposed on advancement or on identification with more experienced members: The Zar doctor is herself possessed by a spirit but has gained control over it. The new member may thus aspire to the same. The real course of an individual member is varied in possibilities. Some members may accept the benefits of initial improvement and remain simply loyal members; others may make use of the possibilities of advancement to leadership positions or may become involved in the economic activities of the group. The benefits of membership depend on the needs of the members: Mentally retarded members of a Zuni Clown fraternity are unlikely to become leaders of the group. Some members with vague psychic disorders may achieve true remission of symptoms. Others with chronic physical disability may improve or simply accept their illness with a new attitude that enables them to overcome its burdensomeness.

The attitude of the healing community towards the "symptoms" that led to initiation varies. In the therapeutic community there is strong pressure for patients to act "normally" and resume functioning in a way that will enable return home. This expectation is found to a high degree in Tensho, where recurrence of original problems is a source of guilty embarrassment, and to a lesser extent in the Zar cult. The Zuni seem to make the greatest allowance for recurrence or continuation of difficulties; this seems to reflect their patient cultural attitude toward deviance and the chronicity of some of the disorders the Zuni healing societies deal with.

The degree of charismatic focus on a single leader varies from one group to another, but charismatic interactions are universal. Several patterns of leadership emerge in our examples. In Tensho the leader is a deity herself (actually a trinity!). Much of the sect's activity revolves about Ogamisama. The sparsity of ritual and the simplicity of Tensho theology are correlates of her availability as a colorful, charismatic, personal leader. With this leadership style a great deal of each member's critical experience revolves about Ogamisama and her attentions. Her instructions, evaluations, and predictions are taken as sacred—they go unchallenged. The leader of the Zar cult is also charismatic, but she is not the group's first leader; thus the association of the person of the leader and the charismatic role is not as complete as with Tensho. The leader is preeminent not as a deity but simply as the best communicator with Zar spirits, her own and those of others.

Individual charismatic leaders do not emerge in the Zuni societies. In these healing communities there is a progression—through extensive training—first to a general priestly rank and then to more specialized therapeutic skills that can be used outside the group. Thus the degree of charismatic focus on individuals is a function of the wider culture. For example, Ogamisama keeps her distance from Tensho members except for brief, intense interactions. Her followers view her as a deity and accept her commands accordingly. These responses play on the Japanese childhood training for worship of a distant, deified emperor. Similarly, the effectiveness and charisma of the Zar group leader plays on an important personal quality admired in the Amharic culture: the ability to negotiate cleverly, even with guile. Doing this in the service of the sufferer wins his awe and allegiance.

But in each case, no matter how intense the individual charisma of the leader, the member and the newcomer are encouraged to be more than themselves. "Come up here like me!" says Ogamisama, herself an ex-sufferer.

INDIVIDUAL PROCESSES

Just as with the hospital therapeutic community, becoming a member of these non-Western groups begins before actual entry. Frequently there is a similar pattern of failure of other measures for dealing with the problem, so that joining the healing community is an act of last resort. Initiation is preceded by some sort of "diagnostic" process. The outcome is to recommend initiation to the group. The group's expectations of permanent involvement, financial payment, and the rigors of initiation must create strong expectations in the sufferer and his kin. In this way at least three of Frank's four healing factors are present by the time of initiation: definition of the ailment as treatable; social agreement on the appropriateness of treatment; faith by the group in its technique. These, along with the evolving process of becoming a member, support the fourth factor: the faith of the sufferer himself.

Just as in the therapeutic community, the first stage of initiation has the common goal of engaging the attention of the sufferer. In the non-Western groups, entry is an initiation, a *rite de passage* to a new social role. In the therapeutic community, the most striking quality of entry is the rejection of transition into the traditional role of mental patient. The ceremonies and initiation rites of the non-Western groups use a variety of powerful techniques to alter consciousness and make the newcomer amenable to the expectations of the group. Tensho uses rhythmic chanting and dancing; Zar uses intoxicants and a whirling dance; Zuni initiation includes dancing, prayers, emetics. The impact of these activities is enhanced in most cases by the involvement of other group members in modeling and reinforcing the newcomer's part in the ceremony. The subjective impact of the ceremony, over-all, is a hypnotic one. It induces a state of mind in which the initiate is likely to be receptive to the cues that are given for his behavior. He is likely to "let go" of suppressed feelings in cathartic outbursts that are acceptably translated into group-approved patterns (e.g., the orgasmic *gurri* dance of the Zar spirit).

These ceremonies combine, in one or a series of intense experiences, both behavior modification and role paralleling. In part this seems to be a function of the limits on caretaking by the group: In Zar and Tensho the sufferer returns to his kin after the initiation, so that there is more pressure for a major conversion experience during the ceremony. In Zuni, where the healing society takes over much of the day-to-day respon-sibility for the sufferer, the process of entry is extended over a long period of training for initiation. From the limited in-formation we have, it appears—as with therapeutic community—that behavior change comes first, followed by learning the norms of the group and accepting membership on a subjective level: "At first they just called me Clown; then I really became Clown." In groups with charismatic leaders, the internal experience of becoming attached to the group is often focused on a first interaction with the leader, as we saw with Tensho. The quality of this interaction usually carries with it some feeling of hopeful self-betterment. Where mem-bership implies priestly status, as for the Zuni, this is implicit. " . . . then I really became Clown" assumes that being a Clown is valuable for self and others.

Role paralleling is important for the initiate and is in turn supported by the possibility of progressing to more responsible, powerful positions. Rank in healing community is a function of experience, charisma, and degree of attaining goals valued by the group. We find that the usual bases of stratification of the wider culture—wealth, caste or class status, gender—do not apply. The sources of status within the healing group are intimately related to the group's major concerns of healing, doctrinal purity, and performance of important group activities. Rank is also a function of healing charisma, which in turn is a function of experience, training, and personal style. Progressing within the organization reinforces involvement and belief, and thus heightens the effect of the groups's expectations and responses—the behavior modification process. After sufficient time, this process is internalized so that the external reinforcements serve more to remind than to induce change.

GENERAL COMMENTS ON NON-WESTERN HEALING COMMUNITIES

First, we can note a variety of patterns of relationship between the healing community and its host society. Where the group is marginal to the social mainstream, it often seems to be filling a social vacuum—providing outlet for oppressed sexes or classes, aiding individuals caught in the stress of acculturation, or providing healing for a problem that a society is neglecting. Where the healing group is more central, three characteristics are found: (1) The wider culture has more of a communal, group-oriented quality (the Zuni); (2) the group has important religious functions as well as healing functions; and (3) the group provides social control and management of difficult behavior.

Whether socially marginal or central, important qualities of the group's norms and psychological style mimic those of the wider culture. Despite this, the boundary between the healing community and the surrounding society is usually distinct. It is as though the fluidity within the group were threatening to society, and the structures of society threatened the group's communitas. This distinct boundary makes it possible for the healing community to act out certain impulses or patterns vicariously for the society (e.g., the scatological behavior of the Clown Fraternity), and for the group to be a place where socially questionable or awkward transitions are made (e.g., divorce by an Amharic woman).

A second observation is that the non-Western groups seem more oriented to chronicity than is the therapeutic community. Membership is open-ended, and the problems of recurrence or lack of behavior change are built into the group's ways. Actual day-to-day involvement tends to be less than full time, so that there is opportunity for long-range reworking of the individual's social roles, both at home and in the group. With the Zuni we see an added level of sophistication in this respect: a variety of groups characterized by specific behavior patterns shared by the members and channeled into ritual observances. The Zuni illustrate, in fact, a highly complex community mental health program within a small population, one apparently capable of handling many forms of deviant behavior without hospitalization or other kinds of total extrusion. In our own mental health centers and programs, we are just beginning to evolve such a variety of programs and specificities of groups for different people with different behaviors and life histories. Part III will illustrate how, in our own culture, healing communities tend to emerge spontaneously to meet needs that are not being met through formal, professional, or government-sponsored programs.

PART III

Non-Establishment Healing Communities in the United States

In Part III we return to the United States and the culture of twentieth-century America. Instead of the therapeutic community in a mental hospital or healing societies in other cultures, the subjects of study are examples of a more diffuse phenomenon, sometimes referred to as the "encounter movement" or the "human potential movement." The cross-cultural excursion of Part II makes it clear that therapeutic community *as a human social phenomenon* can take many forms. It is thus logical to look at our own society for examples of healing community outside defined mental health settings. Actually, non-Establishment healing communities in this country predate the encounter group: Alcoholics Anonymous is the best known. Part III describes recently emerged examples: first, the encounter group as a general phenomenon, a "search for communitas" in a highly technologic, secular society; and, second, two specific healing communities. One of these is Synanon, a spontaneously developed self-help ·community of and for ex-heroin-users; the other is the Psychodrama Workshop, a largely nonprofessional group who have provided an eclectic encounter experience in Palo Alto, California, over the past five years.

224

The subject matter of Part III holds a great deal of contemporary interest for us. Here we are describing groups that have developed in our own culture, in response to the social conditions of our time. The encounter group in particular is a rapidly burgeoning phenomenon that has come to involve millions of participants.

Such popularity and rapid spread imply an unmet need. We found that this was the case for each of the healing communities in Part II. Thus, in discussing the encounter group, we will begin with an analysis of the needs to which these groups seem to be responding. The thesis will be that encounter groups, rather than being radical or revolutionary, actually respond to long-standing needs that have not been met in an era of rapid change. Encounter has been referred to as "therapy for normals." We will be interested in how encounter groups may be "healing communities for normals." The groups summarized in Chapter 14 are time-limited; their existence as social units ends after a day, a week, or several weeks. They will thus be temporary healing communities at most. Chapters 15 and 16 describe two groups that have evolved into more lasting collectivities and that bear greater resemblance to the healing communities described in Parts I and II.

NOTES

1. Groups in other cultures show striking resemblances to one or another of these three. For example, the Orisa cults among the Yoruba population of Nigeria are similar to the Zuni healing societies in many ways. When other remedies have failed to cure the troubling behavior of a disturbed tribesman, he is initiated into the cult of the Orisa, or spirit, he has offended. This initiation makes the sufferer a member of a religious group responsible for performance of annual ceremonies important to the entire community. He is cared for by members of the cult while his behavior is still difficult. Membership in an Orisa cult is lifelong; the sufferer and his family, who pay a sizeable initiation fee, know this. All can take comfort in the fact that although cult initiation is a major step, it means care of the sufferer is

taken over by a group in an open-ended way. He is likely to improve eventually, if not during the three-week initiation period, and in any case becomes a member of an important religious group (Prince). Among the Northeast American Iroquois nation in the seventeenth and eighteenth centuries, there existed a similar pattern of multiple medicine societies with both therapeutic and religious functions (Wallace, 1959).

2. Confession and self-criticism are widespread accompaniments of group involvement: The Chinese emphasis on group discussion of political issues includes considerable doses of public self-scrutiny, while the Catholic Church has long used confession.

CHAPTER 14

Encounter Groups: Searching for Healing Community

Critiques and analyses of modern society have been numerous in recent years. Some of these have followed the Marxist tradition of identifying economic patterns and class structure as central variables. More and more often, however, social and psychological factors have been brought into question (see, for example, Keniston, 1960). This shift has coincided with awareness of the increasing dominance of technological considerations in modern life and with the corresponding realization that both the problems and solutions may lie outside the technological realm. The evolution of industrial society has progressed neither to totally exploitative capitalism nor to a proletarian revolution. Instead, modern life has insidiously become dominated by technological decisions and styles, while material satisfactions have become widely, though not equally or universally, distributed (Roszak, 1969). In the face of this seemingly peaceful and gradual evolution, dissatisfactions seem to grow rather than diminish. When a generation unencumbered by the economic, military, and nuclear war anxieties of the thirties, forties, and fifties came of age, it began challenging many basic assumptions of a seemingly secure society.

Much of the political, military, and economic critique in these challenges is not directly relevant. It is the psychological and social questions raised during the past decade that interest us here. These challenges have been reflected in a variety of radical analyses, for example, in feminist literature, which has questioned psychological, familial, and social role assumptions with vigor and incisiveness. The most vivid challenges have taken the form, however, of radical *action*. Examples of such action include three major movements of the late 1960s: First is the "hip culture" with new ways of dressing, behaving, living, and eating, and its institutions of rock concerts, crash pads, rural communes, and generally redefined patterns of self, family, and relatedness. The second movement is that of radical politics, which has often made a direct connection between dehumanizing institutions at home and useless slaughter in imperialistic ventures abroad.

The third new development, the encounter movement, has cut across the hippie counterculture and radical political movements and included millions of "straight," middle- and upper-income Americans. These groups have sought change at the level of personality and relatedness.

Philip Slater has suggested three common themes in the discontent that these developments reflect:

1. The desire for *community*—the wish to live in trust and fraternal cooperation with one's fellows in a total and visible collective entity.
2. The desire for *engagement*—the wish to come directly to grips with social and interpersonal problems and to confront on equal terms an environment which is not composed of ego-extensions.
3. The desire for *dependence*—the wish to share responsibility for the control of one's impulses and the direction of one's life (Slater, 1970, p. 5).

What makes Slater's analysis profound and useful is that he goes on to elaborate the ways in which attempts to meet these desires are often translated into actions that aggravate rather than resolve the discontent. For example, look at what happens in the area most obviously relevant to our theme —community. The modern American experiences considerable loneliness and isolation. He yearns for acceptance, involvement. As he seeks a solution, he deals with his dilemma in the terms of American culture: He flees "conformity," which he associates with a loss of himself in the group, and strives to make contact with others by espousing the American pattern of individualism, which his rearing and his society tell him over and over will lead to recognition and involvement. But, in practice, individualism translates to career, competition, mobility, and independence from extended family obligations. The rewards of these behaviors are limited and highly symbolic—rank, power, and material goods. Instead of involvement and contact, he may have the admiration of his superiors, the envy of his peers, and the respect of his subordinates. Fearing his isolation even more, the individual then settles for imitation—he espouses the culturally dictated patterns of behavior and interaction that reassure him he is like everyone else, even if he is not liked by everyone else. Thus, where he fled *conformity*, he now espouses patterns of life that reflect uniformity—the mass produced, nationally advertised combinations of suburban home, automobile, hobbies, and social life. The net result is that he has the appearance of involvement without the experience of real contact and community. Compared to his nineteenth-century ancestor, he is richer, more socially and geographically mobile, better able to choose from a variety of external experiences in his leisure. But he lacks the inner experience of meaning, interconnectedness, and stable social position of his more limited predecessor.

Many of these choices and patterns are felt as beyond

individual control. Throughout the individual's life, social reinforcements push him in directions determined by technology and large bureaucracies. It is the misfit or the maverick who deviates from the norm. Psychologically, most environments reinforce a public personality that is rational, detached, undemanding, and superficially friendly. Other sorts of behaviors and impulses, such as idealism, intense feelings of love and hate, spontaneity, whimsy and fantasy, are consigned to a private sphere of experience and not supported by the responses of others in the ordinary social round. In principle, the family is the place where many of these experiences are to be had. In reality, the high level of interdependence and intimacy of the nuclear family limit or deny the possibility of expressing these needs and impulses at home (Keniston, 1960).

What has happened, in fact, is that modern man has not "caught up" psychologically with the radical changes that have followed from a technologically dominated society (Toffler, 1970).[1] The degree of impact of this technological revolution on the individual is often unrecognized. Socially, we have lost "community" in several senses. First, the literal community of village, small town, or neighborhood has been replaced by impersonal, transient living situations—be they suburb, ghetto, high-rise, or even old residential neighborhood. Second, religious and fraternal organizations have become discredited by the attrition of values and the mobility of their memberships. The small business, which had a rich social life, has given way to the larger, more "efficient," and emotionally colder corporation. And as every social commentator reminds us, the extended family has been broken up as a functional unit. Each of these changes has been welcomed as liberation from coercive, limiting, traditional patterns. But this liberation has not been accompanied by new patterns and institutions to replace the psychological and social needs that were being met by the older forms of community.

Specifically, what has been lost or is missing in the present array of social patterns and psychological styles? Socially, we lack varieties of opportunity. The extended family, as well as the neighborhood, provided contacts with persons at a variety of social distances and age levels. Opportunities for finding "surrogate" parents, sibs, or children are diminished. These relationships provide alternative sources of love, support, modeling, and guidance. The loss of these opportunities gives rise to the desires for dependence and engagement referred to by Slater. In addition, the sense of coherence of the community is gone; the vast majority of the population lives in large cities or suburbs where migration is frequent. Psychologically, we lack opportunities for the expression of the "inner" self, especially feelings of intense anger, sadness, joy, or transcendence. To give way to such feelings would risk career, marriage, social status, or reputation.

The emergence of encounter groups from obscurity to widespread popularity in the past 15 years, is one response to these changes, needs, yearnings, and impulses. To refer to an encounter "movement" is misleading. There is no unifying style, organization, leader, or goal. There is, rather, the widespread vacuum of need that one or another sort of group springs up to fill. Certain features of encounter groups are almost universal, however. The emotional atmosphere of meetings is usually intense; interpersonal contact is reinforced, as is the expression of strong feelings. The groups generally range in size from six to 30 persons, allowing face-to-face contact between all members. The groups generally strive for openness, honesty, confrontation, and self-disclosure. As in the therapeutic community, these norms are seen as a way to achieve the general goal of change in one or another area: behavior, attitude, values, or life-style.

BACKGROUND AND DEVELOPMENT

The most common historical starting point for the human

potential movement is a 1946 conference on race relations organized by Kurt Lewin and his associates for the Connecticut Fair Employment Practices Commission. At this conference, small, informal discussion groups were observed and their interactions recorded by the staff. The observations were discussed during evening staff sessions, to which conference members were admitted. It quickly became clear that those attending the conference learned most in these "feedback" discussions. The conference staff, already interested in the small group as a learning situation, were impressed by the powerful educational tools this experience revealed. They went on to develop what became known as the "T (training) -group" as a basic unit for exposing people to group phenomena and increasing their understanding of others and themselves in a group setting. A common format was for people to attend a conference in which they spent many hours a day with the same T-group, over a one- or two-week period. The National Training Laboratory (NTL) was organized to offer such conferences widely. The approach was educational, and the emphasis on learning of leadership and interpersonal skills. Participants in T-groups were generally top- and middle-echelon administrators from the fields of industry, the military, education, or religion, sent to learn these skills in order to increase their individual effectiveness in the organization. A similar program of group dynamics conferences has been developed at the Tavistock Institute in London by A. K. Rice and his associates, using a different theoretical orientation. The "small group," however, continues to play a central role in the learning of group dynamics using the Tavistock approach. In general, participants in these groups found themselves becoming more open personally and with each other, and more expressive of feelings. The conference frequently felt like a small community with a sense of equality that often included the "staff."

In the early 1960s the T-group crossed paths with several therapeutic innovations—and the encounter group, in a variety of forms, emerged. Although the focus of these new groups was much less on group dynamics and much more on personal change, the presence of others engaged in a shared endeavor seemed to reinforce what was happening. George Bach and George Stoller are best known for developing "marathon" group meetings 12, 24, or 48 hours long. In these groups few breaks are permitted; sleep deprivation, along with the strain of constant, intense interaction, is felt to weaken defenses and heighten opportunities for change. The marathon format, itself an elaboration of the T-group conference situation, has been used by a variety of group leaders with different techniques. Bernard Gunther and William Schutz are well known for developing and publicizing structured group techniques designed to promote interaction, heighten affect, and broaden awareness. If the human potential movement has any central figure, it would be the late Fritz Perls, who developed both a new technique for group work—the "hot seat"—and a new therapeutic philosophy—Gestalt. Perls' approach is more an attitude than a specific technique, however, and his many followers have developed a variety of differing styles. Eric Berne developed Transactional Analysis which emphasizes identification of repeating interaction patterns. Through identifying these in group settings, individuals can examine and change their behavior. Synanon and the Synanon "game" (group meeting) emphasize a style of aggressive emotional attack on members, in rotation (see Chapter 15). A great variety of approaches stress nonverbal techniques. This may be done through movement, touching, fighting, swimming, nudity, massage, or exercise.

This wide variety of formats and techniques tends to obscure the commonalities among different encounter groups. These will be familiar to us, for they are again patterns of communitas and healing charisma. The presence of communitas is suggested by the group qualities Carl Rogers describes as common to most encounter groups: "climate of safety," "immediate feeling reactions of each member toward others...tend to be expressed," "mutual trust develops," "possibility of change," "individuals can hear each other . . . learn from each other. . . ." Such a group atmosphere is developed rapidly—over the course of a weekend, for example. Rogers and others emphasize the role of the leader in reducing defensiveness, and modeling an attitude of warmth and concern for every member, regardless of the feelings of the moment. "Such I-thou relationships (to use Buber's term again) occur with some frequency in these group sessions and nearly always bring a moistness to the eyes of the participants" (Rogers, 1970, p. 34). Turner uses the same I-thou concept to characterize relatedness in communitas situations.

Rogers' style is low-key but none the less charismatic, judging by the reactions of group members he cites. Many other encounter leaders are more flamboyant and directive. In either case, healing charisma plays an extremely important role in the group. The norms must be taught anew to each group, with the leader as the primary or sole source of specific healing norms as well as the facilitator of communitas norms. In some groups—Gestalt therapy groups are a good example—the leader interacts with participants largely in a one-to-one process with the rest of the group as sort of Greek chorus. Obviously, in these groups the charisma of the leader is critical. In my observation, healing charisma is different from technical competence with a particular approach. The capacity to affect individuals and engender an elevated spirit in the group as a whole is dependent on healing charisma and its transmission to the members. As Rogers describes this: "So, in situations in which a member is showing behavior which is clearly pathological, I rely on the wisdom of the group more than on my own, and am often deeply astonished at the therapeutic ability of the members" (Rogers, 1970, p. 58).

Even over the course of a single marathon weekend,

group members learn the norms: how to be group members in the way that is expected. They learn a role, even when the role is defined in terms of expressing feelings directly, as they happen. The full group processes of healing community usually can only get started in an encounter group. Similarly, the individual processes of encounter emphasize the saturation of attention and the modification of behavior through intensity, duration, and specific techniques. Role paralleling is limited, especially when the time duration is brief and the leadership style directive and dyadic.

The encounter group as a one-time experience provides a brief, intense immersion in an *ad hoc* healing community. If the participant accepts the techniques and beliefs of the leader and group, he usually develops feelings of closeness to others and becomes more aware of himself and his feelings. During the encounter experience, he often reveals more of his inner psychological life than he does to friends, work associates, or even his spouse. Strong reactions and catharsis are frequently part of the groups' norms and are approved despite their unacceptibility in conventional outside settings. Many participants experience great relief and elation—"peak" experiences—during and after catharsis. Such experiences, together with the closeness engendered by the atmosphere of openness and support of most groups, make many group experiences memorable regardless of the duration of changes.

Eventually—whether after the 24-hour marathon, weekend conference, two-week T-group, or three months of weekly meetings—the group ends. The "community" vanishes; the members return to their homes, jobs, families. The well-known problems of "reentry" and "casualties" suggest the limits of encounter groups. The participant goes back to an environment where the norms developed in the group are not legitimate. He has been stirred, perhaps freed of old conceptions and behaviors. His feelings and reactions to other people are close to the surface. The family and associates to whom he returns, however, have usually not shared such an experience.[2] He may be able to integrate some of the changes into his interactions with others. If distressing things have happened, there is no way to return to the scene. Many aspects of the experience remain only as memories, for there is no sustaining community he can refer back to. Since most real change—intrapsychic or interpersonal—is incremental, much of the intensity and alteration that occurs in encounter groups may diminish with time (Lieberman et al., 1973). Yet the change orientation is only one way of looking at groups, a view that derives from therapy and education. For many, the group experience itself is important, since it provides much that is otherwise missing. Some participants, indeed, find it safer, more comfortable, to have such experiences segmented off from daily life by being part of an encounter group whose existence is time-limited and geographically distant. Nevertheless, for many, the poignancy and difficulty of the reentry experience is great. Participation in other encounter groups may eventually lead to cynicism and boredom rather than relief.[3]

The two groups described in the following chapters represent a possible further evolution of encounter: development of real communities, whether formal or informal, that exist over time. This pattern seems to be emerging more and more widely in the past few years. Fritz Perls, in the last years of his life, founded a communal settlement intended to integrate his Gestalt therapeutic techniques with a way of life. Betty Grover Eisner, a Los Angeles psychologist, has aided long-term therapy groups to live communally or become close-knit networks of interdependent families. The staff of Arica, an integrated program of meditative techniques, has close, communal living arrangements in adjacent homes in San Francisco.

Like many modern phenomena, the encounter movement has been a victim of the faddish tendencies of American culture. The growth of the movement rapidly outstripped the number of qualified, experienced leaders. The groups have much to offer in the way of therapy, education, religion, and community. But time is obviously needed for the leaders, participants, and potential participants to learn how to use these groups and to learn which groups address which of the many needs that motivate participation. One step in this direction is the evolution toward more stable, "settled," and localized groups, or "growth centers." These offer a variety of types of groups, time formats, and styles, Such centers also offer the participant a variety of degrees of involvement. The evolution of more varied activities will be valuable in better meeting and needs of participants. At present there is frequently confusion between the function of encounter groups for healing (i.e., therapy) as against "growth" (i.e., widening of experience).

It is still far easier to identify the origins of the encounter movement than to say where it is headed, or even where it is now. It appears to be outliving the more strident era of radical challenge and youth activism, and becoming part of the program of more traditional institutions of American life. For example, a new form of three-day religious retreat, the *cursillo*, is mushrooming in Christian congregations. Originating within the Catholic community, cursillo has spread to many Protestant denominations. Rather than the theological or meditative focus of past retreats, the cursillo emphasizes self-expression, openness with others, making human contact.

SUMMARY

The encounter group phenomenon is a diffuse movement touching wider and wider circles of American life. Its relevance here stems from those aspects of modern life to which it responds, chiefly the steadily increasing domination of social and psychological life by technological processes. Suppression of feelings, spontaneity, variety and idealism in favor of rationality, control, and cool competence creates a ready "underground" of impulses, needs, and desires in modern American culture. The encounter group offers at minimum some social "first aid" for these frustrations. It reassures participants about the legitimacy of their feelings and the importance to all of human contact and involvement. The groups themselves have many of the features of the healing communities described in Parts I and II. The basic individual and group processes of healing community are present. Like non-Western healing communities, the use of intense, ritualized activity is high and is frequently directed toward a goal of feeling and catharsis. Like the hospital therapeutic community, the groups are time-limited, so that the impact and ambiguous meaning of the individual's experience often remain for him to integrate, for better or worse. In the following two chapters we shall see how two groups, more or less in the encounter movement, have evolved to more lasting communities in very different ways.

NOTES

1. Alvin Toffler's book *Future Shock* is a perceptive analysis of many contemporary problems, but offers simplistic solutions that are typically American. He proposes that the citizen and institutions of the future will have to become adapted to the rapid rate of change and dislocation of modern life. Like the machines whose needs have already come to dominate his life, man will have to learn how to be moved, packaged, and retooled constantly and efficiently. Apart from the amorality of this attitude—which I violently reject—it shows a considerable naiveté about what man is capable of.

2. Special approaches have been used to bring about coordinated changes in the members of social systems, such as organization staffs (Argyris, 1955) or families (Satir, 1969).

3. Jane Howard, a journalist who wrote a book on the encounter movement, *Please Touch*, by attending one type of group after another, illustrates this in describing her own reactions (1970).

CHAPTER 15

Synanon

Synanon, an organization of and for narcotics addicts, developed in the early 1960s in California. It emerged spontaneously, without the support, financial or institutional, of any governmental or medical institution. Although Synanon has much in common with the style of some of the encounter techniques that were developing in Southern California about the same time, it was not developed as an encounter group for outsiders until several years later. Considerable information is available on Synanon and its origins.[1] Synanon is of interest to us for several reasons: (1) It is reportedly far more effective than prior approaches to addiction; (2) it is a self-supporting, live-in community; and (3) it has continued to grow and thrive for over a decade now.

Solutions to the narcotics problem by the established agencies of society have been, at best, ineffective; and at worst, they have intensified the problem. The illegal status of these drugs, the heavy penalties for their use and sale, and the resulting profitability of supplying drugs has led to large-scale criminal organization for distribution. Medical treatment of addiction has been severely constrained by the legal ramifications of narcotics use and the resulting conditions under which addicts come to medical treatment.[2]

The orientations of institutions and of addicts toward institutions, along with the punitive legal attitude to addiction, have conspired to make a therapeutic approach unlikely or impossible. It is worth emphasizing that an important element in this situation of institutional failure is the orientation of the addict. The addict is a person whose time is spent, not with the personalized, bizarre, or self-destructive behavior of the psychiatric patient, but with manipulating others and exploiting situations as completely as possible. When this addict style comes in contact with most institutional treatment programs, it quickly leads to disillusionment and failure on both sides.

BACKGROUND

In this state of affairs it is not completely surprising that a more therapeutic orientation to addiction developed outside established institutions and with the energy of addicts themselves. In 1958 Chuck Diederich, an ex-alcoholic and successful product of Alcoholics Anonymous, initiated an informal weekly discussion group that gradually attracted both alcoholics and addicts in the Santa Monica area north of Los Angeles. This discussion group quickly took on a special style, still associated with Synanon meetings.

"Attack of one another was a key note of the sessions, with everyone joining in. I could detect considerable lying and self-deception in the group. I began to attack viciously—partly out of my own irritations and at times to defend myself. The group would join in and we would let the air out of pompously inflated egos, including my own. The sessions soon became the high point in everybody's week" (Diederich, quoted in Yablonsky, 1955, p. 49).

From the discussion group evolved some cooperative

living and financial arrangements. Once a stable group had developed, the first addicts with active drug habits were taken on. Conditions for joining were total commitment to the group: quitting one's job, leaving one's family, and moving in. Within the first year, a break took place between the alcoholics and the addicts, whom Diederich decided to champion. This freed the group from the AA rules and patterns, making it possible to develop social structures and group norms appropriate to the addicts' needs. Not long after its origins, other critical elements in Synanon's program emerged. It was decided that drugs of any sort, as well as alcohol, were taboo within the growing cluster of Synanon residential units. This rule put full emphasis for the handling of psychological crises, including heroin withdrawal, on psychological and social group resources. It also reduced to almost zero the maneuvering room of the addict around medication. He could secrete a "stash" of some sort of drug and risk immediate expulsion by fellow Synanon members. Since there was no conspiratorial group of fellow-inmates with whom to share his secret, the psychological payoffs of maintaining a stash were markedly reduced. Moreover, regular use of narcotics was made impossible by the members' sophistication about its symptoms.

The meetings that had initially formed the core of the program continued to play a major role when Synanon became a full-time living group. These meetings were scheduled three times weekly. They had one fundamental rule: Any verbal interaction was allowed, as long as it was unaccompanied by physical violence. The meetings continued to emphasize angry, confronting psychological attacks on one member at a time. This group meeting style was in deliberate contrast with more psychoanalytically oriented group techniques, in which gradual uncovering and "insight" are seen as therapeutic foci. Synanon group meetings are premised on the belief that insight, though possibly revealing for an addict, has no therapeutic value for him. What is valued is the process in which he is psychologically laid bare by a group of peers who have firsthand, personal experience of a similar life style. Interestingly, it is these heated Synanon sessions that give new members the sense of being cared about sincerely. The experience of being laid bare is also made more acceptable by the knowledge that it is coming from a group consisting only of other ex-addicts.

The history of Synanon over the 1960s is as exciting and unbelievable as any Horatio Alger story. As cohesion and social structure developed in the growing organization, some of the considerable energy of addicts began to be applied to the survival and expansion of the organization. Members "hustled" the "square" community for cheap or free food, equipment, and new residence space. By now, 15 years after its origin, Synanon has successfully rehabilitated hundreds of addicts; involved thousands of "square" nonaddicts in Synanon group meetings; spread to other parts of California and to the East Coast; made inroads into prisons and other institutions; and is now establishing a large-scale new community based on communal living and interaction in the Synanon style.

NORMS AND COMMUNITAS

Throughout this development, most of the central social patterns and norms of the Synanon organization have remained fairly constant. Small group meetings, now called the "Synanon game," continue to be the core experience. One reason for this appears to be that it is in the small group meetings that important norms of Synanon are maintained. The groups are constantly reshuffled in membership in order to avoid mutual protection among a specific set of members. The constellation of participants in a particular group may be designed to capitalize upon a tension or conflict between two or more members. The "attack" style of these meetings, putting one or a series of participants on the "hot seat," taking apart their facade or behavior, appears to stem from intuitive recognition that the last thing an addict needs is sympathy. The attack is less an attack from another than it is an attack on the defensive facade that the addict maintains. The attacker, fully aware from his own experience of other addicts' capabilities for fooling themselves or others, is in an excellent position to help remove some of these facades.

Through the attack the addict develops the beginnings of openness about himself. That is, he gradually relinquishes some of the stereotypes that he uses to justify his behavior and relation to others, and begins to look at himself and others in a less stereotyped, manipulative way. Since his unprotected self-view may be ugly and his self-esteem abysmally low, attack in Synanon groups is indeed painful and brutal. Yet it is undoubtedly softened by the fact that the same person who is giving the devastating "haircut" is a fellow member with whom many friendly times have been and will be shared. There is no confidentiality within the small Synanon groups. In fact general discussion of what emerges in these meetings is encouraged. As a result of this and of the shifting makeup of the groups, an individual's progress in disclosure and general attitude is widely known throughout the whole Synanon community. Implicit in this is a strong acceptance of membership in Synanon and of oneself as a member. Here again is a fundamental prerequisite of communitas: valuation of the group by every member.

The admission requirements of Synanon also convey and help to bring about the realization of the importance of the whole organization for the individual. Membership is both total and open-ended. An individual may return to outside work or to his family in the course of his development in Synanon, but these decisions are made with the group, not by the individual alone. Generally, this is viewed as a process of several years, and recently Synanon has moved toward bringing the family into Synanon, rather than returning the addict to the outside world. The importance of group membership in Synanon is also illustrated by many of the processes that occur within the organization. Much of the content of formal and informal discussions about members consists of examination of their behavior within the Synanon setting. Frequently implicit in such discussions is the evaluative index of how much a member's behavior reflects his commitment to Synanon. The good Synanon member is one who is working wholeheartedly for the organization and achieving his personal transformation and ambitions through it.

Norms around control are of particular importance in this organization of individuals who have spent lifetimes subverting, challenging, and manipulating legitimate authority. The authority structure of Synanon is neither democratic nor dictatorial. Individuals with seniority—not necessarily in years, but in socially confirmed maturity—are elevated to positions of greater responsibility. Newcomers are regarded as helpless, immature, and incompetent at behaviors that would support their progress in Synanon and are thus treated quite directively. This pattern of authority, though firm and strict, does not qualify as authoritarian because it is openly enacted, relies upon the cooperation of the membership, and is in the best interests of goals the member has espoused. Since the doors are always open, the authority of the organization relies at base upon the commitment of its members. As we shall see, charisma plays a major part in maintaining this pattern of authority.

Work is another important norm of the organization. Initially, work both inside and outside Synanon were critical to its survival. Work served to channel the nonusing addict's immense need for activity and busyness. The emphasis on work reinforces the importance of group membership, and working symbolizes some acceptance of individual commitment to the group. Emphasis on work also corresponds to the general "Protestant ethic" orientation of American society.

As Yablonsky says, "Some of Synanon's philosophy corresponds closely with 'square society'."

BECOMING A MEMBER

The process of entry into the organization is particularly critical with addicts, who have spent a great deal of their lives in institutions, to which they have always related in an alienated, hostile, and manipulative fashion. To deal with this, the entrance procedures for Synanon minimize proselytizing by the organization and force the applicant to prove his interest in joining. A member who came to Synanon after a 3000-mile plane trip from the East Coast commented on his surprise at not being "welcomed aboard," as he had been in so many other institutions and treatments. Instead he was regarded with indifference, allowed to wait many hours for an interview, and once seen, was not allowed to speak but was lectured to at length by Synanon members. Similarly, dropping out is viewed as a failure of the addict, not of Synanon.

In the indoctrination meeting with one of the member-leaders, the newcomer is likely to be grilled and harangued. In the following session reported by Yablonsky, Chuck Diederich talks about 10 times more than the newcomer. Here are selections from his description of life at Synanon:

Now, here's what we offer an addict, in simple terms. We offer an addict an opportunity to work for the Synanon Foundation. When you work for the Synanon Foundation you get the necessities of life: you get shelter as good as we have, you get all the food you can eat, you get cigarettes, you get a pretty nice place to live; and if you continue to work for the Foundation a month, two months, four months, or a year, eventually you'll be a pretty well integrated human being. You've seen quite a few of them around here since you arrived, whether you recognized them or not. The small amount of work that you'll be required to do, any adult could do standing on his head in a hammock in about two hours a day. Your job will probably be from four to five hours a day.

You will get the only therapy that works, more often than not, for narcotic addicts. In addition to your work, we demand certain standards of behavior around here for reasons known to us; not to you, yet. Someday you quite possibly will understand it; you will if you get well, and then you'll see why we are insistent on certain standards of behavior. There is no "we-they" situation here like there is in a prison.

The minute you kick your habit, you become part of the staff. You become one of some hundred or so doctors and then you yourself are a patient and you've got about a hundred doctors around you. This is a new concept.

We provide Synanon meetings three times a week, where you can have catharsis sessions.

You can sit there and call somebody a mother-fucker. There you can say to someone, "How do you stand that mother-fucking Chuck who runs the joint?" That's fine. I want you to do that, in that situation but not in the building or in the men's john. You will behave yourself and you won't throw your weight around yet. Someday you'll learn how to assert yourself in a constructive manner. Now your behavior is quite obviously destructive (Yablonsky, 1965, pp. 200–201).

After this sort of initial exposure, the newcomer is shown around. He sees ex-addicts indentifiable through the scar tissue over their veins or perhaps known to him personally. He seeks out the "connection" that he assumes can be found in such a loose setup. This search is greeted with derisive, negative comments from members who have all gone through the same experience themselves. If the new member has been using heroin, he may begin to experience withdrawal symptoms. Here, too, he will have an experience unlike any he had before in an institution. At Synanon, with its blanket rule against medications, he withdraws "cold turkey." In other settings the addict can often get medication by exaggerating and intensifying his withdrawal symptoms. At Synanon his symptoms are ignored or played down.

> The hi-fi is usually playing, children may be around in the room, he receives warm drinks (eggnog, hot tea), and he is physically soothed with occasional shoulder rubs. People will come over, shake his hand, welcome him, and chat. Most important, he can literally see live evidence of success at Synanon. He may see "clean" ex-addicts with whom he personally used drugs. He is encouraged to achieve the healthy physical and emotional condition of the people he sees before him. He begins to learn about Synanon from people who have experienced his current emotions. He sees real models of achievable success around him. He is interacting with people who understand how he feels, since they themselves were all at one time in his shoes. In addition to understanding his feelings, they sketch for him a positive future which they themselves are literally experiencing. In his confused state, these solid reference points provided by other Synanon members help to minimize his psychic and physical withdrawal pains and speed his involvement in the group (Yablonsky, 1965, pp. 198–199).

During the addict's first days and weeks, he is faced with a difficult choice. If he remains, he must confront heroin withdrawal and the difficult job of accepting a new kind of adaptation to life. If he leaves, he acknowledges that he "can't make it" and thus disappoints whatever small part of him would like to end the addictive life-style. Unlike prisons and hospitals, Synanon is likely to reject him the second time around. The initiation procedures of Synanon appear to have evolved in such a way as to heighten the difficulty of making this decision and yet favor remaining. Elements in this appear to be a mixture of parental controlling and structuring, the enticement of personal growth, and acceptance in a community of individuals whom the addict has every reason to respect. The member's role is defined as that of an employee, a staff member, and therapist for the other members—all at one time. A distinction is made between subordination on the basis of role, such as occurs with hospital patients or prison inmates, and subordination on the basis of maturity or experience in Synanon. The latter is legitimate, as is the coercive side of the initial care of a newcomer and the protective value of being cared for initially.

If he does not walk out, the addict has implicitly become a part of the place. He may have many private reservations, but these will be sensed by others and undoubtedly exposed and attacked at Synanon meetings. He will have to demonstrate his involvement through his work performance. And by "acting like" a devoted member, the addict gradually comes to feel like one. This last is in fact an open part of the Synanon strategy. The longer he stays, the more he will tend to redefine his goals in terms of the Synanon framework of possibilities. Thus whatever personal needs for subverting authority, succeeding sexually, or manipulating people that the addict expressed in his life-style as an addict, he can now express within Synanon. More experienced Synanon members will, through the medium of the Synanon meetings and the ongoing discussions that occur throughout the day, push the addict to meet these impulses in new ways. The seductive ex-prostitute will be torn apart verbally and revealed as a dependent baby. Once revealed, she may be able to allow herself to try relating to men as an adult woman, without the male stereotypes she has maintained, and to experience their responses. A criminal who has channeled his impulses around authority to defiant lawbreaking and rebellion in institutions may find after a time that he can become an enterprising, hustling executive within Synanon. For doing this he will be rewarded, although he will continue to be under close scrutiny for signs of stress resulting from the dissonance between his prior life-style and present position.

LEADERSHIP, ROLES, AND HEALING CHARISMA

Although there is vertical status mobility within Synanon, there is no questioning of the final leadership authority of Chuck Diederich. Descriptions of Diederich's leadership behavior and of his significance for members portray a charismatic leader *par excellence*. He is viewed with awe by many members, especially those recently arrived at the organization. His first one-to-one contact with a newcomer is a critical moment in the addict's Synanon experience, invested with great significance and reexamined at length afterwards. Diederich's behavior is often dramatic and impulsive. The central leadership of Synanon clearly operates around bonds of personal loyalty between Diederich and his initial addict followers.

With enlargement in size, Synanon members no longer have opportunity for extensive contacts with Diederich, but this serves in some sense to heighten the meaningfulness of those few contacts they do have. Furthermore, Diederich has transmitted his charisma to others in the Synanon organization. It is clear from descriptions of their work that they, too, are capable of charismatic behavior with new members.

One aspect of healing charismatic leadership emerges around the idea of Synanon and Diederich as lifesaving.[3] To many addicts, their conversion to a drugless existence and constructive involvement in Synanon is unbelievable. They place the focus of their change on Diederich as a symbol of Synanon, the organization. In this way, Synanon members constantly reinforce Diederich's charisma and at the same time transfer it to the organization as a whole.

The small Synanon groups can be viewed as the medium in which the charismatic process is maintained. In these groups, Synanon members are subjected to the attacking, laying-bare technique that Diederich developed; they also emulate Diederich and other old-timers by using the technique on others. In the groups, the charismatic aura of the individual leader is transformed into a style of interaction that may be shared by all members. In this way the group meetings make possible an emulation of the leader's charismatic behavior.

The core leadership other than Diederich had opportunity during the early years to develop their own leadership skills and styles. This made it possible for others to take over from Diederich some of the administrative and management responsibility for Synanon. These leaders—invested with charisma directly from Diederich, sharpened and tested in the fire of many top-level Synanon meetings and "haircut" sessions, and trained in leadership themselves as administrators in Synanon and as group leaders—could be trusted to carry the message and activities of Synanon to new areas in the community and to new enterprises. But beyond such specific responsibilities, the concept of every member as a healer for every other member is basic to Synanon. Thus healing charisma is universal, enhanced through relations with Diederich and through advancement in the organization.

SYNANON AND SOCIETY

In its early years Synanon was viewed with mistrust and overt hostility, especially by the middle-class residential communities in which it sought living facilities. This was true both in the first years in Santa Monica and in connection with a later satellite program in Westport, Connecticut. In general, relations between Synanon and the outside world might be characterized most succinctly as intensely ambivalent in both directions. Conservative elements in the community have attacked Synanon as a center of free love, a haven for dope fiends who would subvert the morals of innocent young. Sympathetic citizens contribute time and material support to the organization. Synanon, on its part, initially welcomed the public to Saturday night Synanon meetings and more didactic explanations of the organization. At the same time, Synanon monitors the outside participation carefully and strongly discourages nonaddicts and interested others from dabbling in the program, especially from taking any responsibility or authority in it. Later, Synanon "square" groups were organized to provide a way for outsiders and nonaddicts to participate regularly.

The observation has been made repeatedly that in many ways Synanon as an organization simulates the style of the addict in relation to society. It "hustles" for free or cut-rate food and materials; it manipulates "square" institutions for its own needs. It could also be argued that, like the individual addict, Synanon as an organization acts out certain forbidden impulses for the community as a whole. It may be, however, that to the degree that society recognizes Synanon's success in converting hardened addicts to a productive, entrepreneurial way of life in the community, it is threatening. I suggest this as a partial explanation of the massive opposition that Synanon frequently incurs. Synanon successfully converts addicts into middle-class citizens. Breaking down the clear boundary between dope fiend and successful citizen may be disquieting. First of all, when the boundary of deviant and member-of-society-in-good-standing is blurred, the possibility of traversing this boundary both ways becomes more likely. Further, whatever the psychological function the existence of unchangeable deviants in the community may serve for other citizens, it is threatened if the deviant can be converted back.

On Synanon's side it can well be asked, What will be the effect on group cohesiveness and motivation if the organization is too easily accepted? Synanon may maintain some of its distance from the community in order to retain an internal sense of having a hostile social surrounding. Recently Synanon has expanded from ex-heroin-users to accepting more "squares" and "life-stylers" in new enterprises. A major one is development of communities based on Synanon philosophy and technique. As rural utopian ventures, these do retain distance from society in a new way.

SUMMARY

Synanon has features in common with the healing groups previously considered; it has other features it shares with some groups; and in some interesting ways, it is unique. Along with the Zar cult, Tensho, Zuni medicine fraternities, and therapeutic community, we find the group spirit I have been calling *communitas*: Rank exists only in experience in the group; otherwise, every member is equal to every other. Authority is charismatic, as is the motive power behind the seemingly miraculous individual changes Synanon has achieved. One style of special behavior defines proper behavior whether among top leaders or newcomers—the particular aggressive verbal attack of the Synanon meetings. Cohesion and loyalty are intense within the group, and boundaries are carefully maintained.

Like the Zar cult, Tensho, and Tompkins I, Synanon has a central charismatic leader. Diederich and the healing group he developed are charismatic in a wonderfully American way: They have made a comeback from alcoholism and heroin, and have achieved success through the traditional American virtues of energy, persistence, and cleverness. The interaction style is also uniquely American: honest, tough confrontation—to which one learns to stand up like a man. But like the other groups, charisma flows outward from the central leader to others, investing them with healing abilities that they, in turn, can use with newer members.

Membership in Synanon, as in all the groups except the therapeutic community, carries advantages that go beyond healing the original ailment. In fact, no group thus far has carried this feature as far as has Synanon, which completely redefines the lives of those who join. This encompassing way of life probably is the only effective counter to the encompassing quality of heroin addiction in our society. The addict literally need think of little else while he is hooked, since it requires full-time, often day-and-night activity to support his habit. When he arrives at Synanon he *has* little life other than addiction, even if he has clung to the trappings of family and job. Synanon recognizes this by making complete involvement a precondition for membership, and by making restoration to life outside a matter of years.

Like the afflicting spirits of Zar, Tensho, or Zuni, the addict's strengths are put to positive use. But the energy of the addict, which has heretofore enabled him to sustain his addiction, is now transformed into hard work for the organization. As in all these organizations, membership in Synanon is something special: Once a member, one enters the charismatic flow of the group and becomes more than what one was before. Diederich expresses this by likening membership to being a doctor; he is explicit about the healing qualities and prestige of the member's role. Synanon's success at recruiting and transforming its members both fuels the charismatic process by reaffirming commitment and strengthens feelings of the group's efficacy.

Overall, Synanon is very much a healing community. Its uniqueness is primarily in style. The core social organization and program are similar to those we have observed in other groups. The group developed as it did—away from formal institutions—because our society had no way to deal with drug addiction. Making the addict a criminal had not prevented the spread of addiction. As a unique organization of ex-addicts, Synanon moved into the vacuum thus created, developing spontaneously the processes and patterns we associate with healing community.

NOTES

1. The description of Synanon that follows is drawn largely from Louis Yablonsky's extensive study of Synanon's early years, *Synanon: The Tunnel Back,* New York: Macmillan, 1965.

2. The methadone replacement technique of Dole and Nyswander has now been developed as a way to bring the criminal component of the addictive cycle under control by offering replacement of heroin with another, analogous medication (1965).

3. Actually, considering the morbidity and mortality of the untreated addict's life, Synanon and Diederich may well be lifesaving for a fairly sizable percentage of Synanon members.

CHAPTER 16

Psychodrama Workshop of Palo Alto

The Psychodrama Workshop of Palo Alto, California, offers a variety of specialized encounter experiences in a small residential city 40 miles south of San Francisco.[1] The workshop is an organization of 15 to 20 persons who offer a variety of weekly group meetings and weekend marathon sessions, many of which are open to the public for a small fee. Of all the organizations that we have so far discussed, the workshop is the youngest: it began five years ago. The origin of the group and its techniques can be documented relatively easily; further, the workshop is still evolving, so that its present direction and problems may suggest important issues in the development of other new healing communities. The workshop has several features of healing community that we have identified before, for example, charismatic leadership and relationship patterns, and a striving for a close, equal, communitas spirit among members. Other parallels will emerge as we explore various aspects of the Psychodrama Workshop: the ideas and beliefs that underlie its activities, the quality of group meetings, patterns of joining and participating, and its social organization.

Psychodrama Workshop has features in common with Synanon—and some distinct differences. Like Synanon, the workshop has evolved from an occasional encounter group to a stable organization with a permanent location. Unlike Synanon, membership in the workshop does not require the breaking of outside bonds and does not involve shared living arrangements. On the other hand, the workshop espouses attitudes and values that distinguish it from the dominant beliefs of American culture. Born in the heyday of the "counterculture" and using many of the approaches of the encounter movement, the workshop in many ways has institutionalized a set of values and practices different from those of the surrounding society. The workshop's Psychodrama technique is in itself fascinating to the therapist and group leader: It is an amalgam of older psychodynamic concepts with newer therapy orientations and techniques. [2]

BACKGROUND [3]

The Psychodrama Workshop of Palo Alto was formed in 1968 around the leadership of Victor Lovell, a clinical psychologist practicing in the Palo Alto area. The origins of the workshop involve a fascinating convergence of influences: the Freudian psychoanalytic therapy tradition; the psychedelic drug experiences of the early 1960s; the anti-Establishment political rebellions of the late 1960s; the encounter movement, especially that of Fritz Perls and his followers at Esalen; and the long-established psychodrama technique of J. L. Moreno.

During the mid 1960s Palo Alto was at the crossroads of a number of social movements and upheavals. The hippie/drug culture phenomenon had part of its origin in LSD experiments in the Palo Alto area. A small hip subculture like the Haight-Ashbury developed. Considerable numbers of alienated, disaffected, "dropped-out," war-opposing young people settled in Palo Alto, or joined from the nearby Stanford University campus. Part of this subculture was oriented to militant radical political activity focused on the Vietnam War and on local and national institutions that were seen as reflections of a society that could initiate, tolerate, and prolong an immoral conflict. At the same time, another part of the hip culture was searching for alternative forms of political, social, and psychological life.

Two hours to the south, at Big Sur, the Esalen Institute offered a varied program of encounter groups and workshops, attracting many participants from the Palo Alto area and stimulating wide interest in new therapy and growth techniques. By the late sixties an "Esalen at Stanford" program brought many of the leading figures of the human potential movement to the Stanford campus at fees that students and others in the Palo Alto community, including the original Psychodrama Workshop members, could afford. The attractiveness of these new encounter techniques was considerable for those people who had been involved in extensive psychedelic drug use during the early 1960s.

The drug "trip" provided an artificially induced transcendent experience that was compelling to people reared in a secular society. Both the "high," with its positive experiences of oneself, nature, and communion with others, and the "bad trip," with its puzzling, disquieting, frightening, or terrifying experiences, left many questions. In general the drug trip, with its intensification of immediate experience, made people aware of their self-consciousness and defensiveness.

By 1968 many persons who had experienced the gamut of psychedelic effects were looking for new, less unpredictable, less dangerous ways of "getting high." Eastern mystical traditions such as yoga, transcendental meditation, Subud, and Zen gained many adherents. Other persons, influenced by the psychological and interpersonal opportunities that drugs had suggested, became involved with encounter groups. Politically oriented individuals were interested in new approaches to handling group decision-making and leadership.

For several years (between 1967 and 1970) these interests and searches became organized around the "Mid-Peninsula Free University" in the Palo Alto area, which was similar to free universities that developed in many cities and academic communities throughout the country at this time. The "Free U" offered few controls over teachers and course content. Many leaders, with and without professional therapy training, experimented with the techniques of Fritz Perls and other Esalen group leaders. The Free U clientele were eager participants in these groups, especially where they used physical contact and struggle, and encouraged strong expression of feelings. Pervading most of these encounter groups was a set of norms opposite to those of the surrounding middle-class American culture. In these groups the new "counterculture" ethic could be shared, and individuals could give each other social reinforcement for new patterns of behaving and experiencing.

Into this fluid, experimental situation came Hussein Chung, a small, flamboyant, Chinese group leader, also trained in the Indonesian mystical tradition of Subud. In Los Angeles Chung had developed a combination of intense encounter, modeled after Synanon, and psychodramatic techniques, learned in a brief visit to Moreno's psychodrama institute in New York City. Chung was invited to Palo Alto by the Free U to lead groups of Free U staff members. The groups were powerful and popular; Chung and several assistants migrated from Los Angeles to Palo Alto. Soon he opened a "Human Institute" that offered weekly psychodrama groups, frequent extended marathons of 40 hours or more, and a training program for assistants. These played parts in psychodramatic scenes and acted as co-leaders in confronting, attacking, and exposing the defenses and resistances of group participants. In marathons, sleep deprivation, combined with an intense group process, frequently led participants to dramatic explosions of feeling. Chung was a dramatic, aggressive, charismatic leader who worked by augmenting and intensifying feelings and interactions; with the aid of his assistants, he aggressively forced participants into involvement. In addition to Chung's own powerful style, participants were exposed to heavy group pressure and physical assault in the form of slapping, wrestling, and fighting. Expression of positive feeling through hugging and group contact was also encouraged, as was sadness, screaming, sobbing, and other outbursts. The impact of Chung's groups on participants was varied. Many experienced incredible "highs" afterwards that reminded them of drug experiences. Others made major life changes as a result of the groups. Some were relatively untouched, while others became "casualties." The physical bruises and psychic upsets following groups contributed to a highly controversial reputation for Chung and his adherents.

Vic Lovell, a psychotherapist who had "dropped out" of conventional therapy settings to become a leader in the Free U, found Chung's style both shocking and fascinating. Initially critical and wary, Lovell gradually began to participate regularly in a variety of Chung's psychodrama groups as he saw dramatic effects on himself and others. He and others began employing psychodramatic techniques in encounter groups. For some, Psychodrama became almost a way of life, a way to solve the problems of people living or working together. Lovell himself, grounded in a 1950s clinical training of Freudian, psychodynamic orientation, was slow to assume a leadership role in such groups, as he was wrestling with understanding their confusing and often chaotic qualities.

In 1969 Lovell announced the formation of a Psychodrama Workshop for developing and elaborating the new techniques of Chung, Perls, and other encounter group leaders. He recruited a number of talented psychodramatic actors, and the group rented a large Palo Alto mansion where many of the workshop members lived and where the Psychodrama sessions of the new workshop were held. During the first year, the workshop version of Psychodrama tended to be much like that of Chung: unpredictable, explosive, violent, and powerful in impact, both positive and negative. Psychodrama was used to resolve problems of living together, political conflict, and personal development.

Within the first year, tension developed within the group between those interested primarily in radical political action and those interested primarily in personal growth and radical psychotherapy. The political activists left the group to pursue more specifically revolutionary activity elsewhere. In the workshop Lovell began to discourage psychological assault and confrontation for its own sake, and to evolve his own Psychodrama process, merging the encounter Psychodrama techniques of Chung with the therapeutic innovations of Gestalt therapy and bioenergetics.[4] Perls' approach contributed both at the level of technique and of overall philosophy. The Gestalt "hot seat" technique, in which the leader works with one group member at a time, was easily combined with the psychodramatic role of "protagonist," where the director and his assistants create scenes around one person and his problems. The Gestalt "dialogue," in which an individual voices both sides of a conflict or a relationship situation, proved to be a useful entrée into psychodramatic scenes. On a conceptual level, Perls' ideas provided guidance for the direction of Psychodrama sequences, a series of scenes with one protagonist. Psychodrama sequences could be seen as enactments of incomplete internal processes, as Perls viewed the goal of Gestalt therapy. By dramatizing this internal process, it often became intensified and could frequently be developed further. While Freudian psychodynamic theory frequently gave clues to the internal drama, such observations were used by Lovell for guidance in setting up psychodramatic situations, rather than for verbal interpretation to the protagonist. The concepts and technique will be described further in the next two sections of this chapter. Gradually, regularities appeared in psychodramatic sequences; spontaneous innovations became staple scenes in the repertoire. Music had been

used in Chung's group, and it became more and more sophisticated in workshop groups. Theatrical lighting effects were
added.

As time passed, Psychodrama became used less in
everyday life and was limited to group meetings, marathons
(open to the public), and workshop staff meetings. As in
many quickly formed communes in this era, there were tensions and clashes, pairing and break-ups, in the Psychodrama Workshop living situation. Gradually, the number of
workshop members living in the house declined: some
moved out to solidify couple relationships; others simply left
the workshop. New workshop members were taken into the
house less readily, and many had stable living situations
elsewhere. In mid-1972 when the rental lease was lost, the
workshop moved to a new location in a renovated church
meetinghouse in downtown Palo Alto. This building now
provides the home for a larger "growth center," *Prometheus*,
which sponsors other encounter groups and training experiences as well as Psychodrama. Thus, what began as a complete living/working setting has become part of a larger community facility.

In a natural process of self-selection, the workshop has
become less fluid in its membership, more serious and structured about training, and more varied in its program of
groups. Other leaders have emerged to supplement Lovell in
directing groups. Psychodramatic acting is becoming more
"professional." The workshop has begun to recruit members
who have therapy training, and it increasingly attracts
middle-class, "straight" participants to its groups. These
changes parallel both the dissolution of the more organized
aspects of the local "counterculture" and the desire to integrate older ideas with what has been learned in a more experimental era. As this shift occurs, the workshop also struggles
with the degree to which Psychodrama should be therapy and
the degree to which it is an experience unto itself, with responsibility for its healing impact left to the individual par-

ticipant. We shall return to this issue after a description of the Psychodrama experience itself.

THE PSYCHODRAMA EXPERIENCE

Psychodrama Workshop groups are held in four-hour weekday evening meetings, in 40-hour "marathons," or in "minithons" of 12 or 24 hours. Psychodrama groups are held in a large room (20 x 40 feet) that has been constructed from half of what was once a church meetinghouse. The floor is covered by a wall-to-wall carpet of deep red with a light green border; the red is in the form of a giant cross covering most of the room and defining the central space. The furnishings are simple: many pillows arranged in an oval around the carpet border, ashtrays, and in one corner an elevated platform with a control panel for the lighting, two turntables, and a large record collection. Two large stereo speakers at opposite corners of the room focus sound at the room's center. Spotlights, both white and colored, are also focused at the middle of the red rug. Initially and between scenes, "house lights" provide general lighting. Coffee and toilet facilities are available in rooms off the main room.

As participants enter for the group—after paying a fee at the door—music is playing and clusters of people are talking quietly around the growing circle that will total 25 to 50.[5] Participants come to Psychodrama groups in a variety of ways and for a variety of reasons. Most often they have heard about the groups from a friend who has participated. Some have seen a brochure describing workshop activities. The motives are diverse; some participants come for the same sorts of reasons that bring people to therapy: a distressing feeling-state or situation; difficulties in interpersonal relations; personality qualities they wish to change. Other people attend more from a spectator motive; they have heard of the theatrical aspects of the scene. Lonely people may come to be with a group of others, perhaps to make new friends. On a given evening there will generally be a mix of veteran participants, a few newcomers, and some people who have attended a few times before.

Members of the Psychodrama Workshop are not distinguished in any way from paying participants and mix generally with the circle, socializing and welcoming newcomers. After most of the participants have entered and seated themselves, the leader arrives and takes a place at the end of the oval-shaped group, seating himself in a "director's chair" or on the floor. He is dressed casually in a blue workshirt, dark pants, and white sneakers. The music, which has been playing as people have been coming in, is turned off, the outside door closed, and a sense of anticipation comes over the group as attention is focused on the director. He begins with the following statement of rules and expectations:

This is a heavy, intense scene. If you're drunk, if you're stoned on "downers," if you're suicidal or psychotic, or in any condition where you can't take responsibility for yourself, you shouldn't be here. We don't fight fire with water; we don't fight fire with fire; we fight fire with gasoline. We do this in the faith that there's *something inside you* that can put it together when you really feel it.

If you're here, you're committed for the entire session, which means till about midnight. If you try to leave you are subject to being restrained. However, don't try to run out just to see what it feels like to be restrained. (Laughter) The idea is, if you're feeling something strongly—if you are overcome by fear, anger, lust, or tenderness—try to get out in the center and do something with it. Don't start a separate thing by the coffee, in the bathroom, or out on the street.

Sometimes in Psychodrama we have a violent scene. In a violent scene, you are not to hurt the other person. Let me repeat that. *You are not to hurt the other person.* You are not to use anything in the room other than a pillow as a weapon. You are not to use your body in such a way that it becomes a weapon. No judo, karate, boxing; no fighting skills or martial arts employed. We generally have people pushing, shoving, slapping, and things like thàt. If you are really going to get into something, take off your glasses and earrings.

Who would like to work tonight?

At this point there is generally a pause and then one, two, sometimes as many as five or six people move to the center of the room. The director instructs them: "Tell each other what you want to work on." Subject may range from disturbing dreams to problems in relationships, from physical feelings to psychological states of anxiety or depression. The director selects one person to begin, and the others take their places in the circle again.

The director will elicit some further information by a few direct questions, but will then quickly change the format. Most often the next step is a "Gestalt dialogue." The director instructs the protagonist to enact two sides of the conflict or issue he has mentioned, taking a seat alternately on black and white stools placed at the center of the circle. For example, a scene with someone who came forward to work on his struggle with being too self-controlled might go this way:

> *Director:* Put your self-control on the black stool and talk to it.
> *Protagonist:* You make me uptight. I want to get rid of you.
> *Director:* O.K., move—be the self-control.
> *Protagonist (from black stool):* You need me. You can't get along without me. You'd fall apart without me. . . .
> *Director:* Switch.
> *Protagonist:* I don't need you. You keep me back. There are so many things I could do if I could get rid of you.

After several reversals, a workshop member, spontaneously or on cue from the director, slips on to one stool and takes up the dialogue. Taking cues from what the protagonist has said, his own reactions, and signals from the director, the workshop actor may push the protagonist toward some sort of action. In the case of "control" he might try to exert control of the protagonist by ordering him about, or by physically restraining him. Or, a second actor may be introduced to "double" the protagonist, standing behind him and speaking his unspoken thoughts. The protagonist is told to reject the double's remarks if they feel wrong, but to try saying them if they feel right. The double may initiate action, again by picking up on the protagonist's behavior. For example, a protagonist dealing with depression may find his double leaning on him, physically "depressing" him. Usually these provocations lead to some sort of action—a fight, a struggle, a pushing-away—during which the verbal dialogue may or may not continue. The protagonist may push his "control" away, saying, "Get away! Leave me alone!" The "control" actor may escalate by becoming more controlling and authoritarian in words or actions. The intent of this opening scene is to relieve the protagonist's anxiety at being center stage, to get him moving and taking part more spontaneously, and to elicit information about the way the protagonist *experiences* his dilemma. The protagonist may or may not become engrossed in the action.

If this initial scene has aroused strong feelings in the protagonist, the director may "cut" the action and suggest he "flash back to some time in the past when you felt this way." If the feelings have remained low-key, the director will also "cut" when it becomes clear that the action is having little impact. In either case, the next scene will often be more "psychodramatic." Several characters, played by workshop actors, will be cast around the protagonist. The scene may be based on a memory of a family situation with parents and siblings; a recalled school situation; a romantic conflict or triangle, past or present; or an enactment of the struggle between several parts of the self. The director may set up the scene based on his own knowledge of the protagonist, or may ask the protagonist to characterize the roles briefly. The workshop members cast in these roles take their cues from the protagonist, yet offer him a variety of responses to react to. Usually, the director will reverse roles in the scene once or several times. This allows the protagonist to show and to feel how he experiences others in the scene. Doubles may be sent in for one or more people in the scene, especially the protagonist. The actors and doubles work toward exploring and intensifying the feelings of the protagonist. Rather than try to re-create reality, they play off the protagonist's reactions, frequently exaggerating their responses, at other times changing from one emotional stance to another. For example, a cold, aloof parent or spouse may suddenly break down in sobs and turn to the protagonist for support; a lover may walk in on a marital discussion and make friends with the spouse.

Psychodramatic scenes tend to build in intensity if the protagonist becomes immersed in them. An encounter with parents, a romantic triangle confronted, a dialogue with a dead relative can be intensely gripping, hilarious, or frustrating. When the protagonist keeps his distance from the action, refusing to play along with his created "reality," or if the scene becomes repetitive, the director will eventually cut the scene and request "feedback" from the group. Feedback is a stylized form of encounter. Anyone in the group may give feedback—defined as "what you saw and how it made you feel"—to the protagonist. Psychological analyses and interpretations are discouraged. Feedback can be massively critical, compassionate, or both. The protagonist is told to remain silent and receptive; to "take or leave what you want from feedback" but not to argue back or explain. Sometimes a workshop member or other group participant will have a strong enough reaction to the protagonist to come out into the center; this may initiate a new scene or series of scenes, or it may create a new protagonist. If he feels further movement is unlikely, the director may close the protagonist's sequence with feedback and perhaps a summarizing comment.

When a protagonist's involvement and intensity do build sufficiently, the climax often comes in what is called a "crash": a strong emotional reaction and subsequent catharsis. This may happen spontaneously, or the director may interrupt a scene if he sees a protagonist close to such a reaction. The crash may involve a variety of possible feelings—rage, sobbing, hysterical laughter, overwhelming fear. Often there is a sudden shift of feeling or sudden escalation of intensity. Thus, a protagonist during a psychodrama scene may suddenly attack, scream out, or burst into tears.

When the director sees or senses the imminence of a crash, he will clear the center of the room and work in a very different way with the protagonist. He will usually try to intensify the feeling, following cues from the protagonist's nonverbal vehavior or descriptions of physical sensations. Thus, if there is tightness in the jaw, the protagonist may be given something to bite on; or if the director senses restrained rage, he may encourage the protagonist to hit a pillow or kick and hit the floor like a child in a tantrum. Fear may be augmented into terror with the director encouraging the protagonist to scream while gripping the director's wrist. In this initial part of the crash, the director seeks to combine the protagonist's natural experience of the feeling with nonverbal techniques that he knows may open possibilities for a full cathartic release. Most people have had tantrums as a child, or have screamed in terror. The catharsis makes use of these varied psychomotor patterns to create a channel for feelings that have been held back.

Eventually the protagonist tires or shifts into quiet sobbing and lying still. The director will then work very closely with the protagonist, putting his body in a maximally relaxed position, helping his breathing to be deep and regular. The lights will be low. Soft, dreamy music will be played. Often, after such a period of quiet, the director will suggest that the protagonist produce a visual image or fantasy while his eyes are closed and will use this to bring the protagonist gradually back to awareness of the group without giving up his inner state. Sometimes, an earlier scene from the psychodramatic sequence will be reenacted in a different way. For example, a hostile confrontation with a parent may be redone the way it "should have been," with positive, warm feelings expressed on both sides. A marital interaction may be redone with both sides speaking straightforwardly and uncritically of their own needs and feelings. Although the director makes some effort to bring about this sort of closing, he avoids "happy endings" for their own sake.

In a Psychodrama sequence that moves to and through such a crash, the entire group is usually drawn along in the process. When the lights come up, there is an atmosphere of intensity, often of closeness and warmth. Some may have been moved to tears while watching, and others may hold and comfort them. The director almost never asks for, or even allows, feedback at this point. After a few moment's pause he may then progress to another protagonist. Sometimes another participant, stirred by some element of the prior sequence, will wish to work at this point.

That sequence I have just described is an idealized, simplified depiction—one that occurs frequently but not at all inevitably. At any given point during a sequence, there are many different options for the protagonist, the director, for a workshop member, and for the group. Many scenes end without a crash; many times the sequence is completely different from the example given here. Sometimes the director may create a deliberately chaotic scene in which character after character is introduced, humorous music is played, stroboscopic lights are used to create an "old movie" effect, and so on. Such scenes may be stimulated by a frustrating or confusing protagonist, or by a generally frustrated mood in the group. At other times the director may use structured group activities or interactions. For example, he may divide the group into men's and women's subgroups for a period of discussion of an issue raised by a scene. Marathons always include a period of separate men's and women's groups. At other times he may have a protagonist interact with members of the group in ways appropriate to the issue he is dealing with. For example, a person dealing with shyness may be told to go around the room being particularly aggressive or particularly shy, or deliberately seeking rejection. Sometimes the leader will call on a group member who is showing strong feelings, giving the member an opportunity to talk or come to the center.

Psychodrama sequences tend to have a subjective quality, like that depicted in the Japanese story, *Rashomon*, where each observer of a dramatic situation sees and experiences something different. The protagonist, the director, other workshop members, and each group participant may all see and experience something different in a sequence. When a scene builds to a crash, there is usually less variation in individual experience.

Musical background for scenes has one or both of two qualities: either it is suggestive in style and mood, or its words are appropriate to the action. For example, heavy rock music is often played during a fight scene; weird, electronic music is used for a scene accentuating anxiety or madness. During a struggle for dominance, the refrain "When this battle is over, who will wear the crown?" may be heard in the music, or after a crash, "Freedom is just another word for nothing left to lose." During a comic scene, the music may be the *William Tell Overture*, or during a crash, "Greensleeves." The role of music in Psychodrama is like that in film: a counterpoint to the dramatic action. In addition, the music can be suggestive for the actors by anticipating the probable direction for a scene. Certain selections have specific meanings to Psychodrama familiars. The workshop person handling media is an associate director, suggesting where a scene may be headed. Often the director will take this cue, or if he has a different idea, will signal the selection to be taken off.

Lighting is used in a manner generally more like theater than film. As a protagonist gets involved in his initial scene, the house lights and brighter white spotlights are dimmed and extinguished. Sometimes colors will be matched to a scene—dim blues and greens for a "death scene," reds and yellows for angry fighting scenes. At other times it is more the changes in lighting that are significant, for example, a shift in colors each time the protagonist moves from one side of a dialogue to another. In general, both music and lighting serve as reinforcing cues to focus the attention of participants intently on the central scene.

The "best" (by consensus) Psychodrama evenings have a sense of wholeness, which reflects the fact that several protagonists have worked intensively, often on related themes. Sometimes this buildup is powerful enough to sweep almost everyone in the room into the same basic feeling-state. This may be an energetic, "high" feeling, leading to dancing for a long period after the group has formally ended. Or when feelings of dependence and neediness are evoked, physical embraces, crying, and comforting may be widespread and last for an hour or more. On the other hand, when several protagonists have been dealing with feelings of conflict or alienation from others, this too may spread throughout the group and may lead to an evening ending with widespread feelings of separateness or apathy. No matter which of these feeling-states emerges, such evenings—and Psychodrama groups in general—imply that we are all similar vis-à-vis these basic themes of emotional states and that we can all feel our need for love and contact, anger and conflict, movement and energy, sadness and grief. Especially when an evening has evoked one of these areas, many participants feel united in a shared experience. During a marathon, many of these major feeling-areas are touched and shared, contributing to a widening of this emotional unity.

CONCEPTUAL FRAMEWORK

Like therapeutic community, Psychodrama grows from the general cultural experience and psychological orientations of Western (European-American) culture. Yet it obviously has important similarities to non-Western healing groups in its use of catharsis, ritual, and dramatic ceremony. Like Synanon, Psychodrama developed rather spontaneously in response to the needs of a subcommunity that had lost faith in establishment sources of therapy and care. Unlike Synanon, the central figure in the evolution of Psychodrama is a psychologist who has consciously drawn on a variety of therapy approaches in evolving his techniques. No formal, detailed analysis of Palo Alto Psychodrama has been written by Lovell, perhaps because the technique is still developing or perhaps because, like many innovators, Lovell is too involved in the practice of Psychodrama to describe and analyze it. Despite the absence of a codified theory of Psychodrama as Lovell and the Palo Alto workshop practice it, the origins of the approach are of interest for a variety of reasons. The accessibility of both its intellectual history and its present form gives us a special opportunity for further exploration of certain themes.

The techniques and conceptual framework of the Palo Alto Psychodrama approach are drawn from a variety of sources. Like many contemporary psychological approaches, Psychodrama has its roots in the Freudian, psychodynamic conception of human psyche. Psychodrama has undoubtedly drawn more on Freud's early conceptualizations of libido theory and childhood sexuality than on his later structural and ego psychological concepts. Similarly, most of the other influences on Psychodrama—Wilhelm Reich and Carl Jung, for example—were themselves more affected by Freud's early ideas.

Reich took Freud's emphasis on the biological side of psychological phenomena seriously and speculated extensively on the bodily expression and treatment of psychologically experienced distress. Although his later work has been considered beyond the professional pale, Reich has influenced the development of treatments that seek to treat the psyche, or the entire integrated organism, through the body. The phenomena Freud had identified was seen by Jung as part of a larger context of universal psychological-cultural experiences manifest in the material of dreams, myth, and ritual. Jung's interest in using such forms of human expression suggested their value for therapy.

Another important influence on Psychodrama has been existentialist thinking, both as it has developed into a psychotherapeutic influence and as it has become a philosophic and cultural influence. Out of existentialism has grown an interest in a technique emphasizing immediate experience, such as that developed by Fritz Perls in Gestalt therapy. Palo Alto Psychodrama uses a number of Moreno's techniques, as we have already seen. The innovation Moreno introduced—that the "patient," or protagonist, is a participant in the drama—is a significant break both from theater and from therapy. At the same time, it is not unfamiliar, if we think of healing ceremonies described in Part II. Catharsis, too, is found in most non-Western healing and has been an element in Western psychiatry from the day of Mesmer, through Charcot, early psychoanalysis, narcosynthesis, and recently the ideas and techniques of Laing and—directly influential on Psychodrama—Janov, whose "Primal Therapy" has gained much attention of late.

Of all these, the concepts and techniques of Fritz Perls have undoubtedly had the greatest influence on Lovell and his Palo Alto version of Psychodrama. Perls, along with most innovators since Freud, did not attempt to build a complete psychological theory. Rather, he laid out an approach to human and therapy problems, along with a set of specific techniques (Perls et al., 1951; Perls, 1971). Fundamental to Gestalt therapy and central to the Psychodrama scene is the concept of *wholeness*. Perls believed that given the proper state of awareness, "the most important unfinished situation will always emerge and can be dealt with." The potential for completion lies within the individual; the task of therapy is to bring into awareness the unfinished situation and then to facilitate the natural process of completion. This process of self-completion can occur, however, only when an individual becomes one with his immediate experience—when he is "in the here-and-now." In Gestalt and in Psychodrama, being in the here-and-now means especially being in touch with feelings. The connection is suggested by Lovell's opening statement: "We do this in the belief that there is something inside you that can put it together when you really feel it."

Perls believed that anxiety is simply a kind of human energy blocked from more useful, healthy expression. The origin of such blocks, as in Freud's conception of defenses, is in early and repeated childhood experiences—especially those experiences where the expression of feelings led to unpleasant consequences.[6] The translation of anxiety into other forms, more valuable to the individual, is achieved by tapping psychological processes going on at the present moment. This is a second aspect of Perls' self-healing point of view. The human psyche is viewed as a set of ongoing processes, some of which may be stifled and incomplete. The therapeutic process is designed simply to activate these processes and help them to completion. Fundamental to this is the augmentation of the incomplete process as it is encountered at the moment in the therapeutic situation. Since intellectual activity is generally used defensively—to anticipate and avoid psychic pain—Perls and Psychodrama use techniques that bring about activity, that move attention away from self-conscious observing of experience to active un-self-conscious participation in it. This means, specifically, getting people to move, attending to bodily reactions and positions, heightening tension and conflict when they appear, being willing to touch, and frequently shifting the focus to pursue the process.

In Perls' conception of therapy, a person working on a particular issue that is active and important will reach a point of impasse. At this point the therapist tries to heighten the impasse rather than to circumvent, decondition, or analyze it. When sufficient tension develops, a process of "death" or implosion will occur. A part of the self in which a great amount of psychic energy has been invested is being lost. Following this experience there is an explosion of direct feeling, usually grief or sadness, orgasmic release, anger, or joy. We see the same process in the "successful" Psychodrama scene. The movement from anxiety to action, to involvement, to affect, and finally to catharsis is closely parallel. As a further aid in breaking through the period of impasse, Lovell uses (in addition to all the permutations possible with workshop actors) body techniques drawn from Lowen and cathartic techniques of Janov to work with the protagonist at the point where the impasse has taken the form of a bodily "block" (e.g., "a knot in the stomach" or "a lump in the throat"). The physical suggestions and manipulations that relieve these blocks are designed to move the protagonist actively through the impasse to the feeling state that Perls refers to. Subjectively, this is the most intense and "letting go" part of a psychodramatic sequence for the protagonist. He truly "loses himself" in the bodily experience and related affect.

The Psychodrama crash carries Perls' sequence one step further. By its very intensity the experience is a unique one, and the individual is left in a vulnerable psychological state. The quiet period and postcrash fantasy, or Psychodrama scene, serve to bring the protagonist gradually back from an internal experience to a state of awareness of the environment outside himself. One important function of this gradual return from the intensity of the crash is a sense of closure for the experience. Neither Lovell or Perls expects such one-time experiences to be definitive moments of change. They serve rather to open new pathways that show the individual what he can be or can feel. The work of exploring, of widening this potentiality, remains to the individual. The preparation for return to externals serves to protect the new inner experience for the protagonist.

Thus a sophisticated sort of cathartic release is one goal of the psychodramatic experience. This catharsis should not be confused with simple expression of feelings. Although this, too, is valued, the wholeness of the Psychodrama process includes the gradual development of tension and involvement both on the part of the protagonist and the group. Whether or not catharsis occurs, everyone participates. This aspect of Psychodrama—the vicarious involvement of group members—is common to almost all varieties of group therapy and encounter. In Psychodrama the vicarious experience is heightened by theatrical effects and the clearly defined role of protagonist. Unlike theater, where the dividing line between actor and audience is not crossed, the Psychodrama protagonist is drawn from the group. The vicarious process may become so intense that a group member is impelled to become a part of the scene. Knowing that the doors are closed—that flight is impossible—also heightens intensity. For some, threatened by feelings evoked, these conditions may simply intensify a desperate emotional cutting-off from what is being observed. In my experience this is likely to happen on first visits to Psychodrama, especially for people who use intellectual defenses.

For those who become involved, the catharsis of one protagonist is a shared experience. The best way to describe the individual/group relationship is to call it a ritual one. The protagonist and actors become the focus, with the group as a sort of Greek chorus. And indeed, over the months and years, certain psychodramatic scenes recur time after time, giving them a mythic quality. These inevitably involve the more regular and profound experiences of the human life cycle: the transition from childhood to adulthood; bereavement; marital union and dissolution; career change; and so forth. In effect, the psychodramatic enactments of these situations become *rites de passage*. The Psychodrama situation, including the predictableness of the general format of certain scenes, provides the guiding framework for experiencing and releasing some of the powerful emotions that are inevitably tied up with these basic human transitions. Appropriate here is Turner's concept of communitas as the state of the social group during the ritual event. During one of these intense, ritualistic Psychodrama situations, the entire group is identified with the protagonist and his transition; this identification is expressed in the words of a song that frequently accompanies the buildup of tension during a sequence: "Break on through to the other side."

INDIVIDUAL INVOLVEMENT IN PSYCHODRAMA

The first step toward involvement—attending a Psychodrama group—may already be a significant one. If one has heard of the workshop groups and their reputation for intensity, violence, and confrontation, simply going to a first meeting may be an act of some considerable decision. Others attend the first time on a more casual basis, at the suggestion of a friend or through a brochure or other announcement. In the following description of progressively greater involvement in Psychodrama as a social organization, I shall again, for the sake of brevity, use as protagonist an idealized "typical" individual—not any particular person, but one who embodies the most frequent patterns.

Most newcomers do not become protagonists during

their first evening at a Psychodrama group, although some individuals may do so on impulse and undergo a very intense experience by virtue of being unfamiliar with the Psychodrama process. But watching and learning is the typical first evening's experience. Much of that initial experience is confusion. The pace is quick; action and music may develop rapidly and in unexpected ways. Fighting scenes are particularly startling, especially since the intensity of feeling and apparent violence may be great, despite a limited amount of real pain and damage. Gradually, the newcomer begins to distinguish the pacing of scenes and begins to recognize that the roles are being played by workshop members, not by individuals drawn randomly from the group. He begins to sense the behavior expectations of the group. In feedback, astute analyses of a protagonist's psychodynamics will be met with groans and hisses, while simple statements—"I really like you," "You make me feel cold inside," or "You disgust me when you become passive"—are accepted. Similarly, expressions of feeling are accepted and responded to, while withdrawal and closing-up are criticized or ignored.

As he observes the protagonist, the newcomer is learning about that role. He can imagine himself in the scene, how it would feel, what the director and others seem to want. When he becomes a protagonist himself, all this becomes more direct and intense. During a dialogue he is expected to express parts of himself fully and unambivalently. When an actor is introduced, the protagonist is expected to respond as naturally as possible; he also knows he is to accept the actor in the role (e.g., as a father). When he is cast as himself or another person in the psychodramatic scene, he is to "play" that part as he *feels* it. And if he feels strong emotions emerging from within himself, he is to augment and express them. Subjectively, this experience of becoming one with the psychodramatic process occurs in stages. At first, the participant may resist: "This isn't how it was." "I can't do this." Next, he may go along with what is expected, but feel very much that he is play-acting; it is an "as if" experience. Yet, "going through the motions" begins to get responses from others during the scene, and the responses of the actors may begin to build further involvement. He may find he is really becoming angry at an actor, that the family scene really begins to feel like home. Soon, he may "let go" and become part of the action, losing most or all of his self-consciousness. He begins to focus on the psychodramatic action at the center of the room and forget the observing group.

As the protagonist becomes less self-conscious, he begins to react to the scene increasingly in terms of what he is feeling, whether or not that is exactly "appropriate" to the scene. If such feelings become intense, he knows it is desirable to accept them, to lose himself in the feelings. The actors and director will facilitate this, first within the psychodramatic scene, then in a cathartic encounter in which the scene usually drops away. During the catharsis he usually is aware only of feelings, often as body states or movements: screaming, shouting, hitting, biting, squeezing. The catharsis may continue for several minutes, after which it usually decreases in intensity or changes in quality. Eventually, he feels a calming of feelings, often accompanied by dizziness (the result of hyperventilation) and subjective relief or elation. The release and "high" that frequently follow a crash are reinforcing to the whole process. Members of the group will relate to him quite positively after such an experience, sharing their own psychological similarities and making contact, because they too wish to partake in the intensity of the crash.

A frequent pattern of participation in Psychodrama groups is to attend regularly, that is, once or twice a week and weekend marathons once a month, for several months. Over this time a participant will observe many scenes and may "work" in his own scenes intermittently. Some of these may lead to the sorts of cathartic sequence just described; many others will not, but will end with feedback that underscores his impact on others, or will have value to him in the enactment of a meaningful psychodramatic scene. For example, "death scenes" and "good-bye scenes" can often be powerful for the protagonist, although they may not build to a cathartic climax. Over the course of time, the protagonist has opportunity to experiment with his behavior and to apply his experiences as observer and protagonist.

Overall patterns of involvement are extremely varied from one person to another, since the Psychodrama groups are, for the most part, "open"—that is, commitment is made for each session only. Some people attend two Psychodrama evenings each week as well as frequent marathons. Others attend one weekly group regularly over a protracted period of time, using Psychodrama much as they would an individual or group therapy experience. Still others may attend intermittently, with periods of greater or lesser attendance as their life situation shifts. Some participants attend only smaller groups—men's, women's, or closed membership groups. Some participants come as much for the social contact and the opportunities to meet people as for the group experience. Other come simply to watch, to be together with others, and to experience vicariously the intense emotions in the situations portrayed. Many participate in Psychodrama because it tolerates and encourages aspects of the personality that are not sanctioned in most outside situations. As one enthusiast put it, "This is the only place I can be as crazy as I sometimes feel." Similarly, the opportunities for spontaneity, physical closeness, and fighting are attractive to many.

Becoming involved in Psychodrama has a second side —the social relations that exist around the Psychodrama groups and workshop. Here, the process is even more complex, being a function of a person's own social circle, his need and capacity for sociability, and the makeup of the Psychodrama orbit at that time. Frequently, development of one or more strong friendships or relationships with other participants or workshop members becomes a tie to the workshop and an additional reason for attending frequently.

This double involvement, in Psychodrama groups and the workshop social orbit, often coincides with a period of major personal change: job or career shift, marital breakup, moving away from the parental home, breaking out of a role stereotype, "dropping out" of a conventional life-style or resuming one, or internal shifts in self-concept. Psychodrama provides a supportive, experimental framework for making such changes, and Psychodrama groups provide opportunity for dealing with the present-day situation and with the personal developmental issues that are evoked in the process of change. Such a period of active involvement can lead to one of three outcomes: A participant may drop away from Psychodrama, having made whatever changes (or decided not to make the changes) he wishes; a participant may continue to be involved over a longer period, attending groups more for their social than their therapeutic-growth function; or a participant may become a member of the Workshop.

While attendance at most Psychodrama groups and marathons is completely open, i.e., on a "come when you wish" basis, membership in the Psychodrama Workshop is closed, restricted, and requires a considerable commitment of time and energy. To meet the official criteria for membership, the candidate must have attended and "worked in" groups and marathons, and shown potential Psychodrama acting ability. Workshop members may discuss entry informally among themselves and with the potential member. The director may cast him as a double or as an actor in several scenes prior to a decision. The actual decision about inviting someone into workshop is a function of several factors. Involvement in the social network around the workshop is one; approval by Lovell and the great majority of the workshop members is another. A high proportion of workshop members have some sort of tie to Lovell. Some have been or still are his psychotherapeutic clients; others are intimate with him in social relations. Some see an opportunity for informal, first experiences as Psychodrama leaders or psychotherapists under Lovell's direction, and many enjoy the opportunities for acting in what is essentially improvisational theater. On the side of the potential member, joining carries with it special benefits and advantages that attract some more than others: acceptance by a permanent group whose members he likes, the special aura of those who enact Psychodrama roles and lead groups. While workshop membership once was drawn almost entirely from the "counterculture" and the radical political community, membership is now diverse, and many members who had dropped out of the Establishment in past years are in fact themselves in the process of getting work and educational experience, often in the fields of therapy or counselling. Workshop membership requires attendance at a minimum of two evening meetings per week—the workshop meeting and one other Psychodrama group—and also frequent attendance at marathons.

In workshop meetings the member learns the thinking behind the direction of psychodramatic scenes and the improvisational acting techniques of experienced members. For those with little psychological background, the workshop discussions provide a rich introduction to a variety of concepts and theories. At the same time, the member's particular background, style, and skills will be called on for the benefit of the group. In some respects this can be a mixed blessing: Workshop membership can "freeze" psychological development or even induce regressive patterns. This happens in two ways. Certain strong personality traits may be called on over and over in Psychodrama scenes. The improvisational quality of the acting and the pressure for emotional authenticity tend to make the member call on his own natural reactions. Further, the directors tend to call on those workshop members who most naturally fit certain roles. While the member may recognize that he is "acting" and may well wish to develop other traits, casting in scenes reinforces the old patterns. The second factor limiting personal change is a tacit assumption within the workshop that one is supposed to have problems, be in touch with one's psychological distress, frequently expressed in such statements as "We're all pretty fucked up," or "We're all a bunch of losers." This attitude fluctuates with time and coexists with opposite, expansive feelings that members are special, more psychologically "together" than others.

Many members find that they gradually look outside the workshop meetings for therapeutic aid. Some do this by working as protagonists in open Psychodrama groups; others seek psychotherapy with Lovell or outside therapists. The workshop group then may cease to have much value or may provide an arena for general group support, the development of skills, and experience leading groups.

Leadership of groups is determined by Lovell and a volunteering process within the workshop. Lovell may ask individuals to lead groups; he holds a tacit veto power over new leaders. The weekly open groups are led by Lovell or someone whom he has delegated to lead a group and who is willing and experienced. Individuals may also volunteer for leading special groups or segments of marathon groups. Women's and men's ongoing groups or minithons are offered from time to time, run by volunteers from the workshop as individuals or by several leaders collectively. With the increasing introduction of professionals there is the beginning of experimenting and combining group therapeutic approaches with Psychodrama groups.

PSYCHODRAMA WORKSHOP AS A HEALING COMMUNITY

We can recognize the basic elements of healing community in the workshop; yet the intimacy of my viewpoint on the workshop makes it possible to look carefully at the fit between the general pattern and the workings of this specific group. Each healing community we have described has its unique features. For the Psychodrama workshop of Palo Alto these include: its relation to American *values and norms*, the pattern of *charisma* and charismatic relations in the workshop, its particular *stage of development* as an organization, and questions about its role as *therapy*. The workshop was born in an era of challenge to the existing mores of upper-middle-class American society; the activities and attitudes of the groups embody a combination of traditional American and counter-cultural beliefs. The "therapy" provided by workshop groups is a mix of the conventional view of change for the individual, with a striving for change in attitudes more generally—the "healing" of a "sick society." As the counterculture has shifted from a popular movement to a wider cultural influence, the workshop and its members have also undergone changes. Thus, as we examine Psychodrama against the concept of healing community, we must bear in mind that this is an organization in flux.

Communitas is present in Psychodrama at two levels: in the Psychodrama groups themselves, and in the workshop. In the large, open evening groups or during weekend marathons, there are periods during which everyone is united in the experience of some basic human feeling: laughter, anger, grief, joy. Yet the openness of the groups, the fact that anyone may attend and no prior commitment to the group or its beliefs is required, means that any particular group may include individuals who will not share in these experiences. Even if such persons do not speak out, there is a general sense of uncertainty in open groups about who is who. More than any other group, Psychodrama knowingly includes participants who may be highly opposed to its activities. This openness is counterbalanced by the coercive, closed-door commitment made for the duration of the group. ("If you try to leave, you are subject to being restrained.") The result is that communitas in open groups has a pressure-cooker quality. Without initiation rules and rituals, there is a limit to the sense of "we-ness" in the group. This makes the moments of communitas more powerful in open groups: theater becomes ritual; audience becomes congregation.

It is probably more appropriate to look at communitas within the workshop group. Here, there is assurance that every participant is familiar with Psychodrama and espouses much of its beliefs. Each member has had to be accepted by the entire group and has already shown strong interest in continuing involvement.

Within workshop there is an assumption of basic equality among members, of group cohesion, and of loyalty. Behind this assumption, however, is a complex web of relations, intragroup politics that will be described in greater detail around charismatic processes. In fact, the communitas spirit of the workshop group is also intermittent and limited. During periods of crisis, everyone pulls together and communitas is high. At other times, factionalism, jealousies, and manipulations occur that undercut the sense of good feeling about the group as a whole. Some of the limitations on the level of communitas will become more evident as we look at the other group processes of healing community: norms, roles, and charisma.

The norms of Psychodrama are complex and contradictory. The valuation of communitas-reflecting norms —loyalty, faith in the group, openness to others in the group—can be high. The workshop member is not paid; he follows instructions of his free choice; he values his membership and the basic support of the group. Yet another set of beliefs tends to offset communitas norms. These other norms are a mixture of beliefs that emerge from the counterculture and especially from the encounter movement. I like to characterize them as "Dodge City" norms. Like the stereotype frontier town, there is a high valuation in Psychodrama on personal freedom and independence. Each person should be respected as he is, and no controls should be placed on him. In Psychodrama, this is extended to an acceptance of usually disapproved qualities: madness, violence, licentiousness. But as in the frontier town, one ego is bound to bump into another eventually. The approved style for this is aggressive and confrontive, a style derived ultimately from Synanon. Thus, while Psychodrama norms invite poeple to expose their most vulnerable areas, their most hidden feelings and impulses, the Dodge City side of these norms paradoxically may take the form of an assault, and leaves integration of the whole experience in the participant's hands.

The Dodge City norms that can be a brake on communitas in Psychodrama also reflect the Slater paradox that was referred to in Chapter 14: the self-limiting quality of the reaction against loneliness and isolation in our society. It is as though the tension between the competitive outside culture and the potentially cohesive Psychodrama group were internalized in these contradictory norms. This observation brings out an important feature (noted in Part I) of communitas and communitas norms, namely, that the spirit of communitas does impose restrictions on, and demand compromises from, the members of the group. In Psychodrama the unwillingness to accept such restrictions leads to two phenomena that limit that continuity of communitas feeling. First, while the high pressure crashes and their contagion effect brief moments of communitas, they also stir up anxiety. The outside participant often expresses this in terms of the difficulty he has in fitting what he has experienced at Psychodrama into his daily life; the workshop member may become overaroused with the cumulative effects of his intense feelings. Further, to the extent that crashing is an initiation rite and a symbol of proper workshop role performance, members may unconsciously seek to crash as a means of expressing needs for attention and recognition.

The role expectations for Psychodrama participants and workshop members follow from the norms just discussed. Thus the expectations can appear contradictory—in fact, at times they are. But it is also through the enactment of Psychodrama norms over time that some of their paradoxes are resolved. Thus the role behaviors desired at Psychodrama include spontaneity and activity, yet also patience and responsiveness. Workshop members are criticized by one another if they "come off the wall" in a Psychodrama scene, that is, play the scene in terms of purely selfish or self-serving motives. When the Workshop member is acting in someone else's scene, he is to channel his spontaneity into reactions to the protagonist or other actors. His own needs and problems are to be dealt with at another, more appropriate time, perhaps when he is the protagonist. This expectation, in fact, embodies the charismatic component of the Psychodrama role. One is to transcend oneself in the service of the scene. This is true for director, actor, and participant alike. The protagonist is inspired to become involved, to lose himself in the scene by the director's instructions, the actors' responses, and a sense of group expectancy. The actor is supported by the fact that the director has cast him and by his theatrical poise. The director is aided by the group's trust in him and by his workshop members' skill in moving scenes along.

The charismatic process flows through the Psychodrama organization in a broader way also. Workshop membership and directing are looked on with awe by most participants. Thus, attaining workshop status means an investment of specialness for the member; now he is expected to play roles in the open groups. His sense of charisma is renewed each time he volunteers or is chosen for a Psychodrama scene. After a scene, protagonists frequently have intense and often grateful feelings toward the actors who have played in the scene with them. If the member's outside social circle includes many who admire and participate in Psychodrama, the charismatic feeling will carry over. Something analogous may happen to the participant when he first "works" in a group: He may feel strengthened, elated, able to cope with the feelings, people, or problems that were weighing on him previously. Thus when a scene goes at all well, the director, the workshop actors involved, and the protagonist all have a feeling of specialness and elevation above their ordinary sense of themselves.

Most of the satisfactions of participation in Psychodrama relate to this charismatic process. For the protagonist, they are the satisfactions of being the center of attention and of achieving some degree of internal change. For the actor, the satisfactions lie in the chance to perform and in the enjoyment of his roles; for the director, in the drama itself and in the therapeutic change he may bring about. For workshop members, many of the rewards stem from the personal involvement with others. Much of this relates to the sense of personal growth and evolution available in Psychodrama groups and within the workshop. There is a sense of involvement with the organization as a whole, much of which is experienced in relation to Lovell as an individual. This sense of felt, personal involvement varies with each member. Interactions with Lovell and other workshop members vary from one person to the next. There is a constant shifting of relatedness among workshop members, heightened by the lack of explicit structure. Cliques, couples, and individuals change from time to time. This is especially true around Lovell, an intense, attractive man in his late 30s who is not married and whose social life is primarily with workshop members. Relations with Lovell tend to be dyadic, partly as a result of his personal style and partly because each workshop member attains a significant sense of his own status and involvement from his position vis-à-vis the leader. In his double role as director and center of the workshop social network, Lovell has a powerful impact on everyone else. The workshop group of from 15 to 20 members is thus an interconnected system, something like an extended family or kinship network, where changes in relationships in one part of the network cause ripples throughout the network that ultimately affect everyone.

In an earlier discussion of group processes in healing communities, there emerged an important link between communitas and healing charisma. The two can reinforce each other; the specialness of the individual enhancing the specialness of the group, and vice versa. In the Psychodrama workshop this mutual reinforcement seems limited by several things. First, the Dodge City norms place a premium on individuality that is reflected in the unattached life-style of Lovell and many workshop members and participants. Even though many members, including Lovell, actually are deeply involved in the Psychodrama community, the appearance of independence often overrides acknowledgment of the importance of the group. Second, Lovell's dyadic style of charismatic involvement, reflected in the way he works with the Psychodrama groups as well as in his social life, limits his investment of the group as a whole. Lovell reflects this in saying about his leadership position, "I think everybody has power. I think I am dependent on them to get the power. They think I put the trip on them. I think I absorb their energy and give it back to them." While this is an astute analysis of the charismatic process, it suggests that there is only a limited amount of "energy" or healing capacity; that the charismatic interaction of leader and group does not increase the total capacities of each. Third, within the workshop there is a dilemma around continued healing and change. Not only do the permissive norms deter the group members from pushing each other toward mutually agreed-on individual goals, but there is some implicit support for continuing to have problems. The contagion of intense feelings in groups can increase this difficulty. Although the workshop has had, until recently, its own time for members to "work" on their own problems, the absence of an "objective" participant or leader seems to limit the resolution of many problems, especially conflicts within the workshop group. Thus, though the workshop tends to be highly supportive of members during crises or during periods when they are making independent moves toward change, the healing quality of the group is not enhanced. Lovell himself acknowledges this, and increasingly encourages workshop members to seek therapy outside the group.

A resolution to this situation seems to be gradually evolving. Where possible, Lovell is seeking to transfer responsibility and authority to others, both for leading of groups and for administrative operations. There is a growing movement within the workshop toward "professionalization," that is, increasing members' training in both drama and psychology. This development would parallel that which we found in so many other healing communities: The sufferer, after some time in the group, becomes trained as a healer. By providing a route to a "professional" status vis-à-vis their problem areas, the workshop would decrease the rewards to members for being on the sick side of the sufferer/healer line. Then, like the reformed Alcoholics Anonymous or Synanon member, the workshop member might continue to deal with his problem area, but from a position of greater mastery over its destructive potential.

The elements of the individual healing process identified in other communities can also be seen in the workings of Psychodrama. The participant's attention is gained through a variety of means: the closed door, lights, music, dramatic scenes. For the protagonist, these are intensified; the expectancy of the group and the actors' moves create strong pressure to attend to the scene and to inner states. It is as protagonist also that the behavior modification process of learning how to be a Psychodrama participant occurs most intensely. The director's instructions, workshop members' interactions in scenes, feedback, informal talks with other participants—all these guide a newcomer in learning the concepts and language of the group and applying them to himself. As in other healing communities, the sequence seems to emphasize changing behavior first, then understanding why.

The Psychodrama newcomer also learns by observing the behavior of experienced participants and workshop members. He will find himself rewarded for taking initiative when it is within the norms. This is particularly important in aiding participants who are not active, dramatic, and emotionally expressive. Thus in the process of Psychodrama participation, role paralleling occurs as an important mechanism for guiding the individual and for solidifying changes made in the immediate situation of Psychodrama groups.

A final question of interest in considering Psychodrama as an individual healing process concerns the function of the cathartic crash. From our observations it seems that the crash plays two roles for the participant. First, it is a great relief and a unique experience unto itself, often followed by a dramatic change in mood or attitude lasting days or longer. Second, the crash is a signal moment in the protagonist's life, a time when defenses are down and the opportunity for change, at a more profound level, is present. Lovell recognizes this by minimizing external input during and after the crash, trying rather to follow the protagonist's lead. The crash plays a function for the group also; it is a dramatic portrayal of the impact of the Psychodrama process, and a powerful, evocative experience for the observer. The crash is the result of powerful passions that the ordinary social rules suppress; at the same time it signifies that these feelings and impulses, usually to be feared, can be brought under control and used beneficially. In this sense the crash serves as a central ritual experience linking the individual healing experience with the group as a whole.

SUMMARY

The Psychodrama workshop of Palo Alto is a multitechnique encounter group that has existed for five years in a small California city. Its roots are in the counterculture and radical political movements of the 1960s, but it also has origins in traditional psychoanalytic theory and practice and in newer psychotherapeutic techniques. The groups combine a variety of encounter and new therapy techniques into a sophisticated cathartic process. The group meetings of the workshop are charismatically led and have an intense atmosphere of sharing, ritual, and communitas. Psychodrama groups serve the functions of therapy, social club, theater, church. The practices of the group meetings held by the workshop tend to be viewed as somewhat scandalous by many outsiders, but for its participants the opportunities for expression of impulses not tolerated elsewhere is unique. At the moment, the workshop is in a period of transition in which its program and practices are becoming more therapeutically oriented and professionalized.

Scrutiny of Psychodrama as a healing community reveals that it fits the general model, but suggests also that (1) seen firsthand, no group will fit the model ideally; and (2) in the evolution of healing communities, it takes time to reach a condition of stability, especially in a change-oriented society like ours.

NOTES

1. For simplicity I shall use the term "Psychodrama" (capitalized) to refer to the techniques used by this group, which, however, bear only limited relation to the psychodrama technique originated and practiced by J. L. Moreno and his followers.

2. My own vantage point for observing the Psychodrama Workshop of Palo Alto is more personal than that of most of the other examples that have been presented. I have been a participant in some of the Workshop groups, a trainee in Psychodrama technique. Although my observations of the workshop will undoubtedly be biased as a result, this close involvement also provides opportunities not available in most of the other cases presented.

3. I am grateful to Victor Lovell and others in the Psychodrama Workshop for much of the historical information in this section.

4. Bioenergetics grows from the work of Alexander Lowen, a disciple of Wilhelm Reich. Building from Reich's interest in pursuing the biological,

bodily aspects of libido, bioenergetics uses specific exercises and body positions to intensify and release tension.

5. The following description applies primarily to weekly four-hour open Psychodrama groups. During longer groups there may be alternation of leadership, some structured activities and exercises, and less structuring of Psychodramatic scenes as members of the group elect to become protagonists spontaneously when they feel ready. This description of a "typical" Psychodrama group applies most closely to groups led by Vic Lovell. Other leaders have somewhat different styles and procedures. Since Lovell has led groups continuously for over four years, and since other leaders of workshop groups have learned from him, his groups are the most representative examples of Psychodrama. I should also make clear that every Psychodrama sequence is unique, so that the sequence presented here is primarily illustrative.

6. Psychoanalytically oriented readers will see immediately other parallels to analytic ideas in Perls' and Lovell's concepts of psychology and therapy. The "here and now" emphasis of Gestalt is similar to the free associational participation of the psychoanalytic analysand. Many other parallels can be observed; it is possible that the approaches are based psychologically upon one mechanism of human change. Certainly the *style* of involvement is drastically different.

CHAPTER 17

Review

During the past 15 years millions of Americans have participated in some form of encounter group experience. The motives for participating have been varied, but in general they
reflect a search for the missing elements in modern life listed
by Slater: engagement, dependence, and community. Our
examples suggest that although encounter groups do strive to
give such experiences, they also run into a good many problems. The fact that engagement is implied in the very word
"encounter" is probably one reason for the widespread use of
this word. Each of the groups described uses confrontation as
an aspect of procedure. While this style of interaction is given
various rationales, it responds to the widespread desire for
settings in which one person can be authentic with another.
Yet confrontation in itself is not necessarily healing, and it
may well be deleterious to individuals and to group cohesiveness, that is, communitas. For this reason most encounter
groups stress charismatic leadership. The leader can temper
or channel the impact of direct encounter and can bring the
group together despite the divisiveness of confrontation.

Few encounter groups strive for lasting cohesion; the two
specific groups presented are exceptions in their evolution to
communities. Thus most encounter groups create a tempo-

rary community. In this time-limited situation, the intensity
and impact may be considerable, but obviously the role of the
group in individual lives can by only catalytic. The encounter
movement has had to fit into the entrepreneurial American
pattern of selling itself as a valuable or entertaining individual
experience. This leads to constant changes in style, shifts in
popularity of different leaders and techniques, and mobility,
as leaders search for new sources of participants. All these
effects discourage the development of encounter groups as
healing communities. Both Synanon and Psychodrama retained their identities by remaining in one place, dedicating
themselves to a style of group activity that changes gradually,
and involving members for lengthy or indefinite time periods.
This has enabled the development of regular patterns of organization and some degree of ritualization of the encounter
experience.

It is only with the evolution of encounter groups into
such nascent healing communities as Synanon and Psychodrama Workshop that the desires for dependence and for
lasting sense of community are met. Even so, these groups
suffer from both the strong valuation of individuality and the
mistrust of communality that exists in our culture. Synanon
solves this by banding addicts together against a common
enemy, the larger society; Psychodrama Workshop sacrifices
some of its healing potential by stressing a common bond of
misfitedness. By making such adjustments, these groups
begin to offer their members stability and a setting in which
personal evolution can be blended with group involvement.

As I shall suggest in Chapter 23, encounter groups and
healing communities in general reflect the "moral order," the
side of human culture concerned with relatedness and belief,
rather than mastery and manipulation. The encounter
movement is indeed a *movement*, whose day will inevitably
pass. Behind it will remain two sorts of impact: the specific
sort of healing communities that we have discussed here, and
a broader impact on existing social structures—therapies,

hospitals, businesses, classrooms, congregations—for which it offers a recharging with new intensity and meaning. If there is a serious danger in the encounter movement, I doubt that it is so much in its individual "casualties" as in the faddishness with which it has been quickly accepted and can be equally quickly dismissed. Time is needed to evaluate the techniques evolved and to find their best application. And time is needed for the incorporation into more durable organizations of some of the lessons and experiences the encounter group provides.

PART IV

A Model of the Healing Community

A model of the healing community reveals two aspects: (1) the processes experienced by the individual who comes to the group as a sufferer and is inducted into membership; (2) the processes that sustain the group itself and create the atmosphere in which the individual process may occur. The first I call the *individual healing process*; the second, *group and organizational processes*. The individual healing process, which will be the subject of Chapter 18, has three important components. First, the sufferer's *attention* is gained by saturating him with new and intense stimuli. His awareness shifts from his inner state to the group's activities. He is *aroused, induced into activity*, and involved in ceremonial meetings. Second, the sufferer is engaged in a natural *behavior modification process* in which desired behaviors are socially reinforced and undesired behaviors are ignored or punished. As his behavior changes, so may his subjective state of mind. Third, the sufferer learns how to be a member through a process of *role paralleling*: He models his behavior after that of other, experienced members or "staff." Implicit in this concept is a similarity of behavior expectations for all members, regardless of experience or rank. In all three indivdual processes, the group facilitates the sufferer's progress; in the context of a caring

298

group of fellow sufferers, he can transcend himself to engage in the healing process. Roughly paralleling these interactional steps in the healing process are three stages of intrapsychic change: *imitation, identification,* and *integration.* In the first stage, the sufferer copies behavior of others in the group without knowing why the behavior is useful. In the stage of identification, the sufferer has come to feel his group membership as part of himself; his behavior is congruent with his feeling of belonging. Integration is a longer-range result of involvement in the group in which the experience of illness, the member role, and identification with group are blended as a permanent part of the individual's psychological and social life.

Group and organizational processes in the healing community can be understood through examination of the concepts of communitas and healing charisma. These processes are interwoven, thus giving the organization stability and strength for its primary task of healing. There is an interplay of communitas and charisma, involving the norms and roles they define, respectively. The charismatic leader is a focus of this interplay. The group processes and the individual healing processes are mutually supporting. Finally, the healing community is, in varied ways, supported by its interaction with the society in which it functions.

CHAPTER 18

The Individual Healing Process

When a sufferer comes to the healing community, he is invariably withdrawn, preoccupied, and demoralized. No matter what variety of problem or behavior may be involved, it turns the attention of the sufferer inward. He either seems impervious to the activities of others or responds to them in idosyncratic ways. By the time he has reached the healing community, this inward focus of attention has isolated the sufferer from most of the important people in his life and from his neighbors. The acute schizophrenic distorts his perceptions and gives them personalized meanings. Depressed persons are occupied with themes of guilt, despair, and self-debasement that have subjective vividness but little reality to others. The paranoid is acutely sensitive to his environment, but reinterprets its meaning to fit an internally determined view of the world. The chronically physically ill person is preoccupied with his pain or disability, and has often exhausted the patience of those caring for him.

ATTENTION SATURATION

The final, common result of these different patterns of suffering is withdrawal—physically, psychologically, perceptually. The sufferer becomes increasingly enmeshed in his own way of experiencing things and increasingly withdrawn from socially shared patterns. This is the counterpart of the deviance-labeling process. And, in a vicious-circle process, labeling tends to fix the isolation that has developed. Much of the healing process that will be summarized in this chapter can be understood as serving to counteract this pattern of isolation and labeling. Although the techniques used in specific healing groups differ from one another, they have in common a massive effort to recruit the sufferer's distracted attention. They do this by saturating his perceptual experience with varied and intense stimuli. In early meetings or ceremonies there is frequently a bombardment with unusual experiences: sounds, sights, odors, tastes, sensations, and extraordinary patterns of interaction. Rhythmic movement and chanting is required. The insides of his body may be stimulated with hypnotic drugs or purified with emetics or cathartics, and in the therapeutic community the newcomer is met by a verbal barrage of information about the setting, questions about himself from every patient or staff member he encounters, and usually medication intended to make him more receptive to interaction.

This barrage of stimulation, activity, and inquiry takes place "in public," although within the confines of the group. The sufferer knows that this group will become important to him and that its members have been sufferers like him. He sees that many of them have become less isolated and are able to help him—able, also, to serve as models for what is expected from him. Usually he is already aware of the special aura of the group. Thus the sufferer experiences a social saturation, along with his physiological and psychological saturation, during the first ceremonials or first days of hospitalization. Together, these impacts create an experience of *attention saturation*. The individual healing process begins by drawing the sufferer out of his isolated subjective and objective position and getting him to attend to a new environment: the healing community.

Almost simultaneously with the process of saturating the newcomer's attention, the group begins to focus his attention selectively. In the therapeutic community the newcomer is asked, by staff and patients, "Why are you here?" He may be taken, as was Mary Wheeler, directly to a group meeting, where all attention is on a focused, organized discussion process. Many of the non-Western groups use the synchronous activities of chanting or dancing to initiate the focusing of attention as the group desires.[1] The massive saturation of perceptual channels jolts the sufferer from his passivity and inward focus. The ceremony directs his attention in a particular way. Once the sufferer is in phase with others, chances are that he will attend more readily to them or will join them in their rapt attention to the charismatic leader.

Quite early in the process the sufferer is induced to take an active role. In the first Zar ceremony he is expected to perform his own *gurri* dance, following the lead of other experienced members. The question "Why are you here?" implies that the new Tompkins I patient is able to respond coherently. It also begins to convey expectations of member behavior norms—exposing one's problems, in this case. Once the sufferer is in a more active orientation, he is exposed to processes that make the new state autonomous and less dependent on the excitement of initiation alone. In the Zar ceremony this movement to a more cognitive and interactive level occurs with the "diagnostic" interrogation between the Zar doctor and the sufferer's Zar spirit (i.e., the spirit speaking through the sufferer). As he responds with the spirit's answers, the sufferer validates the whole belief of system of Zar and his personal involvement in it. If we remove the rich imagery of Zar mythology and demonology, we find it to be a set of concepts, values, and norms about illness and patienthood. This conceptual system is coherent, organized, and internally consistent. It is shared with the important others involved in the healing situation. Once the patient's attention has been freed and made responsive to the charismatic leader and the healing group, this system becomes an important means for maintaining the outward orientation of attention and for sustaining the sufferer's new way of organizing his percepts.

Two powerful mechanisms are used by most healing communities in these processes of moving the sufferer from passivity to activity: confession and catharsis. In one way or another, the newcomer frequently must acknowledge his own contribution to what has happened to him. In the Zar cult this occurs symbolically in the dialogue with the leader when the sufferer's Zar spirit begins to reveal itself. At Psychodrama the confession takes the form of revealing information or feelings. In the therapeutic community we found increased agreement during the first week with the questionnaire item "I got myself here." Whatever the form, confession has several values. It is a way of accepting membership. It suggests that the sufferer has some control: Since he brought about his suffering, he can reverse it. It provides a mechanism for dispelling the massive, accumulated guilt for letting others down, for not living up to expectations. It signals a possible rebirth through opening himself to new ways, that is, those of the group.

Catharsis has many of the same functions as confession and is often integrated with it. Catharsis may precede confession, as in the *gurri* dance that precedes interrogation of the Zar spirit, or it may follow, as most often happens in Psychodrama. In a sense, catharsis is the affective, physiological side to the moral and cognitive act of confession. It, too, is an active stance in relation to the problem and a means to potential rebirth.

Both catharsis and confession—the whole process of activating the newcomer, getting and focusing his attention —serve to arouse the sufferer. In general, arousal is found in change situations; it seems requisite for the imprinting of new behaviors and beliefs (Frank, 1973). This is true of religious conversion, which, as noted in Part I, is much like the changes some patients in a therapeutic community seem to undergo. It is quite possible that the importance of arousal is primarily physiological: The changes in feeling, attention, belief, and capacity that occur in healing depend on biological changes. This seems to be intuitively recognized in the use of drugs, both in Western and non-Western groups, and in the emphasis on achieving altered states of consciousness without drugs in encounter groups.

Confession and catharsis are most important early in treatment. They are the dramatic content of the *rite de passage* of initiation to the community for both member and group. In Synanon, where the applicant has been altering his physiological state with heroin and has usually been through many medical and penal institutions, the newcomer is dealt with more subtly: Expecting a great fuss over his arrival and drug withdrawal, he is regarded casually and ignored. This alerts him and makes him more interested in any attention he gets. When he is interviewed by a staff member, he finds himself lectured and his answers ignored or scorned; his prior adaptive patterns, designed to manipulate others, are outmaneuvered. He begins to realize "They are better at it than I am," and a respectful feeling of kinship may develop. In his first group meeting, an unexpected, devastating, verbal attack occurs. Unlike other therapies he has been through, this verbal assault may affect him. The pain of attack is unlikely to overwhelm him; he has been through much worse in the course of his addictive career. But he is puzzled and attracted to a group that knows so well his defenses, his ploys, and his experiences.

Universal to healing communities in their initial interactions with a new member is a sequence of events in which his attention is gained by massive stimulation and changes in consciousness; he is aroused through powerful confessional and cathartic rituals, and his attention is refocused on the activities and beliefs of the group. Through this process the newcomer passes over the threshold of membership and is symbolically reborn. Much of the stigma of his prior evolution into a deviant social role is thus removed, and he may see new possibilities ahead.

BEHAVIOR MODIFICATION

The second aspect of the individual experience in healing community is a continuous process, not a separate phase. We saw most clearly in the analysis of events on Tompkins I how the ward community acts as a behavior modifying environment, providing responses to patient actions from the instant of admission. I use the term "behavior modification" in the sense it is used by Skinner and his colleagues (1953), as an outcome of what they call *operant conditioning*. According to this view, the behavior of an organism will be responsive to the effect it has on the environment. If an action is followed by a positive, gratifying environmental response, the organism is likely to repeat the behavior. No reaction at all or a negative reaction from the environment leads to extinction of the behavior. With sufficiently frequent positive reinforcement, a behavior may become conditioned, that is, automatic and independent, as long as a certain level of reinforcement is maintained. Operant conditioning phenomena can be demonstrated in many human situations, including Rogerian "nondirective" therapy (Frank, 1973). The presence of behavior modification does not imply healing; the dehumanized backward patient is also the result of an operant conditioning process. Behavior therapy seeks to apply operant techniques consciously for the patient's benefit.

The processes of behavior modification that have evolved in healing communities were not designed as such, but evolved naturally. The founders of several therapeutic communities have become aware of the process as behavior modification principles have become better known (Saslow, 1965). Thomas Detre, the first director of Tompkins I, describes the ward as setting a "series of hurdles" for patients. If a patient can successfully manage these hurdles, Detre felt, he is ready for discharge. Our observations and findings confirm this but suggest that the behavior modification process of the healing community is much more subtle and complex. In addition to operating within different time spans, the behavior modification process is interwoven with the group processes of the community and with other aspects of the individual healing process.

When behavior modification has been consciously applied to psychiatric ward situations, it has generally remained an individually oriented process in which the patient is reinforced in some sort of desired goods or scrip (Colman and Baker, 1969; Lindsley, 1960; Ayllon and Haughton, 1962; Buehler et al., 1966). In the healing community, the rewards are social: the approbation of other members and leaders in the group.

The charismatic quality of interactions and the general feeling of communitas enhance the potency of the social reinforcers. To be accepted, or praised, by Ogamisama is a highly desired reward for the Tensho member. Similarly, to be granted a privilege advance by the Patient Advisory Board of Tompkins I is gratifying for any patient who is not massively resisting the program. Often such reinforcements take place in a large meeting of the whole community, so that the reward is felt as enhancement in everyone's eyes. Psychodrama groups combine these effects as the protagonist receives both the charismatic reward of interaction with the director and the support and approval of the group during a successful sequence.

In order for him to respond to the group healing framework, the newcomer must be oriented and motivated to this reinforcement system. This is the function of the attention saturation process and the focusing of attention upon the healing community situation. Attention saturation, to be effective, requires that the group be coordinated and that it have a high degree of consensus about its norms. Only with coordination and consensus about expectations is there certainty that appropriate reinforcements will occur in response to particular behaviors by newcomers. The Tompkins I norm system—and the strong effort made to enculturate all patients to it—becomes clearer when we recognize that the behavior modification sequence depends on a consistent response pattern from all members of the community. Patients as well as staff members in the therapeutic community must know how to respond to the behaviors of a new patient. This is true both on the "micro" level of moment-to-moment interaction in conversation or therapy session and on the "macro" level of decision-making about privilege statuses, passes, and discharge that patients and staff negotiate.

Other healing groups evince this pattern of gaining the newcomer's attention, directing it to the healing activities of the group, and then influencing him through a behavioral interplay. At Synanon the newcomer is surrounded by a tight community of committed members who share a special language and ways of interacting. The total commitment required of the newcomer and the consensus about norms make it inevitable that he play the game the Synanon way or leave. As positive rewards, Synanon offers the approbation of a group of ex-addicts, if the newcomer can "make it," and an experience in group interaction that is reinforcing through its hard-hitting, aggressive quality. Similarly in the Zar, Tensho, and Zuni situations, group membership offers a variety of rewards, including contact with inspirational leaders and deities, lifelong membership in a group, economic opportunity, and the chance to become a healer oneself. Each of these groups makes use of these rewards to encourage the behaviors that are expected and that reflect transcendence of one's problems.

The behavior modification processes are thus active manifestations of the norms of the community, moment to moment and week to week. They guide the newcomer in learning a new role as a member of the group. Interactions that are defined as significant by the norms and offer frequent opportunities for small successes not only reinforce the desired behavior, but boost the morale of the initiate. He gains a feeling of mastery and success that is likely to have been absent from his recent experience. The behavior modification system of the community is also a valuable cognitive framework around which people relate. The intensity and difficulty of face-to-face interaction are eased by the availability of structured patterns of response. Thus the greeting on Tompkins I—"Why are you here?"—is easier to use because it is a regular feature of ward life. Similarly, the careful scrutiny of another patient's mood and behavior, prior to granting a privilege change, is facilitated by the ward's expectations of responsible, cautious behavior by those in the Patient Advisory Board. The behavior modification sequence provides guidance not only initially, but as time goes on and the member either prepares to leave the community or begins to find a more permanent place within it. An important element in defining the specific behaviors to be reinforced is the third aspect of individual healing, role paralleling.

ROLE PARALLELING

"Be like me! Come up here with me!" Ogamisama's exhortation expresses the essence of the third healing-group process, *role paralleling*. The newcomer learns how to be a proper member by emulating the behavior of others in the group. These others include not only other sufferers, but members at any level of experience, including the leader. For the roles, norms, and behaviors expected of newcomers, experienced members, and leaders are cut from the same cloth.

For role paralleling to become part of the individual healing process, the new sufferer's attention must be gained. Where behavior modification processes engage him as an interactor, role paralleling gives him a model of behavior to imitate. By watching the behavior of others in the group, the newcomer sees what is expected of him. He can then imitate; he will be reinforced positively if he begins to do this well. The new Zar cult member rises to do the *gurri* dance for the first time after he has seen other members of the cult begin their dances. The therapeutic community patient asks others about their problems after he, himself, has been asked several times. After being verbally devastated several times, the Synanon newcomer will try this on someone else. In each case the person being imitated may be at any level of experience in the group.

The role of the newcomer in a healing group can be contrasted with the patient role in traditional psychiatric hospitals. In the psychotherapy hospital, a deliberate attempt is made to leave patients a wide range of behavior options in their time outside psychotherapy. The hospital setting is used much like the transference relationship, as a place where problems can be reenacted. The newcomer is expected to act like a "patient," not like his therapist. The roles and organizational functions of patient and staff member are complementary: One is sick, the other well; one has problems, the other cares for them. In the custodial hospital, the patient role is even more clearly defined—in a very negative fashion. The patient is not simply sick—he is dangerous. His role is constructed in terms of controls and limits set by the institution. Patienthood itself is a sign of taint, and no connection at all is conceived of between patients and staff.

Contrasting with the ambiguity or negativeness of patient role in the psychotherapy institution or asylum is the positive definition of being a patient in a healing group. Zar possession carries little taint; on the contrary it offers opportunities for personal psychological improvement and also for external improvement of one's life situation. Underlying these fringe benefits of Zar affliction is the generally positive status symbolized by the Zar spirit: This "personal possessive and protective spirit . . . solves the problems of life and beautifies the face with an inner glow." As evidence of this positiveness is the fact that Zar spirits are rarely exorcised. This pattern is universal in our examples. The afflicted Zuni becomes part of a priestly group; the Tensho member gains salvation through his affliction. Drug addiction, viewed with horror as a combination of crime and mental illness by American society, is considered the best qualification for helping other addicts within Synanon. The Psychodrama Workshop member finds that his personality style, which he regarded as a problem in the past, is accepted and used in the roles he plays during Psychodrama scenes.

Carrying the impact of role paralleling one step further is the pattern of promotion from newcomer to member to leader. The new sufferer sees that there are people around him, occupying positions of responsibility and leadership, who have the same malady he has. Nothing can convey the message of role paralleling better than this. Here is a group within which the sufferer can become the healer. Psychologically, this realization makes possible a further step—from *imitation* to *identification*. Like the child growing up, the newcomer can look to others in the group as representing what he may become. For the deviant adult, the possibility of identifying with other members he can observe and respect brings hope for himself and begins to break down his alienation from others.

Role paralleling is frequently an aspect of a behavior modification situation. For example, in the Tompkins I therapeutic community, a new patient is shown around, introduced, and observed by a more experienced, responsible patient. This provides a reassuring, caretaking entry to the ward; at the same time, it is the process that begins the patient's involvement in playing an active therapeutic role. The patient-sponsor who shows the newcomer around the ward is also likely to involve him in a series of frank questions about how he came to be in the hospital. These questions convey the expectations of the community that problems are to be discussed openly and frankly with other patients. Role paralleling is also manifest in some of the general practices of the therapeutic community. Leaderless groups indicate clearly that the staff expects that patients can be therapeutic with one another, following the staff behavior example; the monitor duties give patients the same responsibilities that nurses and aides assume at other times. At Psychodrama a nonworkshop participant may be called on to play a part in another person's scene. In "feedback" the comments of anyone present are legitimate and are expected to follow a pattern of expression modeled by workshop members.

Thus progression in the healing community—first imitation of, then identification with, more experienced members—is in terms of a style of member behavior shared at all levels. People may have different tasks, but all share in common certain principles about proper behavior. Thus, Tompkins I patients are encouraged to be open about their problems and to confront other patients directly. Staff members are similarly expected to be open about individual difficulties having to do with the ward and about difficulties they sense in their colleagues. In general, there usually seems to be a limit put on confrontation with, or challenges to, more senior, experienced members. Tompkins I staff do not discuss personal problems extensively with patients; when Psychodrama Workshop members share "hang-ups" with participants, it is usually done in the past tense. At certain times in most healing communities there may be a break in this pattern. In Psychodrama this occurs when the director and/or workshop members "crash"; in the Zar cult, when the leader does her *gurri* dance. These moments of communitas provide powerful support for the role paralleling process; if they occur too frequently, however, they tend to weaken the healing charisma of the experienced members and route the healing process away from those who are supposed to be in greatest need.

The parallel in role definition makes it easier for new-comers to move from their first patterns of behavior to roles involving greater flexibility and responsibility. Psychologi-cally, role paralleling makes possible the incorporation of qualities of more experienced members of the group through identification. In the therapeutic community we saw this pro-cess begin in Bill Putnam and Mary Wheeler, who, after gradual and intense change processes, respectively, became identified with other patients and staff members. Charles Williams, however, never showed even imitation in the hos-pital, but revealed a degree of identification after discharge.

In a short-term involvement such as Tompkins I, few, if any, patients reach a third psychological stage that is found in many of the healing groups described in Parts II and III, namely, *integration*. In these groups, the malady, member-ship in the healing community, and the personal experience of healing are combined as a permanent change in social position and self-perception. The married female Zar cult member can now attend all-night ceremonies and may con-sider divorce. In our society, where emphasis is put on living successfully in one's nuclear family and working indepen-dently, we try to return the sufferer home to integrate his illness as, at most, an occasional participant in a healing situation (i.e., an "outpatient"). In other cultures—most especially the Zuni—where families are extended kinship groups and where other group memberships play an impor-tant part in daily emotional life, healing group membership is permanent, and integration occurs within the continuing ex-perience of membership. In those groups that have open-ended membership, there tends to develop a family feeling and social structure. Integration involves finding a meaning-ful place in the group, one suited both to personal and group needs. For the individual, integration usually implies a de-gree of compromise around the original problem. The healing process is not usually curative. There is usually a degree of change in the member, especially alleviation of behaviors and improvement in subjective states, which immediately preceded joining. Other therapeutic changes may also occur psychodynamically and in social relations. The rich "family" environment of the group allows the playing out of many issues, some of which may be "worked through" in the manner of psychoanalytic therapy. We saw such a process beginning for Bill Putnam. Ogamisama frequently orders Tensho members to make changes in their daily relations with parents that are likely to have massive impact on the member. Undoubtedly, her intuitive sense that a filial relationship has become unbearable, or that guilt over breaking with family has become too great, makes these manipulations powerful sociotherapy. But ultimately, integration implies some acceptance of residual difficulties, just as in a successful psychoanalysis certain issues are not resolved but adapted to more effectively. Thus the Synanon member, like the Alcoholics Anonymous member, is always an ex-addict. The Psychodrama Workshop member remains "hung up" in certain ways. The Zuni Clown member remains retarded or alcoholic. And the therapeutic community member continues in outpatient care.

The psychological levels of group involvement (imitation, identification, and integration) do not correspond directly to the social levels of group status (newcomer, member, and leader) or to the processes of individual healing (attention saturation, behavior modification, role paralleling). The psychological levels reflect an inner reality that is, in part, expressed in social relations; the social levels reflect possible intrapsychically significant roles that an individual may play in the group. There is some tendency to limit advancement in status level according to the perception of a member's movement at the psychological level. Usually, a member does not become an accepted leader until he has begun to integrate membership into his life pattern. In a sense, behavior modification operates here, too. Status advancement in the group is a reward for evidences of increasing intrapsychic commitment. But this relationship is not rigid. The mentally retarded Zuni may reach a state of integration of his membership in a Clown fraternity without ever aspiring to leadership. Mary Wheeler moved rapidly to a leadership position on Tompkins I on the basis of imitation, but this proved to be untenable. Membership in Psychodrama Wordshop usually requires a strong identification with the organization, and in turn makes possible a more complete integration of workshop status into one's wider social life.

In American healing groups other than therapeutic communities, we see a movement toward more enduring involvements with the group and toward the achievement of integration within the group context. This is true at Synanon, where commitment is open-ended and where, for the successful member, integration occurs *within* the group.[2] It is also increasingly true of other of the encounter movement groups, epitomized by the evolution of communal living-working settings around such encounter leaders as Perls. The same seems to be true of mental health settings that must accept patients who relapse: After a period of years, there inevitably develops a group of returning members. This phenomenon is viewed with concern by mental health workers oriented to brief treatment, that is, to de-labeling the deviant. It can be seen as a positive, or perhaps simply an inevitable, quality of healing communities, one that can be dealt with constructively if role paralleling is developed and meaningful opportunities are provided for integration of the individual in the organization.

SUMMARY

The individual healing processes of healing community are interwoven mechanisms of individual-group interaction. Frequently, the first events are designed to get the new member's attention away from his own thoughts, feelings, and demoralized subjective state. By saturating his attention with stimuli and by administering consciousness-altering drugs, a state of arousal is created that makes the newcomer amenable to involvement with the group and its members. Natural behavior modification sequences are used to guide the member toward desired changes, both in momentary interactions and over longer time periods. Serving as a model for the newcomer in assuming the role of a member of the healing community are the other members, including the leaders. The parallels between the roles of all members provides an encouraging possibility of advancement within the group.

These individual healing processes are supported by the presence of the healing community and its group processes. Communitas implies the cohesion and support that facilitate the early processes of gaining attention and involvement, that define the norms for behavior influence, and that maintain a sense of equality allowing parallels between the roles of members at any level of experience in the group. Healing charisma similarly provides specific extra energy and reward for the behavior modification processes and the inspiration for acting on the possibilities created by parallel roles.

Intrapsychically, these healing mechanisms bring about a sequence of levels of seriousness and committedness. Initially, the newcomer may merely imitate the behavior of others. Gradually, as he begins to accept membership and to be accepted in the group, he identifies with it. Finally, in some groups that allow or demand lifelong commitment, the member finds a new social role that includes his involvement in the group as a major facet integrated into his life round. In the course of this sequence, his previously deviant behavior is altered or redefined in such a way as to undo his isolation and demoralization, and impart hope and a vision of a meaningful existence.

NOTES

1. Studies of kinesics (body movements) and speech behavior indicate that in small group situations movement and speech may be closely synchronized between individuals. The dancing and chanting of a group may heighten this and may thus subliminally propel the newcomer towards a feeling of oneness with the group.

2. Synanon has now begun to develop communities, operated on its therapy lines, where both ex-addicts and others may espouse a life totally within the organization.

CHAPTER 19

Group and Organization Processes

The healing community is a "by your own bootstraps" phenomenon. Somehow these groups manage to lift their members out of subjective demoralization and social deviance, and at the same time to survive as organizations, often with little aid from the societies around them. Healing communities also lack the intrinsic stability of organizations built around bureaucratic or authoritarian relationships, yet they obviously do have stabilizing mechanisms. At the most general level, the strength and stability of the healing community stems from the interrelatedness of its processes. This interrelatedness operates among the special group processes of healing community themselves, between the group processes and the individual healing process, and between the group and the society in which the community exists. Specifically, *the healing community is characterized by the following: (1) an internal sense of specialness attributed both to individuals in their relations to one another (healing charisma) and the group as a whole (communitas); (2) translation of this specialness into charismatic roles and into behavior norms that reflect the cohesiveness of the community and its espousal of a specific set of beliefs and practices; (3) devotion of much attention to healing activities and derivation of much sense of individual and group effectiveness through the posi-*

*tive results of healing efforts; and (4) a varied pattern of relations
between the healing community and its culture, characterized universally by a boundary between members and nonmembers.* In this
chapter I shall review and discuss these features of healing
community.

These four facets of group and organization process will
be developed in terms of the model used in Chapter 9. For
convenience, Diagram 19.1 below repeats the diagram shown
in that chapter.

DIAGRAM 19.1

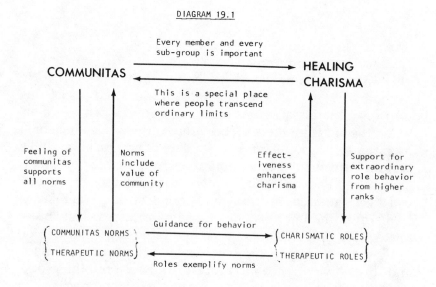

COMMUNITAS

Large group gatherings are emotionally powerful situations. We know the intensity of political rallies, rock festivals,
revival meetings, and the explosiveness of the mob. Observers of group dynamics conferences report that the most

chaotic and unexpected behaviors occur in large meetings with ambiguous expectations (Rice, 1971). Most healing communities have some gathering of the whole membership, often at times of initiation. Such ceremonies or meetings are generally marked by considerable ritual activity on the part of many or all participants, restatements of basic beliefs, and catharsis or confession, or both. The large gathering is a time of affirmation and renewal of the sense of communitas. Members are gathered together, like a congregation, out of a sharing of certain rituals, beliefs, and leaders. Involvement with the group, and often with the leader, is intense. During the ceremony, members are exhorted to participate actively, and this in turn underscores the sense of commitment and significance of the ceremony. Frequently a period of quiet prayer, during which the leader and the group are contemplated by all, alternates with active chanting, singing, dancing, or verbal give-and-take. Through his participation, the member feels related to each other member: Feelings of love for the group and its members are experienced. Put another way, it is in the large group ceremonies that the member symbolizes and experiences how much of his relatedness is engaged with his healing community.

Considering the evolution of human culture, it is not surprising to find large gatherings having such significance. During the greatest part of his evolution, man has lived in small bands of perhaps 25 to 100 individuals. Occasions on which all would be gathered together would tend to give visual reminder of the social involvement and dependency of every person. It is not unreasonable to speculate that the capacity for experiencing strong feelings became attached to such situations, as well as to more intimate attachments. It is also not surprising that such occasions are ones where important beliefs are affirmed and where the leaders of the group are revered.[1]

In the therapeutic community it is the patient-staff meeting or community meeting that serves the purpose of symbolizing the presence of communitas. Some of the activity of the meeting, like discussion of ward problems or individual progress, is pragmatic. A great deal of the meeting's purpose is the promulgation of beliefs by staff and experienced patients, a reaffirmation of the proper style of action and thinking for the members. One central belief being affirmed is the importance of the entire group *as a group*. Every member of the community, patient and staff, is present, all unified for the moment by their shared beliefs. The significance of the situation is often centered in the person of the leader, who may show his most charismatic side in the large meeting. It was in patient-staff meetings of a ward where I was administrator that patients would regularly attribute to me control over the weather, requesting good weather for weekends or blaming me for cold or rain. In another setting where we had deliberately made small subgroups of patients and staff the important focus of involvement, it proved necessary to have at least one large community meeting weekly. Here, the process of the meeting primarily involved the leaders' restatements of norms, often applied to specific situations in the community or to the progress of individual patients.

In many healing communities the significance of the large gathering is heightened by spontaneous or ritualized alteration of consciousness, catharsis, or confession. These actions are characterized by a relaxation of the ordinary norms of self-control, poise, and reputation. Through such actions the member literally places his trust in the community, feeling that he will be protected, accepted, and loved—no matter what happens. By structuring and making legitimate the ways in which these dramas occur in the large gatherings, the communitas norms and specific therapeutic norms play an important part in facilitating such trust. These phenomena clearly play on powerful capacities in the individual for involvement and commitment, and for espousing beliefs.

This explains why the theme of indoctrinating newcomers in the norms of the healing group recurs in all our cases. For Tompkins I, we saw clearly that staff made strong efforts to get patients to accept the ward's norms, or at least to look "as if" they accepted them. Acceptance of the group's norms by the newcomer means that he is one of "us." "We" can trust him accordingly (i.e., know roughly that he will act by our norms and in our interest). The greater the solidarity around values and the narrower the range of belief, the greater such trust will be.

Communitas, as defined by Victor Turner, is an ideal state of society in which all individuals are related as equals, each unique but each as valid as the other. On the surface this ideal would appear dissonant with situations in which certain participants—the newer members, clients, or patients—come to the group with a defect or trait that makes them less able to function than the others in the group. Indeed, the logical consequence of this is seen in most mental hospital situations: There is considerable loyalty among staff and among patients, respectively, but little loyalty or equality between groups. Communitas *is* an ideal, not a real state of things, and much of the activity of the healing community is devoted to striving toward the ideal.

On a pragmatic level, three structural features of healing communities are important in facilitating the continuing influence of the communitas ideal: size, composition, and substructure. Generally, we found that all varieties of healing community tend to remain small enough so that members can know all other members. Not only is this important in terms of the feeling of real relationship to all group members, but largeness in itself eventually leads to hierarchy, bureaucratic rules, and formal roles, all of which are counter to communitas. The composition of a healing community is important for communitas in two ways. First, the sharing of some basic problem or quality that appears in most groups puts everyone "on the same level." Second, the fact that people vary in many ways—experience in the community, progress with their "problem," personality style, skills, and so on —tends to strengthen the group as a whole.

For a variety of reasons, much of the essential activity of the healing community goes on in subgroups. Two of these reasons can be readily identified: (1) Situations that arise in small groups make possible direct interaction of an informal, personal sort; and (2) small groups evoke the sense of family, of trust and belief in the group and leaders. One subgroup in particular—variously known in our examples as staff, workshop, priests, or regular members—is most important in maintaining the community. Attaining membership in this sub-group varies from one setting to another, but almost always requires some symbolic transition or special training. The sense of cohesion and family loyalty within this subgroup, which is the core of the healing community, is usually intense. Correspondingly, conflict in this core group will be seriously destructive to the healing powers of the whole community. Again, the importance of a shared set of beliefs can be seen as limiting conflict in this central group. The bond among the members of the core group has a familial quality. On a ward, for example, director and head nurse often have a father-mother relationship with the other staff members. Much as with new members, the family feeling facilitates closeness, loyalty, and acceptance of common beliefs.

The second sort of subgroup involves one or more of this core group with one or more newer members. In the therapeutic community there are several versions of this second sort of subgroup, including: (1) group therapy, usually led by one or more staff members; (2) family therapy, involving only one patient and his family, with one or two staff present; and (3) family group therapy, with several patients and their families. In Tensho there are small groups that are more cognitive and problem-solving in orientation, and in Synanon the thrice-weekly small group meetings are the place where the most intense, dramatic experiences occur.

The encounter movement is completely built around small groups, with a nonexistent, implicit community in the background. Psychodrama Workshop offers small groups from time to time, and in some ways marathon groups are a special subgroup. In these more intimate situations, behavior modification transactions can take place readily; one member may be focused on more intimately than is possible in larger settings; experienced members may express their charismatic potential more comfortably; and healing charisma may be transmitted outward from the experienced members or staff. These varied functions make subgroups quite important in the life of the larger healing group, although there is variation in how many of these functions take place in the smaller settings.

It is this importance of the subgroup that makes its composition important. Invariably there is a balance struck between giving it a pure communitas quality—"We are all sufferers"—and including enough experienced and norm-sharing members to ensure that it will operate as a subgroup of the whole, not as a potentially oppositional clique. The use of leaderless groups on Tompkins I is an example of this balance. Since the groups have four additional weekly meetings with one ward doctor and other staff, they are frequently reminded about the expectations for how therapy is to be transacted. At the same time, the absence of staff for these two leaderless meetings, which are considered to be therapeutically every bit as legitimate as the others, emphasizes the expectation that patients can be therapists. In other healing groups, a similar mix of older, experienced, specially trained members with more recent adherents assures that the healing charismatic process will be operating. Again, the value to the group, as well as the sufferer, in a prolonged involvement with the group can be seen: The experienced, "well" member provides an important middle group of personnel who can both heal and serve as model for a newcomer.

This discussion of subgroups brings out more clearly why there is intense opposition to cliques and to intense pair relationships, especially heterosexual ones, in therapeutic communities. Such relationships create little islands of individuals who, by virtue of relating closely to one another, can fend off the otherwise powerful influence of the community and its norms. Mary Wheeler's relationship with a patient, uninvolved with the ward, prior to her "conversion," was a way for both of them to remain less affected by the ward. Similarly, the intensity of a romantic attraction absorbs energy that would otherwise be going into group relatedness and personal change, so that it is not surprising that staff rate patients who have had close heterosexual friendships during hospital stay as less improved than others (Almond and Esser, 1965). Obviously, some dyads are inevitable and even desirable, especially in residential settings like Synanon. The reports indicate that, as in the kibbutz, pairing off is accepted but not emphasized unless it seems to compete with group involvement.

Subgroups also provide situations for working out status issues in the healing group. In the ideal state of communitas, there would be no status differences at all. But in reality, there are inevitably status differentiations of some sort, either imposed from outside or related to the fact that there is a learning process in the group that is important in healing. In the therapeutic community set in a typical hospital situation, efforts must be made to overcome the differences in status between doctors, nurses, aides, and patients. The small groups provide a way of doing this, since participants are on a more equal footing in the group meetings. Here nurses are free, at least in principle, to enact their retraining as active therapists, rather than as "doctor's helpers." What status remains and what authority is used depend on the charisma of the small group leader rather than on the privilege of his rank. The issue of authority and its use exists in any social setting, including the healing group. The small group situations make it clear that the basis for the authority of individuals over one another in the group is charismatic, that is, inspirational, rather than coercive or bureaucratic.

HEALING CHARISMA

Healing charisma is a sense of specialness that makes individuals believe they can actually become what they would like to become and makes them believe that another member of the group really has the powers they would like to attribute to him. Specifically in the healing situation, it is that which enables the sufferer first to *believe* he can become, and then actually *to* become, a member of the group, relieved of all or most of his affliction and able to help others with theirs. It is the motive force that enables members to encounter new sufferers, unafraid of their bizarre behavior, and to communicate to them the expectation that they can respond and become members. It is the sense of specialness about himself that lets the leader act dramatically and therapeutically, in the confident belief that he can move and heal others.

One way to understand the psychological roots of healing charisma is to compare it with the processes of dynamic psychotherapy and psychoanalysis. Here, too, a special energy is evoked in the participants, labelled "transference" for the patient and implying for the therapist a special attitude of acceptance, controlled involvement, and countertransference reactions used in the service of therapy. Over the course of a prolonged therapy, the transference feelings of the patient are varied in quality and intensity. Frequently the initial transference reaction is positive, and in early therapy the patient may make striking gains. Some patients may even terminate treatment on the basis of these changes. If treatment continues, this positive feeling becomes the basis for trust in the therapist. Negative feelings begin to emerge as the patient projects prior relationship experiences onto the

therapist. These are worked with through the constant jux-
taposition of the therapist's real attitude and the patient's
reactions. On the therapist's side, the charismatic aspect of
the situation resides in his maintaining an accepting, understanding attitude; controlling his own reactions and using
them to facilitate understanding and show the patient the
impact of the transference; and his consistent involvement in
the relationship. On the patient's side, charisma resides in his
continued trust in the therapist and the therapy process despite the subjective discomfort with the feelings he is experiencing towards the therapist.

In the healing community these same phenomena occur,
but they are parceled out differently. During the initial involvement with the group and the more experienced members or staff, the positive side of the newcomer's reactions are
evoked. The negative side is externalized in the form of a
spirit or problem, and symbolically brought under control in
the course of ritual experiences involving confession and
catharsis. Once under control, the negative feelings, impulses, spirits, or problems are sorted out and redefined in a
more positive way. The Zar spirit is a problem only up to the
point of entry into the cult. There, the spirit is invoked as a
source of greater power. In the process of the group's *gurri*
dance, the member may give expression to passionate and
violent impulses that would otherwise be unacceptable.
Within the framework of the ritual situation, such expression
is considered positive, a step toward control over the spirit
and its power. Over time, this "negative transference" side is
repeatedly subordinated by use of the "positive transference"
to the group and the leader. This usually occurs in special
circumstances of meetings, which through the power of ritual
and strong normative expectations, also favor the triumph of
the sufferer over his difficulty.

Healing charisma draws upon the latent presence in the
individual of an experience of himself as effective, worthy,

and good. We have no way of knowing exactly where in the personal history such experiences occur. They may be in part archetypal, existing as a part of man's constitutional given. They may occur during infancy, when there have been periods of unqualified love in his or her relationship with parents and other nurturant figures, or in later childhood, in a sense of the family circle.[2] These would seem most likely as the original experiences that the healing group seeks to reproduce. For the newcomer, the important figures in the group are the leader, or a member who has charisma like the leader's, and the other members, who welcome him into a fellowship that has a warm, family feeling. This constellation evokes powerful, partly pre-verbal subjective experiences of being at once in the presence of larger, awesome forces, and being important one's self.

Evoking these latent sensations provides the special energy of healing charisma.[3] It is a social energy, since it can be evoked only by the interpersonal experience of entering the healing group. The group uses healing charisma to make the new member feel capable of being more than he thinks he is, transcending his problems, and experiencing that desired sense of internal goodness and satisfaction. Immediately upon evoking this feeling, the newcomer is taught to associate it with the role of group member. Subjective satisfaction with self is immediately translated into an aspect of membership. In this way, healing charisma is an aspect of the primary healing process. Here, however, we are looking at healing charisma as a factor in maintaining the healing group. The discussion thus far indicates that although the newcomer's charismatic experience is dependent upon being in the group, it draws upon things inside himself and thus adds something to the group. Just as in transference-based psychotherapy, there is no psychological sleight of hand going on; the healing charismatic process draws upon something that the sufferer brings with him. Thus the sufferer adds to the group while at the same time benefiting from it. I shall show shortly how the entry of new sufferers adds to the group's charismatic power in general.

Charisma in the healing group does not logically begin with the sufferer's charisma, although I have described the general charismatic potential first. This was done to avoid the usual assumption that charisma resides in the person of the leader. Charisma is a social process; it can never be located simply in an individual, just as individual psychotherapy cannot be effective without the trust and involvement of the patient. What happens is that the charismatic process has a tendency to concentrate on one person. This is most dramatically the case with Tensho, where the leader is a deity. In Zuni, where individualism is frowned on, there is no report of a central leader. What the charisma of the leadership does is to symbolize the group and its power. Supporting the leader, who is the focus of the group, is one way in which the healing charismatic process contributes to maintaining the group. Much of the process that goes on around the charismatic leader is concerned with the group's beliefs. Although these evolve and continue through a shared consensus, it is the leader who voices the beliefs most clearly, who judges ambiguous situations, and who points out new directions.

By being a leader who is more than just a leader, the charismatic person models something that is true, ideally, for everyone in the group. No one is defined solely by his role in the group; instead, like the leader, any member is expected to be more. Much of the member's charisma is provided by the example of the leader and the inspiration he gives in interactions with members. More accurately, the leader evokes the charismatic potential in his followers. From the descriptions of interactions of members of Synanon with Chuck Diederich, or members of Tensho with Ogamisama, it is difficult to understand how the words said could have produced the effects ascribed. Mary Wheeler's profound change after Dr. Detre's one comment to her was similarly surprising. The impact of such interactions on regular members—staff, in the case of the therapeutic community—is to inspire them to become more than their ordinary roles encompass. This recurs as a theme in the descriptions of members in healing groups. Synanon veterans in one breath describe Diederich as saving their lives, and in the next credit him with what they are today.[4] Diagram 19.2 below expresses, in terms of the model of group processes developed earlier, the relationships between the charismatic leader and the elements of the healing community.

It is this expansion beyond ordinary roles that links healing charisma to communitas. If everyone in the group, from newest member to leader, is expected to be something special, unique, and strong—beyond what role would suggest —then a community does exist that is superordinate to that of daily affairs. A patient may also be a caretaker; a nurse may be a therapist; a doctor may be a leader. The feeling that "here I

DIAGRAM 19.2

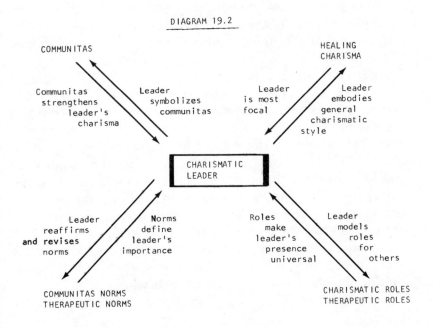

can transcend my assigned role in life" is a universal one. If I cannot be stereotyped by a role definition, then I am more likely to think of myself apart from *any* role, as a unique co-member of the group who happens.to have certain tasks to do.

The person of the leader facilitates this reinforcement between healing charisma and communitas by his behavior, which embodies and models a charismatic role, and by his statements, which enunciate the norms of communitas and the group's specific healing approach.

GROUP PROCESSES AND INDIVIDUAL HEALING

The ultimate focus of charismatic activity—the impact on sufferers—is also an important link in the charismatic process. The evidence that the whole system is working is found in its ability to bring about change or cure. Visible changes —either intense struggle with major problems or disappearance of troubled behavior—are evidence that the charismatic process actually influences people. Such evidence reinforces the members' sense of their own charisma and that of the leader. The leader, in turn, is strengthened by this feeling of effectiveness.[5] The influence of the group on both the individual's behavior and his beliefs supports the group as a whole. Both imply that the group is successful in conveying its beliefs to new sufferers and having a healing impact on them. "Conversion" experiences, whether sudden or gradual, confirm the belief of older members, confirm the effectiveness of "staff" or leaders, and confirm the power of the group. These are all aspects of healing charisma, which is thus renewed by the work of the group with sufferers. The entry of new sufferers from outside the group and their involvement in the primary healing process contribute to maintaining the charisma of the group as a whole.

The individual healing processes delineated in Chapter

18 are, in turn, supported and facilitated by the group processes. The presence of the whole group in healing ceremonies
provides a general enhancement of particular therapeutic
measures. The saturation of new members' attention and
gaining of their involvement calls on the entire network of
group processes, and frequently on the charismatic leader
particularly. Thus, the spirit of communitas as a general atmosphere, made manifest in the norms of group involvement
and healing practice, contributes to putting the newcomer in a
social milieu dramatically different from the one he was in
before. The charismatic aura of group members, manifested
in their behavior and bearing, are intended to evoke the
initiate's charismatic potential also by massive exposure to
new stimuli. The specific responses of members, which comprise the behavior modification process, are guided by the
therapeutic norms and roles maintained in the community.
Role paralleling is facilitated by the charismatic reinforcement
of roles. Diagram 19.3 below expresses, in terms of the model
previously used, the interactions between the individual healing processes and the group processes.

DIAGRAM 19.3

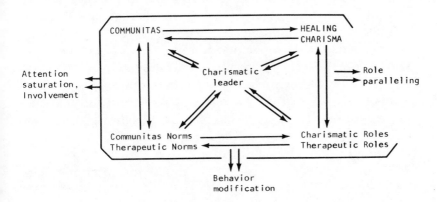

THE BOUNDARY WITH THE OUTSIDE CULTURE

Unlike the relatively consistent interior processes, there is great variability in the relationship between healing communities and the social contexts in which they exist. Some are quite marginal to the mainstream of society; the Zar cult, Tensho, Synanon, and Psychodrama are in this category. Others are more central; the encounter group, the therapeutic community, and Zuni healing societies are progressively more accepted and legitimate institutions in their respective cultures. The marginality or legitimacy we are speaking of is at an explicit level. A culture may be overtly hostile to a group yet give it room to function and flourish. This is the case with Synanon, which, despite its run-ins with neighbors during the early years, is strongly supported by other parts of society. Although "self-sufficient," Synanon is obviously dependent on the environment in many ways for acceptance and resources. The inability of established mental health and legal institutions to cope with addiction creates a sociological "space" and a steady flow of sufferers for Synanon. Similarly, the Zar cult and the Tensho sect cater to individuals and problems not well provided for by other parts of society.

Another variable in the relations of the healing community to society is the overlap in norms. Zuni medicine societies are not only accepted per se, they exist as important groups in a culture that values groups and group membership highly. In other, more marginal healing communities, we still found that patterns inside the group mimicked important cultural patterns outside. This, in fact, was true in some way for every case. Yet some groups, such as Psychodrama, clearly have norms for behavior that are very different from those of the outside society. The expression of violent feeling encouraged in Psychodrama sessions is distinctly frowned on by the surrounding middle-class culture.

Somewhat surprisingly, the viability and internal effectiveness of the group are not directly proportional to the acceptance of society or the sharing of its norms. This is because the absence of support from outside can generate a greater degree of communitas inside the community. A good example of this is Synanon, which over the years has maintained, and if anything increased, its separation from the surrounding society. On the other hand Psychodrama, which keeps its boundary relatively open despite being culturally different, suffers with variations in morale and stability.

A different aspect of the boundary is the acceptance and healing of new members. This process is vital to the group, especially if healing is central in the group's goals. Healing is evidence of the efficacy of the community and thus strengthens it. Similarly, beneficial effects on members are a contribution to the outside society in that such effects reduce the negative impact of the problem behavior that led the individual to the group. Membership may also contribute to the outside world more subtly, by facilitating changes in social arrangements such as job, marriage, or parent relationships. These may not be viewed positively by outsiders who are affected, but the net effect may be to reduce the previously existing social strains.

SUMMARY

The healing community's effectiveness and stability are based on its special social processes. These can be understood in terms of the specialness of the group, communitas, and the specialness of relationships between individuals in the group, healing charisma. Each of these qualities draws on basic human potentials that are frequently subordinated in other settings and situations. Communitas and healing charisma are mutually supporting, and each makes a contribution to the daily life and special ceremonies of the healing community. Individual healing processes are made possible by the special group processes. Least consistent, but still important in the effectiveness and stability of the community, are the relations between it and the surrounding society.

NOTES

1. The physiological impact of social setting has been demonstrated for psychiatric patients entering a mental hospital (Mason et el., 1965), and for normal subjects entering a research ward (Fishman et al., 1962). These effects involve the longer-acting adrenal steroid hormones, not merely immediate, brief biological responses that accompany arousal or anxiety. I am not aware of studies of physiological responses to ceremonial situations, but it would be surprising if such gatherings did not produce considerable effects, possibly beyond the immediate excitement of the situation itself.

2. With delinquents and older sociopathic individuals, the failure of individual, group, and therapeutic community treatments emphasizing these altruistic impulses can be understood in terms of the absence of these early experiences in the life history. Synanon's aggressive, attacking approach to the addict is experientially more comprehensible to him. The success of emotionally "cooler" behavior-modification techniques with some delinquent populations reflects the same thing.

3. I am aware of the inaccuracy of the word "energy" or, in fact, of any term borrowed from natural science to describe the phenomena we are dealing with here. The more accurate statement would have to be phrased something like, "the capacity to evoke unusual behaviors from another person and from oneself."

4. Charismatic leaders may be quite aware of the distortion of the total credit (and responsibility) this sort of statement involves. Often they will directly confront this to demonstrate that what is *in the other* gives power, that the charismatic person is not the sole source of change.

> And, behold, a woman, which was diseased with an issue of blood twelve years, came behind him, and touched the hem of his garment:
>
> For she said within herself, If I may but touch his garment, I shall be whole.
>
> But Jesus turned him about, and when he saw her, he said, Daughter, be of good comfort; thy faith hath made thee whole. And the woman was made whole from that hour (Matt. 9:20–22).

Recall also Vic Lovell's statement that his power is drawn from those he works with in Psychodrama (see Chapter 16).

5. One way in which psychiatric staffs contend with a crisis of confidence in the community is to increase the amount of disturbed behavior they must deal with, usually through increasing the rate of admissions. The resulting busyness not only distracts from the loss of confidence or the problem on the ward, but reinforces everyone's sense of confidence in themselves and in the community by showing the effectiveness of the latter in changing behavior. In one therapeutic community, for example, the announcement that the director and founder was leaving was followed by an increase in admissions and in the amount of disturbed behavior staff had to deal with (Robert Dupont, personal communication).

PART V

Implications

Healing community is a concept with both specific, pragmatic applications and general, universal significance. As
a specific, it suggests approaches and issues in such treatment settings as hospital psychiatric wards and community
mental health centers. As a universal, it has implications for
our understanding of the individual, of organizations, and of
society. Chapter 20 will be concerned with what the general
model of healing community, and the explorations we have
pursued to develop that model, tell us about the workings of
therapeutic communities. I shall try to focus on the themes
and issues that the present analysis indicates are most central
in the functioning of such settings. These include the part
played by communitas as a major dimension in group life,
and the importance of charisma in healing and in meeting the
needs for authority and nurture in the community. Chapter 21
broadens the practical discussion to cover issues relevant to
the wider provision of mental health services. The healing
community in its varied forms proves to include a wide variety of "programs." The motivating needs and institutions
behind various groups are also more varied when seen in the
perspectives of healing communities, and suggest new formats for psychological therapy.

Chapter 22 is an exploration of what the healing group can tell us about man's psychological makeup. Just as we draw conclusions about man's nature from the behavior of patients in the psychotherapy dyad, certain implications can be drawn from the behavior of healing group members. Since this has not been the primary focus of the book, the implications drawn here can be only hypotheses. However, the effort is useful, since so much of our psychological insight is derived from a strict focus on the individual and loses sight of man's considerable capacities for group and interpersonal involvement. Chapter 23 turns back to the healing community as a social institution, examining it not in terms of its mental health function, but as a type of organization. The healing community is here considered as a relative of other institutions with strong manifestations of communitas, like the kibbutz, and as an example of a "moral" as opposed to a "technical" order. Also considered—and speculated on—are the lessons the healing community may have for us at a time when our institutions so often seem to isolate and frustrate us, and so rarely to heal us.

CHAPTER 20

The Practice of Therapeutic Community

There are, without doubt, more psychiatric units using techniques of therapeutic community than ever before. This is partly the result of the fact that therapeutic community or its cousin, milieu therapy, have become the accepted standard for running psychiatric units, and partly the result of tremendous changes in hospitalization patterns for mental illness. Most Americans who become acutely disturbed are now treated on a voluntary basis at private hospitals, community mental health centers, general hospital psychiatric wards, or state hospital admission wards. All of these settings tend to be oriented toward brief hospitalization and restoration to the community if at all possible. Toward this end psychoactive drugs are used widely, along with varying combinations of individual, group, and social therapeutic approaches. Quite often this overall therapeutic combination is referred to as a "therapeutic community." The name used is not so important as whether the setting is therapeutic. The model of a healing community developed in Part IV can be of use in looking at this issue in real treatment settings.

The healing community model is not a standard against which psychiatric wards can be judged but rather a framework within which they can be understood and de-

343

veloped. Changes in hospital care of the last 25 years can be seen as setting the stage for the widespread evolution of the healing community approach to psychiatric disorder. The trend away from large, distant, impersonal state hospitals to more local, open, and intimate settings makes possible the evolution of healing communities. The model discussed here does not delineate necessary components of therapeutic community. Instead it suggests certain universal patterns that may be found within the specifics of any given setting. To put it another way, it is communitas and healing charisma, not group meetings or patient government, that are critical to a therapeutic community. It is the presence of an individual healing process akin to that described in Chapter 18 that is critical, not the particular combination of medication, therapy, and ward program. I shall examine the practice of therapeutic community with the healing group as a framework, looking at such issues as cohesion and norms; the relation of therapeutic community to its setting; patterns of leadership and authority; the handling of dependency; patient roles and careers; the relation of organic therapies (e.g., drugs) to the therapeutic community approach.

COMMUNITAS AND COHESION

In Chapter 2 we argued that the organizational dimension, communitas, was critical to the processes of healing we were analyzing. The importance of cohesiveness—a subjective, everyday sense of communitas—cannot be underestimated for therapeutic community. The effectiveness of a treatment unit organized on therapeutic community principles and its success as an organization are proportional to this sense of shared membership and values. Experience has shown, over and over, that the outward forms of therapeutic community—meetings, patient government, open doors —can exist *without* a concomitant development of healing processes if the community is not cohesive. This observation leads to certain conclusions about the place of individual therapy in a therapeutic community setting. Loyalty to the community as a primary facet of therapeutic community treatment implies a limit on the ideological commitment to dyadic treatment relationships. For the therapist who espouses a dyadic psychotherapy, the subordination of such treatment to the community may force a real and difficult choice.[1] I would argue that the clinician in a therapeutic community must learn how to make individual therapy a *part* of the overall program for patients. The issue here is somewhat subtle: It is not the *practice* of one or another form of dyadic therapy that is at issue in therapeutic community, but the *accessibility of its essence* to those outside the dyad. If the dyadic therapy activity is both special and hidden, then feelings of division, competition, curiosity, and so forth will develop. If, on the other hand, others feel that essential interaction of the dyad is shared with others in some way, then the dyad can coexist with, and reinforce, the community, regardless of whether the content of therapy sessions is public. In practice this means that dyadic therapy rules and relationships embody the same norms shared by the community in general. More subjectively, it means that the dyad and experiences in it are perceived as part of a greater whole, not set off from the rest of the community.

How can we estimate the degree of cohesiveness on a psychiatric unit? First, I would suggest that the question should be addressed to the "core group" of permanent members of the community, be they staff or patients. If this group is tight-knit, mutually supportive, and united in its orientation to treatment, a major degree of communitas exists. Second, this core group must be able to direct its energies outward in dealing with the sufferers who enter the community. It must maintain enough sensitivity to the world outside to protect itself. A core group that is so close and so occupied with itself that it cannot reach out to new sufferers will obviously be ineffective in creating a wider sense of community for all members. Similarly, a core group so committed to itself and its values that it neglects the status of the community with outsiders, will risk organizational extinction (Stotland and Kobler, 1965). Third, the sense of unity, first in the core group and then emanating to the membership as a whole, will be reflected in the sharing of certain orientations toward the treatment process. For Tompkins I we found that staff quite agreed on their concept of optimal patient behavior. We found that, by and large, patients over the course of time adopted similar orientations as they became involved in the community. It does not seem critical that patients be able to verbalize the norm system of the therapeutic community. What is important is that they come to accept it in terms of their behavior in the community, and that they not openly voice beliefs contrary to the therapeutic values of the community. Thus the leadership of a therapeutic community must constantly concern itself with the transmission of its ways to new members, be they staff or patients, that is, with educational activities as well as therapeutic ones. Several of the healing communities used as examples here—especially Tompkins I, and also Psychodrama—never complete these educational activities. Instead, the behavioral changes brought about by the healing community "staff" are considered sufficient. Nevertheless, the communitas feeling within the staff is critical and is part of the overall healing process.

AUTHORITY AND NURTURE

A further set of observations on real treatment settings has to do with the two other important dimensions of organizational life discussed in Chapter 2, control (or authority) and nurture. Real hospital settings inevitably carry with them expectations of authority relationships throughout the organization. In Chapters 3, 18, and elsewhere, I have laid great stress on charismatic leadership and charismatic authority. While charisma can facilitate the authority process, it does not provide answers for the everyday dilemmas of decision-making and social control in the organization. The analysis developed here, along with the model of the healing community, suggests certain considerations in the handling of authority in a therapeutic community. First, to the degree that there is a cohesive core group, it will be less necessary to use directive authority, empowered by rank and hierarchy, to turn therapeutic policy into practice. That is, if therapeutic technique is communicated to staff as a set of norms shared by the leader, the staff, and ultimately the patients, it will be unnecessary to *order* staff to conduct themselves in the desired way. Our model suggests that it is the process of the community, along with its specific therapeutic techniques, that is healing. Therefore, the leader, or whoever is formulating therapy in the situation, can allow himself to be influenced by ideas that emerge from the staff or from the patients. These are the individuals actually experiencing the challenge of engaging patients in the real setting of the treatment unit. A combination of the distance and perspective of a leader and the intimate, everyday experience of staff and patients will lead to the most effective formulations of therapeutic technique. This suggestion does not imply complete relinquishment of authority to lower-ranking staff and to patients. Instead, it is a suggestion that the leader(s) make policy decisions on therapy and other issues *together with* other members of the organization.

The second insight about authority stemming from our conclusions is that both absolute control and absolute permissiveness are deleterious to good treatment. Even the ideal of communitas that we have suggested as a form of social life toward which therapeutic community constantly strives, does not imply absolute freedom. Rather, it does imply a degree of shared belief and conformity that makes extensive external or hierarchical controls unnecessary. The healing community as a whole takes responsibility for the control of potentially harmful behavior. This attitude accepts the fact that most patients admitted to a therapeutic community have, in some degree, come to see themselves as less responsible than usual for their behavior. This approach also avoids any stigmatization of the patient who may behave unusually. Instead, it simply designates certain behaviors as leading to temporary control of the person manifesting them. In my view, maintaining this degree of authority and control is the kindest sort of care. Permissiveness implies acceptance of all the negative, self-destruction impulses of others. Tempered control and influence imply a reluctance to accept the negative side, while hopefully allowing the individual to determine for himself his positive direction. Perhaps the best protection against a misuse of authority is to insist that it be used openly. The authoritarian patterns so pervasive in traditional hospitals depend in good part on authority hiding behind a mystique of hierarchy and professionalism. Authority used in the open is much less likely to be abused, and less likely to be experienced as oppressive.

The handling of authority is important not only for the climate of the organization, but also for the healing process. The power of the group over individuals is built into the behavior modification process. Both arbitrary and permissive use of this authority will weaken this process. I do not mean to gloss over what is actually a profoundly difficult moral issue for psychiatrists and other therapists, namely, that *any* judgment on the acceptability of another person's behavior implies an imposition of one's own views. Ronald Laing and his followers have developed this issue explicitly around the question of interfering with psychotic processes that may, in their view, represent positive transformations of personality (1967). But Laing himself points out that all human interactions involve such impositions; thus there is no way out of the dilemma unless we choose to leave mental sufferers completely to themselves. Once we choose to involve ourselves with patients, we face the existential truth that there is no "neutrality." Further, we must recognize that some of our responses in a therapeutic community situation must be conditioned by the needs of the community rather than the needs of individual patients. It is the therapeutic community's subordination of the individual to the group that some find distasteful. If we accept the need for controls, which is a critical mandate given the mental health facility by society, then the issue is one of where the controls come from. Perhaps it is radical to have these controls come from conformity pressures in the group rather than from traditional medical authority vested in the physician. Nevertheless, it may ultimately offer a more benign form of control.

There is two problems in this pattern. First, vicarious experience of dependency gratification is less satisfying than a direct experience. Second, a one-way flow of nurturance fixes a difference in role definition of staff and patient, respectively. One is well and caring, the other is sick and needy. To the extent that such a division is attractive to patients—who

Another set of issues in therapeutic community can be grouped together under the heading of nurture. The usual image of the distribution of dependent feelings among participants in a hospital setting is that patients are very needy, while staff have their dependency needs gratified elsewhere. On the basis of my own reactions and those of others in a variety of hospital situations, I can state without reservation that staff members always bring some dependent feelings into their work situation. In authoritarian types of hospitals, these impulses are gratified covertly through one's position in a rigid hierarchy. To be told what to do is a form of being taken care of, while to tell others what to do is a form of caring for them. In more benign hospitals that are not therapeutic communities, a major emphasis may be put on nurture, but again only on the care given by the staff to the patients. Staff meets its dependency needs only vicariously.

There are two problems in this pattern. First, vicarious experience of dependency gratification is less satisfying than a direct experience. Second, a one-way flow of nurturance fixes a difference in role definition of staff and patient, respectively. One is well and caring, the other is sick and needy. To the extent that such a division is attractive to patients—who would seem to be getting the best of the bargain—it will limit the possibility of engaging in the individual healing process described in Chapter 18. The patient will not be able to identify with staff and experiment with role behaviors that are parallel to those of staff. To put it more generally, the more a therapeutic community is concerned with *taking care* of patients, the less it will be able to promote healing through imitation and identification with staff. This de-emphasis of nurturance was reflected in the attitudes of patients and staff on Tompkins I. Staff members responded negatively or neutrally to statements that staff should be warm and giving. Patients entered the ward with high expectations of staff nurture, but these decreased with the passage of time.

Reducing the amount of direct nurture in therapeutic community does not diminish the importance of nurture in the organization. In fact, to the degree that staff are no longer having dependent impulses taken care of vicariously, there must be more nurture for staff. This is provided in part by charismatic relations and in part by the cohesiveness of the staff subgroup and the community as a whole. Once again a balance must be struck between the value of warm, supportive relationships among staff members and neglect of patients' needs as a result of intense intrastaff involvement. To a considerable extent, nurture can be replaced by charismatic relatedness. Both tend to be supportive, but in the charismatic relationship, self-esteem is affirmed. The close relationships among staff members in a therapeutic community will also quite literally provide care in times of distress. In fact, one characteristic of staff members' experiences in good therapeutic communities is that they find themselves able to improve their outside life situations and often decide to advance their professional status. Both the lessened caretaking of patients and the increased "therapy" provided for staff are consistent with the concept of role paralleling. The underlying theme is that we all have the same set of needs for being taken care of and for improving (healing) ourselves.

PATIENT CAREERS AND EVALUATION OF THERAPEUTIC COMMUNITY TREATMENT

The description and analysis of patient "careers" developed in Part I provide another set of suggestions for people concerned with therapeutic community. As originally developed by Goffman, the concept of patient career embodied negative, dead-end institutional processing. The analysis of patient careers on Tompkins I demonstrates that deviant careers need not always have such institutional fates. More specifically, the career analyses presented for Tompkins I suggest that any given setting may experience certain regular patterns of patient career. This observation may help those concerned with the evaluation of treatment effectiveness. Rather than evaluating the institution on a case-by-case basis, or on the basis of large, random cohorts of patients, judgments can be made on the basis of recurring patterns of interaction between patient and setting. If it emerges that a given therapeutic community has best results with one sort of patient-hospital type, then the staff can decide deliberately to accept a greater portion of such patients, or to examine their handling of less successful types. Another suggestion prompted by the patient career concept is that of examining post-hospital course. The issue of follow-up outcome is complex, since patients are discharged into a variety of different situations. In terms of the impact of a hospital experience, examination of outcomes for a specific hospital-response type may be valuable. For example, instead of studying the effect of hospitalization on the outcome of acute schizophrenia, one would study schizophrenics with particular hospital career patterns, and particular patterns of pre- and post-hospital experience.

Most evaluations of therapeutic community have been set up as though it were a treatment modality analogous to individual therapy or a drug regimen. But as we have seen at length, therapeutic community is a pattern of organization and healing in which the focus may be the overall life pattern of the sufferer as much as his particular symptomatology. Thus, comparisions of therapeutic community with other treatments such as drug therapy or individual psychotherapy are not highly informative (May, 1968). Spadoni and Smith, who report a "failure" of milieu therapy, are describing what happens when permissive therapeutic community techniques are used without drugs in an institution where medications are universally used to control patient behavior (1969). When patients and staff and the larger institution within which a therapeutic community operates are all accustomed to antipsychotic medications for behavior control, then a no-drug therapeutic community is aberrant and at a disadvantage when outcome is measured by the reduction of psychotic symptomatology. To me, this whole approach is inappropriate. Clinicians must decide separately the questions of how they wish to organize treatment, and whether or not they wish to use the available psychoactive drugs. Tompkins I, for example, chooses to use drugs in almost every case, so that the patient who is not on medication feels deprived (see Chapter 6). Once the decision is made to use one or another treatment, it must be recognized that the treatment will become interwoven with the social structure of therapeutic community. Thus, for example, drugs on Tompkins I are important as (1) specific symptomatic treatment; (2) as a way of controlling socially unacceptable behavior in the midst of a general hospital; and (3) as a form of nurture. For the depressed patient, antidepressive medication may truly relieve psychic pain. Antipsychotic medication will control the behavior of patients who otherwise might not be manageable in a general hospital setting. Most patients experience the tangible pill as something they can "get" from the staff, something that they value over and above the specific physiological effect of medication. As we already noted, individual therapy, with its nearly century-long recognition as a "type" of therapy, becomes something different in a therapeutic community. Confidentiality and central focus on the dyadic relationship must be altered when individual therapy is put in a therapeutic community context. Once again, this need not lead to a choice between two therapies but rather to the recognition that there is a mutually productive complementarity between the dyadic and the social system aspects of group healing.

NOTES

1. Marshall Edelson has described a pattern of organization in which therapeutic community, or what he calls "sociotherapy" and psychotherapy coexist, presumably without competition (1970). Edelson's system does not work smoothly, either in his descriptions or in my own experience as administrator of such a unit (Edelson, 1970; Almond, 1968). At best, combined therapeutic community requires two separate staffs, one for psychotherapy, and additional staff to bridge the gap between the two. This is expensive, awkward, and cannot successfully create a sense of an overall shared community of activities and values.

CHAPTER 21

The Healing Community as a Mental Health Resource

During the last decade in the United States, there has been an extensive decentralization in the care of the mentally ill. This movement was initially stimulated by a recognition that the state hospital systems had become unworkable in relation to goals of brief treatment and restoration of patients to the community. It has led to a variety of efforts toward developing treatment near patients' homes. Psychiatric wards in general hospitals, such as Tompkins I, are one manifestation of this movement. Federally supported community mental-health centers are perhaps the best known and most extensive single development. These are supplemented by a variety of state, county, and privately funded programs. The introduction of national health insurance during the next few years may add yet other kinds of administrative arrangements and supply the impetus for innovation in psychiatric settings. In general, these changes reflect a new attitude toward the mentally troubled person: His deviance is no longer grounds for banishment to distant, custodial institutions. Alternative patient careers to chronic institutionalization are now possible. As I pointed out in the introduction, the first tendency has been to de-label the individual, to separate him from the helping institution quickly. The hope is to avoid both an intrapsychic and a social adjustment to the labeled status. Thus, much of the emphasis in community mental health is upon "crisis intervention," with considerable involvement with family members so that they may better cope with the troubled individual. An extension of this approach, "network therapy," recognizes the limits of the nuclear family unit in this task and engages the aid of extended family, friends, and neighbors of a patient in serious psychiatric difficulty (Speck and Rueveni, 1969).

The next step in this progression is the recognition that de-labeling has limits, that there are many patients and families whose difficulties will not be resolved by brief interventions. Ironically, therapies for less severely impaired individuals already reflect this fact by extending, often for many years, psychoanalysis or group therapy (Freud, 1953; Greenhill and Gralnick, 1966). To meet the needs of persons with a wide range of psychological difficulty will require an institution that can offer open-ended and flexible care and can redefine the meaning of the initial problems positively. The healing community seems to be a logical and natural model for responding to this need.

HEALING COMMUNITIES AND THE RELABELING OF DEVIANCE

The healing community, as a model for mental health organizations, obviously does not imply any specific source of funds or administrative structure. What the model does suggest is that a wide variety of settings, problems, and therapy styles may legitimately be considered healing communities. We can look beyond the usual sources of mental health care to recognize and develop further the network of mental health services in any given locality. This view, it is hoped, can lead to systems of mental health service that are less dependent than at present on government-financed programs. Specifically, if we recognize that such organizations as Synanon, Alcoholics Anonymous, Recovery, Inc., Parents Without Partners, and QT (for postileostomy patients) are all healing communities and that similar organizations can be initiated and facilitated, we may be able to find, within existing community life, rich new resources for mental health. Those responsible for mental health planning, or concerned about the development of new resources in communities, can look to existing voluntary organizations or to groups of sufferers and ex-sufferers as resources. It is my opinion that doing this will reduce some of the serious problems of financial support and limited manpower. The development of new resources on a local basis is made both more important and more likely by the growing acceptance of individuals with obvious mental disturbance. The inconsistency of governmental support points to the importance of such settings being closely integrated into the local community.

Paralleling the increasing acceptance of the humanness of individuals with mental disturbance is a blurring of the previously clear boundary between patient and therapist. Further, the encounter group makes it possible for persons without serious disorders to be involved in a healing situation, and for persons without formal training to be healers. Professional organizations of mental health workers are expressing understandable concern about some of these ventures, which make little effort to screen applicants or guard against psychological "casualties." At the same time, the emergence of these groups points up the unavoidable realization that tens or even hundreds of thousands of mental health professionals will never adequately provide the mental health services needed by our population.

These changes—the de-labeling of mental patients, the blurring of distinctions between professionals and clients, and the emergence of encounter groups—are part of a broad shift in social attitudes. The societal implications of this shift will be discussed in the final chapter as reflecting a resurgence of concern with the "moral order" as against the "technical order." But this shift has important implications for the meaning of therapy or mental health healing. It has been almost gospel in modern mental health planning to seek a return of the patient whence he came, in other words to undo the effects of labeling his disorder. This attitude is reasonable enough when the diagnostic label of schizophrenia, for example, means prognosticating lifelong institutionalization and mental deterioration. The modern, restorative attitude toward mental illness has been part of a curative fervor like that surrounding cancer. This enthusiasm for cure ignores the possibility—so often observed in cross-cultural cases—of an individual's living out a meaningful, often creative, and sociable life after an episode of acute, severe mental disturbance.

Such a view leads to a very different attitude about healing and healing institutions. Treatment and therapy for the mentally disturbed in recent history have operated out of a paradoxical set of precepts. On the one hand, treatment has been aimed at major restitution and change, or cure. The medical prototype here is cancer, or even less appropriate, pneumococcal penumonia. On the other hand, psychotherapy approaches have usually taken a neutral position in relation to the patient's real life situation. The essential transaction between patient and therapist is an exchange of money for a period of time with the therapist, who gives the patient information and some sort of interaction. What the two poles of this paradox have in common is a view of the therapist and the patient as separate, uninvolved individuals who transact around the specifics of the patient's disorder. Psychoanalytic therapies recognize the importance of the relationship but keep it as part of a highly structured interaction, not directly affecting the lives of therapist or patient outside the therapy setting. Such an attitude is consistent with the valuation of individualism in Western society.

The sociologist Philip Rieff has pointed out that in traditional societies, mental disturbance is usually resolved in a different way: by restoration of the sufferer to his community, either in an old role or in a newly devised one (1968). Rieff calls such treatments "commitment therapies," and contrasts them with Western "analytic therapies," referring not to psychoanalysis but to the dispassionate analysis that is the therapist's way of communicating with the patient. "Commitment" refers to the involvement of the sufferer and the healer in the same community. Following from this is a degree of commitment by the community and the therapist to a continuing relationship with the sufferer. The healer in such a situation cannot afford to be "informative and neutral," as is the Western "analytic" therapist. The healer must concern himself with *more* than understanding the sufferer. He must devote himself to creating some sort of transformation of the sufferer and/or his social setting. An example of this is Marvin Opler's description of Ute healing of psychiatric disturbance by shamans (1959). The shaman interprets dreams, not to explore the suffer's unconscious life but to seek guidance in quickly restoring a troubled person to adequate functioning. The Ute, a migratory tribe, cannot afford to have members so disturbed that they are unable to move with the rest of the group. Thus the manipulations guided by dream interpretation of the shaman are critical to both the individual and the group.

If we, too, are coming to have a "commitment" rather than an "analytic" orientation, then the healing community, and the specific cases we have discussed here, will be quite useful. First, there is the issue of time limit. Tompkins I ends its involvement with patients at the moment of discharge, although it seeks to help patients plan a number of aspects of their lives, including work and treatment, following discharge. The non-Western healing groups, Synanon, and Psychodrama all share an open-endedness of involvement. At the same time, many of these groups do not see the initial treatment as a definitive cure or restoration. Evidence is already accumulating that indicates some patients "stick" to the hospital even when it is geared to rapid turnover (Friedman et al., 1966). In community mental health centers, staff have observed that a group of chronic patients gradually become a permanent core group in the center. By the late 1960s some state hospitals were sufficiently pleasant places to live that a subgroup of patients make demonstrable efforts to convince staff that they are too sick to leave (Braginsky et al., 1969). The accumulation of such patients in community mental health centers or psychiatric wards is a "problem" only if they play no constructive role in the institution, if there is a complementarity of controlling, caretaking staff and powerless, and dependent patients. The cases cited here suggest that a solution would be to use such permanent residents and participants as "staff." The challenge to the mental health planner and the psychiatric professional may be how to evoke the strengths of these patients, how to facilitate the emergence of new healing communities. The challenge for a national or regional mental health planner may be analogous to that of providing assistance to proud ghetto communities. Healing communities may not fit smoothly at all times into society. It may become a challenge for the mental health planner to bring certain valuable professional resources to such groups (Ilfeld and Lindemann, 1970).

Helpful in this sort of endeavor would be a recognition of the intrinsic marginality of both the deviant and the mental hospital. We can learn from the lessons of the nineteenth-century asylum, which was pushed out of the mind and presence of the citizen, as well as from the limits of crisis intervention, which seeks to restore every patient to a role of full effectiveness. If the mentally deviant individual, and the institution he becomes affiliated with in a permanent relationship, could be maintained in a dynamic marginal status, we might be able to avoid both the tragedy of ostracism and custodialism, and the disillusionment of readmission and increasing ineffectiveness of performance. If our society could maintain healing communities in such dynamic marginality, it is possible that new, interesting functions might occur in them. We have as models for this the religious, economic, and social-mobility functions performed by all the examples that involved open-ended participation. These examples are illustrative; they do not provide a direct model for the role that might be played by healing communities in our society. But it is not difficult to imagine the hospital serving a variety of such functions, and indeed hospitals that look carefully at their programs tend to develop such variety (Kuldau, n.d.).

The varied patterns in our career studies also suggest a great need for flexible services under the roof of a single healing community. Patterns of American psychiatric care now tend to be a function of administrative rules, Blue Cross regulations, and only in a limited way, patient needs. Twenty-four-hour hospitalization, day care, emergency-crisis services, outpatient treatment—all tend to be separated administratively. As a result, the patient with rapidly changing needs is constantly being introduced to new personnel and new organizational units. The healing community model suggests that this situation will weaken many facets of individual healing and group involvement. What seems needed is an organization small enough to be a healing community, yet flexible in response to patient needs. It is critical that the marginal status of such an organization be maintained and that the healing community not become isolated, because this could well lead to a full circle back to the isolated rural asylum.

SOCIAL CLASS AND THE HEALING COMMUNITY

One aspect of marginality is "liminality," a blurring of such personal attributes as social class differences (Turner, 1969). This, of course, has characterized many charismatic movements, but is manifest also in therapeutic community and other healing communities. The ordinary mental hospital has a highly stratified class structure. At the top of the hierarchy, psychiatrists and senior administrators are upper or upper-middle class either by origin or certainly by virtue of training and pay. Nurses are generally middle class, both in origin and in present status if they are dependent upon their income. Lowest in the hierarchy are aides and attendants, who are almost inevitably of lower-middle, or lower-class, status. Hospital pay scales are such that workers are unlikely to be able to rise out of their economic class status even with many years of experience. Thus, although the psychiatric aide might have 20 years' experience working closely with withdrawn schizophrenic patients, he must frequently defer to the inexperienced nurse, and certainly to the inexperienced psychiatric resident-in-training (Strauss et al., 1964).

When one considers the emphasis placed on experience with patients in mental health professional training, it seems odd that upward mobility is so limited for participants in the hospital staff. Actually, several factors reduce the stress that this paradox might create. First, the educational limits on rising in job status are well known to hospital employees. Second, in most cases the psychological concomitants of class status put limits on upward mobility. It has been documented several times that psychiatric aides score higher for measures of authoritarianism or custodialism than do nurses, and nurses higher than psychiatrists (Gilbert, 1954). While such attitudes may well be the consequence of class status rather than inherent in class itself, they do tend to limit mobility. The authoritarian, custodially oriented aide or nurse will not envision himself as a therapist.

Experience in therapeutic communities and the reports of non-Western healing communities indicate that these class limitations may vanish in the right situation. With proper training, role modeling, and protection in case of mistakes, psychiatric aides are frequently capable not only of managing psychiatric patients competently, but of taking on specific therapeutic functions (Almond and Astrachan, 1969).

At the level of patient, Hollingshead and Redlich demonstrated some time ago that handling of psychiatric disorders is very much a function of the class of the sufferer (1958). Lower-class patients are handled by the police and by the state hospital system; upper-class patients, by private psychiatrists and private hospitals. There is a tendency to reduce the social class status of a mentally ill individual by placing him in an institution. (Many of the reforms in mental health consist of developing a sufficient number of facilities that are pleasant and hotellike, and give the patient middle-class handling.)

One implicit potential of the healing community is to cut across these class-related patterns. Rarely do healing communities within formal, established settings achieve a true leveling of social class for patient or staff. This is certainly true in Western hospitals, even in therapeutic communities. Patients may move to the level of performing some nursing duties; nurses may have some responsibilities usually reserved for physicians; but true access to higher status levels is not directly available. Maxwell Jones improvised a new job classification in his original therapeutic community, the "social therapist," in order to have staff members who were trained on the unit rather than by professional schools. Because of the mobility limits for this rank, the social therapists were generally on the unit for only a year or so. But in Synanon, any addict can rise to a high level in the organization. Whether individuals from lower-class backgrounds frequently achieve senior status in Synanon is not clear from available reports. Presumably, limitations on upward mobility within Synanon would be based on performance rather than on class origins. The example of Synanon is valuable, since it is a naturally developed group with American culture. It should be possible for other, similar healing organizations to maintain the same degree of leveling. If this pattern of organization were to become more common, healing groups could well become a new area of social mobility and work opportunity. What is significant about this possibility is that it would attract some of the more competent ex-sufferers to remain with the group. This, in turn, would facilitate the emergence of healing groups like Synanon, less dependent on professional help for internal training and leadership.

PATIENT CAREERS AND NEW HEALING COMMUNITIES

The unexpected posthospitalization life histories of career-study patients described in Part I bring out a subject that urgently needs further study. Too little is known about longitudinal individual experience of patients and their relations to treatment institutions. We need to know more about the social processes that occur prior to hospitalizations and about the effects of institutional experiences after discharge. Closely related to this is our limited capacity to classify patterns of response to institutions or, more particularly, to different sorts of treatment experience. The typologies developed in Part I for one setting are a primitive beginning. Perhaps more sensitive typologies can be developed, based not upon a single hospital response pattern, but rather upon patterns that emerge over years and decades.

Finally, I must repeat the exhortation of Henry Burdett, the observer and critic of American hospital conditions a hundred years ago, that treatment institutions should be limited in *size* above all else. To the practical experience of therapeutically oriented clinicians over the centuries, I can add observations here of the healing community model from Part IV: The patient-staff group together must be small enough for face-to-face interaction. In settings of more than 50 individuals, face-to-face familiarity is lost, and a sustained sense of communitas is impossible. Similarly, in such large institutions more status levels develop, and the simple pattern of initiate—intermediate member—leader is lost

From a practical point of view, this conclusion might

suggest some reconsideration of the catchment concept for the community mental health center. Among the 50,000–200,000 population serviced by a federally funded community mental health center, there can be expected 500–2000 schizophrenics alone, and many times more sufferers of other diagnostic groups. Thus, were a community mental health center to perform its functions of prevention, treatment, and rehabilitation effectively, it would be dealing with a continuing patient population of thousands rather than dozens. Some further decentralization will be necessary to make the healing group pattern work within the community mental health approach. Perhaps other, nonmental health organizations should be given, as they are among the Zuni, a large share of responsibility for handling the mentally deviant. Some of these organizations may be spontaneous, self-motivated ones like Alcoholics Anonymous, Synanon, or Recovery, Inc. These groups could be aided through small subsidies, provision of facilities, and referrals of new members. The establishment of other local groups could be facilitated.

What existing organizations might become the nuclei of healing communities? Aside from those groups that spring up spontaneously around shared needs, the greatest resource for bringing the healing group approach to a community is religious groups—churches and temples. Secularization and rapid social change have markedly undermined the involvement of congregations in doctrinal and even in ritual aspects of religion. But the need for affiliation, helping, and being helped remains as great or greater than ever. In the wider perspective of healing suggested by Jerome Frank's work or the cross-cultural studies described here, the overlap between religious and healing activities becomes more obvious. The central features of the healing community—shared beliefs; involvement with and caring about fellow-members; charisma, the sense of something out of the ordinary—all these describe the congregation well. In Zuni and the Tensho sect we saw a real overlap of healing and religious groups. American clerics are becoming increasingly aware of the relevance of therapeutic activity to their work. Pastoral counseling has always been a legitimate part of the repertoire of rabbi, minister, and priest. Techniques derived from psychotherapy and group dynamics have been recently introduced to increase the effectiveness of this side of the cleric's work. Sensitivity groups, transactional analysis, and encounter techniques are being used in a variety of ways, including the service itself (Howard, 1970). A Unitarian congregation in Palo Alto, California, has recently facilitated the development of a more elaborate organization with an explicitly healing orientation; this group has many of the features of the healing community, including the possibility of advancement from initiate to leader.

I cannot outline here a program for integrating mental health services with these parareligious groups (see Leslie, 1970). My interest is in pointing out the increasing overlap of interests between religion and mental health, and encouraging interaction in planning and serving particular communities and groups. In our culture the healer, be he medically or academically trained, takes pride in his "scientific" knowledge and technique. Yet in the day-to-day work of healing, he knows that science is only a part of his dealings with people. The pastor, on the other hand, recognizes the limits of his philosophical-theological training in dealing with the psychological and social subtleties of his parishioners' difficulties. Interaction between the two in the development of healing groups for a variety of purposes, may be mutually strengthening.

CHAPTER 22

The Healing Community and Personality Processes

Most of the important psychological concepts of our day come from dyadic therapeutic situations, introspective observations, or experimental situations involving man and machine. Further, most of these concepts have emerged during an era in which scientific, technological concepts have dominated not only the world of nature and machine, but psychology as well. The primary emphasis throughout this volume has been on social processes or on modal individual-group processes. But each of these processes calls on some capacity or responsiveness of the individual. In this chapter I shall speculate on some of these, taking the position that the capacities revealed in the healing community need not be considered derivative ones. That is, I do not assume that the individual attributes revealed are the sole result of early-life family relationships. No psychiatrist can ignore the profound impact of infancy and childhood experiences on all that follows in the individual's development. Increasingly, however, the psychologists of adolescence and adulthood find that the issues to be dealt with and the intrapsychic responses are better understood on their own terms than reduced to analogues of prior developmental phases. The recent contributions of ethology also suggest that many human characteristics predate man and have evolved as part of group life in primates and earlier ancestors of man (Hamburg, 1963).

The personality capacities suggested by group processes of the healing community can be related to single concepts or concept pairs, as follows: Communitas implies the potential in man for devoted *membership* or *group involvement*; healing charisma calls on the capacity for *faith*; together the two processes call forth man's *transcendent* qualities, his capacity for love, in a broad sense, or "I-thou" relatedness. The integral function of norms in the healing community emphasizes the capacity for *belief*, and for belief translated into *action*. Communitas norms in particular suggest the capacity for *conformity* with beliefs shared by a collectivity. The expression of charisma through the special quality of member roles and role behavior in the healing community relates to the capacity of man for interpersonal transcendence, or *altruism*. The healing process of healing community obviously calls upon responsiveness in the individual. Processes of attention saturation and gaining involvement evoke a basic capacity for *immersion*, and letting-go or *release*. Behavior modification and role paralleling both imply *malleability* of belief and behavior. Finally, the intrapsychic processes of imitation, identification, and integration can be discussed in terms of psychoanalytic and ego psychology conceptualizations of the self in relation to others and social values: superego, ego ideal, and identity.

GROUP MEMBERSHIP AND CHARISMATIC RELATEDNESS

Even in an individualistically oriented culture like ours, man's capacity for forming and joining groups is irrepressible. While the rationale for many groups is stated in a way that emphasizes the individual benefit or career function, it is often obvious that membership itself is a primary issue. This is even true in the encounter movement, where the purpose is generally phrased in terms of "learning interpersonal skills" or "personal growth." Yet most of the excitement and satisfaction of encounter experiences is in the acceptance of the group and meaningful participation in the group's activities. In large bureaucracies, which are presumably solely task-oriented, informal groups constantly spring up to circumvent the limits on relatedness imposed by the formal organization. These observations suggest that in adulthood there is a chronic need for a sense of membership in one or more groups that have a communitas quality. It is likely that membership complements the more obvious dependency supports provided in adult family relations.

In a group situation where hierarchy and role play lesser parts in guiding behavior, belief becomes of primary importance. Communitas as a social pattern relies on man's capacity to espouse shared beliefs intensely. In this sense, man's capacity for belief merges into his capacity to relate to social units that are too large to be a composite of several relationships. Strong evidence of this quality of group relatedness is given by the healing community and a variety of related phenomena we will mention in Chapter 23. Man can join together in a moral community that is more than the sum of its members because of their agreement on some shared principles or mythologies. In the healing community, this coming together does not sacrifice the uniqueness of each member. As will be noted in the discussion of altruism, the transcendence of self-interest in healing is not a loss of self. Similarly the group and its members remain distinct but intensely important to one another. Victor Turner, in elaborating on the psychology implicit in communitas, refers to Buber's concept of "I-thou" relatedness:

Only when I have to do with another essentially, that is, in such a way that he is no longer a phenomenon of my *I*, but instead is my *Thou*, do I experience reality of speech with another—in the genuineness of mutuality (Buber, quoted in Turner, 1969, pp. 136–137).

Turner, Buber, and the present observations all indicate that the *I-thou* relation is not limited to two persons, but that *thou* may broaden to *we*. Man's *thou* is within himself, and hence can embrace his experience of one person or a group. These groups tend to generate, or be generated by, charismatic leaders. Such leaders can then personify the individual's relatedness to the group. Weston La Barre, extending Freud's discussion of group psychology, sees the charisma of the leader as "the hero's narcissistic fascination with himself, a mother-given mana and mission . . ." (La Barre, 1970, p. 260). The group member is seen by La Barre as vicariously receiving nourishment from the mana, or charismatic aura of the leader.

I think both of these views speak of the same process and of the same human characteristics. The differences are those of vocabulary and attitude. Turner (and Buber) see man's capacity for moral fusion—in I-thou relatedness or communitas—as a valuable attribute, perhaps the basis of a utopian, or at least happier, social life. La Barre sees the same phenomena in negative terms: "But worship of another man's charisma, when paranoia speaks to paranoia, is also an abdication of the individual ego." These lead to the self-destruction of the individual or the group, according to La Barre. My view is that man has a potential for concentrating his relatedness in a social unit that becomes preeminent for him. In dyadic form, this fusion may manifest itself as the intense dyadic bond of lovers or friends. This bond can be positive, as the basic unit of a happy family; or negative, as in the case of a Leopold-Loeb relationship. Similarly, charismatic groups can be valuable, as we have seen in their ability to influence suffering individuals; malign, as with violent vigilante groups; or self-destructive, as was the case with the American Indian "Ghost Dance" movement that sought to resist with magic the white man's advances on the frontier in the 1890s.

FAITH, CONFORMITY, AND IDENTITY

At its heart the charismatic relationship is able to touch a place in the psyche of the individual that transports him beyond his ordinary patterns and limits. A reverberation occurs between two persons; one is usually ascribed to have some special power and the capacity to set off something special in the other. The other, the less experienced or awakened partner in the charismatic process, is said to have "faith." The word implies both dependence and belief. Yet from an objective point of view, faith resides in the individual and is merely evoked in the charismatic interaction. In Chapter 17, the intrapsychic origins of the charismatic response was hypothesized as deriving from archetypal or archaic psychological experiences. In addition to these sources, there seems to be a need for content, a cognitive framework to which to attach the powerful feelings. In a healing community, the beliefs concern the healing process, just as the reason for the collectivity and the interactions in it are related to healing.

Running through every chapter of this volume has been this theme of *belief*, both as an espousal of the cognitive framework of a group and as the particular essence of each group. I have assumed man's capacity for belief in abstract ideas. We can now look at this assumption, since it has held up well, for what it tells us about *man-as-a-believer*. The beliefs of the healing community may be familiar to some extent for the new member. But, in general, he is dealing with a new set of ideas, or a new relation to them. In other words, the healing community demonstrates that adults are capable of espousing new beliefs in a relatively short time-span. Psychologists of human development have gradually shifted from the

Freudian view that with the emergence of superego in the early years, the major beliefs of life are internalized. There can be no doubt about two major early events having to do with belief: (1) Powerful motivating forces are evoked in the early years, forces that can indeed attach themselves to passionate belief (as well as to other experiences, like romance); and (2) the beliefs the child is exposed to early *do* play a major role through life. But more recently the careful observations of developmentalists show that the capacity for ideological involvement and more complex, "higher" moral thinking emerges only in adolescence and later (Piaget, 1948; Kohlberg, 1973). Erik Erikson clarifies the developmental sequence of man's moral, believing capacity in discussing three concepts: superego, ego ideal, and ego identity. The first is conceived as embodying the capacity for morality itself, "man's *congenital* proclivity toward the development of a primitive, categorical conscience" (Erikson, 1959, p. 148). The dynamic origins of superego reside in the resolution of the Oedipus complex, broadened by Erikson to the developmental tension between "initiative and guilt." The ego ideal derives from interactions and identifications with the important figures during childhood; what is internalized are the beliefs of the family and peer group during the particular historical period of childhood. Ego identity "could be said to be characterized by the more or less *actually-attained-but-forever-to-be-revised* sense of the reality of the self within social reality" (Erikson, 1959, p. 149).

In the healing community, it is the translation of belief, first into norms and then into roles, that relates to the individual's identity. For the specific individual, membership in the group is a process of finding a real place in the organization. This calls upon his ego identity and in turn influences it. I shall return to the concept of identity in discussing individual-group and intrapsychic processes. On the other side of this process of identification with the group and its beliefs is the group's expectation of conformity. " . . . the community, in turn, feels 'recognized' by the individual who cares to ask for recognition; it can, by the same token, feel deeply—and vengefully—rejected by the individual who does not seem to care" (Erikson, 1959, p. 113). Conformity has been discovered in social psychological experiments to be a powerful factor capable of distorting perception, judgment, and moral behavior (Asch, 1958; Milgram, 1968). In fact, the tendency of man to go along with prevailing expectations is so great that these experimental manifestations involved drama- tic evidences of conformity, namely, the adjustment of objec- tive experience and the inflicting of pain on others. The natural tendency to conformity is related to the desire for membership. In an era of rapid change in cultural norms and styles, peer groups have become extremely important sources of context for the conforming impulse. In addition to the dependent reassurance given by membership, conformity with group norms supplies meanings that are ever more important in an era of science and relativism.

In the healing community, special norms have to do with healing activities involving persons whose behavior is de- viant. Not only is the behavior deviant, but it is often aberrant in a way that arouses anxiety in others. This anxiety is allayed by using the healing techniques of the group and the support of healing charisma. The behavior is confronted, and the sufferer is brought into the group. That the deviant behavior is not made reason for rejection or punishment, but instead is made reason for inclusion and massive activity, makes the interaction between member and sufferer an altruistic one. We saw this most vividly in the struggle of the therapeutic community patient dealing with a new patient who had made a disfiguring suicide attempt. Undoubtedly the latent depres- sive, suicidal feelings of the former were stimulated by the thought of interaction, and the first impulse was avoidance. The charismatic therapeutic role definition led the patient to accept his designation as sponsor and to overcome these fears (see Chapter 4).

ALTRUISM

Our culture tends to equate altruism with "selflessness," as though one *gives up* one's self in the altruistic act. The healing community provides a different way of seeing this: The altruistic act may be an *assertion* of self. The improved patient can confirm his status by caring for a newer, more disturbed patient. The alcoholic in Alcoholics Anonymous meets his own need to avoid liquor by seeking out other alcoholics and helping them toward abstention. Thus altruism in the healing group, and perhaps anywhere, is a self-assertive act. The sacrifice of one's time, energy, riches, or even one's life is made for the purpose of confirming an inner image of what one is. For an ex-sufferer, the altruistic activity of healing permits him vicariously to re-experience his suffering and his mastery over it. Seen this way, helping activity is like many other activities in the development of personality: A difficult experience is mastered by a reversal of positions. The child learns to be an adult by "playing" adult to younger sibs or to dolls. Often such play involves teaching the other how to be more "grown up." In doing this, the child also gains a sense of mastery over a situation in which he feels weak and subordinate. Thus the altruistic healing act is a recapitulation of a type of process experienced earlier in life. In the healing group, the helper-sufferer dichotomy is temporary and a part of its altruism is expressed in its being directed toward making a healer of the sufferer.

I find this conclusion—that altruism is an act of mutual benefit—a reassuring one. If altruism, or helping, were a one-way process, we would be left with the dilemma that any individual or group has a limited amount to give. Seeing altruism as a mutually beneficial activity means that it will not be "used up." On the other hand, altruism is not that easily come by: The whole, complex social process of the healing community is needed to provide a framework for sustaining altruism in healing relationships.[1] Thus, though altruism is mutually beneficial, it requires the right conditions. The healing group experience also suggests that altruism is not equivalent to kindness and gentleness alone. At times it is an act of kindness to tell someone else something he will not like to hear.

IMMERSION AND LETTING-GO

In our case examples, we identified over and over an early process in the sequence of individual healing, namely, producing a saturation of the sufferer's attention as the first step in his becoming involved in the healing community. While the means of this process varied widely in therapeutic specifics, common themes included massive inputs of dramatic, unfamiliar, hypnotic, consciousness-altering stimulation. These stimuli, which at first frequently appear to overwhelm the sufferer, evoke from him a dramatic cathartic response. During the course of this catharsis, he frequently "confesses" his problem; then, with the aid of the healer or group, he gains mastery over it. These dramatic initiation ceremonies evoke in the individual a capacity for release and immersion. We have few concepts for such experiences and capacities in our psychological lexicon. Even "altered state of consciousness" tells us little other than that there are different ways of experiencing. One difficulty in describing such states is that they are highly subjective; another is that they are suspect in a culture that values a controlled, self-conscious, objective, "rational" state of mind. If we look for analogues to guide us, we think of William James' descriptions of religious conversions (1958), Maslow's more recent studies of "peak" experiences (1958), and reports of individuals who are in the midst of a romantic love bond (Weingarten and Almond, 1972). In these states, awareness of immediate circumstance is heightened, while prior perspectives on the meaning of experience fall away. There is a feeling of yielding up of control, being in the sway of more powerful forces. This is often experienced subjectively as confusion. At the same time, the self is enhanced, and aspects of inner reality emerge powerfully into consciousness. Often there is a feeling of death/rebirth, followed by a sustained sense of freshness and openness.

In the life history, such experiences are frequently associated with significant life changes. Religious conversion may be the landmark between self-degradation and rededication; falling in love may mark not only the transition to a new relationship, but a change from attachments with parents to age-mates.[2] Many self-descriptions of encounter, Synanon, and Psychodrama experiences have the same quality of rebirth into new patterns of relatedness. For the new member of the healing community, this rebirth may be associated with a life pattern that includes group membership as a major new facet. It is as though the immersion experience jostles up inner patterns of perception, meaning, and attachment, and sets the stage for the *possibility* of something new. The healing community, dealing often with more troubled, dependent persons intrinsically limited in certain ways, provides both stimuli for evoking the experience and a framework for establishing the new patterns.

THE CAPACITY FOR CHANGE

The following stages of individual healing make use of the *malleability* of the sufferer, the intrapsychic quality implicit in Frank's use of the term "influence" to describe a universal quality of therapeutic experiences. Whereas an immersion experience may set the stage, the susceptibility to influence provides internal mechanisms that enable the more gradual process of involvement in the community. Psychologically, the first steps rely on the developmentally early *imitative* capacity, seen in the first year of life. Once the new member has made an imitative response, the group, through reinforcements, can influence the responses. Experimental evidence supports the observation we reported, that behavior changes precede belief changes in this process (Janis and Hovland, 1959; Janis and King, 1954). In fact, it is rare that beliefs are espoused as the outcome of a logical, cognitive process alone. Rather, beliefs are a way of formulating, psychologically, the logic of one's behavior. It makes little sense to go through a Zar ritual or a week of therapeutic community interactions and meetings without espousing the norms that give such behavior meaning and coherence. The progression is from a purely behavioral acceptance of belief, to an internalization of the rules of behavior at an unconscious level (see, for example, Chapters 6 and 7), to an awareness of belief consciously. "At first they just called me Clown; then I really became Clown" (see Chapter 12).

I have characterized the intrapsychic stages of this evolution as progressing from imitation to identification and then to integration. This sequence recapitulates the developmental sequence suggested by Erikson. Following the first responses based on the simple ability to imitate others' behavior, a later developmental capacity is evoked. This is the ability to internalize the image of others as a part of oneself, that is, identification. Role paralleling is the interactive mechanism that enables identification in the healing community to be with any other member, especially those who are already healed. Identification means that whole patterns of behavior and belief become internal, and the individual is thus able to deal with situations for which purely imitative responses do not prepare him. The developmental analogue here is the internalization of parental values and role behaviors used by the child in situations outside the family.

Integration, the final step in the psychological evolution of the group member, also calls upon an earlier life experience: the development of ego identity. Here, the internalizations are of contemporary models, that is, aspects of other group members blended with aspects of the self. Integration presumes two attributes referred to earlier: the capacity to be a group member, and the capacity to espouse beliefs. It requires that these qualities be gradually integrated psychologically with inner needs into a *unique* social role of the particular member in the group. Of course, like identity formation, the process of integration is never complete. Both the individual and the group continue to evolve, and the mutual accommodation between them must be constantly revised.

These individual attributes suggested by the processes of healing communities share the theme of *transcendence*. In one way or another, each has to do with rising above seeming limits. Thus in altruistic and immersion experiences, the individual goes beyond his prior definition of self-interest. In membership and belief, he evidences the capacity to conceive of himself in purely individualistic, pragmatic terms. And in the evolution of a new integration of personality and social position, he demonstrates the capacity for change in a form that benefits himself and others.

NOTES

1. Of course, healing is done in one-to-one relationships as well. But as Jerome Frank has pointed out, the culture in which healing and sufferer live plays an important part in defining the legitimacy of the problem, the healer, and the therapy (see Chapter 13).

2. See Erikson's *Young Man Luther* for an extensive analysis of the context and inner meaning of, and the changes following, one notable immersion experience—Luther's "fit in the choir" (1958).

CHAPTER **23**

The Healing Community and the Moral Order

Critiques of modern society increasingly locate the source of dehumanizing patterns in our culture in man's social organizations rather than in his innate nature. Hospitals create chronicity; prisons teach young offenders to be criminals; bureaucracies abuse those they are supposed to serve; defense departments instigate wars; universities limit freedom of expression in order to protect it. The varieties of modern man's alienation abound, yet remedies are few. Part of the difficulty in finding answers is that we are conditioned by our culture of rapid change to look for "something new." Yet what is missing is something old—the sense of relatedness and meaningfulness that traditional man got from his far less complex and less affluent life. In this final chapter I shall suggest how the healing community, a reemergence of an "old" aspect of human social life, is one model for renewal of human experience.

Students of man's individual or collective behavior repeatedly identify a dichotomy that is fundamental to this problem. Here, we have spoken of it as the dichotomy between *communitas* and *social structure*. But this is only one of its forms, useful in our analysis of groups of about 15 to 100 persons involved in healing activity. At the level of psychic processes, Freud's conceptualization of superego, incorporating parental-community values, and ego reflected a similar division of functions (1960); at the level of society, Toennies' *gemeinschaft* (community) and *gesellschaft* (society) refer to the same thing (1972).[1] One of the broadest and clearest delineations of this fundamental dichotomy is Robert Redfield's discussion of the "moral order" and the "technical order." The moral order concerns far more than morality; it includes the gamut of social and psychological patterns through which behavior is determined by considerations of belief. The technical order consists of behavior deriving from considerations of effectiveness and utility.

> The moral order is therefore always based on what is peculiarly human—sentiment, morality, conscience—and in the first place arises in the groups where people are intimately associated with one another . . . the phrase "moral order" points to the nature of the bonds among men. . . .
>
> "Moral order" includes the binding sentiments of rightness that attend religion, the social solidarity that accompanies religious ritual, the sense of religious seriousness and obligation that strengthens man, the effects of a belief in invisible beings that embody goodness. The moral order becomes vivid to us when we think of the Australian Arunta assembling, each man to do his part, denying himself food, making the sacred marks or performing the holy dances, that the witchetty-grub may become numerous and the whole band thus continue to find its food. Or of the old Chinese family performing the rituals for the ancestors. Or of the members of the boy's gang refusing, even in the face of threats from the police, to "tell on" a fellow member. . . .
>
> The technical order is that order which results from mutual usefulness, deliberate coercion, or from the mere utilization of the same means. In a technical order men are bound by things,

or are themselves things. They are organized by necessity or expediency. Think, if you will, of the orderly way in which automobiles move in response to the traffic light or the policeman's whistle, or think of the flow of goods, services, and money among the people who together produce, distribute, and consume some commodities such as rubber (Redfield, 1953, pp. 20-21).

Thus the moral and technical "orders" are not codified, rigid sets of rules, but are two patterns embedded in the social process of society.

According to Redfield, the moral order is preeminent in folk societies, and throughout the many eons of cultural evolution until the emergence of larger, complex societies. As complexity increased along with the size of interrelated settlements, considerations of utility became more critical. The moral order continues to be a powerful force, but is less preeminent. Redfield suggests that having lost its position as the cement of social life, the moral order becomes more unpredictable and explosive. It operates within social subunits such as the family, the kinship group, social movements, and healing communities. The moral order, manifest as communitas, is characterized by being marginal to the social structure, by fitting into interstices of the routine social process. Groups emphasizing the moral order attract oppressed, poor, deviant, or newer members of society. Examples include the kibbutz, the utopian community, religious sects, "revitalization movements," revolutionary political groups, encounter groups, and communal experiments. These have in common the organizational characteristics of communitas: limited size, egalitarian attitudes, intense loyalty, commitment to shared beliefs.

These characteristics are, for example, very much the major characteristics of the kibbutz movement (Spiro, 1956). All members over 18 are fundamentally equal, despite acknowledged individual differences; individual liberty is valued, within the framework of the settlement's needs; great stress is laid on the particular brand of Marxist thinking espoused by the community; the sense of "hakkara" (an awareness of the kibbutz' dependence upon each individual) is an important aspect of cohesion and social control. The major beliefs of the kibbutzim that are unique are the emphasis on agriculture and on Zionism as determining the location of the settlements in Israel.[2]

The utopian communities of the nineteenth century had either religious or social-philosophical themes. The Hutterites, Doukhobors, Shakers, and Amana settlers were examples of splinter religious groups that banded together around their heretical beliefs (Bach, 1961). Charismatic, prophetic leaders were frequent in these groups. Though the leader's rule on earth might be autocratic, in relation to God and in the afterlife all members were equal. Communal sharing of work, property, and even sex occurred in these groups. The nineteenth-century social utopians—Owenites, Fourierites, Buckmanites—were also communal, with greater earthly equality among members (Nordhoff, 1966; Infield, 1955).

Religious sects from other cultures have been described in earlier chapters. Here in the United States, evangelical, revivalist groups and churches hold meetings characterized by what Turner calls "existential-spontaneous" communitas: a period of hours during which a congregation is united in an ecstatic, transcendent state stimulated by group singing, exhortation, personal testimony, and often faith healing.

Anthony Wallace has used the term "revitalization movements" to describe another, somewhat more complex form of communitas that takes the form of transient social-political-religious movements among populations subject to acculturation or other major upheavals (1956). Classical examples of this phenomenon in American Indian history are the religion of Handsome Lake among late eighteenth-century Iroquois, the ghost dance of the Plains Indians during the late nineteenth century, and the "cargo cults" of New

Guinea (Wallace, 1962; La Barre, 1970; Mooney, 1892-3). Re-vitalization movements consciously intend to revise tradi-tional cultures to meet a crisis of imposed change. The ghost dance was a response to the decimation of the Plains buffalo herds by white hunters in the 1870s; the religion of Handsome Lake was an eighteenth-century response to Christian mis-sionary efforts backed by the whites' military superiority; cargo cults are a native response to twentieth-century accul-turative pressures. In the course of such movements, leader-ship is frequently provided by dramatic, charismatic figures who assure their followers of survival, victory, and restora-tion of lost powers. The movements often transcend tradi-tional structural barriers between kinship groups or tribes. New structures are built within the old, but remain initially quite simple:

> An embryonic campaign organization develops with three or-ders of personnel: the prophet, the disciple, and the followers. . . . Like the prophet, many of the converts undergo a revitalizing personality transformation (Wallace, 1956, p. 273).

Another aspect of the revitalization process is that of translat-ing cultural transformation into group action:

> This group program may, however, be more or less realistic and more or less adaptive. Some programs are literally suicidal; others represent well-conceived and successful projects of further social, political, or economic reform; some fail, not through any deficiency in conception and execution, but be-cause circumstances made defeat inevitable (Wallace, 1956, p. 275).

Related to revitalization movements, perhaps even a form of them, are political movements that develop outside the existing power structure. These tend, especially on the political left, to be utopian, egalitarian, and communal in orientation, with consensual rather than authoritarian or majority decision-making. The recent movements for radical change in racial status, gender roles, and institutional patterns have had these qualities. Although the encounter movement has personal rather than political goals, it has many of the communitas features of group life that mark political groups in which participatory democracy is the rule.[3] Present-day communal experiments have some features of all these different groups and movements; they are almost as varied as they are numerous. Again, the major recurring themes are those of communitas. I shall return to the communal movement below, after further discussion of the healing community among these varied manifestations of communitas and the moral order.

Viewed in the context of these varied groups, the healing community has two important qualities that are more or less distinctive. First, healing communities tend to be more *stable* than many other forms of communitas. Second, healing groups are particularly concerned with the *individual*, with the *psychological* level of experience. The stability of the healing community is related in part to its development of certain internal patterns, particularly those around charismatic processes. But of great importance is the fact that the group performs a meaningful function in treating and handling psychological disorders. This suggests that as a manifestation of the moral order, the healing community is a model for a somewhat more stable pattern. That is, although internally—and to some extent, externally—the group is functioning in the moral order, it is also serving a technical function—management of deviance—for the society as a whole.

The healing community's concern with the psychological level of experience is important in relation to the widespread alienation and disaffection mentioned at the beginning of this chapter. In the large bureaucracies where modern men and women work, the particular, momentary needs of the individual must inevitably be subordinated to the needs of organizational effectiveness. The healing community, like the small therapy group, is small enough to attend to individual needs as they come up. By virtue of its primary commitment to psychological experience, regardless of how it is conceptualized, the healing community can brake the natural evolution (described by Weber) from charismatic to bureaucratic organization. What is valuable here is that the healing group may serve as one model of an organization within a complex society that performs a social function but is responsive to individuals in their uniqueness.

But it is not simply the capacity for individualized response that qualifies the healing community as a guide in the search for a modern utopia. As Alvin Toffler has pointed out, the American of today has a wide choice of "leisure" activities and more time in which to pursue them than have ever been available in any society in man's history (1969). What he desires intensely is the experience of meaningfulness as he expresses himself; he yearns for the experiences discussed by Slater—community, engagement, and dependency (see Chapter 14). These, too, are possible in a healing community. This observation need not be an idealized one; it is in part in the very limits of the healing community that some of these desires may be met. For example, no group can cater to the individual impulses of its membership at every moment and also survive. It is in the constant weighing of individual and group interest that the member may experience the sense of engagement most meaningfully. Through such immediate experience of engagement, the individual senses his involvement in a community of others who care about him and who depend on him. When his desires are not met, he realizes that the needs of others or of the group are directly involved. Since he depends on the group, his deprivation can have a positive significance in reminding him of his interdependence.

The utopian vision with which I conclude is, from a

psychological and social point of view, highly realistic in arguing for a better balance of the moral and technical orders. The healing community provides a possible model either for new groups or for the restitution of existing ones. Among the new groups already in existence are those of the encounter movement, the temporary gatherings of the "counter-culture"—rock festivals, and be-ins, experiments in communal living. These, along with the therapeutic community, give only a hint of the new sorts of groups that could be envisioned. As other economic and ecological factors make undesirable the duplication and waste of present patterns of family life, transportation, and work, new forms of organization will be needed. It is not unlikely that, taking into account economic and ecological considerations, the optimal units of living and working may be the size of healing communities.[4] Within such groups the forms and processes of the healing community would be possible, perhaps as a part of daily life, or as a special aspect of some groups.

The present American communal movement is very much a resurgence of the moral order in which the spirit of communitas is central. The groups tend to be limited in size, egalitarian, opposed to internal hierarchy, accepting of individual idiosyncracy (including psychosis). Individuals' needs to come and go, and to embark on projects are respected, even when they inconvenience the group. Communes strive for reducing per capita economic consumption, while giving greater time and significance to subjective experiences such as psychedelics, meditation, yoga, the natural environment, and contemplation. Implicit in the involvement of each individual is a hope for a charismatic enhancement of self—the discovery, expression, and experience of uniqueness without losing contact with others. Communal groups are also struggling, albeit with some awkwardness, to re-create religious life without making it an experience separate from daily living.

In less than a decade, communes have evolved from the

transient "crash pad," an urban situation motivated largely by mutual convenience, to unintegrated rural settlements, and now to more defined groups and communities. Rurally, these settlements place great emphasis on simplification of living, self-sufficiency, and inner purification. In urban settings, communes, collectives, and communities usually combine service to others, especially the poor, with the economy and interdependence of group life. Two recent directions in these groups are of special interest. First, communal living groups are beginning to emerge from long-term therapy groups (see Part III). Second, complex living-working communities are developing. Coming from two different directions, these two both may arrive at a form of group life that is both economically relevant to the wider society and an expression of the moral order.

To conceive of a society in which communitas groups were common or modal requires a vision of social reorganization on a scale difficult to imagine. In addition to the problems of stability within groups, the evolution of new forms of intergroup relationship would be required. Both are beyond the scope of this volume, although far from unlikely as realities in the near future. But revitalization of existing organizations is as important and is more easily imagined. We must recognize that having attained the capacity for economic survival, man now longs for sources of meaning that are found in the quality of his relatedness to others. If we envision every organization—prison, hospital, factory, or family—as a potential healing community, we may find guides to greater meaning and satisfaction, to the revitalization of the moral order in everyday life.

NOTES

1. These are only two of the many versions of the dichotomy. Parsons and Bales' instrumental/expressive leadership patterns in small groups

(1955), Bion's work/basic assumption modes of group function (1961), Rice's task/sentient functions in organizations are other examples (1964).

2. The kibbutz movement involves only some 5% of the Israeli population. Post-revolutionary China has transformed villages, and developed new communities with similar value schemes. The Chinese phenomena are so varied and the scale of change so vast that it is not possible to place them simply in communitas pattern. Two excellent descriptions of transformations in individual villages have been provided by Hinton (1966) and Jan Myrdal (1965).

3. Ronald Laing has argued convincingly that the distinction between political and interpersonal processes at an intimate level is inaccurate, since the two are closely related (1967).

4. For a prophetic discussion of the architectural and design as well as sociological aspects of this idea, see Goodman and Goodman's book *Communitas* (1947).

In these holy halls revenge is unknown;
If a person falters, love returns him to the path.
A friend takes him by the hand,
And leads him, cheerful and happy, into a better land.

In these holy walls, where one man loves another,
No traitor can reside, because here the enemy is forgiven.
He who follows these principles
Truly deserves to be called a person.

Bibliography

Abroms, Gene M. "Defining Milieu Therapy," *Archives of General Psychiatry* 21:553–560, 1969.

Almond, Richard. "Entrepreneurism and the Social Dynamics of a Research Ward," presentation to the 3-West Clinical Conference, National Institute of Mental Health, Bethesda, January 17, 1968.

————, and B. Astrachan. "Social System Training for Psychiatric Residents," *Psychiatry: Journal for the Study of Interpersonal Processes* 32:277–291, 1969.

————, and A. H. Esser. "Tablemate Choices of Psychiatric Patients: A Technique for Measuring Social Contact," *Journal of Nervous and Mental Disease* 140:68–82, 1965.

————, K. Keniston, and S. Boltax. "The Value System of a Milieu Therapy Unit," *Archives of General Psychiatry* 19:545–561, 1968.

————, K. Keniston, and S. Boltax. "Patient Value Change in Milieu Therapy," *Archives of General Psychiatry* 20:339–351, 1969.

————, K. Keniston, and S. Boltax. "Milieu Therapeutic Process," *Archives of General Psychiatry* 21:431–442, 1969.

————, and D. Kupfer. "Psychiatric Inpatient Research: Social System and Planning Issues," *Journal of Nervous and Mental Disease* 149:398–407, 1969.

Argyris, Chris. *Human Relations in a Hospital.* New Haven: Labor and Management Center, Yale University, 1955.

Artiss, Kenneth L. *Milieu Therapy in Schizophrenia.* New York: Grune & Stratton, 1962.

Asch, S. "Studies of Independence and Conformity. I. A Minority of One Against a Unanimous Majority," *Psychological Monographs* 70:9, 1958.

Astrachan, Boris M., and Thomas P. Detre. "Post Hospital Treatment of the Psychotic Patient," *Comprehensive Psychiatry,* 9:71–80, 1968.

———, M. Harrow, R. E. Becker, A. H. Schwartz, and J. C. Miller. "The Unled Patient Group as a Therapeutic Tool," *The International Journal of Group Psychotherapy* 12:178–191, 1967.

———, A. H. Schwartz, R. E. Becker, and M. Harrow. "The Psychiatrist's Effect on the Behavior and Interaction of Therapy Groups," *American Journal of Psychiatry* 123:1379–1387, 1967.

———, M. Harrow, and H. R. Flynn. "Influence of the Value-System of a Psychiatric Setting on Behavior in Group Therapy Meetings," *Social Psychiatry* 3:165–172, 1968.

Ayllon, T., and E. Haughton. "Control of the Behavior of Schizophrenic Patients by Food," *Journal of Experimental Analysis of Behavior* 5:343–352, 1962.

Bach, Marcus. *Strange Sects and Curious Cults.* New York: Dodd, Mead, 1961.

Beers, Clifford W. *A Mind That Found Itself: An Autobiography.* Garden City, N.Y.: Doubleday, 1935.

Benziger, Barbara Field. *The Prison of My Mind.* New York: Pocket Books, 1970.

Berkowitz, David A. *"Termination and Transfer in a Psychiatric Institution."* M.D. thesis, Yale University School of Medicine, 1969.

Bion, Wilfred R. *Experiences in Groups.* New York: Basic Books, 1961.

Bockoven, J. S. *Moral Treatment in Community Mental Health.* New York: Springer, 1972.

Braginsky, Benjamin M., Dorothea D. Braginsky, and Kenneth Ring. *Methods of Madness.* New York: Holt, Rinehart and Winston, 1969.

Buber, Martin. *I and Thou.* New York: Scribner, 1970.

Buehler, R. E., G. R. Patterson, and J. M. Furniss. "The Reinforcement of Behavior in Institutional Settings," *Behavior Research and Therapy* 4:157–167, 1966.

Bunzel, Ruth L. "Zuni Origin Myths," in *47th Annual Report of the Bureau of American Ethnology.* Washington, D.C.: Government Printing Office, 1932.

Burdett, Henry C. *Hospitals and Asylums of the World* vol. 1. London: Churchill, 1891.

Bursten, Ben. "Family Dynamics, the Sick Role, and Medical Hospital Admissions," *Family Process* 4:206–216, 1965.

Caine, T. M., and D. J. Smail. "Attitudes to Treatment of Medical Staff in Therapeutic Communities," *British Journal of Medical Psychology* 39:329–334, 1966.

———, and D. J. Smail. "Attitudes of Psychiatrists to Staff Roles and Treatment Methods," *British Journal of Medical Psychology* 40:179–182, 1967.

———, and D. J. Smail. "Attitudes of Psychiatric Nurses to Their Role in Treatment," *British Journal of Medical Psychology* 41:193–197, 1968.

———, and D. J. Smail. "Attitudes of Psychiatric Patients to Staff Roles and Treatment Methods in Mental Hospitals," *British Journal of Medical Psychology* 41:291–294, 1968.

Canter, Francis M. "The Relationship Between Authoritarian Attitudes, Attitudes Toward Mental Patients and Effectiveness of Clinical Work with Mental Patients," *Journal of Clinical Psychology* 19:124–127, 1963.

Carstairs, G. M., and A. Heron. "The Social Environment of the Mental Hospital Patient: A Measure of Staff Attitude," in M. Greenblatt, D. J. Levinson, and R. H.

Williams (eds.), *The Patient and the Mental Hospital.* New York: Free Press, 1957.

Caudill, William. *The Psychiatric Hospital as a Small Society.* Cambridge, Mass.: Harvard University Press, 1958.

Colman, A. D., and S. L. Baker. "Utilization of an Operant Conditioning Model for the Treatment of Character and Behavior Disorders in a Military Setting," *American Journal of Psychiatry* 125:1395–1402, 1969.

Cumming, John, and Elaine Cumming. *Ego and Milieu: Theory and Practice of Environmental Therapy.* New York: Atherton, 1962.

Cushing, Frank H. "Outlines of Zuni Creation Myths" in *13th Annual Report of the Bureau of American Ethnology.* Washington, D.C.: Government Printing Office, 1896.

Daniels, D., and J. Kuldau. "Marginal Man, the Tether of Tradition, and Intentional Social System Therapy," *Community Mental Health Journal* 3:13–20, Spring 1967.

———, and R. Rubin. "The Community Meeting," *Archives of General Psychiatry* 18:60–75, 1968.

Denbo, T., and E. Hanfmann. "The Patient's Psychological Situation upon Admission to a Mental Hospital," *American Journal of Psychology* 47:381–408, 1935.

Dent, J. K. *A Bibliographic Index of Evaluation in Mental Health.* Bethesda, Md.: Public Health Service Publications, 1966.

Detre, Thomas. "Remarks to the Faculty of the Department of Psychiatry," New Haven, 1959, Mimeo.

———, D. Kessler, and J. Sayres. "A Socioadaptive Approach to Treatment of Acutely Disturbed Inpatients," in *Proceedings of the Third World Congress of Psychiatry.* Toronto: University of Toronto Press, 1965.

———, Jean Sayres, Nea M. Norton, and Harriette C. Lewis. "The Treatment of the Acutely Ill Psychiatric Patient," *Connecticut Medicine* 25:613–619, 1961.

Devereux, George. "Social Structure of the Hospital as a Factor in Total Therapy," *American Journal of Orthopsychiatry* 19:492, 1949.

Dole, V. P., and M. Nyswander. "A Medical Treatment for Diacetylmorphine (Heroin) Addiction: A Clinical Trial with Methadone Hydrochloride," *Journal of the American Medical Association* 193:646–650, 1965.

Dunham, H. W., and S. K. Weinberg. *The Culture of the State Mental Hospital.* Detroit: Wayne State University Press, 1960.

Durell, J., A. Arnson, and S. G. Kellam. "A Community-Oriented Therapeutic Milieu," *Medical Annals of the District of Columbia* 34:468—474, 1965.

Edelson, Marshall. *Ego Psychology, Group Dynamics, and the Therapeutic Community.* New York: Grune & Stratton, 1964.

————. *The Practice of Sociotherapy: A Case Study.* New Haven, Conn: Yale University Press, 1970.

Ellsworth, R. B., L. Foster, B. Childers, G. Arthur, and D. Kroeker. "Hospital and Community Adjustment as Perceived by Psychiatric Patients, Their Families, and Staff," *Journal of Consulting and Clinical Psychology* (Monograph Supplement) 32:1–41, 1968.

Erikson, Erik H. "Identity and the Life Cycle," *Psychological Issues*, vol. 1, no. 1. New York: International Universities, 1959.

————. *Young Man Luther.* New York: Norton, 1958.

————. *Gandhi's Truth.* New York: Norton, 1969.

Erikson, Kai T. "Patient Role and Social Uncertainty—A Dilemma of the Mentally Ill," *Psychiatry* 20:263–274, 1957.

Esser, A. H., A. S. Chamberlain, E. D. Chapple, and N. S. Kline. "Territoriality of Patients on a Research Ward," in J. Wortis (ed.), *Recent Advances in Biological Psychiatry*, vol. VII. New York: Plenum, 1965.

Etzioni, Amitai. *A Comparative Analysis of Complex Organizations.* New York: Free Press, 1961.

Ferriter, Christine. "Overview of Purpose and Function of a Psychiatric Unit Within a General Hospital (Information to Introduce Student to T I)," New Haven, n.d., Mimeo.

Fishman, J. R., D. A. Hamburg, J. H. Handlon, J. W. Mason, and E. J. Sachar. "Emotional and Adrenal Cortical Responses to a New Experience," *Archives of General Psychiatry* 6:271–278, 1962.

Fontaine, Jean-Guy. "Le 2-Sud, Milieu Thérapeutique," *Laval Médical* 38:853–861, 1967.

Frank, Jerome D. "The Dynamics of the Psychotherapeutic Relationship—Determinants and Effects of the Therapist's Influence," *Psychiatry* 22:17–39, 1959.

————. *Persuasion and Healing: A Comparative Study of Psychotherapy*, 2nd ed. Baltimore, Md.: Johns Hopkins Press, 1973.

Freud, Sigmund. "Analysis Terminable and Interminable," in S. Freud, *Collected Papers* vol. 5. London: Hogarth, 1953.

————, *The Ego and the Id*. Translated by Joan Riviere. New York: Norton, 1960.

Friedman, J., O. Von Merihg, and E. N. Hinko. "Intermittent Patienthood: The Hospital Career of Today's Mental Patient," *Archives of General Psychiatry* 14:386–392, 1966.

Fromm-Reichman, Frieda. *Principles of Intensive Psychotherapy*. Chicago: University of Chicago Press, 1950.

Gilbert, Doris C. *Ideologies Concerning Mental Illness: A Socio-psychological Study of Mental Hospital Personnel*. Ph.D. dissertation, Radcliffe College, 1954.

————, and Daniel J. Levinson. " 'Custodialism' and 'Humanism' in Staff Ideology," in Milton Greenblatt, Daniel J. Levinson, and Richard H. Williams (eds.), *The Patient and the Mental Hospital*. New York: Free Press, 1957.

Gillin, John. "Magical Fright," *Psychiatry* 11:387–400, 1948.

Goffman, Erving, *Asylums*. Garden City, N.Y.: Doubleday, 1961.

Goodman, Paul, and Percival Goodman. *Communitas: Means*

of Livelihood and Ways of Life. New York: Random House, 1947.

Green Hannah. *I Never Promised You a Rose Garden.* New York: Holt, Rinehart and Winston, 1964.

Greenblatt, M., D. Levinson, and R. Williams (eds.). *The Patient and the Mental Hospital.* New York: Free Press, 1957.

Greenhill, M. H., and A. Gralnick. "The Problem of Primary Change in Psychotherapy and Psychoanalysis: Repair vs. Reconstruction," in Excerpta Medica International Congress Series no. 150, *Proceedings of the IV World Congress of Psychiatry,* September 1966, 758–764.

Hamburg, David A. "Emotions in the Perspective of Human Evolution," in P. Knapp (ed.), *Expressions of the Emotions of Man.* New York: International Universities, 1963.

Henry, Jules. "The Formal Social Structure of a Psychiatric Hospital," *Psychiatry* 17:139–151, 1954.

Hinton, William. *Fanshen: A Documentary of Revolution in a Chinese Village.* New York: Random House, 1966.

Hollingshead, A. B., and F. C. Redlich. *Social Class and Mental Illness: A Community Study.* New York: Wiley, 1958.

Howard, Jane. *Please Touch.* New York: Dell, 1970.

Ilfeld, Frederic W., and Erich Lindemann. "The Health Professional and the Community: Pathways Towards Trust," Stanford, 1970, Mimeo.

Infield, Henrik F. "The American Intentional Communities: Study in the Sociology of Cooperation," Glen Gardner, N.J.: Glen Gardner Community Press, September 1955.

James, William. *The Varieties of Religious Experience: A Study in Human Nature.* New York: Mentor Books, 1958.

Janis, I., and B. King. "The Influence of Role Playing on Opinion Change," *Journal of Abnormal Psychology* 49:211–218, 1954.

————, and C. I. Hovland. *Personality and Persuasibility.* New Haven, Conn.: Yale University Press, 1959.

Johnson, D. L., and C. A. Johnson. "Comparative Study of Deviant Behavior of Zuni, Navaho, and Sioux Indian Adolescents." Paper presented at the Biennial Meeting of the Society for Research in Child Development, March 29, 1967.

Jones, Maxwell. *The Therapeutic Community*. New York: Basic Books, 1953.

———. *Beyond the Therapeutic Community*. New Haven, Conn.: Yale University Press, 1968.

Kanter, Rosabeth Moss. *Commitment and Community*. Cambridge, Mass.: Harvard University Press, 1972.

Kelman, H. C., and M. B. Parloff. "Interrelations Among Three Criteria of Improvement in Group Therapy: Comfort, Effectiveness, and Self-Awareness," *Journal of Abnormal and Social Psychology* 54:281–288, 1957.

Keniston, Kenneth. *The Uncommitted*. New York: Harcourt Brace Jovanovich, 1960.

———, Sandra Boltax and Richard Almond. "Multiple Criteria of Treatment Outcome," *Journal of Psychiatric Research* 8:107–118, 1971.

Kennedy, John G. "Nubian Zar Ceremonies as Psychotherapy," *Human Organization* 26:185–194, 1967.

Kiev, Ari. "The Psychotherapeutic Aspects of Primitive Medicine," *Human Organization* 21:25–29, 1962.

——— (ed.). *Magic, Faith, and Healing: Studies in Primitive Psychiatry Today*. New York: Free Press, 1964.

———. *Curandarismo*. New York: Free Press, 1968.

Klerman, Gerald L. "Assessing the Influence of the Hospital Milieu upon the Effectiveness of Psychiatric Drug Therapy: Problems of Conceptualization and of Research Methodology," *Journal of Nervous and Mental Disease* 137:143–154, 1963.

Kluckhohn, C., and D. Leighton. *The Navaho*. Cambridge, Mass.: Harvard University Press, 1947.

Knight, Robert P., and Cyrus R. Friedman. *Psychoanalytic Psychiatry and Psychology: Clinical and Theoretical Papers*. New York: International Universities, 1970.

Kohlberg, Lawrence. *Stages in the Development of Moral Thought and Action.* New York: Holt, Rinehart and Winston, 1973.

Kroeber, A. L. "Psychosis or Social Sanction," in A. L. Kroeber (ed.), *The Nature of Culture.* Chicago: University of Chicago Press, 1952.

Kuldau, John. "Comprehensive Treatment for the Marginally Adapted," NIMH Grant Project MH16981, n.d.

LaBarre, Weston. *The Ghost Dance.* Garden City, N.Y.: Doubleday, 1970.

Laing, R. D. *The Politics of Experience.* New York: Ballantine, 1967.

Lebra, Takie Sugiyama. *An Interpretation of Religious Conversion — A Millenial Movement Among Japanese-Americans in Hawaii.* Ph.D. dissertation, University of Pittsburgh, 1967.

————. "Religious Conversion and Elimination of the Sick Role: A Japanese Sect in Hawaii," presentation at the Conference on Culture and Mental Health in Asia and the Pacific, Honolulu: March, 1969.

————, "Religious Conversion and Elimination of the Sick Role: A Japanese Sect in Hawaii," in William P. Lebra (ed.), *Transcultural Research in Mental Health, vol. II of Mental Health Research in Asia and the Pacific.* Honolulu: University of Hawaii Press, 1972.

Leighton, A. H., and D. C. Leighton. "Elements of Psychotherapy in Navaho Religion," *Psychiatry* 4:515–523, 1941.

Leslie, Robert C. *Sharing Groups in the Church.* Nashville, Tenn.: Abingdon, 1970.

Levinson, D., and E. Gallagher. *Patienthood in the Mental Hsopital.* Boston: Houghton Mifflin, 1964.

Lidz, T., S. Fleck, and A. R. Cornelson. *Schizophrenia and the Family.* New York: International Universities, 1965.

Lieberman, Morton A., Irvin D. Yalom, and Matthew B. Miles. *Encounter Groups: First Facts.* New York: Basic Books, 1973.

Lifton, Robert J. *Thought Reform and the Psychology of Totalism.* New York: Norton, 1961.

Lindsley, O. R. "Changing the Behavior of Chronic Psychotics by Free-Operant Methods," *Diseases of the Nervous System* (Monograph Supplement) 21:66–78, 1960.

Lowen, Alexander. *Betrayal of the Body.* New York: Macmillan, 1969.

Ludwig, A. M., and F. Farrelly. "The Code of Chronicity," *Archives of General Psychiatry* 15:562–568, 1966.

Maslow, Abraham H. *Toward a Psychology of Being.* Princeton, N.J.: D. Van Nostrand, 1968.

Mason, J. W., E. J. Sachar, J. R. Fishman, D. A. Hamburg, and J. H. Handlon. "Cortico-Steroid Responses to Hospital Admission," *Archives of General Psychiatry* 13:1–8, 1965.

May, Philip R. A. *Treatment of Schizophrenia.* New York: Science House, 1968.

Menninger, William C. "Psychoanalytic Principles Applied to the Treatment of Hospitalized Patients," *Bulletin of the Menninger Clinic* 1:35–43, 1936.

Messing, Simon. *The Highland Plateau Amhara of Ethiopia.* Ph.D. dissertation, University of Pennsylvania, 1957.

———. "Group Therapy and Social Status in the Zar Cult of Ethiopia," in Marvin K. Opler (ed.), *Culture and Mental Health.* New York: Macmillan, 1959.

Milgram, Stanley. "Conditions of Obedience and Disobedience to Authority," *International Journal of Psychiatry,* vol. 6, no. 4:259–276, October 1968.

Mooney, James. "The Ghost Dance Religion," in *Bureau of American Ethnology Annual Report.* Washington, D.C., Government Printing Office, 1892-3.

Moos, Rudolph H. *Evaluating Treatment Environments: A Social-Ecological Approach.* New York: Wiley, 1974.

Myerhoff, B. G., and W. R. Larson. "The Doctor as Culture Hero: The Routinization of Charisma," *Human Organization* 24:188–191, 1965.

Myerson, Abraham. "Theory and Principles of the 'Total

Push' Method in the Treatment of Chronic Schizophrenia," *American Journal of Psychiatry* XCV: 1197–1204,
1939.

Myrdal, Jan. *Report from a Chinese Village*. New York: Pan-
theon, 1965.

Nordhoff, Charles. *The Communistic Societies of the United
States*. New York: Dover, 1966.

Opler, Marvin K. *Culture and Mental Health*. New York: Macmillan, 1959.

———. "Dream Analysis in Ute Indian Therapy," in Marvin
K. Opler (ed.), *Culture and Mental Health*. New York:
Macmillan, 1959.

Opler, Melvin E. "Some Points of Comparison and Contrast
Between the Treatment of Functional Disorders by the
Apache Shamans and Modern Psychiatric Practice,"
American Journal of Psychiatry 92:1371–1387, 1936.

Parsons, Talcott and Robert F. Bales. *Family, Socialization and
Interaction Process*. Glencoe, Ill.: Free Press, 1955.

Parsons, Talcott. "Illness and the Role of the Physician: A
Sociological Perspective," in Clyde Kluckholn and Henry
A. Murray (eds.) *Personality in Nature, Society, and Cul-
ture*. New York: Alfred A. Knopf, 1956.

———, and Renee Fox. "Illness, Therapy and the Modern
Urban American Family," *Journal of Social Issues* 8:31–44,
1953.

Perls, Fritz, Ralph E. Hefferline, and Paul Goodman. *Gestalt
Therapy*. New York: Dell, 1951.

———. *Gestalt Therapy Verbatim*. New York: Bantam, 1971.

Piaget, Jean. *The Moral Judgment of the Child*. New York: Free
Press, 1948.

Pine, Frederick, and Daniel J. Levinson. "A Sociopsychological Conception of Patienthood," *International Journal of
Social Psychology* 7:107–122, 1961.

Pittenger, Robert E., Charles F. Hockett, and John J. Danehy.
The First Five Minutes. Ithaca, N.Y.: P. Martinean, 1960.

Prince, Raymond. "Indigenous Yoruba Psychiatry," in Ari

Kiev (ed.), *Magic, Faith, and Healing.* New York: Free Press, 1964.

Rapoport, Robert. *Community as Doctor.* London: Tavistock 1960.

Redfield, Robert. *The Primitive World and Its Transformations.* Ithaca, N.Y.: Cornell University Press, 1953.

Reich, Charles A. *The Greening of America.* New York: Bantam, 1971.

Reiss, David. "Varieties of Consensual Experience Ill. Contrast between Families of Normals, Delinquents and Schizophrenics," *Journal of Nervous and Mental Diseases* 152:73–95, 1971.

————, and Richard Almond. "Assimilating the Patient Stranger," *Journal of Nervous and Mental Diseases,* in press.

Rice, A. K. *The Enterprise and Its Environment.* London: Tavistock, 1964.

————. *Learning for Leadership: Interpersonal and Intergroup Relations.* New York: Barnes & Noble, 1971.

Rieff, Philip. *Triumph of the Therapeutic.* New York: Harper & Row, 1968.

Rogers, Carl. *On Encounter Groups.* New York: Harper & Row, 1970.

Roszak, Theodore. *The Making of a Counter-Culture.* New York: Doubleday, 1969.

Rowland, Howard. "Friendship Patterns in the State Mental Hospital," *Psychiatry* 2:363–373, 1939.

Rubenstein, R., and H. Lasswell. *The Sharing of Power in the Psychiatric Hospital.* New Haven, Conn.: Yale University Press, 1967.

Sapir, Edward. *Culture, Language and Personality.* David G. Mandelbaum (ed.). Berkeley: University of California Press, 1949.

Sarbin, T. R. and V. L. Allen, "Role Theory," in G. Lindzey and E. Aronson (eds.), *The Handbook of Social Psychology,* vol. 1. Reading, Mass.: Addison-Wesley, 488–567, 1968.

Saslow, G. "The Use of a Psychiatric Unit in a General Hospital," in A. F. Wessen (ed.), *The Psychiatric Hospital as a Social System*. Springfield, Ill.: C. C. Thomas, 111–146, 1965.

Satir, Virginia. *Conjoint Family Therapy*. Palo Alto, Calif.: Science and Behavior, 1967.

Scheff, Thomas J. *Being Mentally Ill: A Sociological Theory*. Chicago: Aldine, 1966.

Schulberg, Herbert C. "Inpatient Psychiatric Services in a General Hospital/The Grace-New Haven Experience," in R. Penchansky (ed.), *Health Services Administration: Policy Cases and the Case Method*. Cambridge: Harvard University Press, 1968.

Shils, Edward. "Charisma," in David L. Sills (ed.), *International Encyclopedia of the Social Sciences*, vol. II. New York: Macmillan, 1968.

Sifneos, Peter E. *Ascent from Chaos*. Cambridge, Mass.: Harvard University Press, 1964.

Silverman, Julian. "Shamans and Acute Schizophrenia," *American Anthropologist* 1:21–31, 1967.

——, P. Berg, and R. Kantor. "Some Perceptual Correlates of Institutionalization," *Journal of Nervous and Mental Diseases* 141:651–657, 1966.

Simel, Ernst. "The Psychoanalytic Sanitarium and the Psychoanalytic Movement," *Bulletin of the Menninger Clinic* 1:133–143, 1937.

Simon, Hermann. "Activere Krankenbehandlung in der Irrenanstatt," I, II, III, *Allgemeine Zeitschrift für Psychiatrie* 87 (Nov. 15, 1927): 97; 90a (May 10, 1929): 69; 90b (July 4, 1929): 245.

Skinner, B. F. *Science and Human Behavior*. New York: Macmillan, 1953.

Slater, Philip. *The Pursuit of Loneliness*. Boston: Beacon, 1970.

Sommer, R., and R. Hall. "Alienation and Mental Illness," *American Sociological Review* 23:418–420, 1958.

Soskis, David A., and Malcolm B. Bowers. "The Schizophrenic Experience: A follow-up study of attitude and posthospital adjustment," *Journal of Nervous and Mental Diseases* 149:443–449, 1969.

Spadoni, A. J., and J. A. Smith. "Milieu Therapy in Schizoprenia," *Archives of General Psychiatry* 20:547–551, 1969.

Speck, Ross V., and Uri Rueveni. "Network Therapy—A Developing Concept," *Family Process* 8:182–191, September 1969.

Spiro, Melford E. *Kibbutz: Venture in Utopia.* Cambridge, Mass.: Harvard University Press, 1956.

Stanton, A., and M. Schwartz. *The Mental Hospital.* New York:

Stevenson, Mathilda C. "The Zuni Indians," in *23rd Annual Report of the Bureau of American Ethnology.* Washington D.C., Government Printing Office, 1904.

Stotland, E., and A. L. Kobler. *The Life and Death of a Mental Hospital.* Seattle, Wash.: University of Washington Press, 1965.

Strauss, Anselm, Leonard Schatzman, Rue Bucher, Danuta Ehrlich, and Melvin Sabshin. *Psychiatric Ideologies and Institutions.* New York: Free Press, 1964.

Sullivan, Harry Stack. "Environmental Factors and Course Under Treatment of Schizophrenia," *Medical Journal and Record* 1:19–22, 1933.

Toennies, Ferdinand. *Toennies on Sociology.* Werner J. Cahuman (ed.). Chicago: University of Chicago Press, 1972.

Toffler, Alvin. *Future Shock.* New York: Bantam, 1970.

Torrey, E. Fuller. "The Zar Cult in Ethiopia," *International Journal of Social Psychiatry* 13:216–223, 1967.

Tucker, Robert C. "The Theory of Charismatic Leadership," *Daedalus* 97:731–756, 1968.

Tuke, Samuel. *Description of the Retreat.* London: Dawsons, 1964.

Turner, Victor W. *The Ritual Process.* Chicago: Aldine, 1969.

Vail, David. *Dehumanization and the Institutional Career.*
Springfield, Ill.: C. C. Thomas, 1966.

Vogel, Ezra. "Sociological View on Tompkins I," New
Haven, 1961, Mimeo.

Walk, Alexander. "Some Aspects of the 'Moral Treatment' of
the Insane up to 1954," *Journal of Mental Science*
100:807–837, 1954.

Wallace, Anthony F. C. "Handsome Lake and the Great Revival in the West," *American Quarterly*, Summer 1952,
149–165.

———. "Revitalization Movements," *American Anthropologist*
58:264–281, 1956.

———. "Dreams and the Wishes of the Soul: A Type of
Psychoanalytic Theory Among the Seventeenth Century
Iroquois," *American Anthropologist* 60:234–248, 1958.

———. "The Institutionalization of Cathartic and Control
Strategies in Iroquois Religious Psychotherapy," in M. E.
Opler (ed.), *Culture and Mental Health.* New York: Mac-
millan, 1959.

Weber, Max. *Essays in Sociology.* Translated by M. H. Gerth
and C. W. Mills. New York: Oxford University Press,
1946.

Weingarten, Randolph, and Richard Almond. "A Contribution to the Psychology of Romantic Love: Overview and
Phenomenology," 1972, Mimeo.

Wessen, Albert F. (ed.). *The Psychiatric Hospital as a Social
System.* Springfield, Ill.: C. C. Thomas, 1965.

Wilmer, Harry A. "Toward a Definition of the Therapeutic
Community," *American Journal of Psychiatry* 114:824–834,
1958.

Wynne, L. C., I. M. Ryckoff, J. Day, and S. I. Hirsch.
"Pseudo-Mutuality in the Family Relations of Schizophrenics," *Psychiatry* 21:205–220, 1958.

Yablonsky, Lewis. *Synanon: The Tunnel Back.* New York: Macmillan, 1965.

Zwerling, I., and J. F. Wilder. "An Evaluation of the Applicability of the Day Hospital in Treatment of Acutely Disturbed Patients," *The Israel Annals of Psychiatry and Related Disciplines* 2:162–185, 1964.

Index